QUALITY ASSURANCE IN HOSPITALS

Strategies for Assessment and Implementation

SECOND EDITION

Contributors

Frederick Abbey
Stanley Aronovitch
William Berenberg
Donald M. Berwick
Lois J. Bittle
Robert H. Brook
Maureen P. Carr
Thomas C. Chalmers
Charles G. Child, III
Benjamin Chu
Shan Cretin
Mitchell S. Curtis
Avedis Donabedian
Frederick J. Dorey
Elizabeth A. Draper
Paul W. Eggers
Bruce H. Ente
William R. Fifer
Alfred P. Fishman
George A. Goldberg
Nancy O. Graham
Sheldon Greenfield
Carolyn E. Kalk

Donald Kelly
David M. Kessner
Marian Gilbert Knapp
William A. Knaus
Kathleen N. Lohr
Daniel R. Longo
Marcia Orsolits
Edward B. Perrin
James A. Prevost
Christopher Ramirez
James S. Roberts
Stephen N. Rosenberg
Louise B. Russell
David D. Rutstein
Paul M. Schyve
Linda Simonson
James Singer
Nancy E. Solomon
Bruce C. Vladeck
Douglas P. Wagner
John E. Wennberg
John W. Williamson
Linda G. Worthman
Jack E. Zimmerman

QUALITY ASSURANCE IN HOSPITALS

Strategies for Assessment and Implementation

SECOND EDITION

Edited by

Nancy O. Graham, RN, DrPH

Vice President, Nursing
Lawrence Hospital
Bronxville, New York

AN ASPEN PUBLICATION
Aspen Publishers, Inc.
Rockville, Maryland
1990

Library of Congress Cataloging-in-Publication Data

Quality assurance in hospitals : strategies for
assessment and implementation /
Nancy O. Graham, editor. — 2nd ed.
p.   cm.

"An Aspen publication."
Includes bibliographical references.
ISBN: 0-8342-0139-9
1. Hospital care—Quality control.
2. Hospital care—Evaluation.
3. Medical care—Evaluation.
I. Graham, Nancy O.

RA972.Q34 1990
362.1'1' 0685—dc20
89-18473
CIP

Editorial Services: Ruth Bloom

Library of Congress Catalog Card Number: 89-18473
ISBN: 0-8342-0139-9

Printed in the United States of America

1 2 3 4 5

With Love

To my parents

To my husband

and

To my children

Table of Contents

Preface

Since the first edition of this book was published in 1982, the basic methodological issues in quality assessment remain unchanged, and the evaluation of the relationship of structure, process, and outcome continues. In addition, we are still faced with defining quality, setting standards, and developing appropriate measurement tools. In the 1980s, however, the health care delivery system has been increasingly affected by a number of economic, regulatory, social, organizational, political, and technical factors that have had major impacts on the monitoring and evaluation of health care; hence, the need for a second edition.

This book is intended for those professionals—physicians, nurses, administrators, and students— who need to know current strategies and issues related to quality assurance. It is a practical survey of both external and internal factors.

Major events in the 1980s have profoundly changed the delivery of health care. Concerns about the rapidly escalating rate of health care expenditures are altering attitudes toward quality in health care. When resources were abundant and quality was assumed to be inherent in the system, the quality of care was an issue left to the health professionals. However, in a health care environment characterized by competition, resource constraints, new regulations, and managed care, there is a growing consensus that a better understanding of what constitutes quality care is needed. By far the most sweeping change occurred in 1983 with the advent of the Medicare prospective pricing system, which moved from cost-based to prospective reimbursement. This major change in the financing of health care was the impetus for this growing concern about quality. Can we afford quality? How much can we afford? Can we afford not to have quality? Are efforts needed to ensure that cost-containment pressures do not impinge on the quality of care?

Two additional factors also account for this increased interest in quality: heightened consumer expectations and the growing concern of the medical profession itself. As the general public has become more educated, its awareness of quality issues has increased. Since this new interest is based in part on long-term cultural changes, quality of medical care should remain a major issue to consumers for years to come. The concern of the medical profession is an outgrowth of the emergence of comparative statistics generated by small area analysis. These statistics have shown that hospitals and physicians vary significantly in their practice patterns, which raises the possibility of variations in quality as well. The latest liability crisis has also generated interest in quality issues.[1]

With the rapid advancement of computer technology, we have moved from a peer review system to an emphasis on the development of data bases. The use of computerized case abstract files makes it possible to profile selected information not only on all patients in one particular hospital, but also in many hospitals. In addition, such computerized systems are now being used to assess patterns of performance across hospitals, as well as to evaluate the patterns of performance of an individual provider.[2] Valid comparisons, however, require the ability to adjust for differences in the severity of illnesses and case mixes that might account for differences in outcomes.

The Joint Commission on Accreditation of Healthcare Organizations radically revised its quality assurance standard in recent years. The new monitoring and evaluation process will use severity-adjusted clinical indicators. It will identify organizational characteristics and managerial activities that most directly affect the quality of care, particularly the role of the hospital's governing body. This raises the question of how an institution defines, organizes, and coordinates its services to identify and correct quality problems. Emphasis is placed on the use of quality assurance as a management tool.

The rapidity of change affecting the health care delivery system has raised such questions as

- What is quality?
- How is it to be measured?
- How is it to be obtained?
- How is it to be maintained?
- Can we afford quality?
- How much quality can we afford?
- Can we afford not to have quality?
- What type of information is required by purchasers, providers, and patients to assess quality?
- What progress has been made in the development of a universal data base for the health care industry?

- Can purchasers, providers, and the public balance conflicting expectations in defining, measuring, and controlling quality?
- Can quality improvement and cost reduction be complementary goals?
- What is the effect of regulation on quality?

These and many other questions need to be explored and answered.

It is hoped that this book will help to illuminate some of the issues surrounding these questions and to raise others. With constant questioning, heightened awareness, and continuing research, there is a unique opportunity to greatly improve the quality of health care.

This book is organized into seven parts. Part I establishes the background in quality assessment and assurance and raises some of the questions that surround quality issues. In recent years, the impact of the external environment on quality assurance has increased. The Joint Commission on Accreditation of Healthcare Organizations, Peer Review Organizations, and the general regulatory climate are discussed in Part II. Part III reviews the basic techniques and classic approaches to quality care assessment and discusses how techniques that have been used in other industries can be incorporated into health care. Part IV presents some well-known assessment strategies, chosen for review because they represent interesting approaches to evaluating problems. Internal organizational issues are raised in Part V; these range from data and management issues to the linkage of quality assurance, utilization review and risk management. How to balance cost and quality is a fundamental dilemma of cost containment and a focal point of today's health environment. This issue is discussed in Part VI. Part VII, the last section, raises issues in evaluation research and asks the ultimate question: Where are we going?

NOTES

1. Truman Esmond and Gayle Bulchelor, "Selling Quality Standards in Health Care: Balancing Purchaser, Provider, and Patient Expectation," *Dimensions in Health Care* 88-3:1–5, 1988.
2. Harold Luft and Sandra Hunt, "Evaluating Individual Quality Through Outcome Statistics," *Journal of the American Medical Association* 255(20)(1986):2780–2784.

Nancy O. Graham
April 1990

Issues and Problems in Quality Assessment

Nancy O. Graham

Part I is intended to establish the background for quality assessment and assurance. In Chapter 1, Dr. Graham puts quality of care activities into a historical perspective. More specifically, some of the topics discussed are

- reasons for increased interest in quality assessment in recent years
- the difference between quality assessment and quality assurance
- some of the government regulations regarding quality
- the definition of quality
- major issues related to assessing and assuring quality

In Chapter 2, Dr. Donabedian elaborates on the issues raised in Chapter 1. Before assessment can begin, however, quality must first be defined. The following topics are therefore discussed in this chapter:

- Does one assess only the performance of a practitioner or also the contribution of patients and of the health care system?
- Is monetary cost a consideration?
- What are the causal linkages among structure, process, and outcome?
- How does one specify the components of care to be sampled?
- What is the source of the information?

There are indeed deficiencies in the quality of care currently provided. Professional self-regulation alone has proved inadequate in detecting deficiencies and, subsequently, improving the quality of care. Thus, in recent years, federal regulation has greatly increased to fill these gaps. Both authors discuss the difficulties in defining the many dimensions of quality, as well as the problems in measuring quality once it is defined. The issues

1

of cost and quality are so interrelated that they may be seen as two sides of the same coin. Knowledge of how to define quality, to measure quality, and then to assure quality is still in a somewhat embryonic state. It is imperative that the goals of any quality assurance program are clear and that work proceed in an incremental way, building on what is already known.

Chapter 1

Historical Perspective and Regulations Regarding Quality Assessment

Nancy O. Graham

Since the 1960s, we have witnessed growing interest in the quality of health and medical care on the part of providers, third party payers, health care recipients, and the public at large. This interest has been stimulated by a variety of political, economic, social, and legal pressures. The concern has grown despite our limited ability to define quality, to assess accurately the quality of medical care, and, subsequently, to effect the behavioral changes needed to assure quality.

Quality assessment means measuring the level of quality of care at some point in time, but connotes no effort to change or improve that level of care. Quality assurance, on the other hand, includes the measurement of the level of care provided and, when necessary, the attempt to improve it.[1]

Donabedian states, "Not too long ago the quality of medical care was a matter almost exclusively in the professional domain. Quality is a term too easily bandied about, and there is little hesitation in proposing that quality can be measured, or that it can be enforced as a matter of public and administrative policy. But this mood of almost belligerent confidence is perhaps premature, for there is much about the concept of quality that is elusive, undefined and unmeasured. Our knowledge of how to go about assuring quality is equally frail."[2]

CURRENT INTEREST

The current interest in quality assessment and assurance in the United States is due to a variety of factors:

- increased government funding
- rising costs of medical care

Nancy O. Graham, RN, DrPH, is Vice-President, Nursing at Lawrence Hospital, Bronxville, New York.

- rapid advances in medical science
- demonstrated poor level of quality
- increased consumer expectations with a concurrent rise in malpractice suits
- proliferation of service institutions

Increased Government Funding

The present interest in the quality of health services is related to the entry of the federal government into the health services system as a major third party purchaser of services for the poor and elderly through Medicaid and Medicare, respectively. After the enactment of Medicare in 1965, the federal government established utilization review of hospital and physician reimbursements. It is not surprising that this increase in government participation and funding was followed by a parallel increase in demands for accountability of the cost and quality of the services provided. This utilization review program proved ineffective, however.

In an attempt to correct this situation, PL 92-603 was passed in 1972, creating the Professional Standard Review Organization (PSRO). The PSRO program was enacted into law on October 30, 1972 as part of the 1972 amendments to the Social Security Act. This law created a nationwide system of medical peer review. The PSRO law was intended to assure that services provided under Medicare, Medicaid, and the Maternal and Child Health Act were (1) medically necessary, (2) of a quality that meets professional standards, and (3) provided at the most economical level consistent with quality care.[3] A high degree of variability in its performance led to the program's general ineffectiveness.

In an effort to contain costs, the prospective payment system (PPS) was established in 1983 under PL 98-21. PPS created an even greater need for a strong review system because hospitals now have the incentive to increase admissions (which would increase payments), to increase readmissions, and to inappropriately classify a diagnosis.[4]

The Peer Review Improvement Act (PL 97-248) was enacted into law as a provision of the Tax Equity and Fiscal Responsibility Act of 1982 (TEFRA) in an attempt to address the failure of the PSRO program. The Health Care Finance Administration was directed to develop the requirements for the new Professional Review Organization (PRO). PROs review claims from Medicare services furnished by hospitals to determine reasonableness, medical necessity, quality of care, and the appropriateness of the setting in which the care is given. PROs have greater authority in recommending sanctions against hospitals and physicians than did the PSROs. The statutes make it clear that the congressional intent of the PSRO and PRO programs was two-pronged, addressing cost as well as quality.

Rising Costs of Medical Care

The rapid increase in the cost of medical care is well documented. The national health care bill topped $500 billion in 1987, an increase of 9.8 percent from 1986. National health expenditures, as a share of gross national product, continued upward to 11.1 percent in 1987, nearly double what it was in 1965.[5] With the ever-rising cost of medical care, it is logical to ask a number of questions. Can costs be contained while quality is maintained? What are the trade-offs between costs and quality? Although poor care is usually related to inadequate financing, too much money can also produce poor results, for example, unnecessary surgery or overutilization of hospitals.

Rapid Advances in Medical Science

In recent years, science and medicine have merged in dramatic ways. Personal medical care aroused great scientific, economic, and political interest. Physicians can now diagnose and treat illnesses and can change the natural history of disease in a manner unheard of before. Antibiotics, anesthetics, blood transfusions, immunizations, psychotropic drugs, and many other innovations have changed our orientation toward intervention in the natural course of illness. With the potential for abuse of the new diagnostic and therapeutic modalities, the need for quality controls has become imperative.

Demonstrated Poor Level of Quality

Quality of care studies performed over the past few decades have shown severe problems in the delivery of personal health services. Problems that adversely affect patient outcomes have been found in virtually all institutions in which quality has been examined. For example, studies support the contention that simple routine tasks are not done. Hypertension is often not treated.[6] Iron is not prescribed for anemic children.[7] Improvements in the treatment of such common conditions usually result from the development of better organizational systems and better medical practice habits.

Increased Consumer Expectations with a Concurrent Rise in Malpractice Suits

Another factor in the growing interest in quality assessment activities has been an increase in consumer awareness and sophistication. As consumers become more aware of their economic power, wants become needs and needs become demands. Patients increasingly demand not only more care but good and efficient care as well. The rise in the number of malpractice claims is partly due to the consumers' concerns with these quality issues. They recognize that different organizations and physicians deliver care of varying quality. The fact that more patients are seeking second opinions supports this assertion.

Proliferation of Service Institutions

The current interest in quality assessment in health services in the United States is symptomatic of a broader concern with management of service institutions in general. The public service institutions (government agencies, hospitals, schools, universities, etc.) are the major growth sector in the U.S. economy. The management of these service institutions is seen as the central managerial challenge for the rest of this century.[8] This challenge has now become a mandate from society to health delivery systems.[9] The most obvious manifestations are increasing pressures for cost containment, quality control, and responsiveness to consumer needs.

Managers of health care institutions know that the consequences of inadequate health care are costly. The number of successful outcomes declines and lawsuits occur; staff morale deteriorates; turnover increases; and the institutions acquire a negative public image. In an extreme case, revocation of license and accreditation may threaten a provider's viability. In a saturated or near saturated market, managers have recognized the competitive advantage of offering high-quality services.

Thus, while the forces behind the increased motivation to assess and assure quality of care are many, the major impetus has been a response to the legislative mandate for evaluation of the effectiveness of publicly financed care. In the current state of the art, however, techniques for evaluating and assuring quality trail far behind the demand for such evaluation.

HISTORICAL PERSPECTIVE

Many of the issues discussed here are not new. Health professionals have always been concerned with quality care. Over the years, however, the emphasis has shifted from self-regulation alone to external regulation, with federal policy mandating acceptable quality of care at reasonable cost.

In the 1860s, Florence Nightingale helped to lay the foundation for quality assurance programs by advocating a uniform system for collecting and evaluating hospital statistics. Her statistics showed that mortality rates varied significantly from hospital to hospital.

In 1910, a report by Dr. Abraham Flexner revealed the poor quality of medical education in the United States. This report was instrumental in closing 60 of 155 U.S. medical schools by 1920. It was also influential in introducing more stringent admission requirements and effecting changes in the curriculum. History has shown that this report aided the education of minorities, who previously had not been admitted to medical schools.[10]

One of the key pioneers in assessing quality was Dr. E. A. Codman, who, in 1916, studied the end results of care. This famous study emphasized the same issues that are being discussed today when examining the quality of care, including: (1) the importance of licensure or certification of providers; (2) the accreditation of institutions; (3) the necessity of taking into consideration the severity or stage of the disease; (4) the issue of comorbidity (two or more illnesses present at one time); (5) the health and illness behavior of the patient; and (6) economic barriers to receiving care.

When the American College of Surgeons was established in 1913, one of its explicit goals was the improvement of patient care in hospitals. Thus, in 1918 it inaugurated the Hospital Standardization Program in which the concept of hospital accreditation was put forth as a formal means of assuring good hospital care. The results of the first survey conducted under this program pointed out the severe problems facing hospitals. Of the 692 hospitals surveyed, only 90 (12.9 percent) were approved. However, by 1950, 94.6 percent qualified for approval.

With the growth of the nonsurgical specialties after World War II, and with the general recognition of the success of the American College of Surgeons' program of accreditation, it soon became clear that the approval programs should be supported by the whole medical and hospital field. Accordingly, in 1952 the Joint Commission on Accreditation of Hospitals was established to assume responsibility for the accreditation program. The purpose of the Joint Commission was to encourage voluntary attainment of uniformly high standards of institutional care in all areas (nursing, X-ray, pharmacy).[11]

Some states require accreditation for licensure, and in some regions third party payers, such as Blue Cross, require accreditation as a condition for reimbursement for Medicare. In the 1970s, the Joint Commission expanded its accreditation program to include not only hospitals but also facilities for ambulatory care, long-term care, psychiatric and mental health care, and the care of mentally retarded and other developmentally disabled persons.

In the courts, major precedents that directly relate to quality of care were established. In the *Darling v. Charleston Community Memorial Hospital* (1965) and in the *Gonzales v. Nork and Mercy Hospital* (1966) cases, it was held that hospitals and their medical staffs have the right and obligation to oversee the quality of professional services rendered by individual staff members.[12] In the *Darling* case, under the theory of corporate liability, the Charleston Community Memorial Hospital was held to be independently liable for its own negligence in connection with the negligence of a physician practicing in the hospital. This theory holds that a hospital, because it has the authority to regulate the practice of medicine, has a legal duty to do so. A breach of this duty can constitute negligence independent of that of a physician who practices in the hospital. Thus, quality of care has become an institutional concern, with the focus expanding beyond the individual physician/patient interaction.

Congress is also aware of the need for quality assessment, as shown by the previously mentioned PSRO and PRO laws. The underlying philosophy of these laws is that professionals should take an active, formalized role in determining utilization review patterns (medical necessity and appropriate level of care) and that they should seek improvement in the quality of services rendered. In 1973, the Health Maintenance Organization (HMO) legislation was enacted. This law, among other things, mandated the implementation of a quality assessment system in federally subsidized HMOs.

In 1955, the Joint Commission began to stress the concept of medical audits, and in January 1981, it implemented a new Quality Assessment Standard. This standard required that hospitals integrate their mortality, tissue, transfusion, medical records, and antibiotic committees into a single audit system, along with the delineation of privileges, incident reports, and the monitoring of clinical practice. The standard also required all hospitals to have a written quality assurance plan.[13]

In the fall of 1986, the Joint Commission launched a new project, titled the Agenda for Change. The goal of this program was to develop an outcome-oriented monitoring and evaluation process that would assist health care organizations in improving the quality of care. This program was designed to increase the clinical emphasis of the accreditation process and to stress the importance of performance outcomes, both organization and clinical. As accreditation was extended to health facilities other than hospitals, the name of the Joint Commission was changed to the Joint Commission on Accreditation of Healthcare Organizations to reflect this wide range of health care organizations: long-term care, hospice, ambulatory, home care, and managed care organizations.[14]

DEFINITION OF QUALITY

Two major questions arise when studies to assess medical and health care are considered. First, what is quality of medical and health care? Second, how can it be measured adequately?

The definition of quality is difficult to pinpoint if one wishes to do justice to all its dimensions. Certainly it depends upon the perspective of the definer. Consumers may judge quality by the ability of providers to make a diagnosis and implement a treatment plan. Administrators may judge quality by their hospitals' ability to deliver the greatest number of services at the lowest possible costs. The following case gives an example of a few of the biases that must be considered in defining quality of care.

A patient arrives at a medical center with an upper respiratory infection.[15] The physician, upon examination, finds the patient has unusually high blood pressure, which indicates that follow-up visits are needed to evaluate this patient's hypertension. The patient states that he is fine except for this cold and just wants an antibiotic. The physician explains that antibiotics are not effective against viruses and further stresses the need for follow-up because of the elevated blood pressure. The patient is given a return appointment. The return appointment is broken because the patient is dissatisfied by his inability to get the medicine for which he came to the clinic. The physician is frustrated by the patient's failure to continue treatment because the patient's hypertension renders him more liable to heart and kidney disease. The administrator, meanwhile, is concerned about the high incidence of broken appointments, which reflects upon the use of resources.

The definition of quality encompasses both the technical, scientific aspect and the "art" of the care. The art of care refers to the manner in which physicians conduct themselves in relation to their patients and is sometimes measured in terms of patient satisfaction. Thompson defines quality as the optimal achievable result for each patient, the avoidance of physician-induced (iatrogenic) complications, and the attention to patient and family needs in a manner that is both cost-effective and reasonably documented.[16]

It is impossible to discuss a definition of quality without examining the values of the professionals, the patients, and the institution. The definition of quality depends not only on values but also on the purposes of the review. Is the purpose of the review to contain costs as to satisfy review requirements by some outside agency? Or is it to obtain information that is useful in making decisions about the improvement of care? Or are all these purposes being served? Before one can assess quality, one must arrive at an operational definition of quality and clearly state the purpose of review (improvement in quality, cost containment, accreditation). A definition of quality, then, must ask: quality from whose perspective, based on what values, and for what purpose? Furthermore, the definition of quality is dynamic. It changes as knowledge, values, and resources change.

ISSUES IN QUALITY ASSESSMENT AND ASSURANCE

A number of issues that relate to assessing and assuring quality of medical and health care will affect how these activities proceed over the next decade. One such issue is the cost-quality trade-off—how much more are we willing to spend and for what amount of quality? Another issue involves the relative costs and benefits of the quality assurance activities themselves. With a finite amount of money, how much are we willing to divert from actual health care services to the assessment of health care? Quality assessment has the potential for improving the care given and for enhancing the decisions made. If poorly conceived or mismanaged, however, it can increase health care costs and accentuate quality problems. Attempts should be made at analyzing quality assurance activities in relation to their relative costs and benefits.

The methodological problems in assessing quality are numerous. Reliability and validity measurements, as well as the correlation between the process of care and patient outcome, are elusive. Techniques need to be developed to identify the small percentage of physicians (approximately 5 percent) who appear to be responsible for most of the inappropriate or excessive care.[17] Fraud and abuse investigations need to be strengthened to detect the most flagrant violators.

Most studies relate to the technical aspects of care, that is, diagnosis, treatment, and management. The art of care relates to the manner in which physicians conduct themselves in relation to their patients. Both aspects, however, contribute to overall quality. In general, we emphasize what we can measure, and this certainly has been the case in the quality assurance movement. Thus, in quality assessment systems, emphasis has been on the technical aspect of care to the neglect of the art of care, because few measures of the latter are available. Patient satisfaction and compliance are closely related to the art of care and can have major impact on outcome. Since these areas have received some attention in the literature, they may provide one measure of the art of care.[18-20]

A further problem with assessment methods relates to data accuracy. The Institute of Medicine termed the state of the art of health data collection and analysis "relatively crude." Just how crude became apparent in 1977 when the Institute published the findings of a major study, *Reliability of Hospital Discharge Abstracts*.[21] In this study, the Institute of Medicine evaluated a sample of 3,301 abstracts prepared by five abstracting services for 50 participating hospitals and found a 24 percent error rate with regard to "principal procedure" and a 33 percent error rate with regard to "principal diagnosis." Therefore, it concluded that for any aggregate sample of abstracts, a sizable portion will not be reliable, that is, they will not be coded similarly on repeated occasions.[22]

Since the patient's medical record is a basic source of information in quality of care studies and because data systems rely on items of information abstracted from the medical record, a fundamental question is: How accurately does the abstract reflect the information on the chart? An even more fundamental question is: How accurately does the patient's chart reflect the actual care being given that patient?

It has been stated that the ultimate aim of quality assurance is to lead to behavioral change; however, the best approach for achieving this goal is unclear. Does involvement of local providers in setting criteria and standards make it easier to modify their behavior at a later date? How should feedback of information about level of quality be accomplished—in a formal or an informal manner? And what effect does the method of feedback have on behavior? Little is known about the relationship of various corrective methods (education, payment denial, peer pressure, or administrative change) on behavioral change.

The importance of factors beyond the traditional scope of personal medical care systems (life style, genetics, and environment) is evidenced by the high incidence of motor vehicle accidents, suicide, and lung cancer. A study by Dever found that almost all federal health expenditures go to health care organizations, while the largest percentage of current mortality can be attributed to the influence of life style.[23] As such data indicate, efforts to assess quality must consider the question: Should money go toward assessment or toward changing life styles? Thus, it can be seen that cost problems, measurement problems, and sociopolitical problems make the area of quality assessment and assurance difficult and challenging.

NOTES

1. R.H. Brook, K.H. Williams, and A. Davies-Avery, *Quality Assurance in the 20th Century: Will It Lead to Improved Health in the 21st?* (Santa Monica, Calif.: Rand Corporation, 1975) p. 5530.

2. A. Donabedian, *Needed Research in the Assessment and Monitoring of the Quality of Medical Care*. National Center for Health Services Research Report Series. DHEW Publication no. (PHS) 78-3219 (Hyattsville, Md.: July 1978).

3. M.J. Goran, "The Evolution of the PSRO Hospital Review System," *Medical Care* 17, supplement (1979):1–47.

4. *The Impact of PRO's on Hospitals*. Ernst & Young, Washington, D.C., 1987.

5. S.W. Letach, K.R. Levit, and D.R. Waldo, "Health Care Financing Trends," *Health Care Financing Review* (1989):109.

6. National High Blood Pressure Education Program—Fact Sheet. U.S. DHEW Public Health Service, National Institutes of Health, DHEW Publication no. (NIH) 76-632, 1976.

7. Lloyd Novick, Karen Dickinson, Russell Asnes, Mary Lan, and Regina Loewenstein, "Assessment of Ambulatory Care: Application of Tracer Methodology," *Medical Care* 14 (1976):1–12.

8. Peter Drucker, *Management: Task, Responsibilities and Practice* (New York: Harper & Row, 1973).

9. N.M. Tichy, "Diagnosis for Complex Health Care Delivery Systems: A Model and Case Study," *The Journal of Applied Behavioral Science* 14 (1978):305–320.

10. A. Flexner, *Medical Education in the United States and Canada*, A Report to the Carnegie Foundation for the Advancement of Teaching. Carnegie Foundation Bulletin no. 4 (New York, 1910).

11. R.H. Egdahl and P.M. Gertman, *Quality Assurance in Health Care* (Rockville, Md.: Aspen Publishers, Inc., 1976).

12. *Ibid.*

13. Joint Commission on Accreditation of Hospitals, *Perspective on Accreditation*, no. 3 (Chicago, May–June 1979).

14. The Joint Commission on Accreditation of Healthcare Organizations, *An Introduction to the Joint Commission.* Chicago: Author, 1988.

15. M. Michnick, L. Harris, R. Willis, and J. Williams, *Ambulatory Care Evaluation: A Primer for Quality Review* (Los Angeles: University of California, 1976).

16. Richard Thompson, personal communication, May 1980.

17. Brook, Williams, and Davies-Avery, *Quality Assurance in the 20th Century.*

18. Evan Charney and Harriet Kitzman, "The Child Health Nurse in Private Practice: A Controlled Trial," *New England Journal of Medicine* 285 (24) (1971):1353–1358.

19. Dale Christensen, "Drug-taking Compliance: A Review and Synthesis," *Health Services Research* 13 (Summer 1978): 171–187.

20. Donald Schiff, Charles Fraser, and Heather Walters, "The Pediatric Nurse Practitioner in the Offices of Pediatricians in Private Practice," *Pediatrics* 44 (1) (1969):62–68.

21. Institute of Medicine, *Advancing the Quality of Health Care: Key Issues and Fundamental Principles.* A policy statement by a committee of the Institute of Medicine, National Academy of Sciences (Washington, D.C., 1974).

22. *Ibid.*

23. G.R. Dever, "An Epidemiological Model for Health Policy Analysis," *Soc Indicators Res* 2 (March 1976):453–466.

SUGGESTED READING

Batalden, P., and O'Connor, J.P. *Quality Assurance in Ambulatory Care.* Rockville, Md.: Aspen Publishers, Inc. 1980.

Becker, Marshall, and Mayman, Lois, "Sociobehavioral Determinants of Compliance with Health and Medical Care Recommendations." *Medical Care* 13 (1975):10–24.

Brook, R.H.; Davies, A.R.; and Kamberg, C. J. "Selected Reflections on Quality of Medicare Care Evaluation in the 1980s." *Nursing Research* 29 (1980):127–133.

Brook, R.H., and Williams, K.N. "Evaluation of the New Mexico Peer Review System, 1971–1973." *Medical Care* (Supplement) 14, no. 12 (1976).

Christoffel, T., and Loewenthal, M. "Evaluating the Quality of Ambulatory Health Care: A Review of Emerging Methods." *Medical Care* 15 (1977):877–907.

Donabedian, A. *A Guide to Medical Care Administration*, Vol. 2. New York: American Public Health Association, 1969.

Donabedian, A. "The Quality of Medical Care. Methods for Assuring and Monitoring the Quality of Care for Research and for Quality Assurance Programs: A Review of Emerging Methods." *Medical Care* 15 (1977):885.

Donabedian, A. "The Quality of Medical Care: A Concept in Search of a Definition." *The Journal of Family Practice* 9 (1979):277–284.

Giebank, Gerald, and White, Nicole, eds. *Ambulatory Medical Care Quality Assurance 1977.* La Jolla, Calif.: La Jolla Health Science Publications, 1977.

Gonnella, J.S.; Louis, D.Z.; and McCord, J. "The Staging Concept—An Approach to the Assessment of Outcome of Ambulatory Care." *Medical Care* 14 (1976):13–21.

Greene, R., ed. *Assuring Quality in Medical Care: The State of the Art.* Cambridge, Mass.: Ballinger Publishing Co., 1976.

Health Care Financing Review—Quality of Care. December 1987 Annual Supplement. Baltimore, Md.: U.S. Department of Health and Human Services.

Hughes, Edward, ed. *Perspectives on Quality in American Health Care.* Washington, D.C., McGraw Hill, Inc., 1988.

Institute of Medicine. *Assessing Quality in Health Care: An Evaluation.* Report of a study by a committee of the Institute of Medicine, National Academy of Sciences, Washington, D.C., 1976.

McAuliffe, W.E. "Studies of Process–Outcome Correlations in Medical Care Evaluations: A Critique." *Medical Care* 16 (1978):907–930.

McNerney, W.J. "The Quandary of Quality Assessment." *New England Journal of Medicine* 295 (1976):1505–1511.

Need to Better Use the Professional Standards Review Organization Post Payment Monitoring Program. Report by the General Accounting Office HRD 80-27, December 6, 1979.

Palmer, R. Heather. "Definitions and Data." In *Assuring Quality in Medical Care*, edited by Richard Greene. Cambridge, Mass.: Ballinger Publishing Co., 1976.

White, Nicole; Giebank, Gerald; Nessen, H. Richard. Synopsis of the Conference Proceedings in *Ambulatory Medical Care Quality Assurance*, edited by G. Giebank and N. White (La Jolla, Calif.: La Jolla Health Science Publications, 1977).

Williamson, J.W.; Aronovitch, S.; Simonson, L.; Ramirez, C.; and Kelly, D. "Health Accounting: An Outcome Based System of Quality Assurance: Illustration Application to Hypertension." *Bulletin, N.Y. Academy of Medicine* 51 (1975):727–738.

Chapter 2

The Quality of Care:
How Can It Be Assessed?

Avedis Donabedian

There was a time, not too long ago, when this question could not have been asked. The quality of care was considered to be something of a mystery: real, capable of being perceived and appreciated, but not subject to measurement. The very attempt to define and measure quality seemed, then, to denature and belittle it. Now, we may have moved too far in the opposite direction. Those who have not experienced the intricacies of clinical practice demand measures that are easy, precise, and complete—as if a sack of potatoes was being weighed. True, some elements in the quality of care are easy to define and measure, but there are also profundities that still elude us. We must not allow anyone to belittle or ignore them; they are the secret and glory of our art. Therefore, we should avoid claiming for our capacity to assess quality either too little or too much. I shall try to steer this middle course.

SPECIFYING WHAT QUALITY IS

Level and Scope of Concern

Before we attempt to assess the quality of care, either in general terms or in any particular site or situation, it is necessary to come to an agreement on what the elements that constitute it are. To proceed to measurement without a firm foundation of prior agreement on what quality consists in is to court disaster.[1]

From the University of Michigan School of Public Health, Ann Arbor.

This article was written for the *AMA Lectures in Medical Science;* it is the basis for a lecture in that series given on Jan 11, 1988, by invitation of the Division of Basic Sciences, American Medical Association, Chicago.

Note: Reprinted from *Journal of the American Medical Association,* Vol. 260, No. 12, pp. 1743–1748, with permission of American Medical Association, © 1988.

As we seek to define quality, we soon become aware of the fact that several formulations are both possible and legitimate, depending on where we are located in the system of care and on what the nature and extent of our responsibilities are. These several formulations can be envisaged as a progression, for example, as steps in a ladder or as successive circles surrounding the bull's-eye of a target. Our power, our responsibility, and our vulnerability all flow from the fact that we are the foundation for that ladder, the focal point for that family of concentric circles. We must begin, therefore, with the performance of physicians and other health care practitioners.

As shown in Figure 2-1, there are two elements in the performance of practitioners: one technical and the other interpersonal. Technical performance depends on the knowledge and judgment used in arriving at the appropriate strategies of care and on skill in implementing those strategies. The goodness of technical performance is judged in comparison with the best in practice. The best in practice, in its turn, has earned that distinction because, on the average, it is known or believed to produce the greatest improvement in health. This means that the goodness of technical care is proportional to its expected ability to achieve those improvements in health status that the current science and technology of health care have made possible. If the realized fraction of what is achievable is called *effectiveness,* the quality of technical care becomes proportionate to its effectiveness (Figure 2-2).

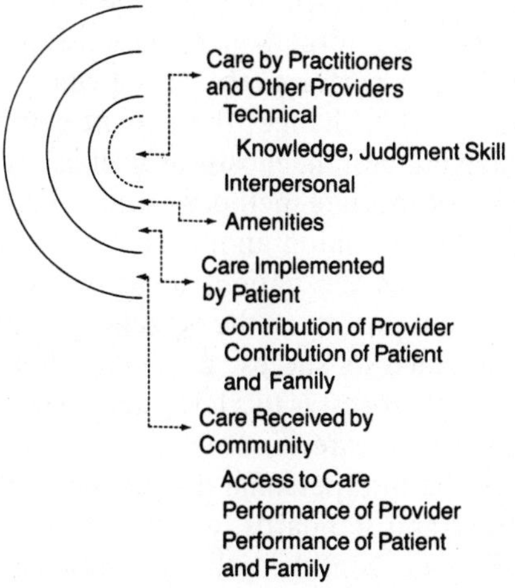

Care by Practitioners
and Other Providers
Technical
Knowledge, Judgment Skill
Interpersonal
Amenities
Care Implemented
by Patient
Contribution of Provider
Contribution of Patient
and Family
Care Received by
Community
Access to Care
Performance of Provider
Performance of Patient
and Family

Figure 2-1 Levels at Which Quality May Be Assessed

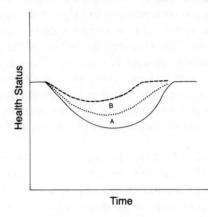

Figure 2-2 Graphical Presentation of Effectiveness (in a Self-Limiting Disease). Solid line indicates course of illness without care; dotted line, course of illness with care to be assessed; and dashed line, course of illness with "best" care. Effectiveness equals $A/(A+B)$.

Here, two points deserve emphasis. First, judgments on technical quality are contingent on the best in current knowledge and technology; they cannot go beyond that limit. Second, the judgment is based on future expectations, not on events already transpired. Even if the actual consequences of care in any given instance prove to be disastrous, quality must be judged as good if care, at the time it was given, conformed to the practice that could have been expected to achieve the best results.

The management of the interpersonal relationship is the second component in the practitioner's performance. It is a vitally important element. Through the interpersonal exchange, the patient communicates information necessary for arriving at a diagnosis, as well as preferences necessary for selecting the most appropriate methods of care. Through this exchange, the physician provides information about the nature of the illness and its management and motivates the patient to active collaboration in care. Clearly, the interpersonal process is the vehicle by which technical care is implemented and on which its success depends. Therefore, the management of the interpersonal process is to a large degree tailored to the achievement of success in technical care.

But the conduct of the interpersonal process must also meet individual and social expectations and standards, whether these aid or hamper technical performance. Privacy, confidentiality, informed choice, concern, empathy, honesty, tact, sensitivity—all these and more are virtues that the interpersonal relationship is expected to have.

If the management of the interpersonal process is so important, why is it so often ignored in assessments of the quality of care? There are many reasons. Information about the interpersonal process is not easily available. For example, in the medical record, special effort is needed to obtain it. Second, the criteria and standards that permit precise measurement of the attributes of the interpersonal process are not well developed or have not been sufficiently called upon to undertake the task. Partly, it may be because the management of the interpersonal process must adapt to so many variations in the preferences and expectations of individual patients that general guidelines do not serve us sufficiently well.

Much of what we call the *art of medicine* consists in almost intuitive adaptions to individual requirements in technical care as well as in the management of the interpersonal process. Another element in the art of medicine is the way, still poorly understood, in which practitioners process information to arrive at a correct diagnosis and an appropriate strategy of care.[2] As our understanding of each of these areas of performance improves, we can expect the realm of our science to expand and that of our art to shrink. Yet I hope that some of the mystery in practice will always remain, since it affirms and celebrates the uniqueness of each individual.

The science and art of health care, as they apply to both technical care and the management of the interpersonal process, are at the heart of the metaphorical family of concentric circles depicted in Figure 2-1. Immediately surrounding the center we can place the amenities of care, these being the desirable attributes of the settings within which care is provided. They include convenience, comfort, quiet, privacy, and so on. In private practice, these are the responsibility of the practitioner to provide. In institutional practice, the responsibility for providing them devolves on the owners and managers of the institution.

By moving to the next circle away from the center of our metaphorical target, we include in assessments of quality the contributions to care of the patients themselves as well as of members of their families. By doing so we cross an important boundary. So far, our concern was primarily with the performance of the providers of care. Now, we are concerned with judging the care as it actually was. The responsibility, now, is shared by provider and consumer. As already described, the management of the interpersonal process by the practitioner influences the implementation of care by and for the patient. Yet, the patient and family must, themselves, also carry some of the responsibility for the success or failure of care. Accordingly, the practitioner may be judged blameless in some situations in which the care, as implemented by the patient, is found to be inferior.

We have one more circle to visit, another watershed to cross. Now, we are concerned with care received by the community as a whole. We must now judge the social distribution of levels of quality in the community.[3]

This depends, in turn, on who has greater or lesser access to care and who, after gaining access, receives greater or lesser qualities of care. Obviously, the performance of individual practitioners and health care institutions has much to do with this. But, the quality of care in a community is also influenced by many factors over which the providers have no control, although these are factors they should try to understand and be concerned about.

I have tried, so far, to show that the definition of quality acquires added elements as we move outward from the performance of the practitioners, to the care received by patients, and to the care received by communities. The definition of quality also becomes narrower or more expansive, depending on how narrowly or broadly we define the concept of health and our responsibility for it. It makes a difference in the assessment of our performance whether we see ourselves as responsible for bringing about improvements only in specific aspects of physical or physiological function or whether we include psychological and social function as well.

Valuation of the Consequences of Care

Still another modification in the assessment of performance depends on who is to value the improvements in health that care is expected to produce. If it is our purpose to serve the best interest of our patients, we need to inform them of the alternatives available to them, so they can make the choice most appropriate to their preferences and circumstances. The introduction of patient preferences, though necessary to the assessment of quality, is another source of difficulty in implementing assessment. It means that no preconceived notion of what the objectives and accomplishments of care should be will precisely fit any given patient. All we can hope for is a reasonable approximation, one that must then be subject to individual adjustment.[4-6]

Monetary Cost As a Consideration

Finally, we come to the perplexing question of whether the monetary cost of care should enter the definition of quality and its assessment.[1,7] In theory, it is possible to separate quality from inefficiency. Technical quality is judged by the degree to which achievable improvements in health can be expected to be attained. Inefficiency is judged by the degree to which expected improvements in health are achieved in an unnecessarily costly manner. In practice, lower quality and inefficiency coexist because wasteful care is either directly harmful to health or is harmful by displacing more useful care.

Cost and quality are also confounded because, as shown in Figure 2-3, it is believed that as one adds to care, the corresponding improvements in health become progressively smaller while costs continue to rise unabated. If this is true, there will be a point beyond which additions to care will bring about improvements that are too small to be worth the added cost. Now, we have a choice. We can ignore cost and say that the highest quality is represented by care that can be expected to achieve the greatest improvement in health; this is a "maximalist" specification of quality. Alternatively, if we believe that cost is important, we would say that care must stop short of including elements that are disproportionately costly compared with the improvements in health that they produce. This is an "optimalist" specification of quality. A graphical representation of these alternatives is shown in Figure 2-3.

Health care practitioners tend to prefer a maximalist standard because they only have to decide whether each added element of care is likely to be useful. By contrast, the practice of optimal care requires added knowledge of costs, and also some method of weighing each added bit of expected usefulness against its corresponding cost.[8] Yet, the practice of optimal care is traditional, legitimate, even necessary, as long as costs and benefits are weighed jointly by the practitioner and the fully informed patient. A difficult, perhaps insoluble, problem arises when a third party (for example,

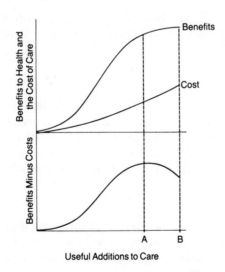

Figure 2-3 Hypothetical Relations between Health Benefits and Cost of Care As Useful Additions Are Made to Care. A indicates optimally effective care; and B, maximally effective care.

a private insurer or a governmental agency) specifies what the optimum that defines quality is.[9]

Preliminaries to Quality Assessment

Before we set out to assess quality, we will have to choose whether we will adopt a maximal or optimal specification of quality and, if the latter, whether we shall accept what is the optimum for each patient or what has been defined as socially optimal. Similarly, we should have decided (1) how health and our responsibility for it is to be defined, (2) whether the assessment is to be of the performance of practitioners only or also include that of patients and the health care system, and (3) whether the amenities and the management of the interpersonal process are to be included in addition to technical care. In a more practical vein, we need to answer certain questions: Who is being assessed? What are the activities being assessed? How are these activities supposed to be conducted? What are they meant to accomplish? When we agree on the answers to these questions we are ready to look for the measures that will give us the necessary information about quality.

Approaches to Assessment

The information from which inferences can be drawn about the quality of care can be classified under three categories: "structure," "process," and "outcome."[1,10]

Structure

Structure denotes the attributes of the settings in which care occurs. This includes the attributes of material resources (such as facilities, equipment, and money), of human resources (such as the number and qualifications of personnel), and of organizational structure (such as medical staff organization, methods of peer review, and methods of reimbursement).

Process

Process denotes what is actually done in giving and receiving care. It includes the patient's activities in seeking care and carrying it out, as well as the practitioner's activities in making a diagnosis and recommending or implementing treatment.

Outcome

Outcome denotes the effects of care on the health status of patients and populations. Improvements in the patient's knowledge and salutary changes in the patient's behavior are included under a broad definition of health status, and so is the degree of the patient's satisfaction with care.

This three-part approach to quality assessment is possible only because good structure increases the likelihood of good process, and good process increases the likelihood of a good outcome. It is necessary, therefore, to have established such a relationship before any particular component of structure, process, or outcome can be used to assess quality. The activity of quality assessment is not itself designed to establish the presence of these relationships. There must be preexisting knowledge of the linkage between structure and process, and between process and outcome, before quality assessment can be undertaken.

Knowledge about the relationship between structure and process (or between structure and outcome) proceeds from the organizational sciences. These sciences are still relatively young, so our knowledge of the effects of structure is rather scanty.[11,12] Furthermore, what we do know suggests that the relationship between structural characteristics and the process of care is rather weak. From these characteristics, we can only infer that conditions are either inimical or conducive to good care. We cannot assert that care, in fact, has been good or bad. Structural characteristics should be a major preoccupation in system design; they are a rather blunt instrument in quality assessment.

As I have already mentioned, knowledge about the relationship between attributes of the interpersonal process and the outcome of care should derive from the behavioral sciences. But so far, these sciences have contributed relatively little to quality assessment. I cannot say whether this is because of a deficiency in these sciences or a narrowness in those who assess quality.

Knowledge about the relationship between technical care and outcome derives, of course, from the health care sciences. Some of that knowledge, as we know, is pretty detailed and firm, deriving from well-conducted trials or extensive, controlled observations. Some of it is of dubious validity and open to question. Our assessments of the quality of the technical process of care vary accordingly in their certainty and persuasiveness. If we are confident that a certain strategy of care produces the best outcomes in a given category of patients, we can be equally confident that its practice represents the highest quality of care, barring concern for cost. If we are uncertain of the relationship, then our assessment of quality is correspondingly uncertain. It cannot be emphasized too strongly that our ability to assess the quality of technical care is bounded by the strengths and weaknesses of our clinical science.

There are those who believe that direct assessment of the outcome of care can free us from the limitations imposed by the imperfections of the clinical sciences. I do not believe so. Because a multitude of factors influence outcome, it is not possible to know for certain, even after extensive adjustments for differences in case mix are made, the extent to which an observed outcome is attributable to an antecedent process of care. Confirmation is needed by a direct assessment of the process itself, which brings us to the position we started from.

The assessment of outcomes, under rigorously controlled circumstances, is, of course, the method by which the goodness of alternative strategies of care is established. But, quality assessment is neither clinical research nor technology assessment. It is almost never carried out under the rigorous controls that research requires. It is, primarily, an administrative device used to monitor performance to determine whether it continues to remain within acceptable bounds. Quality assessment can, however, make a contribution to research if, in the course of assessment, associations are noted between process and outcome that seem inexplicable by current knowledge. Such discrepancies would call for elucidation through research.

If I am correct in my analysis, we cannot claim either for the measurement of process or the measurement of outcomes an inherently superior validity compared with the other, since the validity of either flows to an equal degree from the validity of the science that postulates a linkage between the two. But, process and outcome do have, on the whole, some different properties that make them more or less suitable objects of measurement for given purposes. Information about technical care is readily available in the medical record, and it is available in a timely manner, so that prompt action to correct deficiencies can be taken. By contrast, many outcomes, by their nature, are delayed, and if they occur after care is completed, information about them is not easy to obtain. Outcomes do have, however, the advantage of reflecting all contributions to care, including those of the patient. But this advantage is also a handicap, since it is not possible to say precisely what went wrong unless the antecedent process is scrutinized.

This brief exposition of strengths and weaknesses should lead to the conclusion that in selecting an approach to assessment one needs to be guided by the precise characteristics of the elements chosen. Beyond causal validity, which is the essential requirement, one is guided by attributes such as relevance to the objectives of care, sensitivity, specificity, timeliness, and costliness.[1] As a general rule, it is best to include in any system of assessment, elements of structure, process, and outcome. This allows supplementation of weakness in one approach by strength in another; it helps one interpret the findings; and if the findings do not seem to make sense, it leads to a reassessment of study design and a questioning of the accuracy of the data themselves.

Before we leave the subject of approaches to assessment, it may be useful to say a few words about patient satisfaction as a measure of the quality of care. Patient satisfaction may be considered to be one of the desired outcomes of care, even an element in health status itself. An expression of satisfaction or dissatisfaction is also the patient's judgment on the quality of care in all its aspects, but particularly as concerns the interpersonal process. By questioning patients, one can obtain information about overall satisfaction and also about satisfaction with specific attributes of the interpersonal relationship, specific components of technical care, and the outcomes of care. In doing so, it should be remembered that, unless special precautions are taken, patients may be reluctant to reveal their opinions for fear of alienating their medical attendants. Therefore, to add to the evidence at hand, information can also be sought about behaviors that indirectly suggest dissatisfaction. These include, in addition to complaints registered, premature termination of care, other forms of noncompliance, termination of membership in a health plan, and seeking care outside the plan.

It is futile to argue about the validity of patient satisfaction as a measure of quality. Whatever its strengths and limitations as an indicator of quality, information about patient satisfaction should be as indispensable to assessments of quality as to the design and management of health care systems.

SAMPLING

If one wishes to obtain a true view of care as it is actually provided, it is necessary to draw a proportionally representative sample of cases, using either simple or stratified random sampling. Because cases are primarily classified by diagnosis, this is the most frequently used attribute for stratification. But, one could use other attributes as well: site of care, specialty, demographic and socioeconomic characteristics of patients, and so on.

There is some argument as to whether patients are to be classified by discharge diagnosis, admission diagnosis, or presenting complaint. Classification by presenting complaint (for example, headache or abdominal pain) offers an opportunity to assess both success and failure in diagnosis. If discharge diagnoses are used, one can tell if the diagnosis is justified by the evidence; the failure to diagnose is revealed only if one has an opportunity to find cases misclassified under other diagnostic headings.

A step below strictly proportionate sampling, one finds methods designed to provide an illustrative rather than a representative view of quality. For example, patients may be first classified according to some scheme that represents important subdivisions of the realm of health care in general, or important components in the activities and responsibilities of a clinical department or program in particular. Then, one purposively selects, within each class, one or more categories of patients, identified by diagnosis or otherwise, whose management can be assumed to typify clinical performance for that class.

This is the "tracer method" proposed by Kessner and coworkers.[13,14] The validity of the assumption that the cases selected for assessment represent all cases in their class has not been established.

Most often, those who assess quality are not interested in obtaining a representative, or even an illustrative picture of care as a whole. Their purposes are more managerial, namely, to identify and correct the most serious failures in care and, by doing so, to create an environment of watchful concern that motivates everyone to perform better. Consequently, diagnostic categories are selected according to importance, perhaps using Williamson's[15] principle of "maximum achievable benefit," meaning that the diagnosis is frequent, deficiencies in care are common and serious, and the deficiencies are correctable.

Still another approach to sampling for managerial or reformist purposes is to begin with cases that have suffered an adverse outcome and study the process of care that has led to it. If the outcome is infrequent and disastrous (a maternal or perinatal death, for example), every case might be reviewed. Otherwise, a sample of adverse outcomes, with or without prior stratification, could be studied.[16–18] There is some evidence that, under certain circumstances, this approach will identify a very high proportion of serious deficiencies in the process of care, but not of deficiencies that are less serious.[19]

MEASUREMENT

The progression of steps in quality assessment that I have described so far brings us, at last, to the critical issue of measurement. To measure quality, our concepts of what quality consists in must be translated to more concrete representations that are capable of some degree of quantification—at least on an ordinal scale, but one hopes better. These representations are the criteria and standards of structure, process, and outcome.[20,21]

Ideally, the criteria and standards should derive, as I have already implied, from a sound, scientifically validated fund of knowledge. Failing that, they should represent the best informed, most authoritative opinion available on any particular subject. Criteria and standards can also be inferred from the practice of eminent practitioners in a community. Accordingly, the criteria and standards vary in validity, authoritativeness, and rigor.

The criteria and standards of assessment can also be either implicit or explicit. Implicit, unspoken criteria are used when an expert practitioner is given information about a case and asked to use personal knowledge and experience to judge the goodness of the process of care or of its outcome. By contrast, explicit criteria and standards for each category of cases are developed and specified in advance, often in considerable detail, usually by a panel of experts, before the assessment of individual cases begins. These are the two extremes in specification; there are intermediate variants and combinations as well.

The advantage in using implicit criteria is that they allow assessment of representative samples of cases and are adaptable to the precise characteristics of each case, making possible the highly individualized assessments that the conceptual formulation of quality envisaged. The method is, however, extremely costly and rather imprecise, the imprecision arising from inattentiveness or limitations in knowledge on the part of the reviewer and the lack of precise guidelines for quantification.

By comparison, explicit criteria are costly to develop, but they can be used subsequently to produce precise assessments at low cost, although only cases for which explicit criteria are available can be used in assessment. Moreover, explicit criteria are usually developed for categories of cases and, therefore, cannot be adapted readily to the variability among cases within a category. Still another problem is the difficulty in developing a scoring system that represents the degree to which the deficiencies in care revealed by the criteria influence the outcome of care.

Taking into account the strengths and limitations of implicit and explicit criteria, it may be best to use both in sequence or in combination. One frequently used procedure is to begin with rather abridged explicit criteria to separate cases into those likely to have received good care and those not. All the latter, as well as a sample of the former, are then assessed in greater detail using implicit criteria, perhaps supplemented by more detailed explicit criteria.

At the same time, explicit criteria themselves are being improved. As their use expands, more diagnostic categories have been included. Algorithmic criteria have been developed that are much more adaptable to the clinical characteristics of individual patients than are the more usual criteria lists.[22,23] Methods for weighting the criteria have also been proposed, although we still do not have a method of weighting that is demonstrably related to degree of impact on health status.[24]

When outcomes are used to assess the quality of antecedent care, there is the corresponding problem of specifying the several states of dysfunction and of weighting them in importance relative to each other using some system of preferences. It is possible, of course, to identify specific outcomes, for example, reductions in fatility or blood pressure, and to measure the likelihood of attaining them. It is also possible to construct hierarchical scales of physical function so that any position on the scale tells us what functions can be performed and what functions are lost.[25] The greatest difficulty arises when one attempts to represent as a single quantity various aspects of functional capacity over a life span. Though several methods of valuation and aggregation are available, there is still much controversy about the validity of the values and, in fact, about their ethical implications.[26,27] Nevertheless, such measures, sometimes called *measures of quality-adjusted life,* are being used to assess technological innovations in health care and, as a consequence, play a role in defining what good technical care is.[28,29]

INFORMATION

All the activities of assessment that I have described depend, of course, on the availability of suitable, accurate information.

The key source of information about the process of care and its immediate outcome is, no doubt, the medical record. But we know that the medical record is often incomplete in what it documents, frequently omitting significant elements of technical care and including next to nothing about the interpersonal process. Furthermore, some of the information recorded is inaccurate because of errors in diagnostic testing, in clinical observation, in clinical assessment, in recording, and in coding. Another handicap is that any given set of records usually covers only a limited segment of care, that in the hospital, for example, providing no information about what comes before or after. Appropriate and accurate recording, supplemented by an ability to collate records from various sites, is a fundamental necessity to accurate, complete quality assessment.

The current weakness of the record can be rectified to some extent by independent verification of the accuracy of some of the data it contains, for example, by reexamination of pathological specimens, x-ray films, and electrocardiographic tracings and by recoding diagnostic categorization. The information in the record can also be supplemented by interviews with, or questionaires to, practitioners and patients, information from patients being indispensable if compliance, satisfaction, and some long-term outcomes are to be assessed. Sometimes, if more precise information on outcomes is needed, patients may have to be called back for reexamination. And for some purposes, especially when medical records are very deficient, videotaping or direct observation by a colleague have been used, even though being observed might itself elicit an improvement in practice.[30,31]

CONCLUSIONS

In the preceding account, I have detailed, although rather sketchily, the steps to be taken in endeavoring to assess the quality of medical care. I hope it is clear that there is a way, a path worn rather smooth by many who have gone before us. I trust it is equally clear that we have, as yet, much more to learn. We need to know a great deal more about the course of illness with and without alternative methods of care. To compare the consequences of these methods, we need to have more precise measures of the quantity and quality of life. We need to understand more profoundly the nature of the interpersonal exchange between patient and practitioner, to learn how to identify and quantify its attributes, and to determine in what ways these contribute to the patient's health and welfare. Our information about the process and outcome of care needs to be more complete and more accurate. Our criteria and standards need to be more flexibly adaptable to the finer clinical peculiarities of each case. In particular, we need to learn how to accurately elicit the preferences of patients to arrive at truly individualized assessments of quality. All this has to go on against the background of the most profound analysis of the responsibilities of the health care professions to the individual and to society.

NOTES

1. Donabedian A: *The Definition of Quality and Approaches to Its Management,* vol 1: *Explorations in Quality Assessment and Monitoring.* Ann Arbor, Mich, Health Administration Press, 1980.

2. Eraker S, Politser P: How decisions are reached: Physician and patient. *Ann Intern Med* 1982;97:262–268.

3. Donabedian A: Models for organizing the delivery of health services and criteria for evaluating them. *Milbank Q* 1972;50:103–154.

4. McNeil BJ, Weichselbaum R, Pauker SG: Fallacy of the five-year survival in lung cancer. *N Engl J Med* 1978;299:1397–1401.

5. McNeil BJ, Weichselbaum R, Pauker SG: Tradeoffs between quality and quantity of life in laryngeal cancer. *N Engl J Med* 1981;305:982–987.

6. McNeil BJ, Pauker SG, Sox HC Jr, et al: On the elicitation of preferences for alternative therapies. *N Engl J Med* 1982;306:1259–1262.

7. Donabedian A, Wheeler JRC, Wyszewianski L: Quality, cost, and health; An integrative model. *Med Care* 1982;20:975–992.

8. Torrance GW: Measurement of health status utilities for economic appraisal: A review. *J Health Econ* 1986;5:1–30.

9. Donabedian A: Quality, cost, and clinical decisions. *Ann Am Acad Polit Soc Sci* 1983;468:196–204.

10. Donabedian A: Evaluating the quality of medical care. *Milbank Q* 1966;44:166–203.

11. Palmer RH, Reilly MC: Individual and institutional variables which may serve as indicators of quality of medical care. *Med Care* 1979;17:693–717.

12. Donabedian A: The epidemiology of quality. *Inquiry* 1985;22:282–292.

13. Kessner DM, Kalk CE, James S: Assessing health quality—the case for tracers. *N Engl J Med* 1973;288:189–194.

14. Rhee KJ, Donabedian A, Burney RE: Assessing the quality of care in a hospital emergency unit: A framework and its application. *Quality Rev Bull* 1987;13:4–16.

15. Williamson JW: Formulating priorities for quality assurance activity: Description of a method and its application. *JAMA* 1978;239:631–637.

16. New York Academy of Medicine, Committee on Public Health Relations: *Maternal Mortality in New York City; A Study of All Puerperal Deaths 1930–1932.* New York, Oxford University Press Inc, 1933.

17. Kohl SG: *Perinatal Mortality in New York City: Responsible Factors.* Cambridge, Mass, Harvard University Press, 1955.

18. Rutstein DB, Berenberg W, Chalmers TC, et al: Measuring quality of medical care: A clinical method. *N Engl J Med* 1976;294:582–588.

19. Mushlin AI, Appel FA: Testing an outcome-based quality assurance strategy in primary care. *Med Care* 1980;18:1–100.

20. Donabedian A: *The Criteria and Standards of Quality,* vol 2: *Explorations in Quality Assessment and Monitoring.* Ann Arbor, Mich, Health Administration Press, 1982.

21. Donabedian A: Criteria and standards for quality assessment and monitoring. *Quality Rev Bull* 1986;12:99–108.

22. Greenfield S, Lewis CE, Kaplan SH, et al: Peer review by criteria mapping: Criteria for diabetes mellitus: The use of decision-making in chart audit. *Ann Intern Med* 1975;83:761–770.

23. Greenfield S, Cretin S, Worthman L, et al: Comparison of a criteria map to a criteria list in quality-of-care assessment for patients with chest pain: The relation of each to outcome. *Med Care* 1981;19:255–272.

24. Lyons TF, Payne BC: The use of item weights in assessing physician performance with predetermined criteria indices. *Med Care* 1975;13:432–439.

25. Stewart AL, Ware JE Jr, Brook RH: Advances in the measurement of functional states: Construction of aggregate indexes. *Med Care* 1981;19:473–488.

26. Fanshel S, Bush JW: A health status index and its application to health service outcomes. *Operations Res* 1970;18:1021–1060.

27. Patrick DI, Bush JW, Chen MM: Methods for measuring levels of well-being for a health status index. *Health Serv Res* 1973;8:228–245.

28. Weinstein MC, Stason WB: Foundations of cost-effectiveness analysis for health and medical practices. *N Engl J Med* 1977;296:716–721.

29. Willems JS, Sanders CR, Riddiough MA, et al: Cost-effectiveness of vaccination against pneumococcal pneumonia. *N Engl J Med* 1980;303:553–559.

30. Peterson OL, Andrews LP, Spain RA, et al: An analytical study of North Carolina general practice, 1953–1954. *J Med Educ* 1956;31:1–165.

31. *What Sort of Doctor? Assessing Quality of Care in General Practice.* London, Royal College of General Practitioners, 1985.

External Environment

Nancy O. Graham

Part II examines the dual issues of the impact of the external environment on quality assurance and who is accountable.

Since the early part of this century, concern over quality of health care services has led to extensive and complex external controls. In Chapter 3, Vladeck suggests that this emphasis on controls is the result of the decentralized nature of the nation's health care system and the dominance of the American legal system, with its adversarial orientation. The basic process of external controls of health service involves three separate steps: adoption of standards, surveillance, and sanctions.

One issue raised by Vladeck is whether the processes of high quality health care are, or can be, sufficiently specified as to make external controls both effective and worthwhile. He also suggests that if we are truly concerned about not only measuring the outcomes of health services but assuring that they are as good as possible, we should probably be devoting less energy to measuring outcomes and more to the task of establishing controls on the quality assurance process itself.

In Chapter 4, Roberts et al. discuss the future direction of the Joint Commission on Accreditation of Healthcare Organizations. For example, they indicated that the standards for assessment of quality have moved from an emphasis on implicit review, to standards that required the performance of structural audits, to the current requirements for ongoing, improvement-oriented quality assurance programs. In December 1986, the Joint Commission's Board of Commissioners decided to refocus the paradigm for accreditation by establishing a new project, the "Agenda for Change." This new project was designed to concentrate on key quality-related clinical and management functions, and the ability to monitor the effectiveness with which these functions are performed and outcomes obtained. This chapter describes the objectives, current status, and short-term priorities of the Agenda for Change and the impact it is likely to have on health care organizations.

In chapter 5, Orsolits and Abbey discuss the Peer Review Program (PRO)—its history, the review process, its impact on hospitals, and future issues as they relate to cost, quality, and access.

What individuals, groups, or combinations of review procedures best protect the patients' interests—health organizations, government, private external quality review organizations, or group purchasers of care? The present situation is a patchwork of accountability, resulting in a situation fraught with confusion, competition for turf, and suspicion about motives.[1]

Berwick states that health care regulators must become more sensitive to the cost and ineffectiveness of relying on inspection to improve quality. Those who rely on this approach ("theory of bad apples") believe that quality is best achieved by discovering bad apples and removing them from the lot. Berwick believes that real improvement in quality depends on continual improvement throughout the organization through constant efforts to decrease waste, rework, and complexity. Continual research is also essential to improve all processes.[2]

NOTES

1. K.N. Lohr, K.D. Yardy, and S.O. Thier, "Current Issues in Quality of Care," *Health Affairs* (1988):5–18.

2. D.M. Berwick, "Continuous Improvement as an Ideal in Health Care," *New England Journal of Medicine* 320 (1989):53–56.

Chapter 3

Quality Assurance through External Controls

Bruce C. Vladeck

In keeping with contemporary mores, recent concerns with the quality of health services have focused largely on questions of measurement, comparison, public disclosure, and incentives and disincentives. An era that glorifies markets, deregulation, and the mythology of consumer sovereignty inclines the debate in that direction. But quality *assurance,* both as a process and as an objective, has been often viewed historically as requiring mechanisms for administrative, bureaucratic, or legal controls external to specific providers of health service. It is unlikely, given the realities of the American political system, that pressures to maintain, refine, and even expand such controls will be permanently resisted. Even during the deregulatory Reagan administration, peer review organizations (PROs) have been created and their responsibilities expanded; external review of health maintenance organizations (HMOs) that serve Medicare patients has been mandated; and standards for nursing home licensure are being strengthened while new surveillance processes are being implemented. Congressional proposals have called for still more—and wider and deeper—controls on facilities and physicians and on such processes as AIDS testing.

Concern for the quality of health services did not originate yesterday. Since the early part of this century, the quality of services and service providers has been understood, correctly enough, to have important implications for the health of the public, and thus to constitute an appropriate arena for intervention by public authorities or their delegated private agents.[1] In the legal sense, the issue of health care quality has long been interpreted as closer to that of contaminated milk than of false advertising, and whatever passing fancies may dominate in the political arena, the judiciary has demonstrated admirable restraint in maintaining this tradition.

Note: Reprinted from *Inquiry,* Vol. 25, pp. 100–107, with permission of Blue Cross and Blue Shield Association, © Spring 1988.

There have been efforts to assure quality through external controls for quite some time. While it is, in some sense, remarkable how little systematic knowledge has been gained about such efforts, there are important lessons from that experience, which are the primary subject of this paper.

A recognition of both the inevitability and the justification for external controls on health services should hardly be equated with an uncritical or unqualified judgment about their effectiveness, or benefits compared with costs, however. There are some things that external controls can do rather well, the record suggests, and other things for which they may be intrinsically incompetent or inappropriate. Perhaps more importantly—but posing more difficulties from an analytic perspective—external controls can be designed and administered well, or poorly, or anywhere in between. Summative evaluative judgments about the suitability or effectiveness of external controls that fail to take that most basic fact into account can produce highly misleading conclusions.

In this paper I selectively review the experience with efforts to maintain external controls on the quality of health services, offer some observations about that experience, and then seek to draw some implications for future policy. I begin with an examination of one extreme-case paradigm.

EXTERNAL CONTROLS: A PARADIGM

It has been years since anyone died in a multiple-death fire in a licensed health care facility. Given all the other ways there are to die in health care facilities, and the expense that has been incurred to ensure the protection of patients and staff from fire hazards, that may not constitute an entirely unmixed blessing, but it does represent a particularly clear instance of cause and effect between external controls and an aspect of health services not unrelated to the quality of care.

The Life Safety Code and its impact constitute a useful paradigm for thinking about external controls, because they are characterized by objective, frequently quantifiable standards that reflect a reasonably high level of professional consensus about their content, compliance with which can be readily and objectively verified, and for which compliance is not only valued by providers of service but reinforced by environmental forces and incentives quite apart from the external control process itself.

Distances between smoke partitions or the combustibility of construction materials does not permit much interpretation, subjectivity, or individual judgment. Such standards may, in fact, be as arbitrary and untested as other prescriptions people find more objectionable, but it is hard to see how even the most informed layman would know. Moreover, however abstruse or technical the knowledge base on which they are grounded, most Life Safety Code standards have a certain intuitive plausibility to laymen not expert in fire prevention or suppression, but who have spent most of their lives in man-made structures.

Specific standards for fire protection have, from time to time, been the subject of bitter controversy within specialized branches of the engineering community, but the level of professional consensus about most standards seems, at least from the outside, to be reasonably high. Institutions obligated to conform to the standards do not perceive themselves as victims of the winning party or as injured bystanders in internecine professional conflict. The implementation of new generations of standards has, in fact, frequently been the subject of vigorous controversy, generally concerning the economic impact of such standards and the likely ratio of benefits to costs that the implementation of such standards would entail.

These controversies constitute a sort of subparadigm, which speaks to the frequent allegations that regulation through external controls is inadequately sensitive to the balancing of costs and benefits. For while it is true that technical standards, derived from technical consensus, may be indifferent to a cost-benefit calculus, those who administer external controls, by adopting such standards and then seeking to enforce them, can and often do engage in such calculations. Economists or other political partisans may not like their decisions, but the decisions are ultimately political or administrative rather than technocratic. In the frequent instances in which waivers to Life Safety Code compliance are permitted, cost-benefit calculations about them are made all the time.

However they might feel about the costs of compliance, most health care providers are presumably in agreement with the intent of Life Safety Code regulation. Moreover, even if the administrative apparatus responsible for these external controls is weak or even indifferent, compliance is privately enforced both by liability insurers and by lending agencies that sit athwart potential capital flows to the institution.

To be sure, the Life Safety Code is the apotheosis of so-called structural regulation, which is generally scorned for its putative simplemindedness, inflexibility, and ostensible irrelevance to actual patterns of clinical service and the implications of those patterns for patient outcomes. Injury from a preventable fire is, however, presumably an extremely adverse patient outcome. The real distinctiveness of such structural regulation lies in its relative rarity. One suspects that if the knowledge base underlying health services were substantially more advanced, or medical care itself less permeated by uncertainty than it is, structural regulation would be both more widespread and more widely accepted.

EXTERNAL CONTROLS: A GENERAL OVERVIEW

Providers of health services in the United States are subjected to more external controls than their counterparts anywhere else in the world, and they are more extensive, more intrusive, and more complex. There are two primary reasons for this.

First, there are more external controls in the American system precisely because it is so decentralized, pluralistic, and fragmented. The oversight of providers that occurs elsewhere, formally or informally, within the administrative structures that provide care must be accomplished through external controls in the United States because more comprehensive structures do not exist. Providers in the United States, for instance, derive their income from literally dozens of different sources, each of which either seeks to develop its own external controls on utilization and minimum quality of services or acquiesces in or supports the collective delegation of that role to government bodies. Conversely, it is often argued that large group practices, whether prepaid or not, are able to provide consistently high levels of service quality because of the control mechanisms intrinsic to their basic social and operating structure, which internalize controls that elsewhere must be imposed from outside.[2]

Second, the extent and, to a large degree, the nature of external controls on providers of health services in the United States arise, in a way largely not well understood by those providers themselves, from the nature of the American legal system. Other English-speaking nations share the common law tradition, but none also share the Bill of Rights, especially the Fifth Amendment. Uniquely American concepts of due process, of property rights, and of the appropriateness, and appropriate form, of adversarial procedures both dominate the process of external control and reinforce its proliferation.

In the American legal context, the critical question, in terms of external controls on the quality of health services, is what constitutes evidence. Subjective clinical judgment, which lies, of course, at the heart of actual medical practice—including high-quality practice—rarely generates the kind of objective, documentable, testable evidence that becomes necessary whenever quality is called into question. To impose sanctions, or provide special rewards, or even to provide an official stamp of approval or acceptance, public agencies must extend due process of law to providers, which means observing certain evidentiary standards.[3] Even privately generated and administered external controls tend to observe the same standards, either because public expectations require them to or simply because their lawyers, being lawyers, reflexively demand it.

To be sure, the American legal system has never been insensitive to the special characteristics of highly technical professions, and has long delegated—and continues to delegate—extraordinary autonomy to private professional entities such as the Liaison Committee on Graduate Medical Education or the Joint Commission on Accreditation of Healthcare Organizations (JCAHO)—or, indeed, the National Fire Protection Association. But the legal system is also not insensitive to more general tides in broad public opinion, and as public willingness to unquestioningly accept the unsupervised decision making of professionals erodes, the whole evidentiary apparatus that tends to surround external controls comes with them.

Whether current tendencies toward the development of new external controls might have been prevented had professionals done a better job of self-regulation in the past is a historically interesting, but essentially moot question. More relevant is the notion that intrinsic to the effective performance of at least some parts of professional activities like medicine or nursing are elements of experience, subjectivity, and judgment that might be effectively overseen by appropriate professional mechanisms (e.g., idealized peer review) but which simply do not fit with the standards and biases of formalized, legalized external controls. An experienced and open-minded surgeon probably can judge pretty well the competence of another surgeon by observing him in the operating room or just reading patients' charts, but he is also likely to have a difficult time defending his judgment under adversarial cross-examination. And whether or not he is actually going to be subjected to cross-examination, external control processes will likely require that he act as though he were going to be.

The surrounding legal environment thus pushes external control processes in the direction of that which is objectifiable, measurable, and quantifiable. Of course, other forces in this society and this culture push in the same direction. The result, however, may at least sometimes be that administrators of external controls end up behaving like the drunk who concentrates his search for his lost keys under the lamppost not because he believes the keys are anywhere nearby, but because that's where he has the most light. External controls may focus on relatively secondary or tangential aspects of service quality not because anyone really believes that they constitute high-quality service, but because that is what they are capable of focusing on.

WHAT EXTERNAL CONTROLS DO

The basic process of external control of health services, like other regulatory and quasi-regulatory activities in this society, can be described in three separate steps: the adoption of formal standards, surveillance of providers to assess the degree of compliance with those standards, and imposition of whatever sanctions or incentives the external control agency may employ in response to reported deviations from standards. Each of these steps has its own strengths and weaknesses and its own effects.

Standards

The development of formal standards as part of a process of external control, necessitated by the underlying legal environment, can have important educational and exemplary effects. The mere adoption of a set of formal rules by an authoritative body can both ratify the state of the art surrounding important issues and provide a template for providers of service motivated, by whatever impulses, to adopt the most current practices. In its earlier years, many JCAHO standards filled this role.[4] More recent examples might include mandatory screening of newborns for phenylketonuria (PKU) and other genetic disorders, as now required in most states, and controls on the use of ethylene oxide as a sterilizing agent.

To be sure, formal standards can become technically obsolescent, and thus retard rather than promote more effective health care delivery. They can be excessively and counterproductively stringent, as has probably been the case with many of the requirements imposed on hospices as a condition for Medicare participation. Or they can simply be ill conceived, like the so-called Baby Doe regulations. How serious the adverse effect of poor standards will be depends, to some extent, on how rigorously they are interpreted and enforced. If external control agencies are neither obtuse nor pursuing a punitive political agenda (and sometimes they are one or the other, or worse, both), poor standards will cause only limited damage, although everyone would still be better off with better standards.

Perhaps more seriously, the process of generating standards for health services quality that can be used in the administration of external controls generally devolves into an effort to define a minimum, rather than an optimum, level of acceptable performance. Standards tend to focus on adequacy rather than excellence. And while the old political maxim holds that the excellent can be the enemy of the good, it may also be that where the quality of health services is concerned, the good may be the enemy of the excellent. Given the widespread human tendency to get by, to do just enough, to satisfy rather than maximize, standards set too low or too broad may promote mediocrity. To weed out the completely inadequate, we may sometimes pay the price of promoting the second best.[5]

Still, it is important for administrators, clinicians, and patients to have a set of common expectations about the basic characteristics of the system in which they all participate. Formal standards ratified by external control agents may provide a uniquely useful form for defining such expectations. Some degree of literal standardization is also probably desirable, though probably less necessary than in the past, when other mechanisms for national communication of professional consensus on standards of care were less well developed. In the current environment, indeed, the *process* of developing standards itself is probably more significant, since for many aspects of health services, external control agencies have become the authoritative sources for professional consensus on how care should be delivered. As contemporary debates on new Joint Commission standards for hospital medical staffs or quality assurance activities, or on federal conditions of participation for nursing homes, suggest, the standards-setting process and the policy-making process have become one and the same. Formal standards adopted by authoritative external control agencies not only embody policy, they *are* policy.

Surveillance

No matter how well motivated anyone may be, it would appear to constitute a basic rule of human nature that people and institutions behave better, or at least conform better to shared mores, whether formal or informal, when they believe their actions are likely to be scrutinized by outsiders. The greatest advantage of the surveillance component of the external control process involves precisely that phenomenon. All other things being equal, people behave better when other people are watching.

Of course, surveillance, like most things, can be done in a wide variety of ways, and at widely varying levels of quality. There is substantial literature on the mechanics of surveillance, much of it from areas of endeavor ordinarily thought to be quite far afield of health services, such as police work, but not perhaps entirely irrelevant. Much of the extensive dialogue between PROs and the Health Care Financing Administration, and between PROs and providers of service, focuses on the most narrow and specific details of surveillance strategy, such as sample size and sampling procedures, automatic screens, and categories of cases deemed to require universal review. Similarly, there is heated debate over the optimal period that should elapse between consecutive "annual" surveys of nursing homes.[6] In such debates, the participants obviously believe that different strategies imply different constellations of benefits and costs to providers and surveillants, and that the choice of strategies implies a choice of winners and losers.

This is not the place for an extensive discussion of the issues surrounding surveillance, but the debates themselves illustrate several important characteristics of the surveillance component of the external control process. To begin with, surveillance has costs, both for the external control agency and for providers. The benefits of surveillance, in terms of eliciting improved compliance, probably diminish with increased surveillance activity and, thus, increased surveillance cost. Indeed, the curve may even turn downward if excessively intrusive surveillance engenders a combative posture on the part of providers. Furthermore, not all surveillance activities are equally effective in inducing compliance with standards or in identifying noncompliers. Finally, surveillance has effects secondary to, or even unrelated to, what is commonly perceived as its primary purpose of identifying deficiencies. It may serve an educational purpose for providers and external control organizations alike. It may be used punitively, especially in circumstances where external control agencies feel frustrated in their ability to use formal sanctions. Alternatively, surveillance may substitute for other, more effective or more relevant quality assurance activities when external control agencies are incapable of, or unwilling to perform, more effective activities.

Sanctions

Both external control agencies and providers of service tend to focus much of their attention and energy on the sanctions component of the control process, when in many instances that is the least important part. As has been discussed, much of what can be attained through external control is attained in the standards formation process or the surveillance process. Still, the existence of sanctions, and the possibility they might be invoked, is in at least some sense the engine that drives the entire system. In the absence of sanctions, not only are providers less likely to comply with standards, but the shape of the surveillance process is radically changed, since the quality of evidence required by the need for formal sanctions is no longer necessary.

A case could be made that standards and surveillance are overemphasized in most efforts to address the problem of health care quality through external controls in the United States, and that sanctions are invoked too rarely. Too some extent, this is a result of the legal environment discussed in the foregoing. To impose any sanction that has any meaning on a provider, external control agencies not only must observe the entire panoply of due process requirements, but also are likely to need to invest considerable resources in that process itself.[7] How much preferable, the tendency often is to believe, to rely on the deterrence effect of potential sanctions. But if sanctions are never invoked, they lose their deterrent effect.

Moreover, the widespread presumption in favor of the inherent good intentions of health care professionals and other providers of health services still dominates, perhaps appropriately, not only within the legal and quasi-legal due process systems, but within most external control agencies themselves. These agencies are often staffed by people with the same educational backgrounds and professional disciplines—and possibly the same career objectives—as direct providers of service. In that part of the literature which is most hostile to any form of governmental regulation, the tendency of regulators to identify with and share common interests with those they are regulating is defined as part of the inevitable process of regulatory "capture" by the regulatees.[8] In fact, there is probably some optimal balance between mistrust and sympathy which every external control agency should maintain toward those it is supposed to be controlling, and that optimum is probably difficult to attain and even more difficult to maintain. Moreover, external controls are imposed on activities like health care precisely because those activities are deemed to be so important to the well-being of the public. The art of effective external control often involves trying to improve service provision while still ensuring that those services remain widely available.

Nonetheless, if maintaining the quality of health services is so important to the public, external control agencies, for whatever reasons, have probably not done nearly as much as they might have to protect the public from grossly inadequate providers by levying whatever sanctions they might have had available on at least the most extreme miscreants. In those instances where external control agencies have been suddenly energized by external forces, as in enforcement efforts following nursing home scandals in the early and mid-1970s, the results have, so far as anyone can tell, been quite positive.[9]

The example of enforcement of sanctions on nursing homes also raises another issue about the sanctions process: Not all sanctions are equal, and, as is the case in the criminal justice system, the public may not be well served when the only tools of enforcement are especially blunt and punitive. External control agencies, faced with sanctions they or the reviewing courts believe to be excessively harsh—such as the loss of the license to practice (in the case of an individual practitioner) or the loss of the license to operate (in the case of an institution), necessitating the relocation of patients—may seek informal alternative means to try to induce better behavior from providers. They may rely on exhortation, on bluffing, or on tacit acceptance of indefinite delays in the sanctions-invoking process. The problem with such behavior is that those providers who probably should be expelled from the market catch on quickly, and whatever risk they pose to the public can be indefinitely prolonged.

Thus, those concerned with the external control process have increasingly sought to develop "intermediate sanctions," penalties such as civil fines or time-limited suspensions that reflect both the unacceptability of the provider's performance and the expectation that, once the sanction has served its purpose, the provider ought to have another chance to demonstrate improved performance.[10] Whether the availability of such intermediate sanctions will induce external control agencies to become more aggressive and effective in their enforcement activities, or just provide an additional level of opportunities for temporizing and delay, remains to be seen. The issue, however, of how to make the "punishment" fit the qualitative shortcoming will remain.

EXTERNAL CONTROLS AND HEALTH CARE QUALITY

To summarize the discussion to this point, external controls on the quality of health services, or other services, can work well when it is possible to specify the components or attributes of quality in some detail. To say that they can work well does not mean that they necessarily *will* work well, but making them work well in those instances is something it is at least theoretically possible to do.

The real problem in the use of external controls to assure quality, at least at the current state of the art in health care, is the difficulty specifying the components of quality in a way that can be effectively employed in control processes, either internal or external. In those few instances in which a causal relationship between structural attributes of health care provider and quality of care are well understood, external controls have contributed importantly to quality improvements. The question is what to do about the far more numerous instances in which such causal relationships are not so well understood. To address that question, and to more fully explore the relationship between quality and external controls, it is necessary to complete the classic trilogy[11] and consider the outcome and process dimensions of quality.

The current literature focuses largely on the measurement of outcomes. Not only do outcome standards have considerable intuitive appeal, since presumably the effect of medical care interventions on patients are the real "bottom line" for the health care enterprise, but they fit quite nicely in an era that glorifies market or pseudomarket behavior, since outcomes are presumably what consumers can most readily comprehend and what they care, or are supposed to care, most about. External control processes, by contrast, cannot deal very well with outcomes. The reasons they cannot, I would suggest, raises questions about the utility of outcome measures altogether.

The problem of outcome measures for external control processes is that they do not link cause and effect closely enough to support control processes that fit in the due process environment. To invoke any kind of sanction on the producer of a bad outcome, it is necessary to be able to demonstrate something that the provider did or failed to do that caused or contributed to that outcome. But those things that providers do or do not perform are what we usually call "process."

Indeed, to effectively operate any kind of quality assurance process, whether external or internal, one has to be able to associate outcomes with behaviors. If not, adverse outcomes become random events, acts of nature, or otherwise inexplicable phenomena that one may deplore but about which it is impossible to do anything. Moreover, but not less importantly, if outcomes are not linked to certain processes, it is always at least theoretically possible that such outcomes might be attained through processes that are considered unacceptable by whoever is asking the qualitative question. To take one example, we do care, or at least we should care, whether an outcome has been produced by unethical behavior, but ethics is largely a matter of process.

Indeed, if one looks at instances in which outcome data have actually been put to use, they tend to serve one of two purposes. They are used either in an attempt to employ a crude measure of quality or as a screen or a flag to identify instances on which review of the processes of care should be focused. There is nothing wrong with measuring quality per se, but such measurement has only an indirect and secondary relationship to assuring quality.

The question thus becomes one of whether the processes of high-quality health care are, or can be, sufficiently specified to make external controls both effective and worthwhile. Here, the jury is clearly still out. There are some obvious, simple cases—routine immunizations as part of periodic well-child exams, or measuring blood pressure in many encounters with adult patients—but these are, indeed, the simple cases. Whether efforts, including some currently under way, to provide substantially more comprehensive specification of optimal, or at least minimally acceptable, medical care process will prove useful, or instead bring all the dangers and disadvantages of "cookbook medicine," remains to be seen. The final judgment probably depends, more than anything else, on the progress of biomedical science in altering the balance between the scientific and judgmental components of medical practice.

I have two more observations to make about process. First, there are many characteristics of medical care about which consumers care very much, but which are largely overlooked or ignored in contemporary discussions of health care quality. These include the availability of providers, waiting times for service, and provider courtesy and considerateness—what Donabedian refers to as the "interpersonal" aspects and the "amenities" of care, as opposed to the "technical" aspects.[12] All these are process attributes, although the extent to which they should be subjected to external controls is highly questionable.

Second, and perhaps more important, although it may not be possible, given the current state of knowledge, to administer external controls that address the most important attributes of the process of health care (important in the sense that they most affect outcomes), it may well be possible to intervene at a higher level by creating expectations for the *process* of quality assurance. We may not know enough to adequately specify the processes of optimal health care, but any reasonable notion of professionalism entails beliefs about the unspecifiable—that is, subjective, experimental, and judgmental—components of quality, which include the capacity of professionals to assess one another's work.[13] Again, such beliefs have traditionally found considerable sympathy in the legal system, which is itself largely run by professionals.

It is certainly true that the track record of intraprofessional mechanisms for quality assurance in health care has not been particularly distinguished, and that the failure of such mechanisms underlies much of the contemporary effort to identify alternative mechanisms, whether in the form of the marketplace, formal external controls, or something else. But it may well be that the missing link is effective external control of internal controls, whether at the level of the institution or of the professional group. An external agency may never be able to definitively determine whether Doctor A did the right thing in his care of Patient B, but it can certainly tell whether anyone else with the appropriate, nonspecifiable expertise to make a judgment checked on Doctor A's performance, in a process of checking designed to identify and remedy problems of inadequate performance in a way that does not impose inordinate burdens on either the checker or the checkee.

This consideration of the relationship between external controls and the assurance of health services quality concludes with two paradoxes. First, precisely because it is so difficult to specify comprehensively and exhaustively the attributes of high-quality medical care in all cases, it may be necessary to specify, and enforce, *processes* of quality assurance. Second, if we are truly concerned about not merely measuring the outcomes of health services, but assuring that they are as good as possible, we should probably be devoting less time and energy to the measurement of outcomes themselves and more to the substantially more irksome and frustrating tasks of developing and maintaining internal and external controls on quality assurance *processes* in health care.

NOTES

1. Michael G. Macdonald, Kathryn C, Meyer, and Beth Essig, *Health Care Law: A Practical Guide* (New York: Matthew Bender & Co., 1987), 5:1.

2. Walter McClure, "Toward Development and Application of a Qualitative Theory of Hospital Utilization," *Inquiry* 19 (Summer 1982):117–135.

3. Kenneth R. Wing, *The Law and the Public's Health,* 2d ed. (Ann Arbor, Mich.: Health Administration Press, 1985), chap. 6.

4. James S. Roberts, Jack, G. Coale, and Robert R. Redman, "A History of the Joint Commission on Accreditation of Hospitals," *Journal of the American Medical Association* 258 (Aug. 21, 1987):936–940.

5. National Academy of Sciences, Institute of Medicine, Committee on Nursing Home Regulation, *Improving the Quality of Care in Nursing Homes* (Washington, D.C.: National Academy Press, 1987), chap. 6.

6. "IOM Panelist Flays OMB over Survey Cycle Proposal," *Long Term Care Management* 16 (Dec. 3, 1987):2.

7. Bruce C. Vladeck, *Unloving Care: The Nursing Home Tragedy* (New York: Basic Books, 1980), 162–167.

8. George J. Stigler, "The Theory of Economic Regulation," *Bell Journal of Economics* 2 (1971):3–21.

9. National Academy of Sciences (note 5).

10. *Ibid.,* pp. 155–168.

11. A. Donabedian, "Evaluating the Quality of Medical Care," *Millbank Memorial Fund Quarterly: Health and Society* 44 (July 1966):166–206.

12. A. Donabedian, *The Definition of Quality and Approaches to Its Assessment* (Ann Arbor, Mich.: Health Administration Press, 1980).

13. A. Donabedian, "Advantages and Limitations of Explicit Criteria for Assessing the Quality of Health Care," *Milbank Memorial Fund Quarterly: Health and Society* 59 (Winter 1981):99–106.

Chapter 4

The Agenda for Change— Future Directions of the Joint Commission on Accreditation of Healthcare Organizations

James S. Roberts, Paul M. Schyve, James A. Prevost, Bruce H. Ente, and Maureen P. Carr

INTRODUCTION

The history of the Joint Commission on Accreditation of Healthcare Organizations and its predecessor, the American College of Surgeons' (ACS) Hospital Standardization Program, has been well chronicled.[1,2] One example of professional commitment to self-assessment and improvement, accreditation of health care organizations has been an essential component of the United States health care system since the ACS program was initiated in 1918.

Through the years, the Joint Commission's standards, survey processes, and decision-making methods have evolved in concert with the changes in health care and with experience. For example, standards for the assessment of quality have moved from an emphasis on implicit review, to standards that required the performance of structured audits, to the current requirements for ongoing, improvement-oriented quality assurance programs.[3] More recently, standards related to the plant, technology, and safety management and to infection control have been revised to focus on effective management of these key functions.[4,5]

Over the years there have also been improvements in survey processes, as illustrated by the use of specialized surveyors to evaluate specific standards, expansion of the size of the teams used to survey hospitals, doubling of the length of the survey for small hospitals, and development of survey-scoring guidelines for all Joint Commission accreditation manuals. These guidelines constitute the "rules of the game" and are used by the Joint Commission in judging compliance with standards.

James S. Roberts, MD, is Senior Vice President, Research and Planning for the Joint Commission on Accreditation of Healthcare Organizations.

Paul M. Schyve, MD, **James A. Prevost,** MD, **Bruce H. Ente,** and **Maureen P. Carr** are also associated with the Joint Commission on Accreditation of Healthcare Organizations.

These survey changes, along with expansion of the Joint Commission's internal information handling capacity, have allowed a more sophisticated analysis of survey findings and more consistent differentiation of levels of accreditation—a capability evidenced by the recent creation of a category called "conditional accreditation."[6]

While important, these enhancements (and other significant changes made over the years) have been guided by the same model of accreditation. From its inception, accreditation has been designed to be a measure of organizational capability. Accreditation standards have focused on those organizational structures and processes that experts believe are necessary to an organization's capability to consistently provide quality patient care. Standards have not prompted organizations to evaluate and improve the effectiveness of these activities; nor have the Joint Commission's survey and monitoring processes been able to independently test the effectiveness with which these functions are performed.

A PARADIGM SHIFT

Thus, from 1918 until 1986, the paradigm for accreditation remained unchanged. In December 1986, however, the Joint Commission's Board of Commissioners decided to pursue a significant shift in this paradigm. This purposeful evolution became a major developmental project called the "Agenda for Change"—a project designed to focus the accreditation standards on key quality-related clinical and management functions and to build within the Joint Commission the ability to monitor the effectiveness with which these key functions are performed. The remainder of this chapter describes the rationale for this initiative; its objectives, current status, and near-term priorities; and the impact it is likely to have on health care organizations.

THE GENESIS OF THE AGENDA FOR CHANGE

The 1986 decision to pursue the Agenda for Change resulted from broad-based discontent with the ineffectiveness with which health care organizations were addressing the quality of their care and services—a problem demonstrated both by Joint Commission survey data and by a large and growing body of research showing substantial variation within and across hospitals in the quality of care—no matter what measures were used to assess quality.[7-9]

These survey and health services research findings led the Joint Commission to conclude that

1. The future of health care would include an unswerving demand for health care organizations to be accountable to government, pur-

chasers of care, and the public concerning the cost, quality, and value of the care they provide.
2. This demand, while justified by the amount of societal resources being devoted to health care, was one that the vast majority of health care organizations were ill prepared to meet.
3. The Joint Commission's role as standard setter, evaluator, decision maker, and educator made it a logical vehicle through which national experts could identify the changes needed to meet this demand and stimulate their implementation.

With these conclusions in mind, the Joint Commission initiated the Agenda for Change in early 1987.

OBJECTIVES OF THE AGENDA FOR CHANGE

Viewed in its broadest context, the Agenda for Change involves substantial improvement in all major Joint Commission activities. Educational programs and publications are being modified to ensure that their content is of direct, practical value to the users. Communications with the health care field are being improved, and new communication channels are now open with those who purchase, regulate, insure, and consume health care services. Most pivotal to the future effectiveness of the Joint Commission, however, are the initiatives to refocus and improve standards and accreditation activities. This retooling of accreditation will be the result of the multiyear research and development effort described in the balance of this chapter.

Improving the Accreditation Process

This accreditation initiative involves two major objectives: (1) modify Joint Commission standards to better identify those clinical and organizational functions that are most important to the quality of care, and (2) improve Joint Commission surveys, monitoring systems, accreditation decisions, and evaluation reports to stimulate continual improvement in the performance of these functions by accredited organizations. These objectives are based on the premise that quality patient care will occur only when an organization has a clear understanding of the clinical, managerial, and governance functions essential to high quality care; a determination to constantly assess the effectiveness with which these functions are being fulfilled; and a commitment to continually improve this effectiveness, regardless of its current level.

This premise has its operational translation in the many familiar clinical and managerial functions that health care organizations pursue every day. These functions can be divided into two categories—those that affect patients directly and those that support direct care. Examples of each are shown in Exhibits 4-1 and 4-2.

Without exception, fulfillment of these functions requires the combined efforts of several individuals and, often, many departments within the organization. For example, the initial clinical assessment of a trauma patient involves physicians, nurses, and often other practitioners as well. If this assessment is to result in appropriate triage, it must be performed well by every individual, and the results of these separate evaluations must come together in a unified judgment that is enhanced by the complementary work of each person. Likewise, the accurate delineation of clinical privileges will have a positive impact on quality only if its importance is understood by all those involved; if it receives the tangible resources (e.g., people, information, and proper legal protection) needed to reach objective conclusions; and if opportunities to improve the process are sought systematically and implemented when found. These examples illustrate a fact that is understood intuitively by all in health care—the quality of the care received by an individual patient or by a population of patients is the result of the combined efforts of all those who govern and manage the organization and who provide and support patient care.

While the importance of this concept is understood, most health care organizations have done little to foster such coordination. Prompted in part by the department-oriented construct of current Joint Commission standards, and reinforced by both the natural territorial instincts of human beings and the historical tendency to view quality strictly as a clinical issue, contemporary quality assurance programs often work at counterpurpose to the coordinated efforts essential to good care.

Identifying an approach to overcome this problem was an early priority of the Agenda for Change. Led by a task force of quality of care experts, the Joint Commission adopted the "Principles of Organization and Management Effectiveness," which are shown in Appendix 4-A. The preamble to these principles, reproduced in Exhibit 4-3 serves to emphasize the

---

Exhibit 4-1 Examples of Functions That Affect the Patient Directly

1. Accurate and timely initial clinical assessment
2. Effective use of appropriate diagnostic testing
3. Effective use of appropriate treatment modalities
4. Accurate matching of postdischarge care to patient needs
5. Effective use of preventive care and patient education services

Exhibit 4-2 Examples of Functions That Support Patient Care

1. Consistent and effective involvement of leaders in all phases of quality assessment and improvement
2. Accurate matching of an individual's competence with his/her clinical, managerial, or governance responsibilities
3. Explicit attention to quality in planning and budgeting activities
4. Efficient acquisition and effective use of information for quality assessment and improvement
5. Effective coordination, communication, and conflict resolution within and across departments

critical importance of organization-wide devotion to the continual improvement in the quality of care.

PROJECT STRUCTURE

Using these principles as a blueprint, the Joint Commission has created a structure consisting of (1) panels of national experts that define and develop indicators and standards and (2) pilot site health care organizations that test each indicator for feasibility and value. Guiding and providing policy and technical oversite to the project is the Accreditation Project Steering Committee, a group composed of Joint Commission Commissioners and internationally recognized experts in quality evaluation and organizational change.

Priority is being given to the standard setting and indicator development activities that are outlined below.

Exhibit 4-3 The Preamble to the Principles of Organization and
Management Effectiveness

Total organizational commitment to continuously improve the quality of patient care is the central concern of these principles. This commitment is woven throughout the fabric of the organization, appearing in strategic planning, allocation of resources, role expectations, reward structures, performance evaluations, and the role of the organization in the community. An ongoing, comprehensive self-assessment system supports and promotes continuous improvement in the quality of patient care. This self-assessment system seeks feedback on the quality of care from patients as well as practitioners, from payors as well as other organizational care providers, from employees as well as the community. This system of ongoing monitoring and evaluation of clinical and organizational performance provides information to leadership regarding day-to-day patient care decisions and promotes fiscally responsible organizational change that will improve the quality of patient care.

STANDARDS PRIORITIES

Joint Commission accreditation has been, and will continue to be, based upon an assessment of an organization's compliance with standards—specifications of those functions or objectives that a health care organization must fulfill if its patients are to receive the maximum possible benefit from its services. Accreditation standards have, historically, addressed these functions by defining both the process by which the function should be performed (process standards) and the organizational structure through which it was to be conducted (structural standards).

By contrast, the standards that emerge from the Agenda for Change will focus less on structure, while addressing processes in a much more targeted fashion. Standards that are duplicated or outdated will be deleted. The resulting standards will address only those functions that are critical to the quality of care. Many of these functions already included in the current standards (e.g., accurate assessment of clinical competence; effective quality control of key processes; the effective prevention, surveillance, detection, and control of infections; etc.). These standards will be retained and improved.

New standards will be added if they address key functions not covered in the present standards. The first three such topics have now been identified: (1) leadership activities related to quality, (2) approaches to quality assessment and improvement, (3) information management. Also under consideration is the addition of succinct, yet potentially powerful, provisions that would require organizations to monitor and improve the effectiveness of particularly important components of each of the functions addressed in the standards. For example, current privilege delineation standards require that professional criteria be used as a basis for deciding which clinical privileges an individual should be granted. A useful addition would be to require the hospital to use objective data about individual performance both to judge the adequacy of the criteria and the mechanisms employed to apply them and to improve those that are found wanting.

Another example concerns the establishment of goals for patients in comprehensive physical rehabilitation programs. Current standards require that functional or behavioral goals be established for each patient needing rehabilitative care. An important addition would be to require that the nature of the goals and the effectiveness with which they are established be reevaluated periodically, and that the goals and manner of their establishment be improved based on the findings of the evaluation. Similar attention to goal setting would also enhance the quality of the care provided to patients with chronic mental illness.

Noted above is the Joint Commission's intent to reduce the number of "structural" requirements in the standards. The value of such provisions, once a major component of the standards, is increasingly being questioned.

This change in the Joint Commission's mindset parallels a broader effort within the health care field to focus on measures that are more proximal to the actual quality of care. These tendencies are being reinforced by new laws and regulations that have expanded the scope of practice of many health care professional groups and by the growing need for greater flexibility as health care organizations respond to an environment that demands more efficiency and effectiveness in the delivery of services.

In this environment, compelling questions are being raised about standards that require an organization to be structured in a specific manner; or that reserve important responsibilities for certain designated individuals or professional groups; or that require an organization to provide, as a minimum, a specified set of clinical services.

Each of these standards, along with many others, was created in the honest belief that it would contribute positively to the quality of care. Yet these standards have, at best, an indirect relationship to quality; may be at variance with state law or regulation; may constrain unnecessarily the managerial and clinical flexibility an organization should properly have; and, most important, may give the impression that quality is assured when, in actuality, more direct measures would provide better information. For example, rather than specifying that the governing body has overall responsibility for the quality of care, might it not be more effective for the Joint Commission to require each organization to clearly specify the responsibilities of each leader (or group of leaders) for quality of care (doing so in light of the legal requirements under which the organization operates); require that the organization measure the effectiveness with which these responsibilities are performed; and expect that ineffective performance will be corrected?

Likewise, it is necessary to move beyond the interprofessional conflicts that have characterized the Joint Commission's interaction with some professional groups. Rather than using national standards to define the specific authority of each professional group, it may be more productive to identify patient care functions that must be performed well and to specify the indicators an organization must use to assure itself that performance is optimal. This approach, in embryonic form, is contained in the Joint Commission's "Alcoholism and Other Drug Dependency Services" standards.[10] These standards require the performance of a full patient assessment, but do not specify the professional group(s) by which it should be performed. In place of such requirements are standards that identify the measures an organization should use to judge the accuracy of the patient assessment process. Thus, the standards require the organization to monitor such events as abnormal clinical findings not pursued; frequent changes in treatment plans that are the result of inadequate assessments; treatment plans that are not individualized; and unplanned discharges. Rather than engage in debate as to which group should perform the assessment, the standards prompt the organizations to assure that assessment is being done well.

Because this more direct approach to quality can, at least in many areas of the standards, replace current reliance on structural requirements, it has become an important component of the portion of the Agenda for Change devoted to standards improvement.

This move to standards that focus on key functions and their continual improvement has, in fact, been under way for the last few years. As previously noted, new standards for plant, technology, and safety management were adopted in 1988. From standards that concentrated on inspection as the means to a safe environment, the Joint Commission moved to standards that focused on assuring effective management of the general safety and the fire, equipment, and utilities safety programs.

This approach is also reflected in new standards concerning infection control. Drawing heavily from the results of extensive clinical research, these standards focus organizational attention on targeted surveillance, prevention, and effective response to problems.

While illustrative of the changes needed in Joint Commission standards, these recently modified standards are only a start. There remain a number of key functions that either are not addressed in the standards or are not focused adequately on performance and improvement. These three high-priority areas were cited previously. Work has begun on two of these areas: (1) leadership and (2) quality assessment and improvement methods. While it is early in the development process, the general direction of both of these efforts is already apparent.

A leadership task force has identified and is exploring seven types of activities for possible inclusion in new leadership standards. These activities, shown in Exhibit 4-4 identify the duties that governing body, management, and clinical leaders must perform to assure effective implementation and operation of an organization-wide quality improvement program. Consider the impact on the quality of patient care (and on an organization's ability to compete successfully on the basis of the quality of its care) of

---

Exhibit 4-4 Key Activities of Leaders

1. Promote attention to quality throughout the organization
2. Become personally knowledgeable about quality improvement concepts and methods
3. Explicitly consider quality when making decisions
4. Seek and use feedback and statistics about quality
5. Periodically evaluate their own effectiveness in improving quality
6. Assure the availability of resources and time to assess and improve quality
7. Work together to evaluate and improve quality

such intense attention to quality by all of the hospital's leaders. Think, too, of the reordering of priorities that this level of attention implies. The agenda of hospital board meetings would include much more attention to quality. Chief executive officers would spend a significant proportion of their time (1) learning the concepts and methods of quality assessment and continual quality improvement; (2) promoting quality as a central organizational priority; and (3) using performance information to guide resource allocation decisions, to help establish organizational priorities, and to determine future organizational directions. Clinical leaders would have more of the information they need to gauge the quality of clinical care; would be compelled to work closely among themselves and with the governing body and management to assure the effectiveness of the complex processes and systems that characterize modern health care organizations; and would refocus existing internal education and quality improvement activities to better ensure that state-of-the-art practices are reflected in day-to-day clinical care.

The second area of new standards development concerns the approaches organizations should use to evaluate and improve the quality of care. This challenge is being met by an expert task force consisting of physicians, nurses, health data experts, consumers, hospital executives, and quality assurance managers and individuals interested in the "sociology" of health care organizations. While their work has just started, this task force has begun to concentrate its efforts on the items shown in Exhibit 4-5. Standards covering these subjects will prompt an important evolution from "quality assurance" to continued organization-wide improvement. From quality assurance programs that are departmentally focused, centered primarily on the clinical contribution to quality, and designed principally to identify problems, health care organizations will break down the territory-protecting walls that now prevent necessary cross-organization attention to quality assessment, and will use information to improve all processes (not just to find and cull the "bad apples"). Data will be sought concerning the degree to which the needs of internal and external "customers" and "suppliers"

Exhibit 4-5 New Subjects under Consideration by the Quality Improvement Task Force

1. Involve everyone in quality assessment and improvement
2. Seek opportunities to improve quality—not just problems
3. Evaluate and improve key quality-related clinical, managerial, governance, and support functions
4. Provide greater attention to ethical considerations in clinical decision making
5. Broaden and improve the information base—especially feedback from patients
6. Improve the capability to analyze, display, and use quality-related information

are satisfied, and such information will be used to incrementally but continually improve the processes in which they are linked.

The task force's interest in stimulating a "customer" orientation is *not* a reflection of the marketing orientation that many believe is too prevalent in health care today. Rather, caring attention to patients' ("external customers") perceptions of their needs and to the expectations they have of the care they will receive, will prompt care directly relevant to those needs, and will also reduce those expectations that current state-of-the-art practice cannot fulfill.

The importance of understanding and addressing the needs and expectations of "internal customers" is a practical derivative of the fact that effective performance by each person in a health care organization is dependent upon other individuals performing their work well, and, in turn, is critical to the success of others' efforts. Thus, all those who govern or manage the organization and who provide and support patient care are both suppliers to and customers of many others within the organization. This is simply a new way of thinking about a reality that we all understand—patient care is the combined effort of the whole organization.

Clinical, managerial, and support services are linked in sometimes complex ways. Think of the many people involved in getting the right medication in the right dose to the right patient at the right time. Achieving this feat requires a physician who is intimately familiar with the patient's clinical problems and is knowledgeable about the medication(s) that will address that problem effectively. Then, the physician, nursing staff, ward personnel, pharmacist(s), and sometimes others must each perform interrelated duties well in order to assure that the patient receives the medication in the right dose at the right time. In this system, the physician is both a "customer" of the patient (for symptoms and signs) and a "supplier" to the patient. The nurse is a "customer" of the physician (he/she must understand the medication order) and is often the "supplier" to the physician of important information about the patient and to the pharmacist of the medication order. This medication ordering and delivery system is described in more detail in the publication of the National Demonstration Project on Quality Improvement in Health Care.[11]

This chain of interlinked customer/supplier relationships exists in every process used by a health care organization to fulfill key quality-related functions. An organization's success in providing efficient and effective care will depend on its understanding of the importance of these linkages and its ability to describe, measure, analyze, and improve each important process. An approach that illustrates this systematic process analysis and improvement is being developed by the Hospital Corporation of America.[12]

Through careful attention in standards to the key functions that warrant systematic analysis and continual improvement and by the addition of a data system to monitor the effectiveness with which an organization performs these functions, the Joint Commission will be better able to guide organizations in this effort and to stimulate improvement in their effectiveness.

BUILDING AN INDICATOR-BASED PERFORMANCE MONITORING SYSTEM

Perhaps the most challenging objective of the Agenda for Change is the creation of an indicator-based information system containing data from all accredited health care organizations—a system that will eventually allow each organization to compare its current performance with its past performance and with that of others. These comparisons will stimulate accredited organizations to evaluate the clinical and managerial processes that contributed to their performance and to improve those needing improvement.

Until recently, it was not technically feasible to create a national information resource of this type. The revolution in automated information technology has removed this obstacle. Public insistence that organizations collect, use, and report such information has prompted many but not all organizations to begin to invest in this technology and thereby to improve their internal data collection, analysis, and reporting capabilities. While these changes are necessary, they are insufficient. Also required, but still lacking, is the basic substrate for a useful data system—validated measures of clinical and managerial performance. The identification of such measures is now under way within the Joint Commission.

Joint Commission Use of Indicator Data

To put the Joint Commission's indicator development work in its proper context, one must understand the uses to which indicator data will be put. Annual release by the Health Care Financing Administration of Medicare mortality data—arguably the most important symbol in the 1980s of the change occurring in the U.S. health care system—has prompted essential debate over the most appropriate uses for such information. This issue was examined in a 1988 conference on "The Responsible Use of Mortality Data."[13] Exhibit 4-6 provides a description of the remarkable range of uses that had, to that time, been ascribed to mortality data.

While there is continuing debate concerning the appropriate use of mortality and other performance data, the Joint Commission's interest in such data is quite clear. First, performance indicators can be used as screening measures to identify those few organizations that are likely to have ineffective clinical, managerial governance, or support service processes. Sec-

Exhibit 4-6 Potential Uses Ascribed to Mortality Data

1. Screen for possible quality of care problems
2. Identify high-quality hospitals
3. Test the effectiveness of specific clinical or managerial processes
4. Provide a better public understanding of health care
5. Assist patients, purchasers, and insurers in selecting a hospital
6. Aid selection among competing health plans
7. Stimulate greater competition among hospitals
8. Guide local and regional planning

ond (and more important), they can provide a stimulus to *all* organizations to continue to improve all of their key processes, irrespective of their current level of performance. To test this belief, the Joint Commission is using the combined efforts of expert task forces and hospital participants in alpha and beta testing in the sequence shown in Exhibit 4-7.

Indicator Development

Indicator development began in 1987 with the formation of task forces for obstetrics care and anesthesia care and with an exploration of the feasibility of identifying indicators covering several departments of a hospital (hospitalwide indicators). The latter effort, as initially conceived, was not fruitful and is now being pursued through the development of indicators for specific activities that cut across the organization (i.e., clinical laboratory and imaging services, infection control, perioperative care, and the use of medications). Exhibit 4-8 lists the indicator sets that have been or will be developed and tested for acute care hospitals. Home care, managed care (HMOs), and mental health care (both hospital and nonhospital) are the first three indicator sets that will be developed for nonhospital organizations.

Exhibit 4-7 Indicator Development Sequence

Phase I —Task force development

Phase II —Pilot testing (alpha test)

Phase III—Full testing (beta test)

Phase IV—Implementation

Exhibit 4-8 Indicator Subjects for Hospital Care

- Completing alpha testing
  - Obstetrics
  - Anesthesia
- Entering alpha testing
  - Trauma care
  - Oncology care
  - Cardiovascular care
- Task force development in 1990
  - Medication usage
  - Infection surveillance and control
  - Clinical lab services
  - Imaging services
  - Perioperative care

The process used to identify and alpha test the indicators will be described in detail in a *Primer on Clinical Indicator Development* to be published by the Joint Commission in 1990. This publication will describe the "anatomy and physiology" of indicators and provide a "how-to" guide both for health care organizations that wish to develop indicators for their own use and for professional societies that will develop indicators for the use of their members.

The method of indicator development described in the *Primer* is the end result of the Joint Commission's experience first with the obstetrics and anesthesia task forces and then with those for cardiovascular, oncology, and trauma care. An important product of this progress is a comprehensive "indicator development form" that both identifies the information needed for a fully defined indicator and provides needed structure to the process of indicator development and subsequent testing. The content headings of the form are shown in Exhibit 4-9.

Analysis of the indicators developed by the first five task forces revealed that these patient-focused ("clinical") indicators have the potential of test-

Exhibit 4-9 Indicator Development Form Content Headings

- Statement of the indicator
- Definition of terms
- Type of indicator—sentinel/rate; process/outcome
- Rationale for the indicator
- Delineation of the population(s)
- Source(s) for each data element
- Possible underlying factors
- Existing data bases

ing both the patient care and the support functions shown in Exhibits 4-1 and 4-2. This fact is illustrated by the indicators shown in Exhibits 4-10 and 4-11. Each identifies not only important patient and clinician factors that could underlie variation but also those processes over which the organization has direct managerial control. Assessing both the ability of each indicator to test such functions and the feasibility of using the indicator in a national data system is the objective of the alpha and beta testing described next.

Alpha testing constitutes an initial analysis designed to assess the face validity of each indicator and to gain preliminary information about the cost and feasibility of data collection and the clarity of data element definitions. Beta testing will provide a more extensive and rigorous evaluation of the validity of each indicator and a "dress rehearsal" of the technical, financial, and legal issues involved in data collection, transmission, analysis, and feedback. Only after such careful testing will the Joint Commission (or should any public or private agency) require health care organizations to undergo the expense of modifying their information collection and reporting systems to comply with the specific requirements of an external evaluator.

FIELD IMPLEMENTATION ISSUES

All of the activities noted above have significant implications for both the Joint Commission and accredited organizations. These issues are being addressed by alpha and beta testing and through a number of internal

---

Exhibit 4-10 Indicator Example Trauma

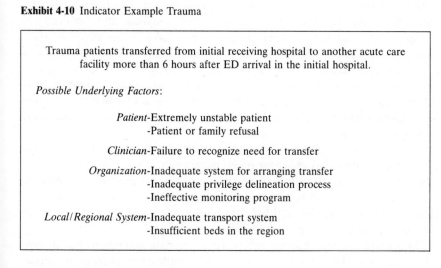

Trauma patients transferred from initial receiving hospital to another acute care facility more than 6 hours after ED arrival in the initial hospital.

Possible Underlying Factors:

Patient-Extremely unstable patient
-Patient or family refusal

Clinician-Failure to recognize need for transfer

Organization-Inadequate system for arranging transfer
-Inadequate privilege delineation process
-Ineffective monitoring program

Local/Regional System-Inadequate transport system
-Insufficient beds in the region

Exhibit 4-11 Indicator Example CABG

Patients undergoing isolated CABG procedures for bypass of a single coronary artery, excluding CABG procedures for only the left main coronary artery.

Possible Underlying Factors:

    Patient-e.g., severe angina, stenosis of proximal portion of left anterior descending or left circumflex arteries, drug intolerance

  Clinician-Inadequate training
             -Inadequate experience
             -Poor decision making

Organization-Inappropriate financial incentives
                 -Ineffective privilege delineation process

working groups; the latter will involve extensive dialogue with those in health care organizations affected by the contemplated changes. Early attention is being given to two important field issues—the data system capabilities of accredited organizations and the readiness of these organizations to move from their current approach to quality assurance to the creation of the environment and methods needed to support organization-wide continual improvement.

An initial assessment of hospital data system capabilities has been completed. Using a 20 percent sample of accredited hospitals, the Joint Commission conducted a mail survey to gather general information about the computer resources now existing in hospitals. The results, which are based on an 83 percent response rate, indicate that quality assurance (63 percent), utilization review (64 percent), and risk management activities (77 percent) are *not* computerized in a large proportion of hospitals; that a majority of hospitals depend upon outside vendors to manage some or all of their information system operations; and that only a modest proportion (8 to 32 percent) of organizations are planning to upgrade important components of their computer capabilities within the next 1 to 2 years. These findings should sober those expecting hospitals to be capable of efficient collection and transmission of new performance information that is not routinely collected in financial/billing systems.

Though general, these results have exposed a potential barrier to full implementation of an indicator-based monitoring system and have led the Joint Commission to plan a more detailed study to examine the content and uses of current data systems; the mechanisms (automated and other) used to collect, analyze, and use data; and future plans for and barriers to the enhancement of these mechanisms.

In addition to the changes necessary in the data systems of health care organizations, the Agenda for Change contemplates an even more important evolution in the manner in which organizations address the issue of quality. Traditionally viewed as a clinical issue (and therefore a responsibility that could and should be delegated to the clinical staff of the organization), quality is increasingly understood to be the responsibility of all components of the organization. This point has significant implications for every facet of an organization's day-to-day life.

It means, for example, that governing boards must take more seriously their own work and their interactions with the organization's clinical and managerial staff. They will need to be explicit about the organization's mission and periodically assess the degree to which the services provided comport with it; gain a clear view of the effect the board is having on the ability of the organization to provide patient care of high quality; provide substantive oversight of the mechanisms used by the organization to evaluate and improve the quality of care and prompt continual improvement when it is needed; and understand that, even in difficult times, an organization must position itself for long-term success while still being prudent about short-term priorities. Boards will need to support the potentially significant changes in the handling of personnel, financial, and organizational structure matters so that these activities will foster—not impede—an environment of organization-wide continual improvement.

Executive managers of hospitals must guide and support boards in these directions and embody similar philosophies in their everyday work. In particular, management—especially the CEO and senior management—must set the example by learning the philosophy and methods of continual improvement; insist that decisions be made with quality explicitly on the table; support their staff with the resources (information, people, and time) necessary to describe, measure, and improve quality-related processes; reevaluate how policy and operating procedures either foster or hinder the cooperative effort needed across the organization; and, most important, play the central role in destroying barriers that are erected around department turf—barriers that are anathema to the communication, cooperation, and conflict resolution needed for continual improvement.

Most of the changes noted above for governing bodies and management also apply to clinical staff. For clinical staff, however, there is the additional challenging task of assuring that the constant evolution in the science of health care is integrated into the day-to-day clinical practice of the organization. Decades of research have shown that new technologies are often adopted prior to full testing, and proven technology and new knowledge are not adopted as soon as they should be. These findings should prompt clinical leaders to reevaluate the effectiveness of internal educational programs (conferences, ward rounds, visiting professors, grand rounds, etc.) and to explore other strategies for achieving behavioral changes.

While these new roles will challenge governing body, managerial, and clinical leaders, they are essential to foster a transformation that many believe is akin to culture shock. The Joint Commission intends to be an important catalyst for this change, and thus must work with accredited organizations to assure a thoughtful and planned process of change.

This effort has begun with the design of a major study of the nature and pace of transition to continual quality improvement. This study will address questions such as the following: How does an organization move effectively from a quality assurance to a quality improvement orientation? What barriers exist and how have they been resolved? What resources, both fiscal and staff, are required? Have organizations found one sequence of steps to be more effective than others in achieving change? Findings from the study, scheduled for completion by the end of 1990, will determine the pace and phasing of the transition, as well as the content and timing of assistance from the Joint Commission that will be needed to facilitate the successful implementation of a new orientation to quality of care in accredited hospitals.

CONCLUSION

The 71-year history of voluntary accreditation has been characterized by progressive change in standards and survey methods, but has retained its concentration on the assessment of organizational capability. The Agenda for Change is a multiyear applied research and development project designed to focus the Joint Commission and accredited organizations on actual performance and its continued improvement.

While plowing much new ground, the first 3 years of this work indicate that the objective can be achieved, thus continuing the positive influence that external evaluation has had on the quality of patient care in the United States.

NOTES

1. J.S. Roberts, J.G. Coale, and R.R. Redman, "A History of the Joint Commission on Accreditation of Hospitals," *JAMA* (1987) 258:936–940.

2. C.P. Schlicke, "American Surgery's Noblest Experiment," *Archives of Surgery* (1973) 108:379–385.

3. J.S. Roberts, and R.M. Walczak, "Quality Assurance: The Evolution and Current Status of the Joint Commission on Accreditation of Hospitals Quality Assurance Standard," *QRB* (1984) 10:11–15.

4. Joint Commission on Accreditation of Healthcare Organizations, *Joint Commission Perspectives 1988*, vol. 8, no 5/6:1, A1–A7.

5. Joint Commission on Accreditation of Healthcare Organizations, *Joint Commission Perspectives 1989*, vol. 9, no. 5/6:7, A25–A29.

6. Joint Commission on Accreditation of Healthcare Organizations, *Joint Comission Perspectives 1989*, vol. 9, no. 3/4:1, 4–5.

7. J.D. Wennberg, and A. Gittellsohn, "Small Area Variation in Health Care Delivery," *Science* (1973) 182:1102–1108.

8. *Confronting Regional Variation: The Maine Approach.* American Medical Association (Chicago, Ill., 1986).

9. M.R. Chassin et al., "Variations in the Use of Medical and Surgical Services by the Medicare Population," *NEJM* (1986) 314:285–290.

10. Joint Commission on Accreditation of Healthcare Organizations, *1990 Accreditation Manual for Hospitals* (1989):3–9.

11. National Demonstration Project on Quality Improvement in Health Care. *Quality Improvement in Health Care* (1989) 1:4–6.

12. P.B. Batalden, and D.E. Buchanan, *Industrial Models of Quality Improvement. Providing Quality Care*, eds. N. Goldfield and D. Nash (Philadelphia: American College of Physicians, 1989).

13. Joint Commission on Accreditation of Healthcare Organizations, *Taking Stock of Mortality Data: An Agenda for the Future* (1989).

Appendix 4-A

Principles of Organization and Management Effectiveness

PREAMBLE

Total organizational commitment to continuously improve the quality of patient care is the central concern of these principles. This commitment is woven throughout the fabric of the organization, appearing in strategic planning, allocation of resources, role expectations, reward structures, performance evaluations, and the role of the organization in the community. An ongoing, comprehensive self-assessment system supports and promotes continuous improvement in the quality of patient care. This self-assessment system seeks feedback on the quality of care from patients as well as practitioners, from payors as well as other organizational care providers, from employees as well as the community. This system of ongoing monitoring and evaluation of clinical and organizational performance provides information to leadership regarding day-to-day patient care decisions and promotes fiscally responsible organizational change that will improve the quality of patient care.

I. Organizational Mission

The organizational mission statement clearly expresses a commitment to continuously improve the quality of patient care. This commitment is translated into measurable objectives and action plans through the organization's strategic, program, and resource planning. The mission statement and plans are mutually developed and regularly evaluated by the governing board and managerial and clinical leadership.* The organization also advocates changes in the external environment that will contribute to improving the overall quality of patient care.

* In hospitals, "clinical leadership" means the elected and appointed leaders of the organized medical staff, and the leaders of the nursing staff and other clinical professional groups.

62

II. Organizational Culture

The organization fosters a culture that promotes widespread commitment to continuously improve the quality of patient care. This culture encourages participation in the improvement process by all who use or provide the organization's services. For all persons, clinical disciplines, and organizational units, the culture promotes self-assessment, open communication, and appropriate participation in decision-making processes, especially by those the decisions affect.

III. Organizational Change

Individuals at all levels of the organization continuously assess and recognize opportunities for change that will improve the quality of patient care. The assessments address the external environment, access to care, adequacy of patient volume to support clinical competence, and quality of care judgments rendered by patients, their families, health care practitioners, other employees, payors, the community, and other organizations providing care. Strategic, program, and resource planning are based on this broad range of assessments. The planning process addresses the financial resources needed to meet short- and long-term goals to improve the quality of patient care. Appropriate changes to improve the quality of patient care are implemented.

IV. Role of Governing Board and Managerial and Clinical Leadership

The organization's commitment to continuously improve the quality of patient care is reflected in the roles and performance of the organization leaders and is expressed in definitions of authority and responsibility, policy, and specific objectives. Leaders articulate the organization's commitment to continuously improve the quality of patient care. Leaders systematically seek, measure, and use the judgments of patients, their families, health care practitioners, other employees, payors, the community, and other organizations providing care as an ongoing method of evaluating and improving the quality of patient care. The organization leaders monitor and promote organizational integration and coordination.

V. Leadership Qualifications, Evaluation, and Development

The governing board and managerial and clinical leadership consist of well-qualified people who possess the knowledge, skills, attitudes, commitment, and vision for assessing and continuously improving the quality of patient care. The leadership regularly evaluates its involvement and effectiveness in improving quality through acquiring, utilizing, and coordinating resources and using information. A well-conceived plan is implemented that addresses both internal and external opportunities for the growth and development of leaders to assist them to continuously improve the quality of patient care.

VI. Independent Practitioners' Qualifications, Evaluation, and Development

The organization has a sufficient number of competent independent practitioners* to provide patient care in accordance with current parameters of clinical practice, who are committed and actively involved in continuously improving the quality of patient care. Independent practitioners are initially assessed and regularly evaluated to determine their clinical competence and performance. A well-conceived plan is implemented that addresses both internal and external opportunities for the growth and development of independent practitioners to assist them to continuously improve the quality of patient care.

* An independent practitioner is any individual who is permitted by law and who is also permitted by the organization to provide patient care services without direction or supervision, within the scope of his or her license and in accordance with individually granted clinical privileges.

VII. Human Resources

Recruitment and retention policies and practices assure sufficient numbers of health care practitioners and others supporting patient care who are competent and have appropriate skills, attitudes, and knowledge and who are committed and actively involved in continuously improving the quality of patient care. The competence and performance of practitioners and others are regularly evaluated. A well-conceived plan is implemented that addresses both internal and external opportunities for the growth and development of all practitioners and others to assist them to continuously improve the quality of patient care.

VIII. Support Resources

Sufficient facilities, equipment, and technology are acquired, regularly evaluated, and maintained to promote a good patient care environment, in accord with the mission statement and strategic, program, and resource plans.

IX. Evaluation and Improvement of Patient Care

The monitoring, evaluation, and continuous improvement of patient care are overseen by the governing board and managerial and clinical leadership and involve appropriate individuals and organizational units. This organization-wide assessment process integrates data from quality assurance, risk management, and utilization review functions and seeks ongoing feedback on the quality of care from patients, their families, health care practitioners, other employees, payors, the community, and other organizations providing care. The analysis of this information is used to develop short- and long-range plans for the organization, its units, and individuals so that changes are made to improve the quality of patient care.

X. Organizational Integration and Coordination

All persons, clinical disciplines, and organizational units recognize their interdependence and their responsibility to work with each other to continuously improve the quality of care. The organization's policies consistently foster appropriate communication, coordination, conflict management, and integration among relevant parties so that changes are made to improve the quality of care.

XI. Continuity and Comprehensiveness of Care

Effective linkages are developed and maintained with external care providers to improve access, continuity, comprehensiveness, and overall quality of the care.

Chapter 5

Impact of Peer Review
Organizations on Hospitals

Marcia Orsolits and Frederick Abbey

INTRODUCTION

Governmental concern about the appropriateness, efficiency, and effectiveness of health care is not new. After Medicare was enacted in 1965, the federal government attempted to control utilization by mandating review of hospital and physician reimbursement. The program was poorly organized and thus proved ineffective.

The Social Security Act Amendments of 1972 established the Professional Standards and Review Organization (PSRO) program, an attempt to create a national utilization review process. Under the program, physician-directed organizations applied for grants to oversee the care given to Medicare patients. However, a high degree of variability in state oversight standards led to this program's general ineffectiveness. The Reagan administration, in its desire to decrease governmental regulation and intervention, proposed eliminating the PSRO program in FY 1982.

Despite this proposal, Congress decided to strengthen efforts to control health care utilization and mandated stricter controls over Medicare reimbursement for inpatient costs by passing the Tax Equity and Fiscal Responsibility Act of 1982 (TEFRA). TEFRA repealed the PSRO program and replaced it with a new initiative, officially titled the Utilization and Quality Control Peer Review Program but commonly called PRO.

With the enactment of the Social Security Act of 1983, Congress established the Hospital Inpatient Prospective Payment System (PPS). Prior to PPS, bills submitted to Medicare were reimbursed as charges. These often were inflated past the actual cost of the care delivered. The ability to control the profit margin in this way was lost when hospitals came under the

Marcia Orsolits, BS, MS, PhD, is the Director of the Department of Nursing Research at the Cleveland Clinic Foundation in Cleveland, Ohio.
Frederick Abbey, MPH, is Senior Manager at Ernst & Young, Washington, D.C.

predetermined, fixed payment system of PPS. Hospitals now had the challenge of redefining the control of their profit margin. The intent of Congress was that hospitals would accomplish this through increasing their operational efficiency. In reality, however, most hospitals responded by attempting to increase volume and maximizing DRG coding. Thus, PPS created an even greater need for a strong review system to counteract the potential incentive hospitals have to increase admissions, increase readmissions (by not performing all procedures in a single admission), and inappropriately classify a diagnosis (in order to maximize reimbursement rules).

The PRO program arose from the failure of the PSRO program to address Medicare's vulnerability to these incentives. In 1984, the Health Care Financing Administration (HCFA) first issued a request for proposals from organizations desiring to become PROs. In fiscal year 1990, HCFA will spend in excess of $300 million to support the PRO program.

A rigorous review of hundreds of proposals resulted in the initial selection of 53 organizations to become PROs. Many of these PROs are transformed Professional Standards Review Organizations (PSROs), although they now have responsibility for a much more comprehensive medical review focused on quality of care, and they must also maintain data sets on institutional, provider, and practitioner performance.

Specifically, PROs review claims for Medicare services furnished by hospitals to determine the reasonableness, medical necessity, and quality of the care, as well as the appropriateness of the setting in which the care is provided. Unlike PSROs, PROs cannot delegate any of the review functions to the hospital; however, federal budgeting pressures and experience with many high quality hospital providers may lead to delegated review in certain cases in the future. The contracts between the PROs and HCFA are based on objective performance criteria; those with the PSROs were not. In fact, about one-third of all PRO contracts are not automatically renewed and are competitively bid to ensure that the cost of the review process is appropriate and that state-of-the-art review techniques and technologies are applied. PROs also have greater authority in recommending sanction activities against hospitals and physicians than did the PSROs.

PRO reviews are done on both a concurrent and a retrospective basis, and most inpatient reviews are performed retrospectively (88 percent).[1] Reviews are done either on-site (at the hospital) or off-site (at the PRO). Although the reviews are restricted to Medicare patients, PROs may also enter into contracts with Medicaid and/or private payers.

PEER REVIEW ORGANIZATIONS (PROs) TODAY

The PROs examine the appropriateness and quality of service in hospitals and certain ambulatory settings; therefore, it is important to pay particular regard to the way in which they operate. Any organization that has access to physicians who can review claims is eligible to contract with HCFA as a PRO. The organization may be for profit or not-for-profit. While physician sponsorship is not required, it is preferred, and *most* PROs do have physicians either as presidents or as chief executive officers.[2]

The PRO must be cognizant of the various dimensions and perspectives of medical care. The PRO governing board reflects this awareness by including physicians, hospital representatives, and consumer representatives among its members. Consumer representation on PRO boards was mandated by the Omnibus Budget Reconciliation Act of 1986 (OBRA) because of increased consumer concern over health care issues and the government's desire to encourage greater individual participation in general health care decision making.

Fifty-nine PRO contracts are now administered by 44 organizations across the United States and its territories. This distribution recognizes that there are considerable variations in the practice of medicine across specific areas; these variations are indicative of local medical culture, epidemiologic patterns, health care resource availability, and hospital utilization. The contracts between HCFA and the PROs are negotiated, fixed-price contracts. The contract selection process involves competitive bidding, which allows more than one organization within a state to bid. The contracts previously were renegotiated biennially, but this period has now been changed to every 3 years.[3] This change is intended to make the program more stable and to encourage closer and consistent relationships between the PROs and health care providers and practitioners.

Organizations desiring to contract with HCFA are under pressure to define objectives that not only respond to the HCFA criteria but also identify specific needs in a given geographic area. PRO performance is evaluated and contracts are renewed, based on how successfully they have met their stated objectives. Each hospital should circulate a copy of its PRO-stated objectives among its medical staff, as outlined in the contract with HCFA. PROs have also begun to market their services to other third-party payers and to some large self-insured employers, among whom interest in medical review is increasing. Therefore, a hospital's relationship and involvement with its PRO may have an impact beyond the Medicare program and therefore are increasingly important. After having successfully negotiated a contract with HCFA, a PRO may subcontract with other organizations.

PROs are required to use physician consultants who have active admitting privileges in one or more hospitals in the area. This ensures that the focus of the review remains on medical care and reflects the current standards of practice present in the community. More specifically, HCFA regulations require PROs to follow these rules:

- Only physicians can make initial determinations denying payments for care or services provided by another physician.
- Physicians must be involved in quality of care reviews and in the sanctions process.
- Physician and nonphysician reviewers are prohibited from reviewing a case if they are directly involved in providing the service or if they have a significant personal or financial interest in the institution in which the services were provided.
- Decisions regarding medical procedures and diagnostic information must be made by a physician.
- Reconsideration of denied admission or poor quality determinations must be made by board-certified physicians in the specialty involved.
- Technical coding issues must be reviewed by individuals with experience and training in current ICD-CM coding.
- Nonphysician health care practitioners must be consulted before making a determination on a case involving services provided by a nonphysician health care practitioner (i.e., physical therapist).

In the near future, there may be a greater need for expert review by professional nurses. The care monitored by the HCFA screens currently encompasses nursing as well as medical care. Perhaps as much as 40 percent of the problems flagged by the screens are nursing care issues i.e., falls, medication errors, nosocomial infections and decubitus ulcers.[4]

To validate the accuracy of the medical determinations made by the PROs, HCFA contracts with an independent organization. This "Super PRO" also is responsible for verifying that nonphysician reviewers are properly applying the PRO criteria for referring cases to physicians for consultation. Four hundred random cases from each PRO are reviewed by the Super PRO in every 6-month period. The PRO is notified as to which cases will be reviewed by the Super PRO and must then obtain copies of those records from the appropriate hospitals. The Super PRO generally has found the PROs to be accurate in their determinations. Hospitals should be aware, however, that there have been instances in which the Super PRO has identified problems and the case has been reopened. This reflects the fact that medical judgments about care rendered continue to differ when medical records are reviewed. Even in the area of medical coding, PROs and the Super PRO have come to different conclusions. In about 10 percent of the cases reviewed by the Super PRO, the actual diagnosis-related group (DRG) assignment was changed from that submitted by the PRO and the hospital.[5] The Super PRO's determination invalidates that of the PRO unless the PRO appeals the determination with HCFA.

Contrary to some misconceptions, the Super PRO does not provide an overall evaluation of how adequately the PRO is funded. Rather, it assesses the PRO's accuracy and provides feedback to HCFA on how well the national standards are being implemented.

PRO Relationship with the Hospital

PROs negotiate agreements with hospitals along the same lines as their agreements with HCFA. In the agreement, the PRO must include:

- review criteria and procedures
- location in which the review will be done (on-site or off-site)
- time frames involved
- documentation required

In addition, because PRO program directives and regulations may change, the PRO's agreement with the hospital should provide methods for its periodic modification.

Hospitals must allocate space to the PRO for its conduct of on-site reviews and must make the medical records available to the PRO at the time of the visit. Generally, when review takes place off-site, hospitals must, within 30 days of its request, photocopy and (for a fixed amount per page fee) deliver to the PRO all required information.

The nature of the relationship between the PRO and the individual hospital varies. Each PRO has different strengths and weaknesses, and each hospital has unique combinations of physician attitudes and administrative policies. These characteristics can effect the tone of the PRO-hospital interaction, and this interaction is the key to the resolution of quality of care disputes.

National Objectives

Both national objectives and PRO-specific objectives are included in the PRO's contract with HCFA. In general, each PRO develops an approach with specific goals designed to meet the following national objectives in the areas of admissions and quality.

Admissions

- Reduce admissions for procedures that could be performed effectively and with adequate assurance of patient safety in an ambulatory surgical setting or on an outpatient basis

- Reduce the number of inappropriate procedures for specific DRGs
- Reduce the number of inappropriate or unnecessary admissions or invasive procedures by specific practitioners or in specific hospitals

Quality

- Reduce unnecessary hospital readmissions resulting from substandard care provided during the prior admission
- Assure the provision of medical services that, when not performed, have significant potential for causing serious patient complications
- Reduce the risk of mortality associated with selected procedures and/ or conditions requiring hospitalization
- Reduce unnecessary surgery or other invasive procedures
- Reduce avoidable postoperative or other complications

While PROs set their own goals and targets based on HCFA's broad objectives, requirements are in place that specify how to identify claims that will undergo a review.

The cases that are selected for retrospective (postdischarge) review are obtained from the routine flow of claims, which generally follows this sequence: Admission → Discharge → Fiscal intermediary (FI) payment of claim → FI transmittal to PRO of data tape of all claims received for a given period of time (usually a month) → PRO flagging of claims to be retrospectively reviewed → PRO review of claim → Possible PRO request to hospital to get the medical records of the cases flagged.

Retrospective Review Cases

Table 5-1 outlines those cases flagged for review on a retrospective basis under the third scope of work. Future scopes may include new categories for review.

Concurrent Review Cases

In addition to flagging cases for retrospective review, PROs are required to do concurrent reviews in either of the following categories:

- *Preadmission Review*—For specific diagnoses the PRO feels should be reviewed because they fall outside the level of standard patterns of practice for that geographic area. The PRO's contract with HCFA stipulates that ten types of diagnosis must be chosen, based on a list

Table 5-1 PRO Retrospective Review

Category for Review	Third Scope of Work (as of 10/1/88)
Random Sample	3%
Transfer (PPS to PPS)	50%
Transfer (Alcohol)	0%
Transfer (Rehab)	0%
Transfer (Swing Bed)	25%
Readmissions	25%—Sample of all readmissions less than 31 days
DRG 468: Unrelated or Procedure	50%
DRG 462: Rehab	25%
DRG 088: COPD	0%
DRGs 385–391: Newborns	100%
DRG 472: Extensive Burns	100%
DRG 474: Tracheostomy	100%
DRG 475: Mechanical Ventilation with Endotracheal Tube	100%
Day Outliers	25%
Cost Outliers	25%
Percutaneous Lithotripsy	0%
Assistants at Cataract	Same
Review of Ambulatory Surgery	5%
Intervening Care	20%

Source: 1988–1990, Third PRO Scope of Work, Office of Medical Review, Health Standards and Quality Bureau, Health Care Financing Administration.

of the most frequently admitted DRGs for that area. For example, cases selected by one PRO for preadmission review include

—cholocystectomy
—major joint replacement
—prostatectomy
—hysterectomy
—permanent pacemaker insertion

The PROs are required to review 100 percent of these cases prior to admission.

• *Preprocedure Review*—For specific procedures the PRO feels should be reviewed because they fall outside the level of standard patterns of practice for that geographic area. The PRO's contract with HCFA stipulates that five types of procedures must be chosen, based on a list of the ten highest cost procedures for that area. For example, another PRO has selected these cases for preprocedural review:

—cataracts
—permanent pacemaker implants and reimplants

—gastroscopies
—bronchioscopies
—colonoscopies

Preadmission and preprocedure reviews should take place 48 hours before the proposed admission or procedure. If this cannot be done, the case is targeted for retrospective review *before* payment. If the proposed admission/procedure is denied, the PRO must contact the physician and the provider to discuss the case.

If an initial denial determination is issued, a request for reconsideration can be made within 3 days. To ensure that the intended care was actually provided, retrospective review is done on all cases that received preadmission/preprocedure approval.

Medical Review Tests and Screens

Once a PRO identifies a case for review, it is required to routinely examine each case from five separate perspectives.

1. *Admission Review*—Is the admission medically necessary and appropriate? If the answer is no, a preliminary notice of initial denial determination is sent to the hospital and the physician (see section on appeals).

2. *Discharge Review*—Was the patient medically stable upon discharge? Was the patient in need of acute care upon discharge? If the answer to the first question is no, and the answer to the second question is yes, a preliminary notice of initial denial determination is sent to the hospital and the physician. If the violation is gross and flagrant, the PRO may also initiate a sanction activity (see section on sanctions). If this violation of discharge criteria is found to be a pattern, the PRO will intensify its review of the cases submitted by the particular hospital or physician.

3. *Quality Review Activities*—Has the PRO screened all retrospectively reviewed cases to determine that the care rendered meets acceptable standards of medical care? This is in addition to the application of the HCFA generic quality screens and discharge review. The PRO must apply the following process for quality review:

- Problem Identification/Timing of Review;
- Determination of Source of Problem (i.e., Physician and/or Provider);
- Assignment of Severity Levels;
- Notification of Quality Problems to Affected Parties;
- Quarterly Profiling and Computation of Weighted Severity Scores; and
- Implementation of Quality Interventions.

4. *Generic Quality Screens*—This category is designed to measure the outcomes of hospital care, which helps to gauge the quality of medical care being provided. For this reason, it is of major interest to the PROs. The generic quality screens measure morbidity and mortality and include:

- *Adequacy of Discharge Planning*
  Was there a documented plan for appropriate follow-up care taking into consideration the physical, emotional, and mental status and needs of the patient at the time of discharge?
- *Medical Stability of the Patient at Discharge*
  Was the patient medically stable at discharge? Stability encompasses blood pressure, temperature, and pulse measurements; abnormal results of any diagnostic services; IV fluids, or drugs given the day of discharge; and purulent drainage of wounds.
- *Deaths*
  Did the patient die unexpectedly during or following elective surgery, following a return to intensive care, or 24 hours after transfer out?
- *Nosocomial Infection*
  Was there a nosocomial infection, indicated either by a temperature increase of more than 2 degrees, more than 72 hours after admission, or by an infection following an invasive procedure?
- *Unscheduled Return to Surgery*
  Was there an unscheduled return to surgery within the same admission for the same condition as the original surgery?
- *Trauma in the Hospital*
  Was trauma suffered in the hospital? Trauma includes unplanned removal/repair of an organ; a fall resulting in an injury; life-threatening complications from anesthesia; life-threatening transfusion error or reaction; a hospital-acquired decubitious ulcer; care resulting in serious or life-threatening complications unrelated to the reason for the admission; or major adverse drug reactions or a medication error with serious potential for harm.

If the case fails one or more of these screens, it is reviewed by a nurse and then by a PRO physician. A review of PRO data suggests that these screens are not always accurate in capturing cases involving poor quality of care. As Table 5-2 illustrates, four out of the six screens can flag cases falsely, i.e., identify cases that are not subsequently found to involve poor quality. Conversely, they may miss cases where poor quality may exist. Therefore, HCFA is developing more sensitive measures to assist PROs in screening cases for poor quality. One such project involves a uniform clinical data set to support morbidity and mortality screening.

Table 5-2 Cases That Failed Generic Quality Screens

| | Per 100 Records | | |
| | --- | --- | --- |
Type of Review	Number of Cases Failing Screen	Number of Actual Problems Found	Percent of Actual Problems Found
Adequacy of discharge planning	2.5	1.62	65.8%
Medical stability at discharge	13.1	0.87	6.7
Avoidable deaths	1.2	0.06	5.3
Hospital-acquired infections	7.1	2.16	30.5
Unscheduled returns to surgery	0.7	0.03	3.9
Avoidable errors in treatment	4.2	0.61	14.4
Total	28.8	5.37	18.6

Note: All reviews were conducted between November 1987 and November 1988, and are based on the 3% random sample of records reviewed by PROs.

Source: Office of Medical Review, Health Standards and Quality Bureau, Health Care Financing Administration.

If the physician finds a quality issue exists, appropriate interventions are initiated. These interventions may include education of the physician involved, a corrective action plan, intensified review of the physician and the hospital, denial of payment, or initiation of a sanction recommendation.

Each PRO is required to have a quality intervention plan that must include a process to notify appropriate personnel in poor quality cases, educational approaches, intensification of review, coordination with hospital quality assurance committees, licensing and accrediting bodies, and a sanction plan.

Denial of payment for substandard care, as well as the notification of beneficiaries of such decisions, is required by law,[6] and proposed regulations for implementation have been publicized. There is some concern, however, that patients receiving such information might sue physicians or hospitals and cite PRO denials as evidence of poor quality delivery.

For this reason, HCFA is proposing a generic letter from PROs to beneficiaries saying only that "the quality of services you received does not meet professionally recognized standards of health care." Beneficiaries would also be informed that they are not liable for any costs associated with the admission, and that the denial decision was made only after the hospital and the physician had been given an opportunity for rebuttal. The notification process, as proposed in the *Federal Register,* is highly controversial, however, and HCFA received over 4,000 public comments on the subject. Hospitals and physicians are concerned that these letters are premature and do not allow sufficient time for the appeal process.

In addition to the admission and discharge reviews and the use of the quality screens, PROs are required to validate systematically the DRG assignment of the case and the medical necessity of the rendered services.

5. *DRG Validation*—Was the ICD-9-CM code supported by the information in the medical record, and does the physician's attestation confirm the primary and secondary diagnoses, procedures, and discharge status? If the answer is no, preliminary notice of change in the DRG assignment is sent to the hospital and the physician. There is then a discussion between the PRO physician and the hospital physician, after which a final determination is made.

If the PRO detects a pattern of incorrect DRG assignment by the hospital, corrective action is taken. This corrective action can include education, intensified review of specific DRGs or specific physicians, and/or initiation of a sanction recommendation.

6. *Items/Services Coverage Review*—Were all items/services used during the stay medically necessary and appropriate? If the answer is no, a preliminary notice of initial denial determination for those items/services is sent to the hospital and the physician.

Each PRO is required to build a data base of information related to review activities. One part of this data base is to profile review findings according to physician, institution, DRG, and so forth. These profiling activities are done on a quarterly basis. Each case is assigned a severity level to help categorize the data bases and determine what form of intervention the PRO should take with a provider or practitioner.

The following severity level system is used; however, the severity level must always be confirmed by a physician reviewer.

- medical mismanagement with significant adverse effects on the patient (Level III)
- medical mismanagement with the potential for significant adverse effects on the patient (Level II)
- medical mismanagement without the potential for significant adverse effects on the patient (Level I)

"Significant adverse effect" is defined as (1) unnecessarily prolonged treatment, complications, or readmission, or (2) patient management that results in anatomical or physiological problems.

Maps through the Review Maze

Review Process

The following charts display the major sequential steps in the medical review process (see Figures 5-1 through 5-5). The process is more involved, but these charts illustrate the route a review should take.

These five charts diagram various aspects of the review process: Chart 1 (Figure 5-1) is a diagram of the routine medical review process.[7] A diagram of the review process when a patient is readmitted to a hospital is shown in Chart 2 (Figure 5-2).[8] The review process when a patient is transferred to a swing bed is illustrated in Chart 3 (Figure 5-3).[9] Chart 4 (Figure 5-4) illustrates the sanctions process involved when a hospital receives a penalty for quality of care problems.[10] The appeals process once a denial of a case is recorded by the PRO is shown in Chart 5 (Figure 5-5).[11]

New PROs are selected through a contract process and there will always be new participants. For this reason, hospital managers must understand how the system is designed to work, so that they can question and challenge any decisions that arise.

Examples of Cases

Case 1—Retrospective Medical Review/Routine

> Mrs. Jones, age 72, was admitted to Get-You-Well Community Hospital for gall bladder surgery. Her surgery went well. She stayed in the hospital 2 days less than the average length of stay for that DRG and was discharged.

The fiscal intermediary (FI) processed the claim, recorded it on tape with all other claims for that time period, and sent the data tape to the PRO. Within 15 days of receipt of the tape, as a part of its routine review function, the PRO chose Mrs. Jones' case as one of the 3 percent random sample of discharges to be reviewed. The PRO requested that a copy of the medical record be sent from the hospital within the next 30 days. Within 15 days of receipt of the medical record, the PRO reviewed Mrs. Jones' case against the five criteria (admissions, discharge, generic quality screens, DRG validation, and item/service coverage). The case passed all criteria and payment of the claim was approved.

Case 2—Retrospective Review/Premature Discharge

> Mr. Smith, age 69, was admitted to Good Health Memorial 10 days after having been released from the same hospital. He was treated and discharged. The FI processed the claim, recorded the data on tape, and sent the data tape to the PRO. Upon review of the tape, Mr. Smith's case was flagged for review because it was a readmission within 15 days of discharge.

The hospital was notified that an on-site review of a number of cases would occur the next week and it was to have Mr. Smith's medical record

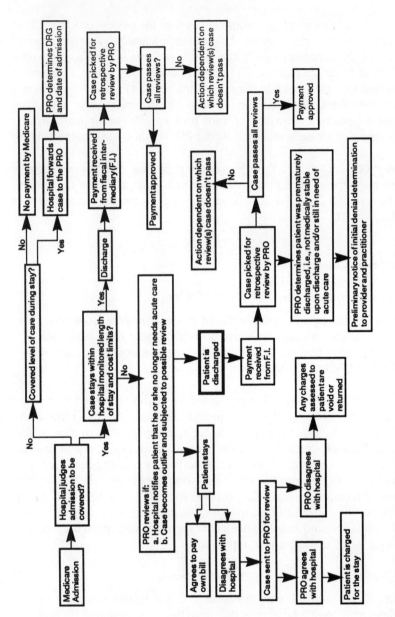

Figure 5-1 Routine Review Process. *Source.* Adapted from *The Impact of PROs on Hospitals* with permission of Ernst & Young, © 1987.

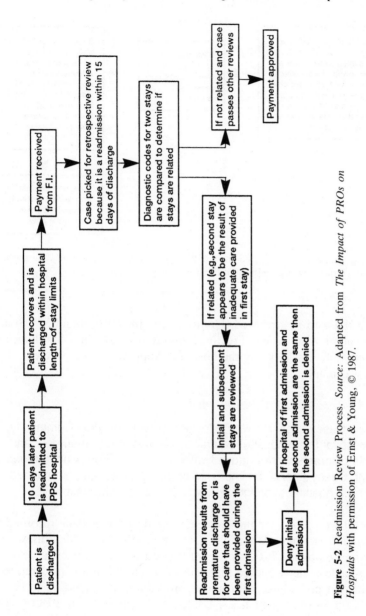

Figure 5-2 Readmission Review Process. *Source:* Adapted from *The Impact of PROs on Hospitals* with permission of Ernst & Young, © 1987.

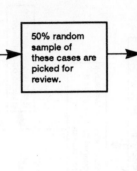

Figure 5-3 Transfer to Swing Bed Review Process. *Source:* Adapted from *The Impact of PROs on Hospitals* with permission of Ernst & Young, © 1987.

among those to be reviewed. Upon review, the PRO found Mr. Smith's second admission was not directly related to his first admission, indicating no premature discharge by the hospital. Approval of the payment of the claim was made.

Case 3—Retrospective Review/Denial

> Mr. Casey, age 76, was admitted to Get-You-Well Community Hospital for removal of cataracts. He was taken to surgery and his cataracts were removed without incident. Following surgery Mr. Casey's condition improved normally; however, he remained in the hospital overnight. He was discharged the next day.

The FI who processed the claim submitted by the hospital recorded the information on tape and sent the data tape to the PRO. Mr. Casey's case was reviewed by the PRO as part of the retrospective review process.

The nurse reviewer noted that cataract surgery is not considered to be an inpatient procedure. All cataract procedures are supposed to be performed on an outpatient basis. Based on this finding, the PRO notified the FI and the hospital that payment for the case would not be approved.

Release of Health Care Data

One of the most volatile issues facing hospital administrators is to prepare for and respond to the release of Medicare data to the public. As a

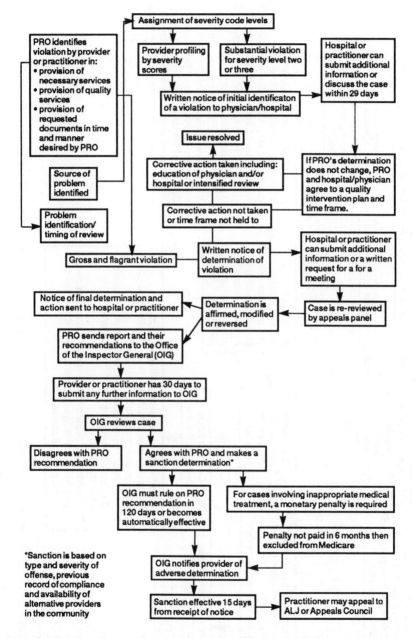

Figure 5-4 Sanctions Process. *Source:* Adapted from *The Impact of PROs on Hospitals* with permission of Ernst & Young, © 1987.

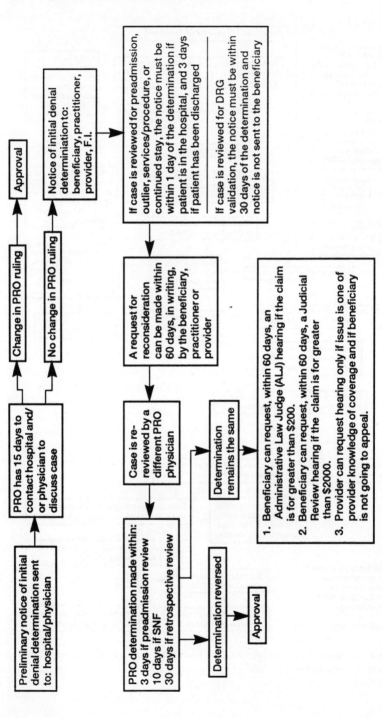

5-5 Appeals Process. *Source:* Adapted from *The Impact of PROs on Hospitals* with permission of Ernst & Young, © 1987.

Preliminary notice of initial denial determination sent to: hospital/physician

PRO has 15 days to contact hospital and/or physician to discuss case

Change in PRO ruling → Approval

No change in PRO ruling → Notice of initial denial determiniation to: beneficiary, practitioner, provider, F.I.

If case is reviewed for preadmission, outlier, services/procedure, or continued stay, the notice must be within 1 day of the determination if patient is in the hospital, and 3 days if patient has been discharged

If case is reviewed for DRG validation, the notice must be within 30 days of the determination and notice is not sent to the beneficiary

A request for reconsideration can be made within 60 days, in writing, by the beneficiary, practitioner or provider

Case is re-reviewed by a different PRO physician

PRO determination made within:
3 days if preadmission review
10 days if SNF
30 days if retrospective review

Determination remains the same

Determination reversed → Approval

1. Beneficiary can request, within 60 days, an Administrative Law Judge (ALJ) hearing if the claim is for greater than $200.
2. Beneficiary can request, within 60 days, a Judicial Review hearing if the claim is for greater than $2000.
3. Provider can request hearing only if issue is one of provider knowledge of coverage and if beneficiary is not going to appeal.

federal program, Medicare is subject to government-wide disclosure rules. Through the PROs, HCFA has access to a nationwide network of data that serves as indicators of the quality of care rendered in hospitals. HCFA is in a position to analyze outcomes of care and to share that information with the public. HCFA's goal is to provide consumers with sufficient information to enable them to make informed health care decisions, such as where to receive inpatient care.

PROs are not federal agencies and thus are exempt from the requirements of the Freedom of Information Act (FOIA), the legislation that guides federal agencies on what and how data are to be released. However, the PROs are bound by regulations that require them to disclose all requested information to HCFA. Since HCFA *is* a federal agency subject to FOIA requirements, the FOIA requirements on data release become effective whenever HCFA receives data from the PROs. For example, in March 1986, HCFA was forced by the FOIA to release PRO data on hospital mortality rates, even though the same information would not necessarily have been released by the individual PROs.

Following HCFA's decision to release the mortality data, much criticism and debate ensued over the issues of disclosure and dissemination of hospital mortality and utilization data. However, the debate has not changed the direction of data disclosure. In 1989, HCFA released its fourth set of hospital-specific mortality data.

The hospital industry has questioned the release of such mortality data as inappropriate. It is debatable whether a single piece of information about a provider's performance presents a balanced view of the hospital or provides a sufficient basis upon which a consumer can make a health care service decision. Current procedures afford hospitals the opportunity to validate and analyze the data and to develop a response. The HCFA's release to the public is accompanied by the hospitals' written responses. HCFA is also considering a variation of this format—releasing data on high-performing hospitals immediately, but withholding data on other hospitals.

The California Example

California's Medical Review, Inc. (CMRI) became the first PRO to make health care data readily available to the public by releasing hospital-specific data for California's 543 hospitals. The statistics released covered discharges from October 1984 through September 1985. They included information on total discharges, total days of hospitalization, average length of stays, average patient age, percentage of female patients, number of deaths, and percentage of deaths for the 24 Major Diagnostic Categories (MDCs). (MDCs group all 470 DRGs into 24 major system categories.)

CMRI releases these data at the end of every calendar quarter. This PRO stresses that the data are to be considered a *starting* point for initial public assessment of hospitals, but cautions that consumers should not judge a hospital's quality of care solely on this information.

CMRI initially briefed hospitals several months before the data release, and each hospital had a 30-day period in which to submit written comments for attachment with its report. CMRI believes releases such as these help to make hospitals accountable to the public for their services and encourage them to assess and improve their quality of care. Such data also serve as a reference point to aid consumers in asking hospitals and physicians the right questions about health care services.

The Ohio Example

Peer Review Systems (PRS) Inc., the Ohio PRO, initiated its own data disclosure in December 1988.[12] PRS announced to the public its intention to focus its medical review on 43 percent of Ohio's hospitals because these institutions exceed hospital health statistics in one or more diagnostic categories. PRS published the list of these hospitals, as well as the diagnostic categories that had high death rates. PRS now provides periodic reports to these hospitals, concentrating its efforts on the 22 facilities that needed to lower their death rates.

Confidentiality Rules

The release of health care data has become one facet of the government's mission. Therefore, it is important to understand the process that PROs are obligated to follow in dealing with the confidentiality issue.

Confidential information is defined as: (1) information that explicitly or implicitly identifies a particular patient, practitioner, or reviewer; (2) sanction reports and recommendations; or (3) quality review studies that identify patients, practitioners, or institutions. Information that identifies a particular institution is *not* included in the definition of confidential information.

The rules require the PROs to disclose to HCFA information on quality and appropriateness of health care services for individual hospitals. PROs are asked to release information on average length of stay, death rates, number of surgical procedures performed in specific catagories, and number of patients in each category who have been readmitted for further treatment.

To assure the protection of the hospital's rights, and to avoid misinterpretations of the data, a PRO must notify a hospital of its intentions to disclose information. It must provide the hospital with a copy of the information and give the hospital 30 days to comment. The PRO must attach these comments to the disclosed material.

The hospital should take advantage of this 30-day period to prepare explanatory statements regarding the data. For example, if the PRO statistics relate to mortality, the hospital should include a response to the data and offer additional information—such as case mix statistics, severity of illnesses treated, or the number and ages of its patients—to enable the public to better interpret the data. In the absence of a national consensus, the hospital may develop its own standards or methods for measuring quality of care and use a data release situation to communicate its quality assurance program to the community.

Severity of Illness Adjustments

DRG payments are based on the average cost of services for a case with that particular diagnosis. One of the major limitations of the DRG payment system is that it has no method of adjustment for exceptions to or variations in resource use within a DRG. While each year HCFA has made coding changes to increase the homogeneity of the DRGs, unstandardized measures of the differences in resource consumption remain. The outlier policies for both cost and day outliers do not appropriately address this issue.

HCFA is evaluating a variety of patient classification systems to augment the DRG system and help measure quality of care. This evaluation process is not likely to lead to an application of any one of these systems; rather HCFA may incorporate the most viable attributes from several of these systems into a system of its own.

Severity is a descriptor of disease intensity. A severity of illness system quantifies this intensity and allows for measurement of a person's illness at a specific point in time. Severity levels are measured several times during a hospitalization: upon admission, during the hospitalization, and after discharge. These measurements should decrease in value as the hospitalization progresses and be at their lowest upon discharge. Severity of illness measurements that fall outside the expected norm should be investigated to determine whether the failure to progress is due to substandard quality of care or untoward disease complications.

Severity measurement can predict the course and expected recovery of a disease. Knowledge of the disease's "typical" course and recovery process assists hospitals in identifying quality problems, appropriate resource utilization, and professional performance. Currently, five major severity systems (products) are available. Each system assigns a numeric severity level and predicts resource consumption for a particular illness. Because of the systems' ability to measure observed versus expected disease progression, hospitals are evaluating these systems to determine whether they could also be used to indicate quality of care.[13] The systems include:

1. *APACHE* II (Acute Physiology and Chronic Health Evaluation) uses a point score based upon initial values of 12 routine physiologic measurements (such as vital signs and blood tests), age, and previous health status to provide a general measure of severity of disease. APACHE II is most effective when applied to critical care patients. The other severity measurement systems generally apply more to the entire hospital patient population. The APACHE II classification system was developed by Knauss and others at the George Washington University Medical Center.[14]

2. *Disease Staging* pertains to two related approaches for measuring severity: (a) Clinical Staging, a method based on a manual review of clinical measurements (such as case history and symptoms) documented in the medical record; and (b) Coded Staging, an automated method based on the coded diagnostic data recorded in the discharge abstract. Both methods share the concept of "staging," which defines discrete points in the course of individual diseases that are clinically detectable, reflect severity in terms of risk of death or residual impairment, and possess clinical significance for prognosis and choice of therapeutic modality. Diseases are divided into four major stages of increasing severity based on the extent of disease and the presence of complications. Both Clinical and Coded Staging are marketed by SysteMetrics, Inc.[15]

3. *MEDISGROUPS* (Medical Illness Severity Grouping System) is an admission-oriented severity grouping system that uses objective clinical findings from medical records to categorize patients into one of five severity groups. MEDISGROUPS is not disease specific; it evaluates the range of signs and findings regardless of the patient's diagnosis. MEDISGROUPS is marketed by MediQual Systems.[16]

4. *Patient Management Categories'* (PMCs') system of severity classification assumes that categories which serve as the basis of hospital payment must not only predict resource use but also reflect the diagnostic and treatment processes applicable to each patient type. First, patients are assigned to up to five disease modules according to the diagnosis in the discharge abstract. Then, patients are assigned to a PMC by comparing the diagnosis and procedure codes against those specified by the PMC software. PMC was developed by Wanda Young at Blue Cross of Western Pennsylvania.[17]

5. *The Computerized Severity Index* (CSI), modeled on the Severity of Illness Index, is based on a six-digit system: the first five digits are the same as the disease condition labels in the current ICD-9-CM code book used by virtually all hospitals in the United States; the sixth digit (1 to 4) describes how severe the disease is on the basis of recorded signs and symptoms, laboratory values, radiological findings, vital signs, etc. This system index was developed by Susan Horn of Johns Hopkins.[18]

IMPACT OF PROs ON HOSPITALS

The impact of PRO review on a hospital affects the major functions of the institution.

Financial

A PRO can affect the finances and reputation of a hospital. For example, the PRO review of the medical records supports or denies payment and recommends sanctions. Based upon the PRO's recommendation, HCFA may deny reimbursement; the denial of payment for services already delivered can generate direct and indirect losses. Direct loss includes denial of payment; indirect loss includes loss of volume resulting from damage to the hospital's reputation within the community and the release of adverse mortality data.

When the PRO reviews the medical record, it also subjects it to a validation of the DRG assignment given by the hospital. Based on the review, the PRO can reassign the DRG, thus affecting the final payment to the hospital.

HCFA may impose sanctions on physicians and hospitals that frequently violate quality and utilization standards. A sanction may be either a monetary penalty or an exclusion from the Medicare program. The provider receives reimbursement for appropriate services, but payment is denied for the services deemed inappropriate or unnecessary. Additionally, the amount denied must be remitted to the government as part of the sanction. For example, if the patient bill is $5,000 and $500 is deemed inappropriate, the provider receives reimbursement for only $4,500 and incurs the remaining $500 as a loss. The median sanction is $3,647.[19] Between 1984 and 1988, the Department of Health and Human Services (HHS) received only 51 recommendations to sanction hospitals from PROs. An exclusion sanction (barring participation in both Medicare and Medicaid) must be for at least 1 year and may be permanent; the average exclusion lasts 18 months.

Operations

PROs contract with hospitals to provide off-site medical record reviews. Substantial hospital administrative time and resources are consumed by the process of providing the medical record to the PRO.

The PRO system relies on appropriate medical record coding and documentation of care. The medical record is the basis for review and, as such, must be complete and accurate. Thus, the medical records staff devotes considerable time to internal chart review. Additionally, hospitals are often inadequately reimbursed by HCFA for the total costs involved in photocopying the charts for off-site review.

Market Position

A PRO can release hospital-specific data to the public at any time after first submitting it to the hospital 30 days prior to release. HCFA first released mortality data in March 1986, and again in December 1987, 1988, and 1989. These data were released by HCFA after the hospitals were given the opportunity to review and comment on the statistics; the comments were published with the data.

The government believes consumers have a right to access information on health care in their community. HHS hopes that the mortality rates have provided consumers with a starting point for health care decision making. Furthermore, HHS anticipates that these and additional data releases will increase the motivation of hospitals to examime quality of care within their institutions.

High mortality rates imply substandard care; when publicized, this implication can seriously damage a hospital's reputation in its community. Both consumers and physicians may be reluctant to utilize the hospital, creating lower occupancy rates.

Human Resources

The reputation, financial stability, and clinical services of a hospital affect the quanity and quality of personnel who staff the institution. Progressive, "high quality" hospitals attract and retain motivated, competent staff members. Professionals with high standards of performance and excellence will seek the same characteristics in their work environment. Conversely, having a reputation as a substandard provider will create difficulties in the recruitment and retention of well-qualified personnel. This situation will become increasingly evident during the current nursing shortage, as hospitals compete with each other and with other delivery systems for a limited supply of nurses.

Quality Assurance

The impact of the PRO system will force hospitals to develop strong, coordinated quality assurance/utilization review programs. It is the responsibility of the Board of Trustees to establish the philosophy of quality care in a hospital. In implementing a strong, effective quality assurance

(QA) program, the board and administration must communicate to the staff, regulatory agencies, and consumers their commitment to quality and ultimate accountability for care delivery.

The Board of Trustees is now being held accountable for the quality of care of a hospital, in addition to its financial well-being. Thus, the Board has the responsibility to ensure that the Chief Executive Officer (CEO) has the appropriate mechanisms in place to provide high-quality care.

The QA department should develop standards, policies, and procedures to provide the staff with clear guidelines to follow when caring for patients. Uniform standards will also enhance the quality of care. Since professionals will be using the same definitions and medical care documentation, the chance of errors resulting from lack of knowledge will be reduced. The credentials of physicians, nurses, and other health care professionals should be verified to ensure accountability for professional services.

FUTURE ISSUES

The policies, procedures, and operations of the PRO program are still maturing. The issue of quality of patient care remains at the forefront of the thinking of all involved—policymakers, consumers, providers, and payers. Recent changes in health care delivery and finance have stimulated new discussions of the interfaces among cost, quality, and access. The competing pressures generated by efforts to contain costs while assuring access will continue to lead to concerns about the quality of care being delivered.

Despite the Bush administration's desire for less regulation, the government continues to expand Medicare regulatory efforts. Each year the breadth and depth of PRO medical review responsibilities increase. Each year, too, more rules are written to maintain quality. Concern is now growing over after-discharge care. In fact, recent legislation mandated that PROs will also review after-care such as skilled nursing facilities (SNF) and home health care. PROs have also been given the new mission of scrutinizing care given to HMO patients. PROs are now actively geared up to begin this review, as it is part of their latest contract with HCFA. This is likely to be the beginning of a process that may end in the PRO's review of an entire episode of illness.

Medical review is not meant to be a challenge to the physician's art, but to be a challenge to both the hospital's administration and its medical staff to effectively and efficiently allocate resources. Success in dealing with peer-review organizations requires a strong partnership between hospital management and the medical staff. It also requires hospitals to develop specific strategies and management techniques to address quality of care concerns.

In 1987, the Health Care Finance Committee requested an objective survey to assist in evaluating the PRO program and the developing quality of care monitoring. Two recent surveys examined the effectiveness of the government's quality assurance program and suggested strategies to build relationships with the PROs.[20] The results of these surveys also provided new insights into the characteristics of what is perceived as a "quality hospital." The factors identified as having a significant impact on hospital quality included professional competence, nurse/physician relationships, nurse/patient ratio, and hospital management style. As a first step, hospitals should become more familiar with their PRO's rules, process, and personnel and perhaps initiate interaction by inviting PRO staff to visit and present their program to administration and medical and nursing staff.

As a second step, a quality assurance commitment by a proactive board will optimize the effectiveness of the professionals involved in patient care and will support the entire organization's ability to meet quality of care standards and patient expectations.[21] PROs as regulators want to promote high quality standards that are implicit within all hospital missions. A hospital's ability to manage health care delivery in the future will increasingly be dependent upon its skill in monitoring and evaluating the quality of services it provides. The challenge is clear—hospitals must contain costs while demonstrating quality to assure everyone access to effective and efficient health care.

NOTES

1. Health Care Financing Administration, Department of Health and Human Services, *Medicare Prospective Payment and the American Health Care System,* Report to Congress, June 1989, p. 33.

2. American Medical Peer Review Association, *AMPRA PRO Directory,* AMPRA, 810 First Street, N.E., Suite 410, Washington, D.C. 20002, April 24, 1989, Directory.

3. U.S. Congress, House, *The Omnibus Budget Reconciliation Act of 1987,* Conference Report to H.R. 3545, 100th Congress, House Report 100–495, section 4091.

4. Marcia Orsolits, "Substandard Care—Better Differentiating of Facility versus Physician Quality Problems," Presentation at American Medical Peer Review Association (AMPRA) summer conference, Boston, July 1989.

5. Unpublished data, Health Standards and Quality Bureau, HCFA Office of Peer Review, Data Set DRG Changes, May 26, 1988.

6. "Medicare and Medicaid Programs, Denial of Payment for Substandard Quality Care and Review of Beneficiary Complaints," *Federal Register* (11) (January 18, 1989):q956 ff.

7. Ernst & Young, *The Impact of PROs on Hospitals,* E&Y no. J. 58693, (Cleveland, Ohio, 1987).

8. Ibid.

9. Ibid.

10. Ibid.

11. Ibid.

12. Peer Review Systems, Inc., 3700 Corporate Drive, Suite 250, Columbus, Ohio 43229; press release kit dated December 19, 1988. (614) 895-9900.

13. J. William Thomas, et al., *An Evaluation of Alternative Severity of Illness Measures for Use by University Hospitals (Vol. 1: Management Summary).* Ann Arbor, Mich.: Department of Health Services Management and Policy, School of Public Health, University of Michigan, December 29, 1986).

14. William A. Knaus, et al., "Apache II: A Severity of Disease Classification System," *Critical Care Medicine* 13 (1985):818–829.

15. Joseph S. Gonnello, et al., "Staging of Disease: A Case-Mix Measurement," *Journal of American Medical Association* 251 (Feb. 3, 1984):637–644.

16. Alan C. Brewster, et al., "Medisgrps: A Clinical Based Approach to Classifying Hospital Patients at Admission," *Inquiry* 22 (Winter 1985):377–387.

17. Wanda W. Young, "Incorporating Severity of Illness and Comorbidity in Case-Mix Measurement," *Health Care Financing Review* (November 1984):23–31.

18. Susan D. Horn, "Measuring Severity: How Sick Is Sick? How Well Is Well?" *Healthcare Financial Management* (October 1986):21–32.

19. General Accounting Office, *Statutory Modifications Needed for the PRO Monetary Penalty,* GAO/HRD 89-18. (March 1989).

20. C.K. Davis, M. Orsolits, and F.B. Abbey, "The PRO's Role in Monitoring Quality of Care," *Trustee* 40 (July 1987).

21. Grujic, et al., "Organizational Control of Hospital Infrastructure Determining the Quality of Care," *American College of Utilization Review Physicians* 4(February 1989).

Part III

Technical Considerations

Nancy O. Graham

Choosing the appropriate method of health care assessment, modified method, or combination of methods is discussed in Chapter 6. Dr. Rosenberg explores the strengths and limitations of evaluating the structure underlying health care, the actual health care process, the outcomes of care, patient satisfaction with care received, and various combinations of these categories. While choosing the appropriate method may be difficult, the task is made easier if the following questions can be answered:

1. What do you mean by quality?
2. What are the objectives of your evaluation?
3. Are you evaluating the care given by your own unit? Or someone else's?
4. What sources of data are accessible and reliable?
5. What resources are available and justified?
6. Are you interested in a specific time frame?
7. What range of diseases and professional inputs interests you?
8. What kinds of quality of care problems do you think you have?

The different strategies for assessing the quality of medical care are reviewed in Part IV. Quality assessment methods differ in *time frame* for review (prospective, concurrent, retrospective), in *data gathering* methods (record review, abstract, observation, interviews, surveys, simulations, claims data), and in *categories* of criteria (structure, process, outcome). One element, however, is common to most of these approaches—the use of explicit criteria. No assessment is possible without some measure of comparison. Criteria are the basic ingredients used to measure the quality of health care.

In Chapter 7, Graham explores criteria formulation, discussing such topics as

- definitions of terms
- implicit versus explicit criteria
- technical terminology
- categorization of criteria
- criteria development

Health care in managed care systems, competition, cost containment, and new regulations are changing how care is provided. In Chapter 8, Berwick and Knapp stress that the time is ripe for new directions in the quality measurement field. Industries other than health care have much to teach regarding the methods for obtaining, analyzing, and displaying data; techniques for problem identification, problem solving, and reassessment; and ideas about organizational factors that produce a high quality product. The authors describe the Quality Measurement Program at the Harvard Community Health Plan, which has begun to supplement traditional concepts and methods in health care quality assessment with new approaches, new models, and new management needs in health care delivery systems.

Chapter 6

Choosing the Assessment Method That Meets Your Needs

Stephen N. Rosenberg

No single method of health care evaluation is "best" in any absolute sense of the term. Each assessment technique has certain strengths that make it useful in some situations, as well as limitations that make it inappropriate for other applications. The most productive way to identify quality deficiencies in a pediatric group practice may be very different from the optimal method for comparing the quality of nursing care in two surgical intensive care units. No single method is "best" for another reason as well: In most settings, as Donabedian mentions in an earlier chapter, effective quality assurance will require the coordinated application of several different approaches.

This chapter will explore the strengths and limitations of each of the basic methods of quality assessment, and will then discuss the factors to be considered in choosing the most effective method (or, more often, the most effective combination of methods) to meet the quality assurance needs of a specific clinical setting.

For the purposes of this comparison, I find it useful to divide the approaches to health care evaluation into four categories:

1. assessment of the process of health care, i.e., what is done for patients by health professionals (and by family members and the patients themselves)
2. assessment of the structure that underlies health care, including physical, human, and organizational resources
3. assessment of outcomes, i.e., the impact of care on health status, as well as on patient knowledge and behavior

Stephen N. Rosenberg, MD, MPH, is an Associate Professor of Clinical Public Health (Health Policy and Management) at Columbia University School of Public Health and he also serves as the Medical Director of the New York City Employee Health Benefits Program.

4. assessment of satisfaction with care on the part of both patients and their care-givers

This categorization expands somewhat upon Donabedian's classic three-way classification, in which all assessment techniques are conceptualized as measures of structure, process, or outcome, and patient satisfaction is considered to be a type of outcome. Adequate physical and organizational structure does facilitate the appropriate process of care, which, in turn, promotes desirable health status outcomes. Patient satisfaction, however, does not appear to flow in the same linear fashion from structure and process.

Instead, satisfaction seems to interact with the other three factors in a fairly subtle manner. Structural factors—often those we consider to be "minor amenities," such as the comfort of waiting rooms—have a direct impact on patient satisfaction. So do certain aspects of process, especially those interpersonal factors we are least likely to measure, such as the courtesy of receptionists. Satisfaction, in turn, affects the continuing process of care, through its influence on the patient-professional relationship, "compliance" with instructions, and the keeping of follow-up appointments. And this feedback has enormous potential for facilitating (or hindering) the achievement of health status outcomes, particularly in the long-term treatment of chronic conditions.

Because of these interactions, it is useful to think of patient satisfaction as a fourth, separate and important area, and to evaluate it along with structure, process, and/or health status outcome.

All the assessment methods described in this book, as well as others in the health care literature, fit into these four categories. Some are variations or modifications of one of the classic approaches (e.g., criteria mapping, a fairly recent adaptation of process assessment). Others, such as tracers or health accounting, represent combinations of two or more of the fundamental techniques. An understanding of the strengths and limitations of the four basic approaches is necessary to appreciate the reasons why modified methods have been modified and combined methods have been combined, and to choose one or more techniques for application in a specific clinical situation.

STRUCTURE

Assessment of the structure underlying health care services involves evaluation of the quantity and quality of three types of resources:

1. physical structure—the actual physical facilities in which care is rendered, the adequacy of supplies, and the amount, type, and condition of equipment

2. personnel—the number of professional, paraprofessional, and support staff of each type; ratios of personnel to patients and of one type of personnel to another (e.g., registered nurses to nurses aids); and the qualifications and experience of staff members
3. administrative and organizational arrangements—the existence and thoroughness of up-to-date procedure manuals concerning such topics as disaster response and infection control, the composition of professional committees, and the adequacy of systems dealing with quality assurance, record-keeping, and the sterilization and resupply of equipment

The most widespread evaluations of structure are carried out by licensing and accrediting agencies. Typically, an agency will make its criteria and standards available to the facilities it oversees, and will schedule most, if not all, of its routine evaluations in advance. When an assessment site visit is scheduled, the agency will ask that certain documents, such as staff rosters and procedure manuals, be submitted before the visit, so that the structural evaluation can get under way in the agency's office. The evaluators will also ask the facility to have certain other documents available at the time of the visit and to have specific staff members on hand to be interviewed.

A structural assessment team is almost always multidisciplinary, and includes administrative staff; an engineer, sanitarian, or other professional capable of assessing the physical aspects of the facility; and the members of other professions whose qualifications, organization, and equipment are to be evaluated. Nurses and physicians are almost always included; pharmacists and medical records personnel are frequently members of the team; and physical, occupational, and speech therapists, dentists, social workers, dieticians, and others may also be involved, depending on the type of facility being audited and the emphasis of the evaluating agency. The team may also include paraprofessional or nonprofessional ancillary staff members.

The site visit typically begins with a meeting in which the evaluation team explains its procedures to the facility's key administrative staff. Members of the facility's governing board will often attend as well. The team then separates with each member assessing a different aspect of the facility: the pharmacist checking out the patient medication profiles and the adequacy of drug stocks, the nurse reviewing staffing levels and qualifications, the administrator reviewing procedure manuals and interviewing administrative staff, the engineer measuring ventilation in patient rooms and checking for compliance with fire codes, etc. The data collection instruments necessary for structural assessment are the checkoff lists used by each team member to record his or her observations.

At the end of the site visit, which may take several days, the assessment team usually holds an "exit conference" with the facility's administrative staff. The team informally presents its major preliminary impressions and seeks clarification of any incomplete or inconsistent findings. Eventually, a written report of the evaluation is sent to the administration and board of the facility. Continued licensure or accreditation may depend on the results of the assessment and/or the adequacy of actions taken to correct any significant deficiencies. More focused follow-up visits may be made, sometimes on an unannounced basis.

Structural assessments have several advantages over evaluations of process, outcome, and satisfaction, which account for their widespread use by licensing and accrediting bodies. They are relatively rapid, relying on straightforward interviews and reviews of existing, easily observable objects and documents. Structural assessments are simple to carry out, so that many tasks, such as checking on the adequacy of supplies and basic equipment, can be delegated to inexpensive ancillary staff members. Because they are rapid and simple, structural assessments tend to be relatively inexpensive.

All of these attributes make structural approaches attractive to state agencies that license hospitals, nursing homes, and other facilities, as well as to the Joint Commission and other accrediting and funding agencies. What makes a structural evaluation *most* attractive to these groups, however, is the fact that it is highly objective. A hospital that loses its license or its accreditation (and therefore its ability to sponsor residency training programs and to participate in Medicare and most state Medicaid programs) might well appeal the findings of process, outcome, and satisfaction assessments, which are—as we shall see shortly—more open to interpretation. However, they will be less likely to appeal if they lose their license because their own staff roster showed only two registered nurses on the midnight-to-eight shift, while their own census report showed 200 patients in-house.

An additional strength of the structural approach is that it can answer certain questions about the quality of care that no other method can address. If you want to know whether there is privacy in the examining rooms of the venereal disease clinic, whether or not the immunization materials in the pediatric office are outdated, or whether the well-child clinic is too cold in the winter, you have to make a site visit and look at these items of structure for yourself. They may be extremely basic, but they are also important. The *process* of care may be perfect in each of these settings, but if the structure is inadequate, the venereal disease patient will not answer questions frankly, injections of outdated measles vaccine (though given at the correct age) will not provide protection, and chilly babies will be crying so loudly that an examination of their hearts and lungs will be worthless. The *outcomes* of these deficiencies, e.g., cases of measles developing years after the ineffective immunizations, may be extremely difficult to measure.

Unfortunately, the structure underlying health care is two steps removed from the ultimate concern of evaluation—health status outcome. This is its primary drawback and makes it a somewhat blunt evaluation instrument. Inadequate structure may make correct process and otpimal outcome less likely or even impossible. On the other hand, satisfactory structure does not guarantee good process and outcome. If there are no scalpel blades in the operating room, the process of care for the next patient with acute appendicitis will no doubt be poor, and his or her outcome will be tragic. Yet the presence of numerous, sharp and shiny scalpel blades does not ensure that the surgeon will not slice into the patient's iliac artery.

For this reason, few articles about structural assessment appear in the professional literature, and agencies such as the Joint Commission would like to add more process and, especially, more outcome tools to their armamentarium. Nevertheless, if we are willing to admit that there are hospitals with woefully inadequate supplies, nursing homes with serious staffing deficiencies, and other situations in which it is impossible to render the best of care because of structural deficiencies, this method of assessment remains an important component of an effective quality assurance system.

PROCESS

The quality of the services provided to patients is usually evaluated by assessing the written evidence of process contained in patient records. Typically, a sample of patient charts is selected and reviewed by health professionals. The sample (which should usually be random or systematic) is often stratified by patient type (age, sex, etc.), by primary diagnosis, or by principal medical procedure (type of operation, etc.). The review may encompass the entire process of care, or it may focus on the care rendered by one type of professional (nurses, residents, consultants, all physicians, etc.).

In the 1960s and earlier, most chart review was carried out by strict peers of the professionals whose work was being evaluated; thus, board-certified neurosurgeons read the chart entries of fellow board-certified neurosurgeons, and so forth. In the early 1970s, however, the Professional Standards Review Organizations developed a model that has since become widely used. This model involves a two-stage review, whereby nurses review the process of physicians' care (or generalist physicians review the care provided by specialists), and only potential problem cases are set aside for a second review by more expensive, difficult-to-recruit subspecialists. While strict peer evaluation may rely on the flexible judgment of reviewers, review by nonpeers is almost always based on explicit, detailed, written criteria and standards developed by peer consultants.

The evaluation of the written record of the health care process is relatively inexpensive, and the method allows for the assessment of a large volume of care in a fairly brief period of time. Patient identifiers can be concealed for confidentiality, and the names of the professionals providing care can also be obscured to remove any possibility of bias or cronyism. Health professionals generally are comfortable with the process approach, since it parallels their educational experience. The findings in an assessment of process lend themselves to meaningful feedback about factors that are amenable to improvement through education and managerial interventions.

The limitations of this approach are largely due to frequent problems of illegibility and difficulty in retrieving records. It is also often claimed that charts may not adequately reflect what was really done for patients. This complaint is especially common from health professionals who have just been told that a review of their patients' records revealed poor quality care: "I give the *finest* quality care, which is why I have such a busy practice and don't have the time to record all the *nonsense* you're looking for in my charts!" This complaint is valid if evaluators base their reviews on trivial or irrelevant criteria. However, there is an emerging consensus that a reasonable amount of relevant information *must* be included in the written record, not just to facilitate evaluation but also as a part of acceptable quality care itself. If a hypertensive patient's blood pressure, weight, and medication, along with the presence or absence of important sequelae of hypertension and side effects of antihypertensive medication, are not recorded during a visit, the physician who sees that patient the following month (even if it's the *same* physician) will be unable to provide optimal care relevant to the progression or stability of the patient's condition. Moreover, this vital information needed for high quality care is of little use if it is illegible or if it is contained in a chart that is not readily retrievable. With these considerations in mind, a carefully constructed evaluation of patient records can provide a fair and reasonable assessment of the quality of the care being rendered.

As an initial screening method to detect possible deficiencies in the process of care, it is sometimes useful to develop profiles of clinical services. Computerized systems, used primarily for billing purposes, often contain enough information about the frequency of follow-up visits for chronic conditions, the tests ordered for patients with specific diagnoses, the prescriptions written, etc., to permit evaluators to flag aberrant patterns of care. This type of superficial process assessment is not definitive, but can identify areas that deserve closer scrutiny.

A very different approach to evaluating the process of care utilizes direct observation by peer professionals. This technique is extremely common in the education of nurses, physicians, psychologists, social workers, and others. It is not widely used in evaluating health professionals after they have been fully trained because it is both time-consuming and expensive. For example, the evaluation of a heart transplant procedure might require the presence of an evaluating cardiac surgeon for 6 hours. The same surgeon might be able to evaluate the written report of the same operation in 10 minutes. The presence of an observer may influence the quality of the care being observed by motivating usually mediocre professionals to perform at their best, or by causing self-conscious professionals to perform at their worst. Furthermore, direct observation is vulnerable to the effects of conscious and unconscious bias: The observer may know the professional being evaluated or may be influenced by such irrelevant factors as age, sex, race, or appearance.

Despite these drawbacks, observation of the process of care can be valuable because it allows access to certain aspects of the process that are rarely committed to writing, such as the quality of patient-professional communication or the amount of time patients spend in waiting areas and examining rooms.

A final approach to assessing the process of care is to interview patients concerning their perceptions of the care they recently received. Patients can provide reliable reports about the presence or absence of basic, recognizable components of care (e.g., "Did the optometrist use a machine similar to this one, and bring this part close to your eyes to test for glaucoma?"). Their perceptions of patient-professional communication may be even more pertinent than a professional observer's evaluation.

Using any of these methods, assessment of the process of care is still one step removed from our ultimate concern, and it is important to remember that many procedures that experts and textbooks consider to be "good process" have never been carefully tested for their impact on health status. New drugs must be proven safe and effective before they can be marketed. Diagnostic and operative procedures, and, indeed, much of what health professionals do at the bedside and in the office, are not subject to such rigorous standards.

OUTCOME

Given the caveats applied to structural and process evaluations, it is no wonder that so much attention is given to perfecting better techniques for evaluating outcomes, especially health status outcomes.

The typical outcome assessment relies on information in the patient record to evaluate health status at some point after care is provided or initiated, e.g., a patient's blood pressure 6 months after the beginning of antihypertensive treatment. Such evaluation is based on samples of records—as in chart review for process assessment—but it is almost always condition specific, since the desired outcomes will be different for patients with different diagnoses.

When outcome information is not recorded or records are not available, an alternative approach is to reexamine patients directly. In the 1970s, for instance, the New York City Department of Health reexamined approximately 12,000 patients each year to find out whether they could see, hear, chew, and walk better after they had received eyeglasses, hearing aids, dentures, and podiatric foot applications under the city's Medicaid program.

Whether information comes from charts or from patient reexamination, an important issue in all outcome evaluation is timing. For instance, patients who received optometric services must be reexamined quickly, so that the normal progression of their sight disorders will not obscure the fact that they received eyeglasses that were appropriate at the time they were fitted. With many other conditions, however, it is more important not to measure outcomes too soon. It would be inappropriate, for example, to evaluate the outcome of antihypertensive treatment after only 1 month. Six months is more reasonable. Actually, the outcomes of ultimate interest here—the avoidance of myocardial infarctions and strokes with successful maintenance of normal blood pressure—cannot be fully measured for decades. From this example, it should be obvious that outcome assessment is often time-consuming. Because of the problems encountered in following patients over long periods of time, it is also often expensive. On the other hand, once a number of careful studies have established the correlations between short-term and long-term outcomes, it is reasonable to use the former in assessment.

Two special types of short-term outcome that are often measured are changes in patient knowledge and behavior as a result of the educational components of health care. Pre- and post-tests (by questionnaire or interview) and direct observation of patients are used to determine whether, for instance, diabetics have learned to properly inject their insulin, whether patients with emphysema have stopped smoking, and whether hypertensives understand and follow sodium restriction diets.

The most obvious advantage of outcome assessment is that, unlike evaluations of structure and process, it is "self-validating": Full and speedy recovery, high cure rates, and return to normal functions are good things in their own right, while death, disability, and complications are intrinsically bad. This is not an unmixed advantage, however. You cannot assume that positive outcomes are necessarily the result of good structure and process, or that poor outcomes are due to flaws in one of these earlier aspects of care. Many health status outcomes are influenced by environmental, genetic, and socioeconomic factors that health care cannot change. Outcome assessment is usually most useful as a first step, followed by a careful exploration to discover what (if anything) in the structure and/or process of care was responsible for positive and negative findings.

SATISFACTION

The last of the four basic approaches is the study of satisfaction among patients and their care-givers (the parents of pediatric patients, and the spouses, adult children, and others caring for older patients).

Mail questionnaires, along with telephone and in-person interviews, can be used to answer three important questions: whether and to what degree people are satisfied with care, what subgroups are satisfied or dissatisfied, and, most important of all, *why* they are satisfied or dissatisfied. Because the information-gathering techniques are the same, these questions are often accompanied by measures of patient knowledge and attempts to learn patients' perceptions of the process of the care they have received.

Like health status outcomes, satisfaction is "self-validating," in that it is valuable in its own right. As discussed earlier, it is also an important intermediate factor that influences the ongoing process of care and, ultimately, health status outcomes. Patient satisfaction studies are often dismissed as "subjective," but information about why patients are satisfied—which aspects of their care are perceived positively and negatively—can be enormously helpful in improving the effectiveness of any health care program, not to mention the attractiveness and financial situation of a health care facility.

MAKING A CHOICE

Consideration of the relative merits and limitations of the four basic approaches to quality assessment should support my earlier contention that no one method is best in any absolute sense. Each technique is optimal under certain circumstances. Choosing the appropriate basic method, modified method, or combination of methods for a specific setting is difficult, but the task is made easier if you can answer the following eight questions:

1. *What Do You Mean by "Quality"?* The quality of health care can be defined in many ways, and it is important that those who are providing the care in question and those who will be evaluating it reach an agreement on the appropriate definition before the evaluation begins. If not, the results of the evaluation may be viewed as irrelevant by the very people who need to use these results to improve care.

   An excellent way to begin working toward a consensus is to review the "levels" of quality described in the earlier chapter by Donabedian. An evaluation of the process of care, using patient records, may be the most appropriate approach if you define quality in terms of the technical proficiency of services provided by health professionals. If your definition is broader and includes interpersonal aspects of care, it will probably also be necessary to observe care directly or to query patients about their impressions. If the definition of quality focuses on the impact of care on a community (which might be the case if the staff of a health department clinic were doing the defining), an outcome-oriented assessment would be called for.

2. *What Are the Objectives of Your Evaluation?* Evaluations are carried out for a number of very different reasons, each of which may require a different approach. If you are just beginning your quality assurance activities and your objective is to identify problem areas needing closer scrutiny, you will want to use an assessment method that is quick and inexpensive, such as a profile of process patterns or a retrospective review of short-term health status outcomes that are known to be recorded in patient charts. You will probably not want to do extensive peer observation or develop criteria maps (a very detailed approach to process assessment) to attain this objective. On the other hand, you might want to use one of these more time-consuming but definitive approaches if you already know that a certain serious or chronic quality deficiency exists, and your objective is to uncover and correct the underlying causes.

3. *Are You Evaluating the Care Given by Your Own Unit? Or Someone Else's?* If people are motivated to assess and improve the quality of care they themselves are providing, they can use a wide range of relatively subtle and subjective techniques such as direct observation or flexible peer review of charts without detailed written criteria. If, on the other hand, you are evaluating someone else's care (as licensing, funding, and accrediting organizations do), you need to use methods that are highly objective and not open to alternative interpretations, such as structural assessment or the evaluation of carefully defined and documented health status outcomes like mortality or birthweight.

   This question is a tricky one: Evaluators from one unit in an organization who set out to study the work of another unit may feel that they are doing an internal assessment of part of their own facility, but the people whose work is being assessed are very likely to see the evaluators as outsiders.

4. *What Sources of Data Are Accessible and Reliable?* A careful exploration of this question may reveal limitations on the assessment methods that can be used. You cannot do a structural assessment of the offices of private practitioners who will not let you in the door, a chart review in a hospital with a disorganized record room, or a reexamination study in prison health when many of the patients have already been paroled.

5. *What Resources Are Available and Justified?* Some assessment methods require a large amount of professional—even subspecialist—

time, while other methods can be carried out by more plentiful, less expensive staff. Some methods may require the use of computer hardware and softwear or special skills like bilingual interviewing. Are these resources available to you? Are they justified? It may be reasonable to expend a great deal of money and staff time developing and implementing a methodology that will be used continually or repeatedly, but the same investment may not be justified for a one-shot evaluation.

6. *Are You Interested in a Specific Time Frame?* Certain assessment methods must be used retrospectively, or concurrently, or prospectively, while other methods may be used in more than one of these ways. If you are interested in comparing the quality of last year's care with the quality of care you are delivering now (after an intensive inservice education program), you cannot evaluate both time periods through direct observation, and you probably cannot interview patients from both periods, but you can review their medical charts.

7. *What Range of Diseases and Professional Inputs Interests You?* An outcome assessment can provide information about the impact of the entire multidisciplinary staff on the health status of diabetic patients. However, it will not tell you anything specific about the contribution of dieticians, endocrinologists, and nurse educators. Their individual roles would be better assessed with a process tool. To apply process or outcome methodologies in an emergency room would probably require separate studies for the victims of heart attacks, head trauma, and poisoning, but a structural assessment could provide information about the adequacy of emergency equipment and staff for the care of patients with numerous different acute disorders.

8. *What Kinds of Quality of Care Problems Do You Think You Have?* This question, though the most subjective, may be the most important. If informed staff members can honestly discuss their hunches about the kinds of significant problems they suspect, the appropriate assessment technique to confirm or refute their suspicions, as well as to provide information useful in improving care, may be obvious.

In most situations, consideration of these eight questions will lead you to choose a combination of evaluation methodologies. Your definition of quality may well be multifaceted, your evaluation may have more than one objective, several data sources may be necessary to provide all the information you need, or you may suspect the presence of diverse quality deficiencies.

When two or more assessment techniques are combined—in formal systems such as tracers, or in an informal, eclectic manner—the strengths of one method can make up for the limitations of another. Each approach will raise certain questions or provide only partial answers, and a different approach will be necessary to furnish a complete picture.

The opportunities for combining the modifying evaluation techniques to meet the needs of individual situations are almost endless. As you read through the chapters on specific methods of assessment that follow, think about the possibilities: Are there situations in which a tracer study should combine peer observations and patient satisfaction instead of chart review and health status outcomes? Would it be useful to evaluate elements of structure as part of the health accounting approach? The field of quality assurance is a young one, and the choice of appropriate methods for specific situations is enlivened by opportunities for creative innovation.

Chapter 7

Criteria Development

Nancy O. Graham

Any discussion of quality assurance is likely to be clouded by differences in terminology. The terms *occurrence screens, generic screens,* and *clinical indicators* are often used interchangeably.[1] These indicators or screens are referred to as "flags," denoting the need for more in-depth reviews by objective and measurable criteria. Examples of such indicators include unexpected deaths, adverse drug reactions, patient falls, and so forth.

One definition of standard is a level of care or practice. These standards are often set by professional associations as the optimal method of treating or diagnosing. The second definition of standard is an expected level of compliance. The element being reviewed should (100 percent) or should not (0 percent) be expected to be met. In some cases, *standard* may be interchanged with the term *threshold,* stating an expected level of compliance.

To further confuse the matter, *criteria* and *standards* are terms that are sometimes mistakenly used interchangeably. Explicit criteria are predetermined elements of health care against which the aspects of the quality of a medical service may be compared. For example, a criterion statement may be that a pathological examination of the removed tissue should be performed after an appendectomy. Standards are professionally defined expressions of the range of acceptable variation for a criterion. For instance, it may be acceptable for pathology reports to indicate that the tissue was normal on 10 to 20 percent of the appendixes removed. If pathology reports indicate that normal appendixes are never removed, it might mean overly conservative measures are employed and thus certain cases of appendicitis are missed. Too many reports of normal tissue might imply

Nancy O. Graham, RN, Dr PH, is Vice-President, Nursing at Lawrence Hospital in Bronxville, New York.

unnecessary surgery. Another example can be seen in the assessment of the quality of care for patients with a diagnosis of streptococcal sore throat. It may be decided that one criterion is the presence of a positive throat culture in *all* patients with that diagnosis. The criterion is the positive throat culture; *all* is the standard (100 percent of the charts reviewed should indicate a positive culture).[2]

Criteria may also be implicit, i.e., the subjective opinions of the person doing the evaluation. The professionals use internalized criteria of what they consider good practice. Implicit review is helpful in complex cases where disease severity, comorbidity, genetics, or environmental factors complicate the management and make explicit review too complicated.

Which type of criteria should be used? Assessment of quality care based upon explicit criteria is likely to produce the most stringent judgment because, by definition, they must be quantifiable. Rosenfeld suggests that there is enough experience documented in the literature to indicate that reliability is improved through the use of explicit criteria.[3] In addition, the use of explicit criteria makes it possible for personnel less highly trained than physicians to screen the cases under review. Brook and Appel, on the other hand, point out that assessment of quality of care based on explicit criteria may require many more medical services than can be substantiated by rigorous experimental studies.[4]

Morehead and Donaldson advocate the use of implicit criteria.[5] Because of the infinite variation in the reaction of the human body to illness, they feel it is important for assessments to have flexibility in the judgment of individual cases.

Criteria of either type are based on values. It is impossible to discuss quality without examining the values of the professionals, the patients, and the organization. Written criteria are clear statements of current values and beliefs regarding quality patient care.

Unlike criteria, goals are general statements describing broad or abstract intents, states, or conditions. A goal is a statement of a desirable status or condition that is too general for evaluative purposes. In order to evaluate goal achievement, it is necessary to develop related criteria that can be measured. If the goal is "diabetic patients will understand their physiological condition," the criteria for measuring the extent of the patients' understanding might be that they

1. correctly calculate the prescribed diet at least three times prior to discharge
2. respond correctly to hypothetical problems involving the alteration of insulin, activity, and diet in the event of illness, fever, or severe emotional distress
3. correctly describe signs and symptoms of insulin reaction and diabetic

acidosis, their causes, and what to do in the event of either phenomenon.

All of the criteria listed are statements of patient behavior that can be measured insofar as they are visible and can be assessed.

The focus of the evaluation must be remembered when the types of criteria are developed. Are the activities of the institution, the physician, the nurse, or the patient being evaluated? In addition to considering values and focus of review, the evaluator must also be cognizant of the purpose of the review. Is the purpose to identify major deficiencies in care? Or is the purpose to make a comparative evaluation? So long as there is agreement among the physicians—whose care is being examined—that the criteria reflect what they consider to be optimal quality of care, an educated guess will very likely identify any deficiency. Guesswork is less acceptable, however, if comparative evaluation is the purpose of review. Criteria used in this type of assessment must be widely accepted and applicable to practice patterns across a variety of sites and patient populations.

As discussed in Part I, the conceptual approach most often used to discuss the quality of care is the system espoused by Donabedian—structure, process, and outcome (see Chapter 2). Structural criteria involve institutional and provider characteristics. An example of a structural criterion is "physician will be Board-Certified." The process of care is basically what happens in the course of treatment; it is usually considered the professionals' management of patients. An example of a process criterion is "the patient is helped to ambulate every 2 hours the first day after an operation." Outcome is the evaluation of the end results of care in a specific time frame. Examples of intermediate outcome criteria are "the fifth day after gastric surgery, the patient is on a full diet and oral temperature is below 100°F."

Since criteria are basic ingredients in measuring the quality of health care, a certain technical vocabulary relative to criteria is required.

TECHNICAL TERMINOLOGY[6]

Normative

Normative judgments underlie all criteria, no matter what their source. Normative criteria are derived from opinions of what constitutes good care, for example, from textbooks or from expert panels. They are based on whether a group of providers believes patients or populations ought not to receive a specified service. A limitation of the use of normative criteria is the lack of knowledge regarding whether process criteria have a direct relationship to positive health outcome.

Empirical

Empirical criteria or standards, which are derived from actual practice, are often expressed as distributions, averages, ranges, and other statistical measures. They are a concrete reality. For instance, the impact of a confirmed observation that shorter lengths of stay in the hospital have no apparent adverse effects among comparable patients is very great. However, a shorter length of stay cannot be accepted as a criterion for quality unless its results have been compared with those of a longer stay.

Essential

Based on research, essential criteria are predictive of specific outcomes; for example, research has proved that penicillin kills streptococci. However, there are several limitations to the use of essential criteria. First of all, the number of known relationships between process and outcome is small. Second, it is difficult to confirm that positive outcome is related only to the medical care process and not to other potential influencing factors (environment and life style). Finally, within the practice of most physicians, the number of patients with conditions that lend themselves to essential criteria assessment is too small to provide a performance profile on the physician.[7]

Consensus

Because criteria must be measures of valued outcomes, a certain degree of agreement among recognized leaders in the profession about certain criteria is necessary for a convincing evaluation. There is consensus that penicillin is given for streptococcal throat infection; therefore, a convincing evaluation can be made regarding treatment of this condition. On the other hand, there is disagreement, not consensus, regarding the management of breast cancer.

Validity

The validity of criteria depends on whether the criteria measure what they were intended to measure, i.e., their demonstrated relationship to outcomes. For instance, when a record review is done, the following questions could be asked: Does it measure quality of care? Does it measure the quality of the record keeping? Are they synonymous? To provide another example, is a lower infant mortality rate a valid indicator of the quality of care? Or does the lower rate have to do with environmental factors, such as level of income or education?

Stability

The validity of almost all criteria of medical care is temporary and conditional. Not only are criteria redefined as medical science and technology change, but they are also influenced by changes in the organization of medical care services and by social developments that affect values and expectations relevant to medical care. For these reasons, criteria—especially those that are normatively defined—need to be constantly reformulated. For instance, the treatment for tuberculosis has changed dramatically over the years.

Transferability

Questions have been raised concerning the applicability of criteria formulated from one group or setting to all groups and settings. There has been particular dissatisfaction with the application to general practice of criteria elaborated by specialists who practice in academic settings. This problem is related to the need for consensus among professionals in different settings.

Configuration

There are two kinds of phenomena or characteristics to which criteria are applicable: monotonic and inflected. Monotonic phenomena are those about which it can be said, "the more the better" or "the less the better." It is obvious, for example, that the lowest possible mortality rate is best. Similarly, it may be asserted that 100 percent of patients with suspected myocardial infarction should have an electrocardiogram. With monotonic phenomena, the direction of movement that determines goodness is normatively defined.

Inflective phenomena have an optimum value or range. Below and above this range or value, quality is said to decrease. Slee suggests that the optimal range for pathologically positive tissue in primary appendectomy surgery may be 80 to 90 percent.[8] A percentage lower than this may mean that conservatism is excessive and that inflamed appendixes are allowed to go untreated. The problem with inflected phenomena is that optimal values cannot be stated a priori, but must be determined empirically. Length of stay is an inflected phenomenon in which both overstay and understay indicate inappropriate use.

Level of Stringency

One factor to consider in deciding how stringent to make a criterion is whether it is discriminating. The criterion may be so strict that no practice in real life can meet it; at the other extreme, it may be so lenient as to be nondiscriminating. For example, in the study of general practice by Clute, physicians could not be categorized according to how they checked blood pressure, took temperatures, or immunized patients because all physicians did them well.[9]

A factor related to stringency is yield. Yield is the number of cases found on the basis of chosen criteria. It is important to keep in mind the output (the find) in relation to the efforts expended in reviewing the cases.

Content

The dimensions of care selected for assessment and the value judgment attached to them constitute an operational definition of quality in a given study or system of quality appraisal. It becomes important, therefore, to identify the dimensions that are included in an evaluation system and to determine that they cover the range of dimensions necessary for a well-rounded view of quality. Studies of quality differ with respect to the number of dimensions used and the exhaustiveness with which each dimension is explored. For example, does the study assess the technical aspect of care (diagnosis, treatment, and follow-up), or the art of care (the physician-patient interrelationship), or both?

Reliability

Criteria are considered reliable when they are clearly and succinctly written and when the results can be reproduced in a repeat assessment by the same person or other persons. Specific instructions can increase the reliability of criteria. The following are some instructional examples:

• operational definition of fever—oral temperature of 100° or above
• synonyms—generic as well as drug manufacturer's name

- frequency—ambulated three times on the first postoperative day
- time frame—results interpreted and reported within 24 hours
- exception—patient did not keep follow-up appointment
- probable location of data—laboratory slip in chart

Feasibility

Feasibility includes the acceptability, cost, and ease of implementation. For example, it is assumed that diabetic patients benefit from health education; however, this criterion is seldom found in the records, and the information may more accurately be obtained from the patients.

CATEGORIZATION OF CRITERIA

There are a number of different ways in which criteria may be conceptualized. For example, they can be categorized as optimal, minimal, branched, or generic.

Optimal Criteria

In developing criteria for optimum care, there is a tendency to develop a long laundry list of criteria. This may yield an unwieldy and meaningless list of items with minimal relevance to any particular case. Moreover, the list may have few items that can be used to discriminate among the various levels in quality of care.

Minimal or Critical Criteria

Minimal criteria often leave out much that is essential to certain subcategories of patients and yield so few items that the exercise may be worthless.

Branched or Contingent Criteria

The codification of decision-making rules is required for branched criteria. This codification, although difficult to establish, is a fairly precise tool for assessing technical competence.

Generic Criteria

Criteria that are used to screen patient records are generic, whether they concern diagnosis or procedures performed. Examples are fever over 101° and hospital-induced trauma.

DISCUSSION

Format

The format in which criteria are framed plays a crucial role in determining the type of deficiency liable to be uncovered. The need for meaningful practice guidelines may conflict with the desire for maximum professional freedom, and this conflict may become a source of tension. Explicit criteria may tend to force medical care into a more or less rigid mold. In order to construct criteria to meet these sometimes opposing demands, it might be useful to consider the use of several sets of criteria progressively. For example, a simple list could be used for initial screening. A more elaborate algorithm in conjunction with peer review, using implicit criteria, could follow.

Quantification

Tables 7-1 and 7-2 show a format that could be used in the application of criteria lists to the assessment of process results. In the quantification process, a mark (+ or −) would be placed next to individual criteria that have been met or not met. Then the evaluator has a choice. Each item may be weighted equally, deriving the arithmetic average, or a differential weight may be assigned to the several items and a weighted average obtained.

Table 7-1 Physical Examination Criteria Met by Provider

Physical Examination Criteria	Dr. A	Dr. B	Dr. C
Temperature taken	+	−	−
Throat examined	−	+	−
Neck examined	−	+	−
Ears checked	+	+	+
Chest listened to	+	−	+
Heart listened to	+	−	−

Table 7-2 Summary of Means of Weighted Scores for Levels of Care, Excluding Management by Provider

Level of Care	Possible Maximum Score	Dr. A	Dr. B
Number of persons		136	138
Overall weighted score	68	52.5	61.7
History	15	8.1	13.3
Physical examination	15	12.4	14.9
Laboratory	33	27.2	28.5
Diagnosis	5	4.8	5.0

There are some problems with this quantification methodology, however. A given score can be obtained by different combinations of performance and nonperformance of the several criteria on the list. In addition, the quantification issue can be further complicated by questions of qualification: Are these different combinations equivalent? Is a score of 65 "good," "fair," or "poor"? What is the basis for the weighting and how valid are the weights?

Social Process

The social process, including group interaction that leads to the formulation of and agreement on explicit normative criteria, needs further investigation. It would be useful to know how leadership is exercised, dissent handled, and differences resolved. The effect of the participation of health professionals other than physicians, such as administrators and even consumers, should be studied. The content of the criteria, as well as the process of arriving at them, might be affected when nonphysicians are included.

CRITERIA DEVELOPMENT

Partisans of the national approach to criteria development feel that basic, national standards are needed in this age of rapid communication. They further claim that criteria writing is time-consuming, so why reinvent the wheel? On the other hand, critics of the national approach point to regional differences in modes of diagnosis and treatment that may be ignored if nationally developed criteria are used. The use of national criteria may also deny appropriate recognition both to different schools of thought and to the art of medical practice. The national approach may discourage experimentation with a variety of approaches to disease. In addition, there are regional differences in the availability of resources, such as sophisticated equipment, and in opportunities for consultation.

Many believe that, in addition to overcoming the disadvantages of nationally developed criteria, locally developed criteria are more likely to be accepted. At the local level, professionals can influence the measures by which their own performance will be assessed. Partisans of both methods agree that essential criteria should be nationally promulgated.

A criterion should answer the question: What does a physician, nurse, or patient have to do or demonstrate in order to achieve satisfactory care or status? Written criteria should start with action verbs that describe the specific desired behavior or clinical status, e.g., assess, teach, observe, monitor, or record. The action verb should be followed with the content involved, e.g., assess character, depth, and rate of respiration; observe dressing for evidence of bright red blood; or monitor amount of urinary output per hour.

The California Medical Association and California Hospital Association developed a guide for criteria formation.[10] They ask the question: Can the criterion RUMBA?

VERIFYING OR CLARIFYING CRITERIA RUMBA—OR CRITERIA FOR CRITERIA

Relevant. Each criterion must be specifically related to the objective of the study. It should be the most efficient or effective indicator of good care for this particular group of patients. It should not represent a routine test or standing order.

Examples: Does this criterion apply to this phase or would it more appropriately be part of another audit of this topic with a different objective? Could this criterion also be applicable to another diagnosis/procedure? Is it routine care (such as pre-op chest X-rays) for all surgical patients or specific to cholecystectomy patients (such as operative cholangiograms)?

Understandable. Each criterion may be written in specific medical terminology, but must be worded explicitly as a complete statement to eliminate any possibility of misinterpretation.

Examples: Should any other words be added to this criterion? Does "chest X-ray" mean "chest X-ray ordered" or "post-op chest X-ray shows no atelectasis"? Does "fever" mean 99° or 100° orally or rectally?

Measurable. Each criterion should include the time frame of the activity, the frequency of the activity, and/or the specific range of test data expected.

Example: "Temperature recorded every 4 hours during first 24 hours post-op"; "hematocrit not less than 33 percent prior to surgery."

Behavioral. Each criterion should be an indicator of the activity of a specific group of practitioners or patients in order to identify what or whose behavior should be changed.

Example: "Nurse's notes during first 24 hours post-op will document presence or absence of vaginal discharge."

Achievable. Each criterion should be realistic given the present state of the art, the local patient population, and the hospital staff's capabilities.

Example: Mortality from pneumonia may be expected to be higher in a small rural facility serving a population consisting largely of elderly patients.

NOTES

1. D. Longo, K. Cicione, and F. Lord, *Integrated Quality Assessment: A Model for Concurrent Review* (Chicago: American Hospital Publishing, Inc., 1989):23.

2. M. Mechnick, L. Harris, R. Willis, and J. Williams, *Ambulatory Care Evaluation: A Primer for Quality Review* (Los Angeles: University of California, 1976).

3. L.S. Rosenfeld, "Quality of Medical Care in Hospitals," *American Journal of Public Health* 47 (1957):856–865.

4. Robert Brook, and F. Appel, "Quality of Care Assessment: Choosing a Method for Peer Review," *NESM* 288 (1973):1323–1329.

5. M.A. Morehead and R. Donaldson, *A Study of the Quality of Hospital Care Secured by a Sample of Teamster Family Members in New York City* (New York: Columbia University School of Public Health and Administrative Medicine, 1964).

6. Avedis Donabedian, *A Guide to Medical Care Administration*, vol. 2 (New York: American Public Health Association, 1969).

7. Nicole White, Gerald Giebink, and H. Richard Nessen, "Synopsis of the Conference Proceedings," in *Ambulatory Medical Care Quality Assurance 1977,* edited by G. Giebink and N. White (La Jolla, Calif.: La Jolla Health Science Publications, 1977):4.

8. Virgil Slee as quoted in *A Guide to Medical Care Administration, vol. 2: Medical Care Appraisal* by Avedis Donabedian (New York: American Public Health Association, 1969): 69.

9. K.F. Clute, *The General Practitioner: A Study of Medical Education and Practices in Ontario and Nova Scotia* (Toronto: University of Toronto Press, 1963).

10. California Medical Association/California Hospital Association, *Quality of Patient Care Workshop Manual* (Los Angeles: CMA/CHA, 1975).

SUGGESTED READING

Donabedian, Avedis. National Center for Health Services Research, Report Series. *Needed Research in the Assessment and Monitoring of the Quality of Medical Care.* DHEW Publication No. (PHS) 78-3219, Hyattsville, Md., July 1978.

Donabedian, Avedis. "Criteria and Standards for Quality Assessment and Monitoring," *Quality Review Bulletin* 12 (1986):99–108.

Holden, Lela M. "Quality, Standards, and Criteria. A Physician and Nurse Perspective," *Journal of Nursing Quality Assurance* 3(1989):27–33.

Rosenberg, E. William. "What Kind of Criteria?" *Medical Care* 13 (November 1975):966–975.

Chapter 8

Theory and Practice for Measuring Health Care Quality

Donald M. Berwick and Marian Gilbert Knapp

INTRODUCTION

Quality assurance in health care is an enterprise strangely disconnected from the object of its study. Despite a distinguished intellectual tradition now decades old, the routine assessment of quality is rarely linked with the day-to-day management of health care systems or with the decisions made by individual and aggregate purchasers of health care. In other industries, it would be unacceptable for such a situation to exist. It would be as if neither the producers nor the buyers of automobiles regularly assessed, for purposes of making their decisions, whether the cars they made and bought ran reliably and well.

New directions in the delivery of health care are pressing the industry to reevaluate how quality is assessed, to consider how information about the quality of care delivered may ultimately be used, and to challenge existing notions of the definitions of quality. Health care in managed care systems, competition, regulation of cost, resource constraints, and new regulations are changing how care is provided. We are reducing the length and frequency of hospital stays, cutting capital and operating margins, and forcing economies in ambulatory care. Corporate producers of health care, profit and not-for-profit, seem somehow threatening to the traditional model of the individual doctor serving the individual patient. In the course of things, we are unmasking enormous variation in the patterns of care from region to region and from doctor to doctor, and there is the temptation

Note: Reprinted from *Health Care Financing Review,* 1987 Annual Supplement, HCFA Pub. No. 03258, Office of Research and Demonstrations, Health Care Financing Administration, U.S. Government Printing Office, Washington, D.C., December 1987.

Note: The authors are grateful to Ms. Deborah Alessi for her assistance in preparation of this article.

to conclude that the lowest resource users provide a goal toward which all should strive.

Important questions have been raised demanding thoughtful answers. Physicians and patients ask about the sanctity of the doctor-patient relationship; patient advocates fear that needed care may be withheld if there is money to be saved; patients ask if the lowest cost care is really the best; and the purchasers of care for groups wonder which is the best choice for their clients. The current state of the art in health care quality assessment does not offer tools to answer these concerns. We cannot currently tell wise decisions from faulted ones; we cannot choose those economies that leave patients safe and satisfied and avoid those which unacceptably damage care. The development of a quality measurement system is now an urgent agenda in health care. Meeting the need for managerially relevant quality assessment in health care requires new perspectives and new tools. The field to date has built a respectable array of resources, some of which can be incorporated into future designs, but the resources do not yet form a pattern.

To build the future, it is useful both to review the past experience in health care quality assurance and also to look to other industries that have long histories in the assessment of quality.

HISTORY

Modern quality assurance in health care has two central strands of inquiry. One seeks definition of the object of scrutiny: What exactly is to be studied? The other seeks methods: How to study quality. The dominant figure in the first area is Avedis Donabedian, considered by many the father of the academic enterprise of quality assessment in health, and the author of a recently completed three-volume summary of the field as of the early 1908s.[1-3] Donabedian, among others, offered the categories of "structure," "process," and "outcome" as the three classes of potential objects of investigation.[4] "Structure" is a general term for the nature of the resources that, assembled, provide health care, including, for example, the mix of manpower, the credentials of the providers, the facilities, and the rules of procedure. "Process" refers to intermediate products of care, such as patterns of diagnostic evaluation, access to care, rate of utilization, and choice of therapies. "Outcomes" are end products of care, the health status, longevity, comfort, and, perhaps, the satisfaction of its clients.

Traditionally, structure, process, and outcome are, in that order, increasingly difficult to study and increasingly important. Indeed, many investigators in the field have assumed, tacitly or explicitly, that the first two—structure and process—are appropriate objects of scrutiny only to the extent that they are demonstrably related to valued outcomes. Through this logic, quality measurement has been closely associated with such other domains of research as technology assessment, clinical evaluation, and randomized clinical trials, enterprises that seek to prove that certain processes (or resources) yield particular outcomes.

The second major theme in the quality assessment literature deals with methods of investigation: Having chosen an object of scrutiny, how good is the performance? Three general methods have been explored over time: implicit review,[5-7] explicit review,[8-13] and the use of sentinels.[14-18] Implicit review processes use experts who are able to recognize good care (structure, process, or outcome) when it occurs, or, in some cases, groups whose joint knowledge or judgment is thought better than any individual's. Implicit review procedures may assign scores to records of care or otherwise judge in global terms how well a system or provider dealt with individual cases or groups of patients. Both explicit and implicit reviews may involve sophisticated group techniques for selecting problems for review and for forming consensus on the quality of care.

Explicit review involves specifying criteria for care and review of records or observations to check on the degree to which what happens conforms to these prior criteria. By its nature, explicit review is better suited than implicit review to using nonprofessional staff to conduct the actual reviews of care. Professionals (often using group discussion or implicit techniques) write the standards and train nonprofessionals to rate the care. Explicit review has the advantage of clarity, compared with implicit review, but the disadvantage of oversimplification and, in the worst examples, clinical irrelevance. Recent researchers have attempted to modify review procedures to incorporate clinical algorithms and branching logic into criteria maps,[19] as distinguished from simple criteria lists,[20] in the hope that the more complex rules for rating care may produce results that are clinically more plausible and useful. In one report,[21] criteria maps were, indeed, shown to be superior to lists in predicting which clinicians made correct decisions in sorting chest pain patients who required hospital admission from those who did not.

Implicit and explicit review have remained largely separate streams partly because they seem to produce different results. In direct head-to-head comparisons, explicit and implicit reviews of the same cases have yielded some significant discrepancies in ratings.[22] Which is superior is a matter of continuing debate, with practicing physicians, in general, favoring implicit processes and managers and regulators favoring explicit criteria and scoring systems.

A third, somewhat different, school of method proposes the use of sentinels as the major form of quality review. The advocates of this technique attempt to define classes of unacceptable or red-flag events and then to perform detailed investigations of the events, using implicit or explicit methods. Such case reviews can range freely among issues of structure, process, and outcome; and they can address problems at individual or systemic levels. Perhaps the clearest such model is the morbidity and mortality rounds held in many departments of surgery, but other schemes have been proposed at larger scales. To some extent, the review techniques developed and recommended by Wennberg and his colleagues,[23] who search particularly for statistical outliers in rates of utilization, are connected with this notion of surveillance for sentinel events. Sentinel events can also be used directly as indicators of quality when they are judged to be outcomes that ought to be avoided by a sound health care system.

Donabedian's three volumes,[24-26] in which the field of quality assessment in health care is summarized, provide an impressive pedigree. Why then is quality assessment not yet in the life's blood of health care? Why, if we ask whether cost containment is hurting quality, or whether health maintenance organization "A" is better than health maintenance organization "B," must our answers be so impoverished, or at least so anecdotal? What should happen next in the field if the measurers are to become more useful to those who manage health care—for example, physicians and other health professionals; clinical department managers and chiefs of service; medical and administrative facilities managers; regulators; purchasers of care; and patients who more and more will wish to exercise choice in managing their own health care? A logical next step for health care assessment is to look to other industries to learn from their experience, their successes, their techniques, and perhaps their failures.

LEARNING FROM OTHER INDUSTRIES

Other industries have a long history of assessing quality and use measurement more self-consciously and systematically than health care does. Industrial quality measurement techniques have benefited from nearly 5 decades of trial, development, evaluation, and reevaluation on the way to their current state of sophistication.

The discipline of industrial quality control has drawn energy from the pressures of the marketplace and the demand of consumers that products and services be continually improved. Similar pressures now confront health care providers, and important lessons lie in the extensive experience of other industries in the applied technology of quality control and assurance.[27-29]

Lesson I: Importance of Design

In the history of industrial quality assessment and control, the first quality assessor was the consumer. A product was usually distributed without being subjected to a quality control process, and the only mechanism for knowing if the product was unacceptable was if the consumer complained or abandoned it. In time, industry's response was to institute systems that would attempt to intercept substandard products before they were distributed in order to prevent abrasion of consumers and loss of market share.

As health care delivery has become more organized and more competitive over the past decade, consumers of health care now have the opportunity to select among care delivery systems to find one that best meets their needs. Health care is learning, as other industries have learned, that to use consumer dissatisfaction as an index of quality is both hazardous and costly.

Early internal quality control mechanisms placed an inspector at the end of a production line to weed out those items that did not meet a specific set of criteria. Completed products that might in some way harm the consumer or cause dissatisfaction were discarded before they could reach the marketplace. Although this system may prevent the consumer from receiving faulty goods, it is a costly form of quality control. It offers some protection for the consumer, but, because unacceptable products are still being produced, risks are high. In addition, such inspection systems do little to correct inefficiencies throughout the line of production, may displace responsibility for meeting criteria to a separate entity remote from the production line, and require that the ultimate cost of the product be higher than necessary.

Recent advances in industrial quality assessment and control concepts have moved responsibility for identifying and fixing problems further and further up the production line. Quality control mechanisms are more and more being placed at interim stages in the production process. Modern quality control engineers now try to control quality in the actual design of the product. Corporate mottos such as "Do It Right the First Time" or "Quality by Design" are not just slogans for boosting morale; they also reflect modern notions of the most efficient strategies for quality assurance. High quality design is more efficient in the long run than thorough inspection at the end of the production line.

Lesson II: Multidimensionality of Quality

As industrial quality control has come to understand the importance of higher quality in design, so also has it come to regard the quality of a product or service as a fundamentally multidimensional concept. Here, too, health care can learn from other industries.

Over the past few decades, quality assurance in health care has invested heavily in efforts to demonstrate the relationships between the elements of care—structure and process—and the outcomes of care. The assumption that better health care produces better health outcomes has been the foundation of much of the search for operational definitions of quality. According to this view, the measurement of process is actually a surrogate for the measurement of the real goals of health care: improved health status, function, and comfort.

Making health status outcome so central to the definition of quality has at least three serious limitations. First, it burdens the exploration of quality with the agenda of virtually all clinical and health services research. If assuring quality means assuring that what we do really works, then we can only assess quality when the production functions are known. As Donabedian has pointed out, if we know the relationship between, say, process and outcome, then measuring process is quite acceptable as a surrogate for measuring outcomes.[30] If we do not know the relationship between process and outcome, then measuring outcome is not a useful indicator of system quality, because we cannot use the information to determine which aspects of process to preserve and which to change. On reflection, making an understanding of effectiveness a prerequisite for measuring quality is probably a formula for paralysis. We simply know too little today about what in health care actually does produce health.

Second, there is good reason to believe that a great proportion of health care probably does very little to alter the course of illness or to preserve life or function. In the average ambulatory encounter, at least, the physician is usually dealing with acute, self-limited diseases, for which definitive treatments do not exist and for which a wide variety of diagnostic and therapeutic strategies are equally innocuous. For many encounters, the patient's major objective is to gain reassurance, to feel cared about or listened to, or to undergo a nearly ritualistic ruling out of unlikely major diseases. Unless we define outcome very broadly, to include many elements of the patient's feelings, attitudes, and satisfaction, then the tyranny of outcome in defining quality risks calling much of the activity in health care wasteful, useless, and scientifically unsupported. But doctors and patients know better; they know that, often, what health care delivers is not outcome—in the sense of improved longevity or function—but rather process, itself.

In this regard, health care is like other important consumer goods. The quality of an airplane flight lies foremost in a safe conclusion, but it also connotes the ability to obtain a reservation at a time when it is needed, the courtesy of the staff at each contact, the ease of making connecting flights, and the quality of the food. Such a broader notion of quality, incorporating many different and potentially independent dimensions, raises the important possibility that reasonable and fully informed people may disagree about the quality of a health care provider and goes far beyond the simpler notion that the quality of a health system is coextensive with its safety or ability to produce longer life.

Lesson III: Importance of Organizational Culture

Quality assurance in other industries has now moved back through the production or service line into the very structure of the organization. Industry has learned that, in order for quality assessment to be effective and efficient, it is not enough to develop new techniques of measurement and control to be implemented at various points of manufacture but that there also must be an investment in a corporate culture geared toward producing a high quality product. Industries have silenced arguments against the cost of quality assurance mechanisms as they have learned that, although such systems do require an investment, they return high dividends through reduced customer attrition, through fewer losses from unusable products and less need for rework, and through greater efficiency in the production process. Commitment from senior managers to invest in producing a high quality product is one key to successful quality control. Managers must commit to assisting every employee to improve quality continually. Resources must be available to develop ways of identifying and fixing problems. Goals must be clearly stated, with mechanism to assure that they are understood by all. Employees must have the means to meet these goals and adequate training to enable them to do their jobs effectively. Objective measurement is necessary to know whether goals are being met and where improvement is most feasible. Feedback of the results of measurement must be prompt and must reach those managers, supervisors, and other staff who are responsible for production. Reports must appear in clear, useful, and usable format.

Health care can also learn lessons from other industries about the ways in which measurement data are collected and about the statistical techniques used for analysis. Traditionally in health care quality assurance, the primary source of data for the assessment has been the medical record. Although rich in information, the medical record as an assessment source is widely acknowledged as being flawed by differences in record-keeping systems and variations in recording practices. With health care now expanding its view of what constitutes care in an organized delivery system, it can draw upon methods for collecting data such as those used in service industries—banks, hotels, or airlines. Service industries use three techniques, in particular, that deserve increased exploration in health care: surveys, observations, and simulations.

Perhaps the greatest achievements of industrial quality assurance lie in the practical statistical methods that have been developed for sampling and for modeling performance. Like health care, for example, many industries face the challenge of finding flaws that are extremely rare. Industrial quality control engineers use well-developed techniques for calculation of failure time or of the probability of deficiency, yet these same techniques are rarely used in the assessment of health care. Industrial quality assurance pays strict attention not only to average performance but to variance and loss functions which include terms for reliability. Health care, too, ought to be sensitive, not just to the average performance level of a person or system but also to the variability in that performance.

The time is ripe for some new directions in quality measurement in health care. The next decade of development should not only draw on the distinguished intellectual achievements of the field but should seek, as well, to make the measurement enterprise more useful to the managers and decision makers whose choices and strategies will shape the system we shall pass on to the 21st century. Other industries have much to teach us, if we will think inventively about analogies and similarities. To fail to develop ways to measure and publish wisely the performance of our health care systems will place us at the mercy of ill-informed choices, and may, in the end, cause sacrifice of the legacy of caring that we should seek to preserve.

HARVARD COMMUNITY HEALTH PLAN

At the Harvard Community Health Plan (HCHP), a 300,000 member staff model health maintenance organization (HMO) located in the greater Boston area, the Quality of Care Measurement Program has begun to supplement traditional concepts and methods in health care quality assessment with new approaches, applicable new models, and management needs in health care delivery systems. Using concepts and techniques from a variety of industrial settings, the quality assessment function has been relocated in the corporate structure, has expanded its view of the very definition of quality, and is now developing new technical methods for obtaining data, conducting analyses, and producing reports.

HCHP's Quality of Care Measurement (QCM) Program has a reporting relationship to the highest internal policymaking levels. This position declares and emphasizes that the commitment to providing high quality care is a serious endeavor valued by the corporation as a total system for delivery of care. Further, renaming the former quality assurance program "Quality of Care Measurement" emphasizes the distinction between assurance and measurement. The assurers of care are the providers of care, the physicians, nurses, technicians, and support staff who, on a day-to-day basis, manage the care and service provided to patients, along with the other staff and managers who create the environment in which sound care is possible. The measurers of care provide objective information that is useful to the clinicians as an aid to practice management.

HCHP has embraced a multidimensional view of quality defined from multiple perspectives, including that of the consumer. In the Quality-of-Care Measurement Department, new techniques of gathering data, such as observation, simulation, and patient survey, are being rigorously designed and tested to develop new methodologies that will supplement traditional ones.

Redesign of the quality measurement program at the Harvard Community Health Plan began with a specific conceptual framework for the definition of health care quality and a conviction that any system of assessment should focus on those attributes of care that the Harvard Community Health Plan values for its members and that integrates both professional and lay views of the elements of high quality.

The primary components of the definition of quality remain excellent technical care and favorable health status outcomes. However, other areas of performance, such as providing access to care, receive high weight as additional important aspects of quality. The multidimensional view of quality at the Harvard Community Health Plan includes, at a minimum, measures of technical process, health status, outcome, access, coordination of care, ambiance, interpersonal relationships and satisfaction, support staff training, and staff morale and satisfaction.

Because the Harvard Community Health Plan offers many different products of care (encounters with well patients, care of those with symptoms, care for emergency problems, hospitalizations, psychotherapy, perinatal care, and encounters in such intermediate care areas as laboratories, pharmacies, and radiology suites), the Quality of Care Measurement Program may measure performance in each type of encounter with respect to any of the relevant attributes of care. For each type of encounter, different attributes may deserve different weights: technical process is more important than interpersonal demeanor in a cardiac arrest, but interpersonal qualities may be much more highly valued in a well-child care visit, where the risks of faulty process are much lower and reassurance is often a key goal. Each system (indeed, each patient) may attach different weights to these desired attributes, and intelligent, completely informed consumers may rationally disagree about which of two systems demonstrates better overall quality.

This multidimensional view of the quality of care raises important issues of measurement. Medical records are the traditional source documents for the assessment of outcomes and technical process, but they are not useful for the assessment of such other dimensions as access, interpersonal care, or ambiance. New dimensions require new measurement strategies.

Primary among these strategies and tools are surveys to obtain information about patients' perceptions of care received. Building on work done by other health service researchers, the Harvard Community Health Plan is developing and using scaled questionnaires that can help consumers of health care tell about the care they received. Items on these questionnaires ask about appointment access, waiting time in the waiting room, ambiance, support staff warmth, provider warmth, provider skill, continuity of care, the patients' sense of sharing in the control of care, and a summative satisfaction rating. In addition, members are asked about their intention to keep the same health care provider and the intention to remain an HMO member.

The Quality of Care Measurement Program currently uses two modes for administering these questionnaires. One type of instrument is administered onsite in clinical units as patients exit from their visits; the intent is to gather immediate impressions of the encounter and to focus on the single care event. Collection occurs at regular cycles throughout the year, and attempts are made to collect a completed survey from each visitor. Response rates using this technique range from 75 percent to 90 percent. All Harvard Community Health Plan sites are surveyed during the same time period to assure comparability and reduce confounding effects of events outside of the HMO's control—such as bad weather. Once collected, the data from several thousand surveys are entered into a microcomputer system and analyzed using standard statistical packages.

The other form of survey administration is through the mail. The Harvard Community Health Plan uses mailed questionnaires primarily for evaluating services that do not occur onsite, such as hospitalizations. Specialized surveys have, so far, been developed for medical and obstetrical hospitalizations. Hospital surveys have a broader focus than the visit surveys; during the obstetrical survey, for example, patients are asked to rate their prenatal care, initial labor contact, hospital admission process, labor and delivery care, postpartum care, hospital ambiance, patient education, and length of stay. In addition, patients rate the various clinicians they see, such as obstetricians during pregnancy, nurses in labor and delivery, and pediatricians in the hospital.

All surveys include demographic information such as age, gender, length of HMO membership, race, socioeconomic status, and whether the HMO visit was for well or sick care. Where appropriate, these data are used as covariates in stratified analyses.

Once survey data are collected, the turnaround time for data entry, analysis, and report generation is less than 4 weeks. The goal of most Quality of Care Measurement work is to give information to involved managers and clinicians in a time frame consistent with their management needs. Survey reports go first to the chiefs and supervisors of involved services and thereafter to the medical directors of facilities and to other senior level managers.

Direct observation as a data collection technique has been little explored in health care quality assurance, though observation is a common method of assessment of service in the hotel and airline industries, in which trained observers sample actual transactions and rate them according to previously established criteria. At the Harvard Community Health Plan, observations have been used to rate the quality of the ambiance of the facilities. Observers use rating forms (modeled on those used by the hotel industry) to gather observations about cleanliness of public areas, noise levels, protection of patient privacy, and clarity of signs. Observations of service behaviors among support staff have also begun.

Simulations pose much greater difficulties but also hold greater promise. They are used routinely in some service industries where trained individuals pose as users and report on what customers actually experience. The Harvard Community Health Plan has proceeded cautiously in the use of simulated clinical events. Initial efforts have included attempts to schedule simulated appointments for a variety of types of visit. Quality-of-Care Measurement staff are trained in the use of written scenarios that request appointments for routine or urgent visits. Appointments are made and then immediately cancelled. Such simulations offer a realistic view of a member's attempt to get an appointment and afford a better estimate of true access than do more traditional nonintrusive methods.

Displaying information in a digestible format, one that is easily grasped in one glance, has been an important goal of the QCM Program, which continues to experiment with various display methods. Figure 8-1 shows data collected on waiting times in an HCHP unit.

In December 1985, QCM data and member comments indicated a problem with extended waiting times. Once the problem was clearly documented, managers attempted to determine the probable cause of the problem and to recommend a solution, which required restructuring the workflow during the winter of 1986. During February, the waiting times dropped from an average of 34 minutes to 10 minutes. During the spring and summer, installation of a new computer system caused a rise again in waiting times, but by September the new systems were in place. Waiting times remained constant thereafter at an acceptable level, and member complaints ceased. Regular measurements using standardized procedures displayed in simple formats have been standards in industry for decades. In many instances, as in this example, these techniques are easily transferred to a health care setting. They can help managers identify problems, measure trends, and demonstrate improved performance.

Measures of technical process and outcome, still the most important dimensions of quality, are being developed to ensure the capture of accurate, consistent data. Working closely with senior medical managers and clinician groups to formulate criteria and standards of care, QCM designs mechanisms to measure performance against such criteria. Currently, clinical data are collected in a number of routine ways, some involving searches through the Harvard Community Health Plan's automated medical record systems and some involving detailed, traditional explicit manual reviews. Computer programs have been written for the automated medical record to identify categories of patients whose records are then scanned to determine if appropriate management has occurred. For example, software in the automated record system identifies women with abnormal pap smears

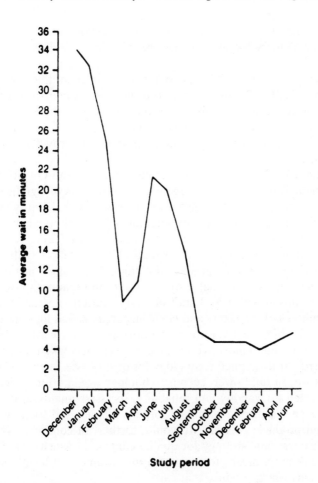

Figure 8-1 Average Patient Waiting Time in the Same Care Delivery Unit for Selected Months: 1985–87

and automatically notifies clinicians if appropriate follow-up has not occurred in a time interval specified by Harvard Community Health Plan clinical staff. Similar systems exist for following up negative rubella screens, diabetic patients, patients on lithium, patients on coumadin, and children with urinary tract infections. These reminders to the physicians have been designed primarily as a tool for physicians to use in managing patients, but the program also collects data on the proportion of patients whose care meets the established criteria.

A data base system that has been built on a microcomputer now includes information on all recent Harvard Community Health Plan deliveries—approximately 2,000 births so far. Reports are generated from this system to display prenatal care patterns, Cesarean section rates, complication rates, rates of high-risk pregnancies, birth weights, and neonatal death rates.

The examples mentioned here provide an overview of the type of work under way at HCHP. Goals in the short term are to develop measurements in all of the identified dimensions of quality, to test them, assess their value, eliminate those that are not viewed as being useful, and, ultimately, to weight dimensions according to their importance to provider and patient populations.

In addition to its general measurement activities, the Quality-of-Care Measurement Department also organizes case reviews of significant incidents. These in-depth studies have proven very useful in identifying broad inefficiencies in systems or areas of potential hazard. Although much more subjective in nature, the historical reconstruction of a failure reveals rich information about how, when, and where problems are most likely to arise. Quality-of-Care Measurement staff also initiate and assist in the design and implementation of special projects, serve on organization-wide task forces, and consult with HMO staff in a large variety of situations, often with committees of managers and clinicians organized at local care sites.

The Quality-of-Care Measurement effort at the Harvard Community Health Plan, though innovative in some respects, has taken only the first steps toward a truly applied technology for quality assessment and control in health care. In full flower, such a technology would offer a wide range of tools, tested for validity and reliability, to assess quality in its several dimensions and to display results in formats familiar and friendly to purchasers and producers of care. It would, further, fit comfortably into an overall organizational strategy for quality control, in which measurement is not an end but a means for continual improvement of health care and of the systems which produce that care.

NOTES

1. A. Donabedian, *Explorations in Quality Assessment and Monitoring, Volume I, The Definition of Quality and Approaches to Its Assessment* (Ann Arbor, Mich.: Health Administration Press, 1980).

2. A. Donabedian, *Explorations in Quality Assessment and Monitoring, Volume II, The Criteria and Standards of Quality* (Ann Arbor, Mich.: Health Administration Press, 1982).

3. A. Donabedian, *The Methods and Findings of Quality Assessment and Monitoring, an Illustrated Analysis* (Ann Arbor, Mich.: Health Administration Press, 1985).

4. A. Donabedian, "Evaluating the Quality of Medical Care." *Milbank Memorial Fund Quarterly* 44, (Part 2) (July 1966).

5. B.S. Hulka, F.J. Romm, G.R. Parkerson, Jr., et al., "Peer Review in Ambulatory Care: Use of Explicit Criteria and Implicit Judgments." *Medical Care* 17(Supplement) (1979): 1–73.

6. M.A. Morehead, R.S. Donaldson, et al., *A Study of the Quality of Hospital Care Secured by a Sample of Teamster Family Members in New York City* (New York: Columbia University, School of Public Health and Administrative Medicine, 1964).

7. M.A. Morehead, "The Medical Audit As an Operational Tool." *American Journal of Public Health* 57 (Sept. 1967): 1643–1656.

8. R.H. Brook, and F.A. Appel, "Quality-of-Care Assessment: Choosing a Method for Peer Review." *New England Journal of Medicine* 288 (1973): 1323–1329.

9. R.H. Brook, "Critical Issues in the Assessment of Quality-of-Care and Their Relationship to HMO's." *Journal of Medical Education* 48 (1973): 114–134.

10. P.A. Lembcke, "Medical Auditing by Scientific Methods: Illustrated by Major Female Pelvic Surgery." *New England Journal of Medicine* 162 (Oct. 13, 1956): 646–655.

11. T.B. Fitzpatrick, D.C. Riedel, and B.C. Payne, "Criteria of Effectiveness of Hospital Use." In McNerney, W. J., and Study Staff, eds. *Hospital and Medical Economics: Services, Costs, Methods of Payment and Controls,* vol. 1 (Chicago: Hospital Research and Educational Trust, 1962).

12. B. Payne, T. Lyons, L. Dwarshius, et al., *The Quality of Medical Care: Evaluation and Improvement* (Chicago: Hospital Research and Educational Trust, 1976).

13. J.W. Williamson, "Evaluating Quality of Patient Care: A Strategy Relating Outcome and Process Assessment." *Journal of the American Medical Association* 218 (Oct. 25, 1971): 564–569.

14. P.A. Lembcke, "Evolution of Medical Audit." *Journal of the American Medical Association* 199 (Feb. 20, 1967): 543–550.

15. M.C. Sheps, "Approaches to the Quality of Hospital Care." *Public Health Reports* 70 (Sept. 1955): 877–886.

16. A. Ciocco, et al., "Statistics on Clinical Services to New Patients in Medical Groups." *Public Health Reports* 65 (Jan. 27, 1950): 99–115.

17. A. Ciocco, "On Indices for the Appraisal of Health Departmental Activities." *Journal of Chronic Diseases* 11 (May 1960): 509–522.

18. D.D. Rutstein, W. Berenberg, T.C. Chalmers, et al., "Measuring the Quality of Medical Care: A Clinical Method." *New England Journal of Medicine* 294 (1976): 582–588.

19. S. Greenfield, C.E. Lewis, S.H. Kaplan, et al., "Peer Review by Criteria Mapping: Criteria for Diabetes Mellitus: The Use of Decision Making in Chart Audit." *Annals of Internal Medicine* 83 (1975): 761–770.

20. B. Payne, T. Lyons, L. Dwarshius, et al., *The Quality of Medical Care.*

21. S. Greenfield, S. Cretin, L. Worthman, et al., "Comparison of a Criteria Map to a Criteria List in Quality-of-Care Assessment for Patients with Chest Pain: The Relation of Each to Outcome." *Medical Care* 19 (Mar. 1981): 255–272.

22. B.S. Hulka, F.J. Romm, G.R. Parkerson, Jr., et al., "Peer Review in Ambulatory Care."

23. J.E. Wennberg, and A. Gittlesohn, "Variations in Medical Care among Small Areas." *Scientific American* 246 (1982): 120–134.

24. A. Donabedian, *Explorations in Quality Assessment and Monitoring, Volume I.*

25. A. Donabedian, *Explorations in Quality Assessment and Monitoring, Volume II.*

26. A. Donabedian, *The Methods and Findings of Quality Assessment and Monitoring.*

27. P.P. Crosby, *Quality Is Free: The Art of Making Quality Certain* (New York: McGraw-Hill Book Co., 1979).

28. J. Juran, *Managerial Breakthrough* (New York: McGraw-Hill Book Co., 1964).

29. W.E. Deming, *Quality Productivity and Competitive Position* (Cambridge, Mass.: MIT Center for Advanced Engineering Study, 1982).

30. A. Donabedian, *Explorations in Quality Assessment and Monitoring, Volume I.*

Methods of Assessment and Monitoring

Stephen N. Rosenberg

The preceding chapters of this book have placed quality assurance in historical and theoretical frames of reference, and have presented the basic methods of health care assessment in general terms. Part IV will provide some concrete examples of assessment and monitoring programs.

The basic approaches to the evaluation of health care structure, process, outcome, and satisfaction were fully developed by the early 1970s. Since then, most efforts to improve the techniques of assessment have taken two forms: (1) modifying the basic approaches and (2) combining two or more of them. Both of these strategies have the same goal—to build on the strengths of the basic approaches while minimizing their limitations.

Modifications have overwhelmingly focused on the techniques of process and outcome assessment; one classic example of each of these modified approaches is included in this section.

The traditional method of assessing the process of care through review of the health care record utilizes a "laundry list" of explicit criteria, leaving no room for individual variations in practice style or patient needs. The alternative—loose, unwritten, implicit criteria—lacks objectivity and reliability. The most important modification of traditional process assessment is criteria mapping, which attempts to resolve this dilemma by using explicit criteria, but in a contingent (branching) format, instead of a linear "laundry list." With a criteria map, only the criteria that are relevant to a specific patient (or a specific provider's practice style) are considered in determining an overall score.

Sentinel health events represent a major modification of the traditional method of assessing health status outcomes. This method screens for the occurrence of preventable diseases, avoidable complications, and untimely

Stephen N. Rosenberg, MD, MPH, is an Associate Professor of Clinical Public Health (Health Policy and Management) at Columbia University School of Public Health and he also serves as the Medical Director of The New York City Employee Health Benefits Program.

deaths in order to create a simple, inexpensive "alarm system" that detects problems in access to care or the quality of care received. The authors intend this screening system for negative outcomes to supplement other methods, which strive to increase the number of positive outcomes.

The following chapters present three very different ways to combine methods of assessment. The tracer approach examines process and outcome for a small set of conditions that are carefully selected to shed light on the quality of all conditions and all components of care. At least one tracer condition in the set should involve each age and sex group in the population served, and at least one should test each aspect of care (e.g., diagnosis, patient management, follow-up). An explicit review is then made of process and outcome for each tracer condition in the set.

Health accounting, the second approach, is a five-step, cyclical process in which priorities are set, desired outcomes are stipulated, and actual outcomes are measured. If desired and actual outcomes differ, a definitive assessment is carried out to determine the reason or reasons for this difference, corrective actions are taken, and outcomes are reassessed. The cycle continues until actual outcomes reach an acceptable level. The method is extremely flexible, combining measures of outcome with whatever method of "definitive assessment" is relevent in each situation: chart audit for process review, assessment of structure, evaluation of patient knowledge or satisfaction, and so forth. By including corrective actions and reevaluations, health accounting becomes not just a method of quality assessment but a model for quality assurance.

The third example of combined methods is based on an evaluation of intensive care units at 13 teaching hospitals by Knaus et al. These investigators carried out linked assessments of structure, process, and outcome. By examining all three aspects of care, they were able to identify the specific aspects of structure and process that affected patient mortality.

After reading five concrete examples of current assessment methodologies, the reader should be ready to consider the impact of quality assurance on a particular health care institution and on the health care system as a whole. The two concluding chapters in this section focus on these issues. Wennberg, who pioneered the study of small-area variation in practice patterns, reviews the effects of differences in structure and process (which may or may not result in variations in outcome) on costs for individual hospitals and area-wide systems. Chu explores the choice of methods available and their application in one specific area of care—ambulatory medicine. These last two chapters also serve as a bridge to the next section of the book, which will consider organizational issues in quality assurance.

SUGGESTED READING

Cleary, P.D., and McNeil, B.J. "Patient Satisfaction as an Indicator of Quality Care." *Inquiry* 25(1988):25–36.

Gardner, E. "Measuring Degrees of Illness." *Modern Healthcare* (1988):22–30.

Gonnella, J.S.; Louis, D.Z.; and McCord, J.J. "The Staging Concept—An Approach to the Assessment of Outcome of Ambulatory Care." *Medical Care* 14(1976):13–21.

Rosenberg, S.N.; Gorman, S.A.; Snitzer, S.; Herbst, E.V.; and Lynne, D. "Patients' Reactions and Physician-Patient Communication in a Mandatory Surgical Second-Opinion Program. *Medical Care* 27(1989):466–477.

Rubin, L., and Kellog, M.A. "The Comprehensive Quality Assurance System." In *Ambulatory Medical Care Quality Assurance,* edited by G. Grebank and N. White, 147–167. La Jolla, Calif., 1977.

Chapter 9

Comparison of a Criteria Map to a Criteria List in Quality-of-Care Assessment for Patients with Chest Pain: The Relation of Each to Outcome

Sheldon Greenfield, Shan Cretin, Linda G. Worthman, Frederick J. Dorey, Nancy E. Solomon, and George A. Goldberg

Quality assessment activities have been mandated and take place routinely in hospitals across the country, yet most of the methods used have not been validated and yield results which many physicians consider to be an inaccurate reflection of the true quality of care. Several recent studies have fueled the doubt surrounding the usefulness of either process (what is done to and for patients) or outcome assessment of quality of care.[1-4] However, critical analysis of these studies indicates that the failure to find a relationship between process and outcome when one is expected is due in part to the manner in which each is measured.[5-7]

We have previously described the criteria mapping method,[8,9] which uses the specific clinical data for individual patients to derive an assessment of the quality of their medical care. The primary objective of this study has been to test two methods which assess the quality of the process of care—the explicit criteria list[10,11] and the criteria mapping technique—by comparing each of them with an appropriate outcome.[12-15] For both process methods, information about compliance with a set of criteria is abstracted from the patient's medical record; the methods differ primarily in the type of information required in order to fulfill the criteria statements. Typically, explicit list criteria specify comprehensive medical history, physical examination, laboratory procedures and management for patients with a

From the Department of Medicine, School of Medicine, and the School of Public Health, University of California, Los Angeles. Presented in part at the annual meeting of the American Federation for Clinical Research, San Francisco, California, May 1, 1978. Supported by a grant (HS 02467) from the National Center for Health Services Research.

Note: Reprinted from *Medical Care*, Vol. 19, No. 3, pp. 255–272, with permission of J. B. Lippincott Company, © March 1981.

Note: We are indebted to Dr. Marshall Morgan for invaluable assistance in developing the map and to Dr. James Smith in developing the lists; we thank Drs. Robert Brook, Michael Pozen, Steven Schroeder, and Martin Shapiro for their critical and constructive reviews of the manuscript; Drs. Marshall Rockwell, Charles McElroy, and M. Lee Pearce for their support; Dr. Robert Elashoff for statistical advice; Joan Wills, Sylvia Jasso, Melody Benris, and Maureen Ostrowski for technical assistance.

given diagnosis, and require only that the criteria be mentioned or documented in the record. In contrast, the criteria map organizes criteria into a branching logic format that uses the *results* of tests, physical examination, and historical inquiry to create subgroups of patients. Additional information is sought when positive clinical findings indicate the need for further investigation or management. For example, if the presence of rales has been noted by the physician, then information concerning history of this finding and extent of the rales upon examination is required; these criteria do not apply when rales are absent or not mentioned. The chest pain criteria map utilizes the branching logic format to evaluate the work-up of a patient symptom; the criteria list technique, on the other hand, is almost always based upon diagnoses.

This study is a prospective comparison of the ability of the two process methods to evaluate one important dimension of the process of care for patients who present to the emergency department with chest pain: the diagnostic work-up and subsequent decision to admit or discharge the patient. The outcome used to evaluate the quality of this decision concerns whether the patient, following the receipt of emergency department care, demonstrated an acute condition for which admission to the hospital was deemed necessary. If process scores can be shown to predict the patient's outcome, then directing physician review to those cases in which the process is determined to be inadequate ensures review of cases in which patients have poor outcome.

METHODS

Patient Population

The study population was defined as all patients aged 30 years and older with a chief complaint of chest pain, who presented to either of two Los Angeles emergency departments on randomly selected days from April through August 1977 and from January through April 1978. One emergency department is part of a large university teaching hospital; the other is located within a voluntary community hospital and is staffed primarily by full-time emergency physicians, many of whom maintain university affiliations. Patients were identified by review of all emergency department medical records.

A total of 485 patients was entered into the population. A schematic outline of the study population is presented in Figure 9-1.

Two hundred and fifty-two patients were admitted to the hospital as a result of emergency department encounter and 233 were discharged to home following their examination. Sixty-four discharged patients were ex-

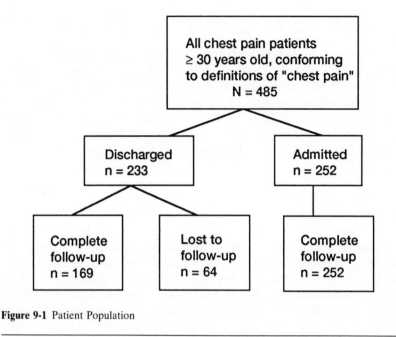

Figure 9-1 Patient Population

cluded from data analysis because outcome follow-up was not obtained. The excluded patients did not differ significantly from the remaining 169 discharged patients in age distribution, sex, prior history of myocardial infarction, or map and list scores.

The remaining 169 discharged patients and 252 admitted patients constitute the patient population reported here (N = 421). One hundred and twenty-five of these patients were transported to the emergency department by ambulance, while the remaining 296 arrived by other modes of transportation. Two hundred and twelve patients presented to the community hospital emergency department; 209 to the university hospital. The 421 patients had a mean age of 59.9 years, and males constituted 52.3 percent of the population. A history of previous myocardial infarction was noted in the records of 20.4 percent.

Data Sources

The emergency department medical record was the source of data used to define compliance with process criteria. Each patient's emergency department record was abstracted according to both list and map criteria by each of two research assistants. All discrepancies between the two abstractions for each process method were identified and resolved by agreement among both abstractors and a third research assistant. Reliability between two independent abstractions was 94.3 percent for list items and 93.5 percent for map items.

Following process abstraction, outcome measures for admitted patients were abstracted from the inpatient medical record. The outcome indicators for discharged patients were ascertained by means of a home electrocardiogram and a questionnaire, which included symptom-relief and patient-satisfaction measures. The home electrocardiograms were obtained an average of 6.5 days following the emergency visit; 97 percent were obtained within 15 days of the emergency visit. Median time to follow-up was between 4 and 5 days.

Process Assessment

A criteria map and criteria lists were developed separately in consultation with two emergency department cardiologists. Two groups of physicians were then convened separately to discuss and ratify each criteria set. Ratification was directed to ensure that differences in criteria formats did not result in differences in medical standards between the map and lists. Following the panel meetings, the ratified criteria were redistributed within each group of panelists for further review, and modified to achieve consensus within each criteria set.

Criteria Map

The chest pain map contains three major types of items: signal findings, subsequent findings and recommended disposition. Signal findings are items containing patients' clinical findings which need to be followed up, if present. Every signal finding is abstracted for every patient. These signals incorporate the clinical data which classify the patient population into a number of subgroups, according to how the patients presented. In the chest pain map, there are about 40 different subgroups of patients, classified by electrocardiographic findings, shock, chest X-ray findings, characteristics of the chest pain, associated symptoms, and findings upon physical exam. Subsequent findings are used to define further the clinical status of the patient with the signal finding. For each subgroup defined by signal and applicable subsequent findings, the map directs appropriate disposition (admit/discharge).

In Figure 9-2, a sample portion of the chest pain map, the signal findings are shown in the left-hand column. In this example, there are five different initial subgroups identified: patients with chest pain and four different types of premature ventricular contractions, and patients with chest pain and atrial fibrillation. For the patients with atrial fibrillation, the subsequent

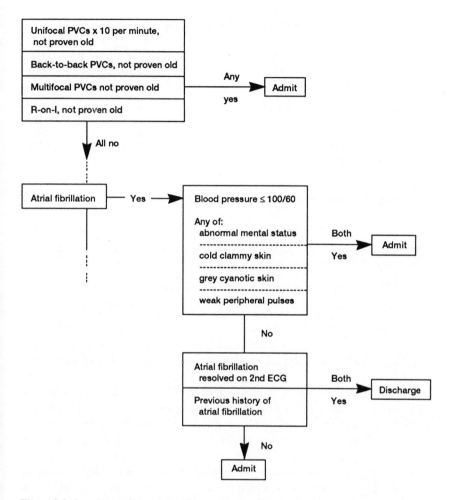

Figure 9-2 Sample portions of the chest pain criteria map. Positive responses to an item defining a patient subgroup (left-hand column) lead to the next item to the right. Negative or undocumented information responses are directed down to the next vertical item.

findings to the right should have been pursued and documented in the patient record. Admission is indicated if the patient was in shock (signified by low blood pressure and one of several other signs of decreased perfusion), if the atrial fibrillation did not resolve, or if the patient had no previous history of atrial fibrillation.

The map scoring system was developed to weight the clinical findings abstracted in the map to reflect the degree to which admission is indicated. For each subgroup, the signal finding and applicable subsequent findings were redrawn into a simple probability tree. Three physicians were inter-

Table 9-1 Estimated Risk and Map Scores for Selected Subgroups of Patients

Subgroup: Patients with Chest Pain and:	Consensus Estimate of Probability of Acute Serious Disease	Resultant Map Score*
Unifocal PVCs ≥ 10/min., not proven old	.60	60
Back-to-back PVCs, not proven old	.70	70
Multifocal PVCs, not proven old	.70	70
R-on-T, not proven old	.70	70
Atrial fibrillation, with shock	1.00	100
Atrial fibrillation, without shock	—	—
and no previous history of atrial fibrillation		
and atrial fibrillation unresolved on 2nd ECG	.93	93
or positive previous history of atrial fibrillation		
and atrial fibrillation resolved on 2nd ECG	.05	05

*Map scores presented here are for patients with *no* other positive clinical findings.
PVC: premature ventricular contraction.
ECG: electrocardiogram.
R-on-T: Premature ventricular contraction which falls on the T-wave of the preceding beat.

viewed independently to elicit their estimates of the proportion of patients who have each of the subsequent findings associated with the signal findings, and finally, the proportion with those findings who have admissible disease.

Following the independent estimation, these physicians were convened to derive consensus estimates. From the information on the probability trees, tables were prepared presenting the risk estimates depending upon whether subsequent findings were present, absent or not documented. In Table 9-1, the physician estimates of risk and resulting map scores are shown for the patient subgroups depicted in Figure 9-1. The probability trees for each of the 40 patient subgroups are the building blocks from which the predictive score was constructed. For patients with one signal finding, the map score is 100 times the probability of admissible disease.

Some patients fall into more than one of the subgroups. Such patients will have separate scores for each signal finding which must be combined into a single risk score. To make the process of calculating scores manageable, the subgroup scores are combined under one of two limiting case assumptions. Pairs of signal findings are either assumed to be manifestations of the same disease or manifestations of independent conditions. When the signals are assumed to arise from a single disease process, the overall probability is taken to be the maximum of the two subgroup probabilities. For each set of independent findings, the overall probability of admissible disease is given by the expression:

$$P = 1 - (1 - P_a)(1 - P_b)$$

where P is the overall probability of admissible disease and P_a and P_b are the probabilities of admissible disease based on findings a and b, respectively. The map score is 100 times P, the overall probability of admissible disease. The map score, then, reflects the seriousness of the clinical findings of the *patient,* and the degree to which the patient is at risk of disease for which hospital admission is indicated. Map score ranges from 0 (low risk of admissible disease) through 100 (high risk of admissible disease). The correlations of map scores based on the three independent physician estimates were all between .89 and .90. Correlations between consensus scores and individual scores ranged from .93 to .97. The data reported below are based on the consensus scores.

The criteria map technique is used to evaluate care by comparing the physician's actual decision to admit or discharge a patient against the patient's map score. In a quality-of-care review, discharged patients with high map scores and admitted patients with low map scores would be identified for physician review.

Explicit Criteria Lists

From the literature, we selected a well-researched and well-documented methodology for explicit criteria list development and weighting,[2,4,10,16,17] and reviewed available published process criteria lists.[18-22]

Four separate lists were developed, each of which was designed to evaluate the workup and decision to admit the patient. Three of the lists were based upon frequent and important diagnoses for patients with chest pain: acute myocardial infarction, pulmonary embolus and pericarditis. The fourth list, labeled "other chest pain," was designed for patients with a wide variety of emergency department discharge diagnoses and impressions, such as "chest pain, probably musculoskeletal," or "chest pain, etiology unknown." Patients were assigned to one of the four lists based upon emergency department discharge diagnosis. The "other chest pain" list was applied to the majority of patients discharged from the emergency department; the lists for suspected myocardial infarction and pulmonary embolus were applied to most of the admitted patients. An excerpt from the list for other chest pain is presented in Exhibit 9-1.

Explicit criteria lists were scored using a weighted average of items in the manner previously described by Morehead,[23] and by Lyons and Payne.[24] A score of 100 represents complete documentation of the criteria. Judgments of relative importance of criteria were made independently by three physicians. The three independent estimates were then combined into a consensus weighting. Correlation coefficients between scores based on different physician estimates ranged from .72 to .95. We report the consensus scores here.

Exhibit 9-1 Excerpt from Criteria List for "Other Chest Pain"

I. History

   A. Characteristics of pain
      Positive or negative mention of all of the following:

      1. Onset
      2. Duration
      3. Location
      4. Radiation

      Plus positive or negative mention of any two of the following:

      5. Quality/character
      6. Intensity
      7. What accentuates/alleviates the pain

   B. Other symptoms
      Positive or negative mention of any five of the following:

      1. Associated GI symptoms
      2. Associated respiratory symptoms
      3. Diaphoresis
      4. Light headedness/syncope
      5. Palpitations
      6. Paresthesias
      7. Hemoptysis

List scores were interpreted according to their conventional use: low-scoring patients should have a greater chance of inappropriate disposition than high-scoring patients. For both admitted and discharged patients, high scores indicating a completely documented workup should result in appropriate disposition of the patient.

Outcomes

The primary dependent variable in this study was the presence of *admissible disease*. We chose this outcome to evaluate the decision to admit the patient because it can be applied to all patients with the complaint of chest pain, regardless of ultimate diagnoses. Because the outcome of discharged patients was assessed at home, while that of admitted patients was abstracted from inpatient medical records, different indicators of the admissible disease outcome were used for these two groups of patients.

The indicators of admissible disease used in this study are given in Exhibit 9-2. For discharged patients, these include death or hospitalization within 5 days of the emergency department visit, or acute ischemic changes on follow-up electrocardiogram. Home electrocardiograms were interpreted independently by two internists who both screened each electrocardiogram for abnormalities. Any electrocardiogram interpreted as abnormal and changed from the emergency electrocardiogram by either internist was

---

Exhibit 9-2 Definition and Indicators of Admissible Disease

Definition

Admissible disease is defined as the occurrence, following receipt of emergency care, of a condition or event for which the patient should have been admitted to the hospital.

Indicators for discharged patients

1. Death within 5 days of the emergency visit from a cause related to the complaint of chest pain.
2. Hospitalization within 5 days for a complaint related to chest pain.
3. Changes on the follow-up electrocardiogram that indicate acute ischemic heart disease, thereby suggesting that the patient was experiencing an acute episode at the time of the emergency visit:
   a. An acute myocardial infarction by standard electrocardiographic criteria.[25]
   b. Any change in nonspecific ST-T findings compared with emergency department electrocardiogram.

Indicators for admitted patients

1. Any of the following 26 hospital discharge diagnoses indicating an acute serious condition:
   cardiopulmonary arrest
   cerebral embolus
   acute cerebral insufficiency
   cerebrothrombosis
   cerebrovascular accident
   cholecystitis

cholelithiasis
complete heart block
acute congestive heart failure
coronary insufficiency
coronary occlusion
dissecting aneurysm
empyema
myocardial ischemia
lactic acidosis
lobar collapse
acute myocardial infarction
pneumothorax
pulmonary edema
pulmonary embolus
respiratory failure
subacute bacterial endocarditis
subarachnoid hemorrhage
third degree heart block
ventricular fibrillation
ventricular tachycardia

2. Any of 12 events or procedures occurring during the hospitalization, indicating an acute, serious condition:

   assisted ventilation
   cardiac arrest
   chest tube
   cardiopulmonary resuscitation
   DC cardioversion
   death
   pulmonary angiogram
   shock
   Swan-Ganz catheterization
   temporary pacemaker
   tracheostomy
   ventricular ectopy

submitted for further review to a cardiologist at the patient's source of emergency care. The cardiologic evaluation was accepted as the final judgment. For admitted patients, admissible disease was indicated by one of 26 hospital discharge diagnoses or the occurrence of one of 12 procedures or events during hospitalization.

Data Analyses

The distribution of map and list scores for admitted and discharged patients with and without admissible disease were analyzed using a t-test. Because the admitted and discharged patients were not combined for these analyses, the null hypothesis for both map and list scores was that the mean score would be the same for patients with admissible disease as for those with no admissible disease. However, a test on means gives little information about the distributions of the scores in each patient group. For this reason, the usefulness of the map or list score in discriminating between patients with and without admissible disease cannot be measured by the results of a t-test. Discriminant analysis must be performed in order to determine what percentage of patients can be classified correctly into the two groups: those with admissible disease and those without admissible disease. In addition, we need to know if the map score improves the classification that would be obtained if only demographic variables (age, sex, history of myocardial infarction) were used to predict risk. Discriminant logistic regression analysis was used to investigate these questions. Multiple logistic regression analysis is used to estimate a relationship between continuous and discrete independent variables (map and list scores, age, sex and history of myocardial infarction) and a dichotomous dependent variable (the presence or absence of admissible disease). In the statistical model on which the logistic analysis is based, the independent variables are assumed to be related to the probability that the dependent variable will take on one of its two possible values. This relationship is assumed to have a mathematical form which ensures that whatever the values of the independent variables, the estimated probability (of admissible disease) will always be between zero and one. In particular, the logistic model assumes that

$$P = \frac{\exp [B_o + B_i X_i]}{1 + \exp [B_j + B_j X_j]}$$

where:

P   is the probability of admissible disease;

B_o is a constant term which measures the "irreducible risk" of admissible disease;

X_i's are the independent variables (map score, list score, age, sex and history of myocardial infarction); and

B_i's are the coefficients which, when standardized, indicate the importance of each independent variable as a risk factor.

We performed a series of logistic analyses to isolate the relative predictive value of each independent variable. Maximum likelihood methods were used to estimate the coefficients, B_i. Using the estimated coefficients and the particular values of the independent variables, the logistic equation generates an estimated probability P for each patient. The probability P can be used, like the map score, to classify patients into two categories: those likely to have admissible disease (Category I) and those unlikely to have admissible disease (Category II). This is done by specifying a cutoff level for P; any patients whose combination of independent variable values leads to an estimated value of P above the cutoff would be assigned to Category I; those with an estimated P below the cutoff would be assigned to Category II. The accuracy of the classification will vary with the choice of a cutoff level. One approach is to select a cutoff which maximizes the percentage of all patients correctly classified, subject to the constraint that a minimum percentage of patients with admissible disease and a minimum percentage of patients without admissible disease must be classified correctly. In our analyses, we examined the degree to which the logistic using the map score plus age, sex, history of myocardial infarction, and list score was better able to classify patients than map score alone.

RESULTS

Discharged Patients

Among the 169 discharged patients, eight were identified on follow-up as having a new finding or condition indicating that they had admissible disease at the time of initial presentation to the emergency department. Five of these patients had acute ischemic ST-T changes on the emergency department electrocardiogram which had become either more marked or improved on the home electrocardiogram; the other three patients were hospitalized within 1 to 4 days after the emergency department visit with diagnoses of pneumonia, acute pulmonary edema, and marked ventricular irritability.

Figure 9-3 displays the distribution of explicit criteria list scores for discharged patients. Patients who have no admissible disease are shown above the horizontal axis (mean = 61.0); patients with admissible disease (inappropriate disposition) are shown below the axis (mean = 55.1). There

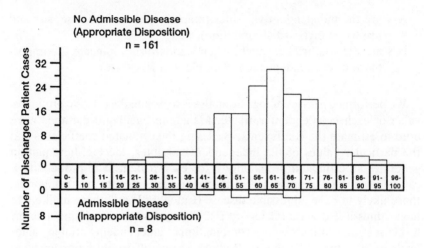

Figure 9-3 Explicit criteria list scores for discharged patients. Above the horizontal axis are the scores of patients who had no admissible disease upon outcome determination; thus disposition was appropriate. The scores of those patients with admissible disease are shown below the horizontal axis. N = 169.

was no statistically significant difference between mean list score for these two outcome groups (p = 0.20, Student's t).

The distribution of criteria map scores for all discharged patients is shown in Figure 9-4. The median score for all 169 patients is 2. Since a low map score means that the patient was at low risk of admissible disease, we would expect to see a preponderance of low map scores among discharged patients. Patients who had no admissible disease are shown above the horizontal axis. These patients have a mean map score of 19.2. Patients with admissible disease are shown below the horizontal axis. These patients have a mean score of 39.9. The difference in mean scores for these two groups of patients is significant (p = 0.02, Student's t, adjusted for unequal variances).

Admitted Patients

Of the 252 admitted patients, 101 were found to have admissible disease. Forty-eight of these 101 patients were discharged from the hospital with the diagnosis of acute myocardial infarction.

The distribution of list scores for admitted patients is shown in Figure 9-5. The overall median is 52.5. The mean score for those with admissible disease was 47.5, and 50.7 for those with no admissible disease. The relationship between list scores and admissible disease was not statistically significant (p = 0.122, Student's t).

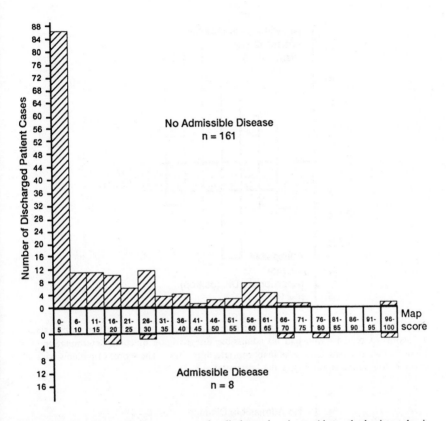

Figure 9-4 Chest pain criteria map scores for discharged patients. Above the horizontal axis are the scores of patients who had no admissible disease upon outcome determination; thus disposition was appropriate. Low map scores indicate "safe to discharge." The scores of patients with admissible disease are shown below the horizontal axis. N = 169.

The distribution of map scores for admitted patients is displayed in Figure 9-6. For patients with admissible disease, the map scores should be higher than for those with no admissible disease. The mean map scores (54.25 for those with no admissible disease and 70.7 for those with admissible disease) were significantly different (p < 0.0001, Student's t).

Logistic Results

Table 9-2 presents the standardized coefficients of the logistic regression equations. (The results using understandardized coefficients parallel these and are not presented here.) From the results of the two simple logistic analyses (using first map score alone and then list score alone), it is clear

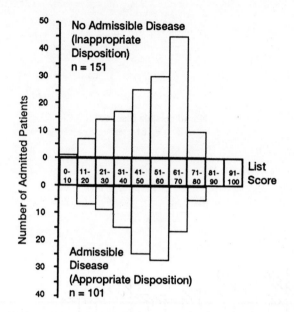

Figure 9-5 Explicit criteria list scores for admitted patients. Above the horizontal axis are the scores of patients who had no admissible disease upon outcome determination. For admitted patients, this represents inappropriate disposition. The scores of patients with admissible disease are shown below the horizontal axis. N = 252.

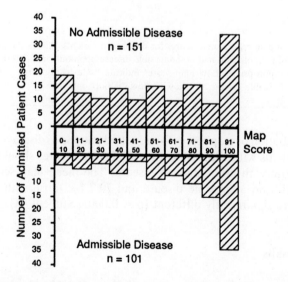

Figure 9-6 Chest pain criteria map scores for admitted patients. Above the horizontal axis are the scores of patients who had no admissible disease upon outcome determination. For admitted patients, this represents inappropriate disposition. The scores of patients with admissible disease are shown below the horizontal axis. N = 252.

Table 9-2 Results of Logistic Regressions, Standardized Coefficients*

			Independent Variables Allowed to Enter			
Variables	Map Only	List Only	Map Plus Demographic Variables	List Plus Demographic Variables	All Variables	Demographic Variables Only
Map score	8.1	—	6.7	—	7.7	—
List score	—	−4.4	—	−3.3	−4.3	—
Age 50 to 70	—	—	−1.7	−3.2	−0.6	−2.1
Age <50	—	—	−2.3	−4.2	†	−2.1
Sex						
Male = 1	—	—	2.7	3.2	2.4	2.6
Female = 2						
Sex–Age 50–70 interaction	—	—	2.7	3.0	2.5	2.5
History of myocardial infarction	—	—	†	†	†	
Constant	−10.3	1.6	−10.2	−0.9	−2.1	−4.2

*Coefficient/(Standard error).
†Allowed to enter, but did not enter.
—: Not allowed to enter.

that the map is a stronger predictor than the list. When only the map score is allowed to enter the regression, the standardized coefficient is more than 8, indicating a very significant relationship. Since the coefficient has a positive sign, the higher the map score, the higher the probability of admissible disease. Although the list score failed to predict admissible disease within either the admitted patient population or the discharged patient population, the list score was associated significantly with admissible disease in the combined patient population. However, the coefficient of the list score is negative, indicating that low list scores (that is, incomplete documentation) are associated with a high probability of admissible disease.

Age, sex, history of myocardial infarction, and interactions between these variables were included with the map and list scores as additional independent variables in a series of stepwise procedures. Because we found that age had a nonlinear relationship with risk, discrete age variables were used. In these regressions, variables were entered into the equation in the order of their importance in significantly improving the patient classification. The multiple logistic results confirm the importance of the map score as a predictor of admissible disease. When the additional variables are allowed to enter, map score is still the most significant predictor, with a standardized coefficient of 6.7. The age and sex variables and one age–sex interaction are also important predictors, but the history of myocardial infarction never entered any of the stepwise regressions. The positive sign for the sex variable indicates that overall, males are more likely than females to have admissible disease. The age–sex interaction term indicates that there is an increased risk of admissible disease for males age 50 to 70 compared with females of the same age, while the risks in the over 70 age group are comparable for males and females.

When all variables are allowed to enter, the map score standardized coefficient is again the most significant, with a value of 7.7. The list score coefficients also are stable. These results confirm the importance of the map score as a predictor and further indicate that the map score is measuring a different contribution to the risk of admissible disease than the list score or the age–sex variables.

We also looked at the predictive power of the age–sex variables alone. Again, the standardized coefficients are very similar to those in the other multiple logistic regressions.

In addition, we examined the ability of the map alone, the list alone and the various multiple logistic scores (P) to correctly classify patients with and without admissible disease. Table 9-3 presents these results in summary form. To understand the contribution of the map, the list and other independent variables to our ability to classify patients correctly, we must first look at how well various random classification rules would perform. First, since only 26 percent of all our patients have admissible disease, it

---

Table 9-3 Logistic Results: Percent of Patients Correctly Classified

	% of Patients with No Admissible Disease Correctly Classified (True Negatives)	% of Patients with Admissible Disease Correctly Classified (True Positives)	Overall Correct Classification
Randomized classification			
0% admissible	100	0	74
50% admissible	50	50	50
26% admissible	74	26	61
Classification based on simple logistic			
Map score only	77	67	75
List score only	72	51	67
Classification based on multivariate logistic			
Demographic variables only			
Cutoff 1	54	81	61
Cutoff 2	75	46	68
List, age, sex	75	61	71
Map, sex, age	83	65	78
Map, age, sex, and list	81	65	77

is possible to classify correctly 74 percent of the patients by simply predicting that every patient will be free from admissible disease (0 percent admissible). Unfortunately, this rule results in the incorrect classification of every patient with admissible disease. Two other random classification rules are included in Table 9-3 for comparison purposes: one in which each patient is equally likely to be labeled as having or not having admissible disease (equivalent to flipping a fair coin to classify each patient) and one in which each patient has a 26 percent chance of being classified as having admissible disease (equivalent to flipping a biased coin with the same probability of having admissible disease as was found in our overall patient population).

In the results that follow, the classification of patients based on the logistic analyses used a cutoff which maximized correct classification subject to the constraint that at least 60 percent of the patients with admissible disease and at least 60 percent of those without admissible disease had to be correctly classified.

When compared with the random assignment strategies just discussed, the classification of patients based on map score alone is better both in terms of overall correct classification and, most important, is significantly better than any random rule in correctly classifying patients who do have admissible disease. Using the list alone is worse than using the map score alone in overall classification, in classifying those with admissible disease, and in classifying those without admissible disease. For patients with admissible disease, classification based on list score is equivalent to flipping a coin.

Because the age–sex variables are discrete, the resulting logistic score is also discrete. As a result, it is not possible to "fine tune" the patient classification based on demographic variables alone. No cutoff achieved 60 percent correct classification in both those with and without admissible disease. The two best classifications are shown in Table 9-3. Because no intermediate classification is possible with these discrete variables, one is forced to choose between an extremely poor classification of those with admissible disease or an extremely poor classification of those without admissible disease. In neither case do the demographic variables achieve an overall correct classification approaching that of the map score.

When the list score is added to the demographic variables, overall correct classification is improved by only 3 percent. Adding the map score to the demographic variables results in a 10 percent increase in overall correct classification. However, compared with using the map score alone, there is an increase in the correct classification of those without admissible disease, at the expense of somewhat worse performance in classifying those patients with admissible disease.

DISCUSSION

One approach to determining whether a method of medical process assessment actually does measure the quality of care performed by physicians is to examine the extent to which the audit results are correlated with actual patient outcome.

In order to demonstrate such an association between process and outcome, four requirements must be met. Medical process must actually have an effect—that is, good medical process must "improve" outcome; the process measure must reflect the care accurately; the outcome measure selected must be sensitive and specific to the care given and be attributable to that care; the study must be designed so that there is sufficient variation in both process and outcome to demonstrate a statistically significant relationship. These four requirements were met in this study.

Admissible Disease As an Outcome

The selection of outcome measures to validate medical care process assessment methods is a critical step. In selecting admissible disease as an outcome measure, we first assumed that for chest pain patients seen in an emergency department setting, the major purpose of the diagnostic workup is to assess whether a patient should be hospitalized. Another objective is to initiate appropriate treatment. In most quality-of-care studies, outcomes which reflect the expected result following treatment are used. These measures are indications of the patient's health status, and may be labeled "good" or "bad" outcomes. However, these traditional outcomes cannot be expected to relate to the quality of the diagnostic workup.

The admissible disease concept then was selected for three reasons: the need to define an outcome measure that would be sensitive and specific to the diagnostic workup for chest pain patients; the need to measure that outcome at an appropriate time to reflect the emergency visit process, instead of later, intervening events either at home or in the hospital; and the need for a measure that could be applied equally well to admitted and discharged patients.

Although the concept of admissible disease is applicable to both admitted and discharged patients, it is difficult to ensure that the concept is measured equitably in both groups. The data available on admitted patients are more comprehensive than those elicited by interview and electrocardiogram on discharged patients. It is possible, therefore, that admissible disease was "missed" in discharged patients; however, most of the indicators for hospitalized patients are serious enough that they would have been detected in the discharged patients.

Explicit Criteria Lists

Although the two process methods used in this study differ remarkably in their approach, we selected the explicit list technique as a standard for comparison because it is widely used and reported in quality-of-care studies attempting to establish a relationship between process and outcome. When our outcome of admissible disease is used to evaluate the disposition decision in the emergency department, the presence of admissible disease must be interpreted differently, depending on whether the patient was admitted to the hospital or discharged home. Table 9-4 shows the significance of finding admissible disease in admitted and discharged patients.

By its nature, the criteria list equates "quality" with the completeness of the medical record; charts that are less complete have low scores, and are identified as poor quality. Among admitted patients then, a low list score (poor "quality" care) should be associated with inappropriate admission to the hospital (or the absence of admissible disease). A high list score (good "quality" care) should be associated with appropriate admission (or the presence of admissible disease). Among discharged patients, list score should have the opposite relationship with admissible disease. Low list scores (poor "quality" care) should be associated with inappropriate discharge (the presence of admissible disease).

In neither the admitted nor the discharged population did the list score show any significant relationship with the admissible disease outcome. Furthermore, among the admitted patients, the trend was in the wrong direction: low list scores were associated with the *presence* of admissible disease.

In an emergency department quality-of-care study using lists, the admitted cases selected for review are usually those with incomplete documentation; yet our data indicate that these low-scoring cases are those for whom admission to the hospital is most justified.

The direction of the association between list scores of the admitted patients and outcome suggests the hypothesis that the scores are negatively correlated with admissible disease, not because list score reflects quality of care, but because sicker patients receive less documentation. Although

Table 9-4 Admissible Disease in Admitted and Discharged Patients

	Patient Disposition	
Outcome	Admitted	Discharged
Admissible disease	Appropriate	Inappropriate
No admissible disease	Inappropriate	Appropriate

it is impossible to infer causality from these data alone, it seems implausible that thorough documentation results in a lower incidence of admissible disease.

In an emergency department, it is quite reasonable that sicker patients receive less comprehensive—or, at least, less well documented—workups than those who ultimately have no serious illness. This reflects the conditions of chart recording in the emergency department. The obviously ill patient may receive immediate attention and be admitted to the hospital quickly. Documentation of only a few critical items is necessary to provide evidence of the patient's need for admission. On the other hand, a patient with no obvious distress might well receive an extensive workup, either ending in discharge home if there were no positive findings, or ending in admission if the investigation yielded a questionable result. In either case, the extensive workup should result in a high list score and low chance of admissible disease.

In the logistic analysis, when the admitted and discharged patients are pooled, the relationship between low list scores and the presence of admissible disease was significant, although it was not as significant or as accurate a discriminator as the map. Given the lack of association within either the admitted patient or the discharged patient group, and the significantly lower list scores for the admitted patients (who constitute more than 90 percent of those with admissible disease), the relationship may be an artifact. The association between high list scores and the absence of admissible disease may simply reflect the higher list scores of the discharged patients, whose care will tend to be better documented due to the possible legal consequences of an inappropriate discharge.

Although the observed relationship between list score and the admissible disease outcome in the pooled patient population is interesting from a research standpoint, it is unimportant from a practical quality-of-care perspective. The list cannot function as an effective quality assurance tool unless it can identify the right cases for review within the admitted patient group and within the discharged patient group separately.

Our findings indicate that medical care evaluation studies using lists are at best equivalent to the random selection of charts for review, and, in the worst case, may be identifying admitted cases *least* in need of review.

Criteria Map

Map scores were significantly associated with patient outcome. Since the criteria developed in the criteria mapping format predict patient outcome, the criteria mapping method can be used in monitoring the quality of care for one important dimension of emergency care, namely, the decision to admit or discharge the patient. Because of biological variation and because of the hazards of using only medical records to assess care, physicians must be the ultimate arbiters of care. The chest pain map can identify cases for physician review that include an enriched sample of the discharged cases with suboptimal care and a large fraction of inappropriate admissions.

The analyses consistently indicate the importance of map score as a predictor of admissible disease. The addition or substitution of other variables such as age, sex, and history of myocardial infarction did not consistently improve our ability to predict patient risk. In the one instance where overall correct classification of patients was improved, the classification was worse within the subgroup of patients with admissible disease. Clinically, the correct classification of patients with admissible disease is more important than the correct classification of those without. For this reason the map score alone is a useful classification tool and its performance is not uniformly improved by the addition of demographic variables.

The map's ability to measure care by applying only the relevant criteria to the various subgroups within a given patient population is augmented by the scoring system. While scoring the map depends on the subjective probabilities estimated by physicians, the relationship between map score and outcomes was present whether the score was based on individual physician estimates or on the consensus estimate. This is due in part to the large number of patients who received a map score of 0 and who were subsequently found to be free of admissible disease. The substantial agreement among the individual physician estimates, especially in the most frequently encountered subgroups, further explains this consistency. Finally, the highest map scores resulted from patients having multiple findings. In these cases the product of several probabilities led to high scores which were relatively insensitive to differences in the individual estimates.

IMPLEMENTATION

Hospitals implementing the criteria map technique to assess process for chest pain patients would select for physician review the charts of patients likely to have received inappropriate care: those with high scores who are not admitted and those with low scores who are admitted. Selection of the map cut point for review should be done separately for admitted and discharged patients, and depends upon the perceived importance of a false positive (unnecessary review of a case) relative to a false negative (not reviewing a case that should have been reviewed). For example, in our study, review of discharged patient cases with a map score of 15 or more includes all patients who had subsequent evidence of admissible disease, but also includes many cases who did not. Decisions at individual institutions should account for the trade-off between the potential risk to a small number of patients inappropriately discharged and the costs of physician review. Similarly, for admitted patients, the importance of identifying potentially unnecessary admissions should be balanced against review time and willingness to make changes in hospital admitting practices. The positive relation of map score to outcome, however, ensures that judicious selection of the cut point will produce an enriched sample of cases which appropriately require physician review.

The map score prediction of admissible disease can be improved. For example, the scoring probabilities were estimated by local physicians. Although they showed considerable agreement, they may have overestimated the risk associated with certain findings. For commonly occurring constellations of findings, data from the present study will be used to revise the probabilities. Moreover, peer review of patients with high scores but no admissible disease on follow-up may influence physicians to reestimate the probabilities. Further data may also be generated by studies of the efficacy of diagnostic processes;[26] incorporation of these data into the map scores should improve their specificity. We are currently extending this study to another hospital with different patient and physician populations.

Criteria maps, ones that are very simple with a few branches[27] and those that are very complex, can examine all parts of medical process, including diagnosis, treatment, and complications. The map examined in this study, the chest pain criteria map, is able to detect a clinically important relation between process and outcome of the quality of care. We conclude that the chest pain criteria map is a valid measure of technical quality, and, because of its association with outcome, is a useful method to assess and improve quality of care.

NOTES

1. W.J. Fessel and E.E. Van Brunt, "Assessing Quality of Care from the Medical Record." *New England Journal of Medicine* 286 (1972): 134.

2. R.H. Brook, *Quality of Care Assessment: A Comparison of Five Methods of Peer Review.* Rockville, MD, Department of Health, Education and Welfare, 1973 (DHEW publication no. (HRA) 74-3100).

3. F.J. Romm, B.S. Hulka, and F. Mayo, "Correlates of Outcomes in Patients with Congestive Heart Failure." *Medical Care* 14 (1976): 765.

4. F.T. Nobrega, G.W. Morrow, R.K. Smoldt, et al., "Quality Assessment in Hypertension: Analysis of Process and Outcome Methods." *New England Journal of Medicine* 296 (1977): 145.

5. R.H. Brook, "Quality—Can We Measure It?" *New England Journal of Medicine* 296 (1977): 170.

6. A. Donabedian, "The Quality of Medical Care: Methods for Assessing and Monitoring the Quality of Care for Research and for Quality Assurance Programs." *Science* 200 (1978): 856.

7. W.E. McAuliffe, "Studies of Process—Outcome Correlations in Medical Care Evaluations: A Critique." *Medical Care* 16 (1978): 907.

8. S. Greenfield, C.E. Lewis, S. Kaplan, et al. "Peer Review by Criteria Mapping: Criteria for Diabetes Mellitus." *Annals of Internal Medicine* 83 (1975): 761.

9. S. Greenfield, M.A. Nadler, M.T. Morgan, et al. "The Clinical Investigation and Management of Chest Pain in an Emergency Department: Quality Assessment by Criteria Mapping," *Medical Care* 15 (1977): 898.

10. H.C. Thompson and C.E. Osborne, "Development of Criteria for Quality Assurance of Ambulatory Child Health Care." *Medical Care* 12 (1974): 807.

11. B.C. Payne, T.F. Lyons, L. Dwarshius, et al., "Quality of Medical Care: Evaluation and Improvement." Chicago: Hospital Research and Education Trust, 1976.

12. R.H. Brook, A. Davies-Avery, S. Greenfield, et al., "Assessing the Quality of Medical Care Using Outcome Measures: An Overview of the Method." *Medical Care* 15(Sep Suppl) (1977): 1.

13. S. Greenfield, N.E. Solomon, R.H. Brook, et al., "Development of Outcome Criteria and Standards to Assess Quality of Care for Patients with Osteoarthrosis." *J Chronic Dis* 13 (1978): 375.

14. A.I. Mushlin, F.A. Appel, and D.M. Barr, "Quality Assurance in Primary Care: A Strategy Based on Outcome Assessment." *J Community Health* 3 (1978): 292.

15. J.W. Williamson, "Evaluating the Quality of Patient Care: A Strategy Relating Outcome and Process Assessment." *JAMA* 218 (1971): 564.

16. B.C. Payne, T. Lyons, E. Neuhaus, et al., "Evaluation and Improvement of Ambulatory Medical Care." Hyattsville, Maryland: National Center for Health Services Research, 1978. (Grant R01 HS01583).

17. B.S. Hulka, F.J. Romm, G.R. Parkerson, et al., "Peer Review in Ambulatory Care: Use of Explicit Criteria and Implicit Judgments." *Medical Care* 17(Mar Suppl) (1979): 1.

18. American Medical Association. *Sample Criteria for Short-Stay Hospital Review: Screening Criteria to Assist PSROs in Quality Assurance.* Chicago: AMA Criteria Development Project, 1976.

19. Arthur D. Little, Inc. *EMCRO: An Evaluation of Experimental Medical Care Review Organizations.* Volume V: *Selected EMCRO Criteria.* Cambridge, Mass.: Arthur D. Little, Inc., 1976.

20. *Quality Care Guidelines*, Utah Professional Review Organization, Salt Lake City: Utah Professional Review Organization, 1973.

21. *Guidelines for Patient Care Appraisal*, Yale-New Haven Hospital, New Haven: Yale-New Haven Hospital, 1974.

22. Multnomah EMCRO. Untitled manuscript. Portland, Oreg.: Multnomah Foundation for Medical Care, 1975.

23. M.A. Morehead, "The Medical Audit as an Operational Tool." *Am J Public Health* 57 (1967): 1643.

24. T.F. Lyons and B.C. Payne, "The Use of Item Importance Weights in Assessing Physician Performance with Predetermined Criteria Indices." *Med Care* 13 (1975): 432.

25. G.A. Rose and H. Blackburn, *Cardiovascular Survey Methods.* World Health Organization Monograph Series No. 56, Geneva: World Health Organization, 1968.

26. M.W. Pozen, R.B. D'Agostino, J.B. Mitchell, et al., "The Usefulness of a Predictive Instrument to Reduce Inappropriate Admissions to the Coronary Care Unit." *Annals of Internal Medicine* 92(Part I) (1980): 238.

27. S. Greenfield, S.H. Kaplan, G.A. Goldberg, et al., "Physician Preference for Criteria Mapping in Medical Care Evaluation." *J Fam Pract* 6 (1978): 1079.

Chapter 10

Measuring the Quality of Medical Care: A Clinical Method

David D. Rutstein, William Berenberg,
Thomas C. Chalmers, Charles G. Child III,
Alfred P. Fishman, and Edward B. Perrin

The lack of measuring sticks of accomplishment has bedeviled all concerned with the improvement of medical care. If the objective of medical care is the maintenance of health and the prevention and treatment of disease, we are constantly faced with a series of questions. What is the relative value of each of the increasing number of preventive and therapeutic agents, the ever more complicated diagnostic instruments, the changing responsibilities and roles of the physician and allied health personnel, the evolving complexity of surgical procedures, the recommended modifications in life style, and the multiplying public health programs? This set of questions has been made more immediate by the increasing discrepancy between available economic resources and the exponential growth in the cost of medical care. Measurements of outcome have to be developed to establish and to document the priorities that must be set for all medical care activities and for expenditure of funds. Continuing advances in science and technology and the constantly changing social scene will require that the priorities be kept up to date.

A method for the measurement of the quality of medical care has been proposed.[1] Its implementation is outlined in this report. A definition of terms is first necessary. *Medical care* is used in its broadest sense. Included are the application of all relevant medical knowledge; the basic and applied research to increase that knowledge and make it more precise; the services of all medical and allied health personnel, institutions, and laboratories; the resources of governmental, voluntary, and social agencies; and the cooperative responsibilities of the individual himself. *Quality* is the effect of care on the health of the individual and of the population. Improvement in the quality of care should be reflected in better health. But quality must

Note: Reprinted with permission from *New England Journal of Medicine,* Vol. 294, pp. 582–584, Massachusetts Medical Society, © March 11, 1976.

be differentiated from the *efficiency* of medical care. Both are important, but they must not be confused. Whereas quality is the output of the medical care machine in the form of better health, efficiency has to do with how well the parts of the machine work, how well they work together, and at what cost. In a word, quality is concerned with outcome, and efficiency is related to the process of care.

Most current measurements of medical care are concerned with efficiency. Compliance with standards of individual and institutional practice, such as those of the American Specialty Boards and the Joint Committee on Hospital Accreditation,* and the process analyses, such as those of the Professional Standards Review Organizations, are mostly concerned with efficiency. Thus, nursing time must not be wasted; laboratory services must be rapid, precise, and provided at minimal cost; the tests ordered must be congruent with the diagnostic requirements of the patient's illness; and patient and physician waiting time must be kept to a minimum. Duplication must be eliminated in superspecialist facilities such as open-heart surgical services, radiation treatment centers, and coronary and intensive care units. Hospital beds must be saved for the patients who really need them. Indeed, efficiency must be maintained at the highest possible level. But making medical care more efficient does not necessarily improve its quality. Improvement in quality has to be verified by the direct measurement of the improved health of the individual and of the population served.

Most previous efforts to measure quality have failed because of the almost insurmountable difficulty of establishing objective criteria for the measurement of increasing gradations of positive health. There are no easily measured quantitative definitions of "bad health," "average health," or "good health." Our proposed system overcomes this difficulty by establishing quantitative negative indexes of health. Cases of unnecessary disease, unnecessary disability, and unnecessary untimely deaths can be counted. Their occurrence is a warning signal, a sentinel health event, that the quality of care may need to be improved.

The value of negative indexes of health has long been established. The use of the maternal mortality rate and the infant mortality rate has been fruitful in saving many lives. But the use of those indexes is limited because they apply only to mothers and babies. We now propose to add negative indexes based on all unnecessary diseases, disabilities, and untimely deaths to make it possible to evaluate the total spectrum of health and medical care.

The occurrence of an unnecessary disease, disability, or untimely death is a sentinel health event that justifies carefully controlled scientific search

---

*Recently (1974), the Joint Committee on Hospital Accreditation introduced retrospective hospital audits, which include measurements of outcome—e.g., complications of disease.

for remediable underlying causes. This approach has been successful in the past. The classic maternal mortality studies of the New York Academy of Medicine[2] in the early 1930s established the pattern. As soon as a maternal death was reported in New York City, the facts were carefully collected and assembled, and the circumstances were reviewed and evaluated by a group of outstanding obstetricians in New York City. The application of the principles derived from that study was followed by a sharp decrease in maternal mortality in New York City,* throughout the country, and indeed throughout the world.

Some will criticize a quality control system based on negative indexes because it cannot in the beginning quantify the positive and some of the more subtle and personal aspects of health. But just as the investigation of an airplane accident goes beyond the immediate reasons for the crash to the implications of the design, method of manufacture, maintenance, and operation of the plane, so should the study of unnecessary undesirable health events yield crucial information on the scientific, medical, social, and personal factors that could lead to better health. Moreover, the evidence collected will not be limited to the factors that yield only to medical measures of control. If there is clear-cut documented evidence that identifiable social, environmental, "life style," economic, or genetic factors are responsible for special varieties of unnecessary disease, disability, or untimely death, these factors should be identified and eliminated whenever possible. Finally, the implementation of the proposed system should serve as a stimulus to identify objective outcome indexes of the more subtle and personal aspects of health.

The identification of the reasons for the "airplane crashes in health" is far simpler, more definitive, and less costly in time, money, and personnel than the global approach of observing entire populations for the occurrence of factors that impair health. Thus, following the pattern of the New York Academy of Medicine maternal mortality study, the Committee on Perinatal Welfare of the Massachusetts Medical Society conducted a similar kind of investigation of infant deaths and was able to determine in the years 1967 and 1968 that approximately one-third of the infant deaths in Massachusetts were preventable by medical means.[3] It would have been much more difficult to follow the large population of pregnant women in Massachusetts to discover the factors that contributed to those unnecessary infant deaths.

With the assistance of specialists in many fields of medicine, we have prepared a list of conditions (Tables 10-1, 10-2, and 10-3) for use as sentinel

---

*The maternal mortality rate in New York City had been at a relatively constant level of 58.9 per 10,000 live births in 1910 and 64.3 in 1933, the year of publication of the Academy report. Thereafter, the rate decreased by half almost every 5 years to 29 in 1940, 16 in 1945, and to 8 in 1950, and then declined asymptotically to 3.3 per 10,000 live births in 1973.

Table 10-1 Clear-cut, Immediate Use of Quality-of-Care Indexes*

8th Rev No.	Condition	Unnecessary Disease	Unnecessary Disability	Unnecessary Untimely Death	Other	Notes†
000	Cholera	P		P,T		
001	Typhoid fever	P		P,T		
003.0	Other salmonella infections w/ food as vehicle of infection	P		P		
005.1	Botulism	P		P		
010-019	Tuberculosis (all forms)			T		
010	Silicotuberculosis	P	P	P,T		P—Occupational
013	Tuberculosis of meninges & central nervous system	P		P,T		Sensitive index
020	Plague			T		
021	Tularemia			T		
022	Anthrax			T		
026	Rat-bite fever			P,T		
032	Diphtheria	P		P		
033	Whooping cough	P		T		
034	Streptococcal sore throat & scarlet fever					
037	Tetanus	P		P		Including neonatal tetanus
040M-044M	Acute paralytic poliomyelitis with or without paralysis or other complications	P	P	P		
050	Smallpox	P		P		
055	Measles	P		P		
056	Rubella	P	P	P		Disability in offspring
060	Yellow fever	P		P		
073	Psittacosis	P		P,T		
080	Epidemic louse-borne typhus			T		
081.0	Endemic flea-borne typhus			T		
082.0	Spotted fevers			T		
090	Congenital syphilis	P	P	P,T		

Table 10-1 *Continued*

8th Rev. No.	Condition	Unnecessary Disease	Unnecessary Disability	Unnecessary Untimely Death	Other	Notes†
091	Early syphilis, symptomatic			T		
093M-094M	Major complications of syphilis	P,T	P,T	P,T		
098	Gonococcal infections			T		
102	Yaws	P		P,T		
124	Trichiniasis	P		P		
126M	Hookworm disease w/anemia	P		P,T		
127.0	Ascariasis	P		P		
140	Malignant neoplasm of lip	P		P,T		P—Pipe smokers & sun exposure
141.1, 141.2, 141.3, 144,145.0	Malignant neoplasm of dorsal & ventral surfaces, borders & tip (not base) of tongue, floor of mouth, or buccal mucosa	P		P,T		P—Tobacco smokers & cud & betelnut chewers
161	Malignant neoplasm of larynx	P		P,T		P—Cigar & cigarette smokers
162	Malignant neoplasm of trachea, bronchus, & lung	P		P		P—Cigarette smoking, occupational exposure
163.0	Malignant neoplasm of pleura	P		P		P—Asbestos exposure
173	Other malignant neoplasms of skin	P		T		Other than melanoma, P— radiation & sun exposure
180	Malignant neoplasm of cervix uteri			T		
188	Malignant neoplasm of bladder	P		P		P—Aniline dyes & cigarette smoking
190M	Malignant neoplasm of eye—retinoblastoma		T	T		Genetic—screening and treatment
	Neuroblastoma (< yr of age)			T		Early recognition & treatment
	Wilms' tumor			T		Early recognition & treatment
193	Thyroid carcinoma	P		P		P—Radiation exposure
205	Myeloid leukemia	P		P		P—Radiation exposure
240.0	Endemic goiter	P				Iodine deficiency
242	Thyrotoxicosis with or without goiter			T		

Code	Condition				Notes
243	Cretinism of congenital origin				
244	Myxedema		T	T	
260-269	Avitaminoses & other nutritional deficiencies	P	P,T	P,T	Not associated with neoplasia or malabsorption
268	Nutritional marasmus	P	P,T	P,T	
274M	Gout—tophaceous	T	T	T	
278.0	Hypervitaminosis A	P	P	P	
278.2	Hypervitaminosis D	P	P	P	
280	Iron-deficiency anemias	P	T	T	Good public health index
281.0	Pernicious anemia		T	T	
281.1	Other vitamin B_{12} deficiency anemias		P,T	P,T	
281.2	Folic acid deficiency anemia		P,T	P,T	
281.3	Vitamin B_6 deficiency anemia		P,T	P,T	
284	Aplastic anemia	P	P	P	P—Benzene exposure, chloramphenicol
320.0	Bacterial meningitis (*Haemophilus influenzae* Group B, pneumococcus, streptococcus Group A, *Staphylococcus aureus*)			T	Early recognition & prompt treatment
375.0	Glaucoma, chronic (primary)		T		
381M-383M	Otitis media or mastoiditis (or both)		T	T	
390-392	Active rheumatic fever		P	P	Prevent recurrences
426	Pulmonary heart disease	P	P	P	P—Occupational & environmental exposure
460M-466M	Acute respiratory infections, influenza, pneumonia, & bronchitis			T	Deaths < age 50 unless associated with immunologic defects or neoplasms
470-474, 480-486, & 490M					
491,492 & 519.3	Chronic bronchitis, emphysema, or chronic obstructive lung disease	P	P	P	P—Cigarettes & other environmental risks

Table 10-1 *Continued*

8th Rev No.	Condition	Unnecessary Disease	Unnecessary Disability	Unnecessary Untimely Death	Other	Notes†
493	Asthma			T		T—Self-inhalation therapy deaths < age 50
500M	Hypertrophy or disease of tonsils & adenoids				X	Tonsilectomy rates
515M-516M	All pneumonoconioses	P	P			
540-543	Appendicitis			P	X	Appendectomy rates
550M-553M	Inguinal or other hernia of abdominal cavity with or without obstruction			T		Deaths < age 65
574M	Acute or chronic cholecystitis with or without cholelithiasis			T		Deaths < age 65
598	Stricture of urethra		T	T		T—Gonococcal infection
620-629	Disease of uterus & other female genital organs				X	Hysterectomy rates
680-686	Infections of skin & subcutaneous tissue			T		
692	Other eczema & dermatitis	P	P	P		P—Environmental & occupational exposure to specific agents
710	Acute arthritis due to pyogenic organisms	P	T	T		P—Secondary to pyogenic infections
712.0M	Blindness—juvenile rheumatoid arthritis		T			Uveitis
720.0	Acute osteomyelitis	P	T	T		
720.1	Chronic osteomyelitis	P	T	T		
	Congenital anomalies associated w/rubella	P	P	P		Including cataract, patent ductus arteriosus, deafness, & mental deficiency
774M-775M	Rh incompatibility	P	P,T	P,T		

Code	Condition			Notes
780-789	Symptoms & ill-defined conditions		X	Bad diagnosis (unless specified as "cause unknown")—index of poor quality
630M-678M	All maternal deaths (including abortion)		P	
760-778	Infant mortality, general		P	
310M-315M	Mental retardation induced by:	P		Parent education & genetic counseling (see Table 10-2)
	Maternal nutritional deficiency			
	Rubella (Maternal)			
	Rh incompatibility			
	Tay-Sachs disease			
	Man-made (including occupational) diseases induced by (with examples):			
	1. *Toxic agents*, including direct chemical hazards (carbon tetrachloride); carcinogens (vinyl chloride); mutagens (lead); teratogens (thalidomide); pesticides (cholinesterase inhibitors); contact irritants (occupational dermatoses); dusts (pneumonoconioses); contact sensitizers (nickel); water contaminants (polychlorinated biphenyls); air pollutants (sulfur dioxide).			
	2. *Physical hazards*, including radiant energy (medical, industrial, & war); noise (rock & roll), & vibration (jack hammers).			

Table 10-1 *Continued*

8th Rev No.	Condition	Unnecessary Disease	Unnecessary Disability	Unnecessary Untimely Death	Other	Notes†
3.	*Artificial environments,* including space travel, airplanes, caissons, air conditioned sealed buildings, & intensive care units.					
4.	*Accidents* (manifold varieties inducing injury).					
5.	*Biological hazards,* including laboratory accidents, antibiotic-resistant microorganisms, & contact allergic dermatitis (plants & wood).					

*P denotes prevention, P? prevention controversial, T treatment, T? treatment controversial, & X additional index.
†The symbol "P—" or "T—" in the Notes indicates that the prevention or treatment is limited to the circumstances described by the phrase that follows the symbol.

Table 10-2 Limited Use of Quality-of-Care Indexes*

8th Rev No.	Condition	Unnecessary Disease	Unnecessary Disability	Unnecessary Untimely Death	Other	Notes†
004	Bacillary dysentery	P		P,T		
005	Food poisoning (bacterial)	P		P		
070	Infectious hepatitis	P		P		
573.0M	Serum hepatitis (Type B)		P			
084	Malaria	P?	P?	P?,T		Early treatment of falciparum infection
153-154M	Malignant neoplasm of large intestine, rectum, & rectosigmoid junction			T		
184.0	Malignant neoplasm of vagina	P		P		Young women—diethylstilbestrol therapy in mother
201	Hodgkin's disease			T		Lower stages of malignancy in young people
204.0	Lymphatic leukemia, acute			T?		
250.0	Diabetes mellitus w/mention of acidosis or coma			T		Above specified death rate & hypoglycemic death due to overtreatment
286.0	Hemophilia	P	P	P		
306.6	Enuresis		P?,T			
345.1	Epilepsy, generalized convulsive		T	T		
400-404	Hypertensive disease		T	—		Above specified rates
410.0M, 410.M, 411.0M, 413.0M, 430.0M, 431.0M, 432.0M, 433.0M,	Hypertensive disease with vascular complications of heart or brain	P	P	P		Relates to excess of complications due to the hypertension

Table 10-2 Continued

8th Rev No.	Condition	Unnecessary Disease	Unnecessary Disability	Unnecessary Untimely Death	Other	Notes†
434.0M, 435.0M, 436.0M, 437.0M, & 438.0M,						
521.0	Dental caries	P				P—Adequate fluorides & reduced sugar intake
531M-532M	Ulcer of stomach or duodenum with or without hemorrhage or perforation			T		Deaths < age 55
626	Disorders of menstruation		T?			
627	Menopausal symptoms		T			
	Rheumatoid arthritis		P			
712M	Curvature of spine	T	T?			
746-747.9	Congenital anomalies of heart & great vessels			T		Early recognition & referral

				Notes
310M-315M	Mental retardation induced by:	P?		
	Blood-group incompatibilities other than Rh		T	
	Cerebral palsy		T	
	Metabolic disorders, including:			
	Phenylketonuria			
	Aminoacidurias			
	Neonatal sepsis		T	
	Toxoplasmosis		T?	
	Herpes simplex infection			
E850M-E859M	Accidental poisoning by drugs & medicaments, including all contraceptives	P	P	Includes iatrogenic disease & deserves special study
E930-E936	Surgical & medical complications & misadventures	P	P	Includes many varieties of iatrogenic disease & deserves special study
	Nosocomial infections	P	P	
	Iatrogenic disease—A category of the man-made diseases (not eligible for Table 10-1).			

*P denotes prevention, P? prevention controversial, T treatment, T? treatment controversial, & X additional index.

†The symbol "P—" or "T—" in the Notes indicates that the prevention or treatment is limited to the circumstances described by the phrase that follows the symbol.

Table 10-3 Categories Demanding Better Definition and Special Study

8th Rev No.	Condition	Unnecessary Disease	Unnecessary Disability	Unnecessary Untimely Death	Other	Notes
291,303, 304,571 E950-E959, S960-E969	Examples: Severe medicosocial problems including alcoholism, alcoholic psychoses, alcoholic cirrhosis of the liver, drug dependence, child battering, & suicide & homicide					
290-309	Mental disorders					

health events in national and local geographic areas and in individual hospitals. In selecting a particular condition as a sentinel health event, we have assumed that if everything had gone well, the condition would have been prevented or managed. The chain of responsibility to prevent the occurrence of any unnecessary disease, disability, or untimely death may be long and complex. The failure of any single link may precipitate an unnecessary undesirable health event. Thus, the unnecessary case of diphtheria, measles, or poliomyelitis may be the responsibility of the state legislature that neglected to appropriate the needed funds, the health officer who did not implement the program, the medical society that opposed community clinics, the physician who did not immunize his patient, the religious views of the family, or the mother who didn't bother to take her baby for immunization. Permanent crippling from chronic disabling diseases such as rheumatoid arthritis can be the result of inadequate instruction and demonstration to the patient of an exercise regimen, lack of facilities for physiotherapy, or the unwillingness of the patient to cooperate in the never ending struggle against frozen joints and contracted muscles. Death from cancer of the lung may be due to the patient's unwillingness or inability to give up cigarette smoking, the reassuring statements put out by the advertiser or manufacturer of cigarettes, the absence of an effective health information program in the public schools and in the community or, more rarely, from an error in diagnosis or from poor surgical care. The reader may develop further examples.

It is clear that the physician cannot be solely responsible for many of the errors of omission and commission that result in a sentinel health event. Nevertheless, in every kind of unnecessary disease, disability, and untimely death, the physician has the initial and also some continuing responsibility. He is the only one competent to provide the leadership and the professional guidance to the politician, the administrator, industry, the public, and to the patient himself. They may not, of course, take the physician's advice, but that does not relieve him of the responsibility for the input of the scientific facts and the professional knowledge that are directly relevant to the improvement of human health and to the prevention of community decisions that may result in unnecessary disease, disability, or untimely death.

The Working Group, in collaboration with representatives of the National Center for Health Statistics, the Center for Disease Control, and the Veterans Administration, and after consulting specialists in many fields, prepared a list of conditions to serve as indexes of the quality of care (Tables 10-1, 10-2, and 10-3) in accordance with the following criteria:

1. The list is designed for international use. Conditions are included whether or not they exist in the United States at present. For example, cholera is listed because it is an important international health problem.

2. The list of conditions is selected whenever possible from the Eighth Revision, International Classification of Diseases Adapted for Use in the United States,[4] to provide ease of comparison with existing health tabulations and to take advantage of current computer programs in such organizations as the National Center for Health Statistics, Center for Disease Control, Veterans Administration, and individual hospitals such as the Massachusetts General Hospital. Where the total scope of the condition is not congruent with an item on the list, the symbol "M" for "modified" appears immediately after the number. Thus, No. 274 in the International Classification of Diseases, "Gout" and No. 274M in Table 10-1 is "Gout—tophaceous." If the condition does not appear in the Classification, no number is assigned in Tables 10-1, 10-2, and 10-3.

3. In the columns of Tables 10-1 through 10-3 distinction is made between unnecessary disease, unnecessary disability, and unnecessary untimely death. Moreover, in each category an attempt is made to indicate whether it is preventable or treatable (or both). As an example, No. 000, Cholera, is a preventable unnecessary disease (P), whereas an unnecessary untimely death from cholera can be avoided through both prevention (P) and treatment (T). Thus, sanitary control can prevent a case and at times a death from cholera; moreover, if a case of cholera does develop, adequate treatment with the salt/glucose mixture should prevent an untimely death. The symbol "P—" or "T—" in the Notes indicates that the prevention or treatment is limited to the circumstances described by the phrase that follows the symbol. Thus, in No. 161, Malignant neoplasm of the larynx, the "P—" is followed by "Cigar and cigarette smokers," indicating that prevention is relevant only to such exposure.

4. The conditions on the list are classified in three separate tables:

Clear-cut and immediate use. Conditions listed in Table 10-1 can now be used as indexes of the quality of care in national or local areas or in individual hospitals. A condition is selected for listing in Table 10-1 only if the occurrence of a single case of disease or disability or a single untimely death would justify, as is true for a maternal or infant death, an immediate inquiry into the question, "Why did it happen?"

Most of the conditions listed in Table 10-1 are single entities. But four subcategories at the end of Table 10-1 deserve special mention. Maternal mortality and infant mortality, although listed as single entities, comprise manifold conditions that have been classified in obstetric and pediatric publications and will not be detailed here. Mental retardation results from many different mechanisms, including some that are both unnecessary and undesirable, as specified in Table 10-1. Finally, the man-made (including occupational) diseases[5] constitute an enormous group of induced injuries and illnesses that could not be reproduced in this summary report. However, the major subcategories of the man-made diseases with examples are listed in Table 10-1 as are selected examples from the International Classification of Diseases—e.g., No. 188, Malignant neoplasm of the bladder, P—Aniline dyes or cigarette smoking, or No. 284, Aplastic anemia, P—Benzene or chloramphenicol. Suffice it to say that a single case of disease or disability or a single untimely death in any of the entities included under maternal mortality or infant mortality, or among the conditions listed under mental retardation, or the occurrence of any of the man-made diseases should serve as a sentinel health event.[6]

We designed Table 10-1 to meet certain needs of the National Center for Health Statistics, the Center for Disease Control, the Veterans Administration, and individual hospitals. The National Center for Health Statistics, through its program of ongoing surveys, and the Center for Disease Control, through its program of disease surveillance, are already concerned with various aspects of the quality of medical care in the United States. The National Center for Health Statistics can now review the interview questions, examination procedures, and laboratory tests and discover whether its ongoing health surveys are identifying the conditions about which something can be done. It is also the repository of all vital statistics from the United States. The Center is now studying the use of the statistics for monitoring purposes. One immediate use is the tabulation of all unnecessary untimely deaths among those reported in all the death certificates from the 50 states. The Center for Disease Control will determine which of the conditions listed in Table 10-1 are amenable to surveillance. Indeed, if appropriate funding were available, both agencies are already organized to conduct pilot field testing of the proposed method of measurement of the quality of care to determine how the indexes in Table 10-1 may be used in ongoing continuous evaluation of the quality of medical care in the United States and its subdivisions.[7]

The Veterans Administration has already begun to apply the proposed method to its maintenance of high quality of care within Veterans Administration hospitals. Analyses are under way of the records of patients who have been discharged from the hospitals to identify the occurrence and distribution of the unnecessary diseases, unnecessary disabilities, and unnecessary untimely deaths listed in Table 10-1. Individual hospitals such as the Massachusetts General Hospital are conducting similar analyses of the diagnoses and outcome in the records of their discharged patients. Fortunately, the required information is immediately retrievable through existing computer programs in many hospitals. One of the great advantages of our proposed method is that the quality measurements can be tabulated with only minor modification in existing data collection procedures.

Although Table 10-1 is a list of sentinel health events that can be applied immediately to the measurement of the quality of care, the flowering of basic science, the growth in medical knowledge and technology, rapid social and environmental mutations, and the changing pattern of medical practice will demand constant surveillance of the conditions that it lists. Revision will be required at specified intervals to keep the list up to date.

Limited use. We have listed conditions in Table 10-2 when prevention or management is highly effective but when more than a single case of disease or disability or a single death is required to initiate an immediate inquiry. Much special study will be required to establish criteria for identification of unusual deviations from minimum rates of unnecessary undesirable health events. This category of conditions is so extensive that Table 10-2 is perforce limited to selected examples from subcategories as follows: (1) When there is a need for experimental study of the entire spectrum of a condition to determine how it may be used as an index (e.g., hypertension with or without vascular complications of heart and brain); when special study is required of discharged inpatients to determine expected level of success (e.g., surgical removal of malignant neoplasms of the large intestine or rectum); when control is effective only at certain stages or under special circumstances (e.g., malaria or Hodgkin's disease); or symptomatic conditions in which prevention or treatment would be effective but not in every case (e.g., enuresis, disorders of menstruation, and menopausal symptoms).

This report is concerned primarily with conditions that can be recognized in the general population as well as in the hospital. But there is a need for systematic studies within the individual hospital. Conditions in Table 10-2 that lend themselves to such study include E850M-E859M, Accidental poisoning by drugs and medicaments including all contraceptives; E930-E936, Surgical and medical complications and misadventures; nosocomial infections; and iatrogenic disease. Most important, the close supervision of the patient within the hospital makes it possible to recognize unnecessary undesirable health events that could not be identified in the general population. Studies on these questions are already in the planning stage.

Categories demanding better definition and special study. There are categories of conditions that may seriously affect health in which prevention or diagnosis and treatment are not well enough defined and in which outcome cannot be precisely enough predicted to use them as indexes of the quality of care (examples in Table 10-3). The cooperation of specialists in medicosocial problems and psychiatry is needed to identify individual conditions that could be used as indexes of the quality of medical care in these more complicated categories of human disease.

In the meantime, the indexes of the quality of medical care listed in Table 10-1 should be immediately useful to those actively engaged in formulating the answers to some of the quantitative questions that are germane to the improvement of individual and national health.

NOTES

1. D.D. Rutstein, *Blueprint for Medical Care.* Cambridge, The MIT Press, 1974, pp. 161–224.

2. New York Academy of Medicine, Committee on Public Health Relations: *Maternal Mortality in New York City: A Study of All Puerperal Deaths 1930–1932.* New York, The Commonwealth Fund, 1933, p. 290.

3. D.M. Muirhead, *Report on Perinatal and Infant Mortality in Massachusetts 1967 and 1968.* Committee on Perinatal Welfare of the Massachusetts Medical Society, December 1971.

4. United States Department of Health, Education, and Welfare, National Center for Health Statistics: Eighth Revision, International Classification of Diseases (1965 Revision) Adapted for use in the U.S. (PHS Publication No. 1693) Washington, D.C., Government Printing Office, 1967.

5. D.D. Rutstein, "The Epidemiology and Control of Man-Made Diseases." *Ann Life Insur Med* 5 (1974): 25–334.

6. A. Hamilton and H.L. Hardy, *Industrial Toxicology.* Third edition. Acton, Massachusetts, Publishing Sciences Group Incorporated, 1974.

7. D.D. Rutstein, *Blueprint for Medical Care,* pp. 174–198.

Chapter 11

Assessing Health Quality— The Case for Tracers

David M. Kessner, Carolyn E. Kalk,
and James Singer

The question is no longer whether there will be intervention in health services to assure quality, but who will intervene and what methods they will use.

Almost 40 years ago, Lee and Jones[1] defined quality of medical care by eight "articles of faith": scientific basis for medical practice; prevention; consumer-provider cooperation; treatment of the whole individual; close and continuing patient-physician relation; comprehensive and coordinated medical services; coordination between medical care and social services; and accessibility of care for all people. Today, these unarguable goals have greater active support than when they were first stated. The focus of health policy makers and consumers is shifting from concern over the bald costs of care to concern for getting their money's worth. Indeed, if anything, the raising of the public consciousness in health matters has hardened the goals; the "accessibility of care" is giving way to the "right to care," and the right to care implies the right to quality care.

During the past decade and a half, the conceptual issues in evaluating health care have been stated and restated many times.[2-13] The basic requirements for a pragmatic evaluation method include a statement of the objectives of the program; standards to define quality of care; data on delivered care that can be compared to standards; careful attention to the nature of the measurement units; assessment of the reliability of the analysis; consideration of the cost of the method; and a plan for integrating evaluation into the organization of health services.

The last requirement is most critical. Evaluation can neither assure quality nor improve care unless it is part and parcel of the delivery system, an ongoing agent for change when change is necessary and a tool for educating

Note: Reprinted with permission from *New England Journal of Medicine*, Vol. 288, pp. 189–194, Massachusetts Medical Society, © January 25, 1973.

178

providers and consumers alike to the strengths and weaknesses of the system.

In July, 1969, the Institute of Medicine (then called the Board of Medicine) of the National Academy of Sciences undertook a program—entitled "Contrasts in Health Status"—to evaluate health services received by different groups of people in our population. In developing a method for assessing health care status, the Institute focused on the premise that specific health problems could serve as "tracers" in analyzing health delivery. When combined into sets, they provide a framework for evaluating the interaction between providers, patients, and their environments. They also would yield easily understood data to be fed back into the health delivery system.

THE TRACER METHOD

The tracer concept was borrowed from the formal sciences. Endocrinologists, for example, use radioactive tracers to study how a body organ—such as the thyroid gland—handles a critical substance such as iodide. They measure how the gland takes up a minute amount of radioactive iodide, and assume that the organ handles natural iodide in the same manner.

For measuring the functions of a health care system, the tracers needed are discrete, identifiable health problems—each shedding light on how particular parts of the system work, not in isolation, but in relation to one another. The basic assumption remains the same—namely, how a physician or team of physicians routinely administers care for common ailments will be an indicator of the general quality of care and the efficacy of the system delivering that care.

The use of specific health problems to analyze health services is not new. In a study of the medical clinic of a university hospital in the early 1960s, for example, Huntley et al.[14] analyzed charts for completeness of patient workup and proportion of abnormalities that were not followed up. More than one-fourth of the patients with a diastolic blood pressure of 100 mm of mercury or higher were given no special tests relevant to hypertension, and approximately one-half of these patients had no diagnosis related to the cardiovascular system.

Other analyses using specific diseases include those by Ciocco et al.,[15] and Morehead and their coworkers,[16,17] Brook[18] and Payne.* These studies all used specific health problems as indicators of either process or outcome variables, or a combination of process and outcome, in the delivery of ambulatory health services.

---

*Cited by Brook.[18]

The tracer methodology developed by the Institute of Medicine differs from previous efforts in several ways. These include the manner in which tracers were selected and combined in sets; specification of criteria for care; and, in application, concurrent assessment of the health professional, the community that he serves, and the people to whom he delivers services.

The tracer method measures both process and outcome of care, which we consider important in any evaluation scheme. It is impossible to pinpoint the strengths and weaknesses of process without knowing the outcome, but outcome alone can be misleading if the patient receives unnecessary diagnostic tests or inappropriate therapy.

SELECTING TRACERS

The first important difference from previous methodologies is that tracers are selected and combined according to criteria. In an attempt to give a rational and uniform basis for selecting the tracers, six criteria were established that would screen out health problems that are not appropriate tracers. In order of importance, the criteria are as follows:

1. *A tracer should have a definite functional impact.* The over-riding purpose of the tracer approach is to focus on specific conditions that reflect the activities of health professionals. Conditions that are unlikely to be treated and those that cause negligible functional impairment are not useful.
2. *A tracer should be relatively well defined and easy to diagnose.* Dermatologic conditions have a clear functional impact. The difficulties, however, of defining clear-cut pathologic entities lessen their utility as tracers. In contrast, it is relatively easy to identify a population of patients with a hematocrit below a specified level and further to diagnose those with iron-deficiency anemia.
3. *Prevalence rates should be high enough to permit the collection of adequate data from a limited population sample.* If an adequate number of cases cannot be studied, it is difficult to evaluate even the most important variables in relation to the set of tracers.
4. *The natural history of the condition should vary with utilization and effectiveness of medical care.* Ideally, in evaluation of a delivery system, the conditions under study should be sensitive to the quality or quantity (or both) of the service received by the patient. It is inappropriate to use conditions for which health services do not alter the progress of the disease.

5. *The techniques of medical management of the condition should be well defined for at least one of the following processes: prevention, diagnosis, treatment, or rehabilitation.* There is danger in using tracers to look at the process of care if minimal standards for medical management cannot be agreed upon.
6. *The effects of nonmedical factors on the tracer should be understood.* Social, cultural, economic, behavioral, and environmental factors can influence the prevalence and distribution of many diseases. Thus, the epidemiology of the tracer should be relatively well understood and the population at risk easy to identify.

We screened 15 candidate traces and selected a set of six—middle ear infection and hearing loss, visual disorders, iron-deficiency anemia, hypertension, urinary tract infections, and cervical cancer—that met the specified criteria. As a set, the six tracers can be used to evaluate the ambulatory care received by a cross-section of the population; the set provides at least two individual tracers relevant to both sexes and four age groups (Table 11-1).

The activities of a health-service delivery organization are categorized in five major groups (see Table 11-2). Each major activity is required for management of at least two tracers. This allows us to sample the varied activities of a delivery system from multiple perspectives and thereby strengthens the validity of extrapolating from the analyses of the tracer set to the delivery system as a whole. For example, if there is little or no screening for four of five tracers that require screening, the concordance of this finding suggests that this medical process needs improvement.

Table 11-1 Age-Sex Groups Represented by Accepted Tracer Conditions

Tracer Condition

Age (Yr)	Middle-Ear Infection	Hearing Loss	Visual Deficiency	Iron Deficiency Anemia	Hypertension	Urinary Tract Infection	Cervical Cancer
Female:							
<5	+			+			
5–24	+	+	+				
25–64				+	+	+	+
≥65				+	+	+	
Male:							
<5	+			+			
5–24	+	+	+				
25–64				+	+		
≥65				+	+	+	

Table 11-2 Aspects of the Process of Primary Ambulatory Health Care Highlighted by Accepted Tracer Conditions

Process Activity	Tracer Condition						
	Middle-Ear Infection	Hearing Loss	Visual Deficiency	Iron Deficiency Anemia	Hypertension	Urinary-Tract Infection	Cervical Cancer
Prevention		+		+			
Screening		+	+	+	+		+
Evaluation: History & physical examination	+				+	+	+
Laboratory				+	+	+	+
Other testing		+					
Management chemo-therapy	+			+	+	+	
Health counseling		+		+			+
Speciality referral	+	+	+			+	+
Hospital-ization					+	+	+
Follow-up case	+	+		+	+	+	+

CRITERIA FOR CARE

A critical requirement for evaluating health services is the establishment of criteria against which services delivered can be compared. Without formal criteria, objective evaluations and analyses are impossible. Yet establishing criteria has an inherent danger—that of the risk of locking the medical profession into a rigid mode of practice.

We believed criteria for treating the tracer conditions could avoid rigidity if they were formulated on three premises: they should outline minimal, or base-line, care; they should be pragmatic, taking into account unavailability of sophisticated diagnostic equipment; and they should be periodically revised and updated.

Also, in formulating the criteria, we recognized that no single plan could cope with the variation in clinical presentation that the practicing physician faces. Thus, the criteria should be viewed as a plan broadly applicable to populations of patients, not as a management formula for individual patients. We made no attempt to rank the importance of various processes involved in delivering care. It is naive to suggest that a history is more or less important than a physical examination or appropriate laboratory tests. Accurate diagnosis depends on integrating critical historical, physical, and laboratory data.

Minimal care criteria for hypertension in adults—applicable to urban or suburban practice—are shown in Exhibit 11-1. They were formulated by practicing family physicians and specialists.

EVALUATION BY TRACER

Tracers can be used to evaluate health service organizations—such as neighborhood health centers—which have responsibility for providing care to a defined population; they can also be used by an individual physician to evaluate his own practice.

To illustrate the application of the tracer methodology, we have outlined a hypothetical community served by a hypothetical neighborhood health center. We will assume that the community is located in the central city and its 42,000 citizens are predominantly blacks, with a median family income of $5,000 per year and a median educational attainment among adults of 11 years of completed schooling. Some of the data in the illustration are real (developed in pretests of the tracer method); some are not. The latter represent, rather, our generalized experience and "best guesses" in constructing a situation typical of those likely to be found by evaluators of urban health delivery systems.

Services in a Hypothetical Community

Because we have selected a neighborhood health center for our evaluation, the first thing we will want to know is how well the center reaches the at-risk populations among those whom it was designed to serve. For this analysis we will need current census figures of demographic and socioeconomic characteristics of the community population, and the age and sex distribution of the persons enrolled in the neighborhood health center.

When we examine the age distributions of the residents, we find more than 40 percent of the population is under 25 years of age, almost 70 percent under 45, and about 10 percent 65 or older. By sex, 54 percent of all residents are females, but the distribution varies with age from 51 percent females in the group under 45 years to 65 percent females in those 65 years and over.

These characteristics are crucial to our selection of tracers. For tracers, we will want to use common ailments treated by the health system; we will want to examine routine, not unusual or exotic, care provided by the health center. And without knowing the predominant age and sex distributions

Exhibit 11-1 A Minimal Care Plan for Hypertension

I. Screening
   A. *Method*. The systolic pressure is recorded at the onset of the first Korotkoff
   sound, and the diastolic at the final disappearance of the second or the change
   if the sound persists.
   B. *Criteria*. An individual patient is judged in need of evaluation for elevated
   blood pressure if the mean of three or more systolic or diastolic pressures
   exceeds the age-specific criteria specified below:

Males & Females	Systolic (mm Hg)	Diastolic
18–44 years	140	90
45–64 years	150	95
65 or older	160	95

II. Evaluation
   In the evaluation of elevated blood pressure, the history and physical examination data listed below should be obtained early in the evaluation.
   A. *History*. (1) Personal and social history; (2) family history of high blood pressure, coronary-artery disease, or stroke; (3) previous diagnosis of high blood
   pressure (females, toxemia of pregnancy or pre-eclampsia) and time of first
   occurrence; (4) previous treatment for high blood pressure (when started and
   when stopped, and drugs used); (5) chest pain, pressure, or tightness; location,
   length of symptoms, frequency of symptoms, effect of deep breathing, description of feeling (crushing, smothering, strangling), symptom temporarily
   curtails activity, and pain radiates into left shoulder, arm, or jaw and is accompanied by nausea, shortness of breath, or fast or fluttering heart beat; (6)
   feet swell; (7) shortness of breath; (8) patient awakens wheezing or feeling
   smothered or choked; (9) patient sleeps on two or more pillows; (10) prior
   history of kidney trouble, nephrosis, or nephritis; (11) history of kidney infection; and (12) prior X-ray examination of kidneys.
   B. *Physical Examination*. (1) Weight and height; (2) blood pressure—supine and
   upright; (3) funduscopic; (4) heart—abnormal sounds or rhythm; (5) neck—
   thyroid and neck veins; (6) abdomen—standard description, including abdominal bruit; and (7) extremities—peripheral pulses and edema.
   C. *Laboratory*. (1) Urinalysis; (2) hematocrit or hemoglobin; and (3) blood urea
   nitrogen or serum creatinine.
   D. *Other Tests*. (1) Electrocardiogram; if the patient is less than 30 years of age
   or if diastolic pressure is 130 mm of mercury or greater; and (2) rapid-sequence
   intravenous pyelogram.

III. Diagnosis
   A. *Essential Hypertension*. As described in above under I B (Criteria) provided
   there is no evidence of secondary hypertension.
   B. *Secondary Hypertension*. Hypertension secondary to renal, adrenal, thyroid,
   or primary vascular disease.

Exhibit 11-1 continued

IV. Management

All drugs are prescribed in acceptable dosages adjusted to the individual patient, contraindications are observed, and patients are monitored for common side effects according to information detailed in AMA Drug Evaluations 1971 (first edition). Fixed-dosage combinations should not be used for initial therapy.

A. *Mild Essential Hypertension (Diastolic Pressure of 115 Mm of Mercury).* (1) Initial treatment with thiazides alone in a diuretic dose; (2) if pressure is not reduced by 10 mm of mercury or to lowest level that patient can tolerate without symptoms of hypotension in 2 to 4 weeks, alpha-methyldopa, reserpine of hydralazine is added to thiazide.

B. *Moderate Essential Hypertension (Diastolic Pressure of 115 to 130 Mm of Mercury).* (1) Initial treatment with thiazide and alpha-methyldopa, reserpine, or hydralazine; (2) if no response after 2 to 4 weeks, change to thiazide-reserpine-hydralazine or thiazide-guanethidine combination.

C. *Severe Essential Hypertension (Diastolic Pressure of 130 Mm of Mercury of Keith-Wagener Grade III or IV Funduscopic Changes).* Refer to specialist or hospitalize (or both).

D. *Secondary Hypertension.* Treat, or refer for treatment of, primary condition.

E. *Undetermined Etiology or No Response to Treatment.* Hypertension of undetermined cause or not responding to treatment regimens above requires further evaluation, to include: (1) determination of serum sodium and potassium; and, if not previously performed, (2) rapid-sequence intravenous pyelography.

of community residents, we cannot estimate the prevalence of the tracer diseases or judge their suitability for analyzing routine care.

To find out how well the center serves the community, we need only compare the current census data with a similar analysis of persons enrolled in the health center. In an actual evaluation, we would compare community residents to the center's 9,000 enrollees for each age-sex group. In this example, however, we will focus on two groups: all persons under 15 and men 25 to 64 years of age.

Table 11-3 shows that the health center serves about one-fifth of all community residents. It is used to different extents, however, by the two age groups that we have selected. Nearly one-third of the children under 15 years of age but less than 15 percent of the men 25 to 64 years old are enrolled. This simple analysis clearly points out a segment of the population—young to middle-age men—that has been underserved, an important finding for our assessment of the center's effectiveness.

The Quality of Care

To assess the quality of care given to men 25 to 64 years old, we will need to select tracers and apply them to a sample of medical records. The

Table 11-3 Comparison of Community Population with Selected Health Center Enrollees

Group	Community Population	Health Center Enrollees	% of Community Population Enrolled
Total population	42,000	9,000	21.4
Males & females, 0–14 yrs of age	9,200	2,900	31.5
Males, 25–64 yrs of age	9,900	1,400	14.1

tracers that we select are critical to the evaluation; ideally, they should consist of a set of two or more tracers for each age-sex group. In that way we can view the services provided to the group from two or more perspectives and avoid the risk of isolating anomalous conditions. For simplicity, however, we will use only one tracer, hypertension, in this illustration and will focus on screening and diagnostic and therapeutic processes.

A review of the literature indicates that the prevalence of hypertension in black men of this age is about 23 percent.[19] When we extrapolate from the community census, we can estimate that there will be approximately 2,300 men with hypertension in the community.

Next, we review a sample of the medical records of this age-sex group according to our treatment criteria for hypertension. Performing the review are persons, not necessarily professionals, who are familiar with the medical care process and who have received 2 weeks of intensive training. It is assumed that about 78 percent of the enrolled men have been screened, and 250 cases are identified—for a prevalence rate of 23 percent in the screened population. From this analysis we can state that more than one-fifth of the enrolled men were not screened; high-risk persons had not been pinpointed for screening because prevalence rate among screened patients was the same as would be expected among a randomly selected sample of enrollees; and the center is caring for only 11 percent of the estimated hypertensive men in the community.

It is possible, of course, that some of the 300-plus unscreened men actually were screened, but that the findings were not recorded or that appropriate follow-up examination was carried out but not indicated on the chart. Implicit in the use of the tracer method, however, is the assumption that good medical records are a requisite for good medical practice.

In evaluating therapy given to the 250 identified patients with hypertension, we select and abstract a random sample of their medical charts according to the treatment criteria. The abstracts are recorded on a precoded form for ease in processing. It is assumed that this analysis finds that in

30 percent of the cases fixed-dosage combination drugs were used in initial therapy. Information such as this concerning the process of medical care is critical in assessing the quality of health services. It does not substitute for measures of outcome, such as whether or not the blood pressure actually declined, but provides important information concerning appropriate treatment.

IMPACT OF EVALUATION

There are three purposes to evaluation: to support good medical practice by identifying its efficacious and efficient elements, to indicate areas of practice in need of improvement, and to provide ongoing education to physicians about their own practices. But these purposes are not served if the evaluation results are not fed back into the delivery system and acted upon.

The results should enter the decision-making process at the point where standards are set for acceptable levels of care. We have not attempted to impose our judgment in standard setting. Decisions concerning an acceptable level of performance in, for example, history taking (should the required minimal history be taken for 20 percent or 80 percent of the potential hypertensive patients?) must be made by the individual physician, the physicians as a group, or the consumer-physician governing board.

In our hypothetical health center, 23 percent of the enrolled high-risk population had not been screened for hypertension, and only 11 percent of the estimated morbidity in the community had been identified. There may also be some question about the adequacy of the center's medical records. Certain remedial actions should be considered: institute case finding among a small sample of community males to estimate the number of persons with high blood pressure who are receiving care elsewhere in the community; restructure health center procedures to obtain blood pressures on all high-risk enrollees; and consider use of structured medical records to obtain a minimal data base on all patients.

The analysis of drug therapy in hypertension provides basic information that physicians, health center administrators, medical directors, or consumer boards need to improve care. It points out that something may be amiss in the way a class of drugs—in this case, antihypertensive agents—is prescribed routinely. By implication, it suggests that inappropriate drug therapy may occur in the treatment of other common ailments and that the center's drug therapy program should be analyzed in greater detail.

CONCLUSIONS

Tracers provide a workable conceptual framework and data base for assessing the quality of health services. Like any system of evaluation, however, this one will need to be adapted to and tested in live, nonacademic practices. In addition, tracer sets and care criteria will need to be developed—for example, to assess care given to the elderly, adolescents, and persons with emotional disorders. It is especially important to note that no system of evaluation, including tracers, can be instituted nationwide immediately to satisfy the emerging political craving for quality assessment. Comparative testing of all evaluation methods is needed first. Such comparative tests can serve, however, as a first logical step to move evaluation from the perpetual research-demonstration-research cycle to utility and problem solving.

NOTES

1. Lee RI, Jones LW: The Fundamentals of Good Medical Care: An outline of the fundamentals of good medical care and an estimate of the service required to supply the medical needs of the United States (Publications of the Committee on the Costs of Medical Care No. 22). Chicago, University of Chicago Press, 1933.

2. Altman I., Anderson AJ, Barker K: *Methodology in Evaluating the Quality of Medical Care: An Annotated Selected Bibliography, 1955–1968*. Revised edition. Pittsburgh, University of Pittsburgh Press, 1969.

3. Donabedian A: Evaluating the quality of medical care. *Milbank Mem Fund Q* 44(3):166–206, 1966.

4. *Idem*: Promoting quality through evaluating the process of patient care. *Med Care* 6:181–202, 1968.

5. *Idem*: The evaluation of medical care programs. *Bull NY Acad Med* 44:117–124, 1968.

6. *Idem*: A *Guide to Medical Care Administration Vol.* II. *Medical Care Appraisal—Quality and Utilization*. New York, American Public Health Association, Inc. 1969.

7. *Outcomes Conference I-II: Methodology of Identifying, Measuring and Evaluating Outcomes of Health Service Programs, Systems and Subsystems*. Edited by CE Hopkins, Rockville, Maryland, Department of Health, Education, and Welfare, Health Services and Mental Health Administration, 1969.

8. Klein MW, Malone MF, Bennis WG, et al.: Problems of measuring patient care in the out-patient department. *J Health Hum Behav* 2:138–144, 1961.

9. Kelman HR, Elinson J: Strategy and tactics of evaluating a large-scale medical care program. *Med Care* 7:79–85, 1969.

10. Kerr M., Trantow DJ: Defining, measuring, and assessing the quality of health services. *Public Health Rep* 84:415–424, 1969.

11. Klein BW: *Evaluating Outcomes of Health Services: An Annotated Bibliography* (Working paper No. 1). Los Angeles, School of Public Health, California Center for Health Services Research, University of California, 1970.

12. Shapiro S: End result measurements of quality of medical care. *Milbank Mem Fund Q* 45(2):7–30, Part I, 1967.

13. United States National Center for Health Statistics, *Vital and Health Statistics, Conceptual Problems in Developing an Index of Health* (PHS Publication No. 1000. Series 2, No. 17). Washington, DC, Government Printing Office, 1966.

14. Huntley RR, Steinhauser R, White KL, et al.: The quality of medical care: techniques and investigation in the outpatient clinic. *J Chronic Dis* 14:630–642, 1961.

15. Ciocco A, Hunt GH, Altman I: Statistics on clinical services to new patients in medical groups. *Public Health Rep* 65:99–115, 1950.

16. Morehead MA: Evaluating quality of medical care in the Neighborhood Health Center Program of the Office of Economic Opportunity. *Med Care* 8:118–131, 1970.

17. Morehead MA, Donaldson RS, Seravalli MR: Comparisons between OEO neighborhood health centers and other health care providers of ratings of the quality of health care. *Am J Pub Health* 61:1294–1306, 1971.

18. Brook RH: A Study of Methodologic Problems Associated with Assessment of Quality of Care. Thesis, Department of Medical Care and Hospitals, Johns Hopkins University, 1972.

19. *Essential Hypertension: A Strategy for Evaluating Health Services*. Edited by DM Kessner, CE Kalk, Washington, DC, National Academy of Sciences (in press).

Chapter 12

Health Accounting: An Outcome-Based System of Quality Assurance: Illustrative Application to Hypertension

John W. Williamson, Stanley Aronovitch,
Linda Simonson, Christopher Ramirez,
and Donald Kelly

This paper describes a system of quality assurance known as Health Accounting and briefly introduces its application in three early studies of diastolic hypertension at Baltimore City Hospital and Johns Hopkins Hospital, Baltimore, Md. An advanced application of Health Accounting at HMO International, a for-profit, prepaid medical-care corporation in Los Angeles, is presented in some detail.

The Health Accounting system of quality assurance developed as a collaborative effort between 23 clinics and hospitals throughout the United States and Dr. John W. Williamson and his staff at Johns Hopkins University. The project reported in this paper is one of 57 encompassed in this experience. Underlying these studies is the premise that it is important to make explicit the assumptions of causality between medical care and health results in patients.

Health Accounting is a five-stage cybernetic strategy, as shown in Figure 12-1. The first stage consists of the formulation of priorities in study topics by a team appointed from those most familiar with the clinic or hospital. Using formal procedures for small group estimates, those topics which have the most potential to improve the health of patients or reduce expenditures for medical care are selected.

Presented as part of a *Symposium on Continuing Medical Education* held by the Committee on Medical Education of the New York Academy of Medicine, October 10, 1974.

This study was supported in part by grants 5 ROI HS 00110 and 5 TOI HS 00012 and research grant PH 43-68-948 from the National Center for Health Services Research and Development, Rockville, Md., by grant 5 DO4 AH 00076 from the National Institutes of Health, Bethesda, Md., and by the Milbank Memorial Fund, New York, N.Y.

Note: Reprinted with permission from *Bulletin of the New York Academy of Medicine*, Vol. 51, No. 6, pp. 727–738, © 1975.

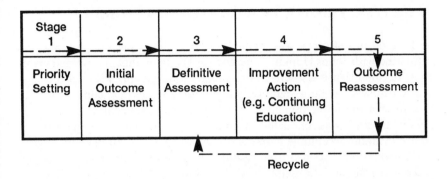

Figure 12-1 Stages of the Health Accounting Project in Its Strategy to Assure an Improved Outcome

In the second stage the outcome of medical care is initially assessed for the chosen topic. This assessment is designed by a second team of qualified staff members of the clinic with the aid of an outside specialist in a field relevant to the topic to be studied. An assessment design is developed which incorporates explicit estimates of the total benefit to health which can be causally related to the diagnostic and therapeutic medical intervention used at that facility. These estimates provide a basis for predicting the potential health impact of the study; they also provide standards for evaluating the outcome. Measures of the health results in patients are obtained in follow-up studies by an evaluation assistant called a health accountant. The health accountant is a high school graduate with perhaps 2 years of college who has demonstrated the problem-solving skills and personality characteristics required to gather data and interview patients. The results measured by the health accountant are compared with the standards previously established by the team. If serious discrepancies are found, further action in the subsequent stages of the strategy are usually recommended.

The third stage consists of more definitive evaluation studies by a variety of relevant methods to identify correctable determinants of the unsatisfactory outcomes. Again, the design is provided by staff members on the study team and the measures are made by the health accountant.

The fourth stage consists of planning and implementing a formal effort to improve the deficient outcomes. A number of educational or administrative measures might be applied.

The fifth stage consists of a replication of the original assessment of results in patients to determine whether health standards have now been met. If not, stages three, four, and five are repeated one or more times until acceptable improvement has been achieved or it is clear that any subsequent gain will not be worth the further effort required.

EARLY EXPERIENCE IN HYPERTENSION STUDIES

In 1966 this strategy was applied by Dr. Williamson in a city hospital affiliated with Johns Hopkins University.[1] The team that determined priorities decided that consecutive emergency room patients with diastolic hypertension would be a significant focus for a study of quality assurance because of the improvement in health that might be achieved. A 1 year follow-up study was conducted. Among other standards of health outcome, the maximum acceptable case-fatality rate was set at 10 percent. Figure 12-2 reveals that the measured case-fatality rate was more than double the accepted standard. Subsequent analysis indicated that much of this was attributed to a lack of follow-up care and poor compliance by patients which might have been prevented.

In 1971 Robert H. Brook evaluated an independent cohort of hypertensive patients from the same city hospital emergency room.[2] In a 5-month follow-up study, he confirmed the magnitude of the problem and the presence of similar correctable determinants. His findings are shown in Figure 12-3. Of 71 patients treated at the time of the follow-up, 46 percent had uncontrolled blood pressure because of inadequate treatment. Of the remaining 34 patients in the cohort, 56 percent had uncontrolled blood pressure due to the absence of treatment. Again, inadequate follow-up and poor compliance were the major factors involved.

In 1972 Dr. Thomas S. Inui attempted to improve the resulting health of hypertensive patients by the focussed education of physicians providing care in the medical clinics of Johns Hopkins Hospital. In a controlled evaluation study,[3] he demonstrated significantly improved compliance and follow-up care in the group of patients whose physicians received this education. Figure 12-4 shows the dramatic decrease in the number of patients with uncontrolled blood pressure after physicians attended educational programs which concentrated on the behavioral aspects of the

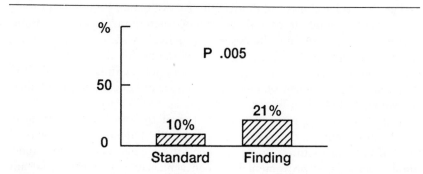

Figure 12-2 Case-Fatality Rate for Hypertension Found in a City Hospital Affiliated with Johns Hopkins University in 1966. One-Year Follow-Up by Williamson of 87 Patients

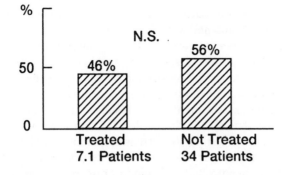

Figure 12-3 Uncontrolled Blood Pressure among an Independent Cohort of 105 Hypertensive Patients in 1971. Five Month Follow-up by Brook. (Same Hospital as in Figure 12-2)

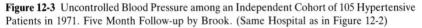

management of patients. This study won the Beryl J. Roberts Memorial Prize, which is given every 3 or 4 years by the American Public Health Association for outstanding writing in the field of public health education.

These early studies seem to support the validity of the procedure for estimating priorities. The judgment of our original study teams on the efficacy of treatment for hypertension has since been verified by the findings of the Veterans Administration cooperative studies.[4]

HMO INTERNATIONAL HYPERTENSION PROJECT

In 1972 an independent Health Accounting system of quality assurance was organized by the California Medical Group, a subsidiary of HMO International in Los Angeles. The following report describes part of their

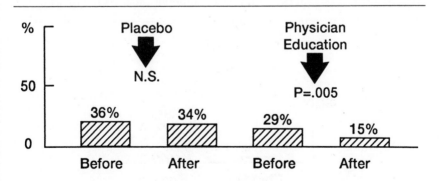

Figure 12-4 Uncontrolled Blood Pressure among 102 Hypertensive Patients in Medical Clinics of Johns Hopkins University in 1972 with and without the Education of Physicians. Two-Month Follow-up by Inui

experience with this approach in two of their 21 clinics; the results of these studies have been combined in this presentation.

In stage one a team of physicians and administrative personnel was organized to identify those assessment topics in which activity in quality assurance might produce the most improvement in the health of patients. Hypertension was one of the five topics identified.

In stage two initial assessments of the results of treatment of hypertension were done. The clinical study team decided that it was unacceptable for more than 5 percent of their hypertensive patients to have uncontrolled high blood pressure. Figure 12-5 indicates that the finding of 36 percent of patients with uncontrolled high blood pressure was seriously deficient for the 248 consecutive walk-in patients found to have hypertension in a 1-month sample.

In stage three the determinants of the deficient outcomes were analyzed more definitively, using two questionnaires administered by the health accountants; one was directed toward the physican and the other focussed on the patient. The questions were few and concentrated on those factors for which the efficacy of medical care interventions for essential hypertension were documented and established. Table 12-1 illustrates the results of some of the knowledge items on the physicians' questionnaire. None of the 14 physicians queried had inadequate textbook knowledge of hypertension pharmaceutics; all were well-informed on that subject. However, 10 were not aware of the poor compliance or poor blood pressure control of their own patients. Table 12-2 indicates that 11 of the 14 physicians failed to mention the education of patients when they listed necessary interventions for the ideal management of hypertension.

The second questionnaire containing knowledge items was directed toward the patients. The results had to be projected from the combined clinic data to a total group of 248 patients because all the patients (52) were studied in one clinic, while only a random sample (100 of 196) was

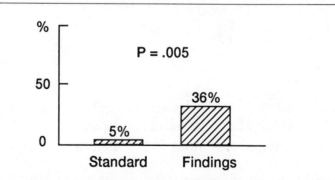

Figure 12-5 Uncontrolled Blood Pressure Found in the Initial Assessment of 248 Patients Participating in the Study by HMO International

Table 12-1 Hypertension Questionnaire of Physicians on Knowledge Items

	Physicians*
Inadequate drug information	0
Unaware danger of hypertension not related to symptoms	4
Overestimated national control of hypertension and compliance	8
Overestimated control of hypertension or compliance by his own patients	10
Total with inadequate information†	11

*N = 14
†Counting each physician only once.

studied in the second clinic. From the sample group of 61 who saw the health accountant in the second clinic, a total of 120 patients was extrapolated and added to the 28 patients who saw him in the first clinic, to obtain an extrapolated total of 148 patients seen by the health accountant in both clinics. Similarly, the group of 100 remaining extrapolated patients who saw only the physician was obtained by adding the total number of patients in the first clinic (24) and the extrapolated sample of the second clinic (39 extrapolated to 76).

Table 12-3 illustrates the projected results from knowledge items in the patients' questionnaire. Of the extrapolated 148 patients who visited the health accountant and completed the questionnaire, 23 were not aware that they had hypertension; 14 were not aware that high blood pressure is a serious health risk; 30 were unaware of the form or dosage of the drug they were receiving to control hypertension; 120 were unaware of the possible toxic effects of that drug; and 137 erroneously related the danger of hypertension to symptoms, not understanding that their first symptom

Table 12-2 Hypertension Questionnaire of Physicians on Value and Attitude Items

	Physicians*
Omitted the education of patients among aspects of ideal care for hypertension	11
Questioned the criteria for hypertension determined in a study by the Veterans Administration[4-6]	5
Rejected clinical diagnostic standards for evaluating the outcome of treatment	1
Rejected the blood pressure outcome project or the role of the health accountant[2]	1
Total who were possibly deficient	11

*N = 14

Table 12-3 Hypertension Questionnaire of Patients on Knowledge Items

	Patients*
Unaware that they had hypertension	23
Unaware that hypertension is a serious risk to health	14
Unaware of the form or dosage of the drug they were receiving to control hypertension	30
Unaware of the possible toxic effects of the drug they were receiving to control hypertension	120
Unaware that the danger of hypertension is not related only to symptoms	137
Total with inadequate information†	140

*N = 148 (extrapolated)
†Counting each patient only once

might be a preventable stroke, if not death. Table 12-4 indicates that more than half of these patients were not obtaining adequate therapy for their high blood pressure. These findings constitute a set of correctable determinants of uncontrolled hypertension, the unacceptable health outcome originally measured.

In stage four an educational effort was implemented by the health accountant. Each physician was given a specific educational prescription based on the inadequacies shown in the questionnaire. Depending on his answers, the physican was made aware of the compliance and blood pressure control rates of his own patients or was given reprints of the Veterans Administration's cooperative studies about the efficacy of hypertension treatment[4-6] or of studies based on data from the surveys of the National Center for Health Statistics, which revealed the lack of relation of levels of blood pressure to symptoms. Patients participated in a similar educational program based on those items which they answered incorrectly on the questionnaire. The health accountants had the patients return, first

Table 12-4 Hypertension Questionnaire of Patients on Behavior Items

	Patients*
Not taking any medication for hypertension	39
Taking medication for hypertension sporadically	25
Taking medication for hypertension only if symptoms occur	16
Total obtaining inadequate medication†	80

*N = 148 (extrapolated)
†Counting each patient only once

weekly and then every 6 weeks, for checks of blood pressure and re-evaluations of their understanding of and compliance with the critical items included on the questionnaire. New problems or lack of response to therapy resulted in an immediate referral to the physician.

In stage five a reassessment of health outcomes indicated that the educational effort had been an apparent success. Figure 12-6 indicates that the proportion of patients in the entire group whose blood pressure was out of control dropped from 36 percent in August 1973 to 19 percent in August 1974. Although this was a significant improvement, it still was higher than the acceptable standard set by the clinic staff. Consequently, these patients were recycled to stage three to identify other correctable factors. Here two independent groups were identified: (1) the 148 extrapolated patients who had responded to the health accountant's request to return to complete the questionnaire and participate in the educational program based on its results and (2) the 100 extrapolated patients who refused to return to fill out the questionnaire, preferring to come in only for their regular appointments with their physicians, who were therefore the main sources of their education. Figure 12-7 reveals the startling differences in improvement in the two groups. Those patients educated by the physician showed a drop from 39 percent uncontrolled to 29 percent; those educated by the health accountant dropped from 34 percent uncontrolled to 13 percent. More than twice as many patients who saw the health accountant had their hypertension brought under control. This difference in rate of improvement was statistically significant at the $p = 0.05$ level.

DISCUSSION

These findings do not establish any solid causal relation to explain the improvement noted. However, they do provide a more specific delineation

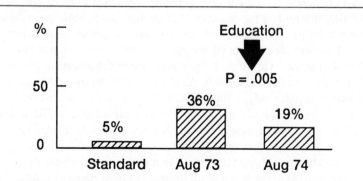

Figure 12-6 Uncontrolled Blood Pressure Found in a 1-Year Follow-up of 248 Patients Participating in the Study by HMO International

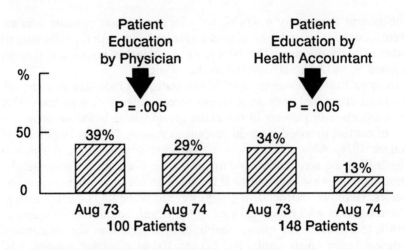

Figure 12-7 Uncontrolled Blood Pressure Found in a 1-Year Follow-up Recycle of 248 Patients Participating in the Study by HMO International

of where future effort might be directed to achieve further improvement and consolidate the gains made. The California Medical Group plans to implement the Health Accounting hypertension program in six additional clinics and, if equally successful, throughout their clinical system.

This report has examined only one of eight high-priority topics being approached in this fashion. In these other areas the same five-stage cybernetic system of Health Accounting is being applied and its impact is being measured in terms of the improved health of patients. This overall quality assurance system will be expanded gradually to encompass an increasingly larger number of patients in areas where assessment of present practice indicates that a substantial improvement in health might be possible.

This experience has again confirmed the practicability of the Health Accounting method in the assurance of quality. Systematic consideration of causal relations between medical care and outcomes in the health of patients has provided a crucial means of cutting through the enormous number of irrelevant variables so often included in the assessment of quality and continuing medical education. As illustrated in the questionnaires used in our hypertension study, a limited number of items related to the critical behavior of physicans and patients can have an impact in terms of improved health. These studies represent the application of specific educational prescriptions based on educational diagnoses resulting from studies of quality assessment; this is in sharp contrast to many traditional courses in continuing education, where it is not at all unusual to hear papers on topics such as "Changes Caused by Hydroxy-6 Dopamine and Alpha Methyl P-Tyrosine in the Tachyphylactic Effect of Indirect Sympathometics on Perfused and Isolated Organs of Rats." While such topics may be of use to some practitioners, the more relevant topics of the compliance of patients and inadequate follow-up are too often neglected. Health Accounting thus far has proved successful in focusing efforts in assessment and education on relevant variables that are more likely to facilitate the improved health of patients. The exciting potential of exploiting this strategy remains a challenge for all future effort in these fields.

NOTES

1. Williamson, J.W.: Evaluating quality of patient care: A strategy relating outcome and process assessment. *J.A.M.A.* 213:564–69, 1971.

2. Brook, R.H.: *Quality of Care Assessment: A Comparison of Five Methods of Peer Review.* DHEW Pub. No. HRA-74-3100. Washington, D.C., Department of Health, Education, and Welfare, 1973.

3. Inui, T.S.: *Effects of Post-Graduate Physician Education on the Management and Outcomes of Patients with Hypertension.* Thesis, Baltimore, The Johns Hopkins University, 1973.

4. Veterans Administration Cooperative Study Group on Antihypertensive Agents: Effects of treatment on morbidity in hypertension, pt 1. *J.A.M.A.* 202:1028–34, 1967.

5. Veterans Administration Cooperative Study Group on Antihypertensive Agents: Effects of treatment on morbidity in hypertension, pt 2: Results in patients with diastolic pressure averaging 90 through 114 mm. Hg. *J.A.M.A.* 213:1143–52, 1970.

6. Veterans Administration Cooperative Study Group on Antihypertensive Agents: Effects of treatment on morbidity in hypertension, pt 3: Influence of age, diastolic pressure and prior cardiovascular disease: Further analysis of side-effects. *Circulation* 45:991–1004, 1972.

Chapter 13

Academia and Clinic: An Evaluation of Outcome from Intensive Care in Major Medical Centers

William A. Knaus, Elizabeth A. Draper,
Douglas P. Wagner, and Jack E. Zimmerman

Intensive care began with the concentration of acutely ill, postoperative patients in one room of a hospital where they could be closely watched. As new monitoring, treatment, and surgical procedures became available, hospitals increased their number of intensive care units, expanded requisites for admission, and increasingly relied on specially trained staff to provide care.[1]

Today, intensive care units appear in virtually all acute care hospitals in the United States and their staffs treat patients who receive medical or surgical care for various diseases. The diversity of diseases and differing arrangements among hospitals for providing such care, however, have limited the precision of evaluation.[1-3]

In response to this need for precision, we developed a severity of disease classification system to estimate the pretreatment risk of death in severely ill patients. In previous multi-institutional and international studies, data from the Acute Physiology and Chronic Health Evaluation (APACHE) system showed strong and stable relationships between severity of illness and subsequent probability of death from various diseases commonly treated in medical and surgical intensive care units.[4-10] We have refined and simplified this system into the APACHE II, which uses information from fewer, readily available measurements but maintains the accuracy of the original system.[11] As suggested by Horwitz and Feinstein,[12] the system is designed to stratify patients prognostically by risk so that different treatment programs can be more accurately compared.

Using the information on the risk factors of acute physiologic disorders, chronic health status, and age that is classified by the APACHE II system,

From the ICU Research Unit and the Departments of Anesthesiology and Computer Medicine, The George Washington University Medical Center; Washington, D.C.

Note: Reprinted from *Annals of Internal Medicine*, Vol. 104, pp. 410–418, with permission of American College of Physicians, © 1986.

along with information on other factors such as diagnosis, indication for admission, and surgical status, we compared treatment courses and outcomes of patients in intensive care units at 13 hospitals. All hospitals had similar technical capabilities in their units but differed in organization, staffing, commitment to teaching, research, and education. We then examine whether these substantial differences in the structure and process of intensive care[3] influenced effectiveness of care, as measured by hospital mortality rates.

METHODS

Hospital Data

Table 13-1 lists the 13 hospitals in alphabetical order. Each responded to a written request to participate in the study; they therefore were self-selected. The criterion for participation was that they provide resources necessary for data collection on a minimum of 150 unselected patients admitted to intensive care units. In one hospital, data were collected for 27 months from 1979 to 1981. In all other hospitals, data were collected

Table 13-1 Characteristics of 13 Hospitals with 19 Medical and Surgical Intensive Care Units (ICU)

Hospital	Total Hospital Beds	Total Adult ICU Beds	Adult ICU Patients in Study	Type of ICU Studied
	←	n	→	
Cooper Medical Center (New Jersey)	522	14	14	Mixed medical, surgical
George Washington University Medical Center (Washington, D.C.)	511	24	16	Mixed medical, surgical
Medical College of Georgia	706	21	6	Medical
Johns Hopkins University (Maryland)	1025	36	7	Medical
Maine Medical Center	533	32	20	Mixed medical, surgical
University of Maryland Hospital	729	31	10	Surgical
Massachusetts General Hospital	1092	90	20	Surgical (2 units)
Polyclinic Medical Center (Pennsylvania)	556	14	6	Mixed medical, surgical
St. Francis Hospital (Oklahoma)	802	40	16	Mixed medical, surgical
South Shore Hospital (Massachusetts)	280	28	16	Surgical; mixed medical, surgical (2 units)
Stanford University Hospital (California)	633	65	57	Medical, surgical, cardiac surgery (3 units)
University of Virginia Medical Center	683	44	16	Surgical
University of Wisconsin Hospital	548	36	32	Medical; surgical, mixed medical, surgical (3 units)

for 2 to 10 months (average, 5 months) in 1982. Multiple units in four hospitals were examined as single entities because they had only minor differences in methods of operation. We did not include coronary care units in the study.

After a hospital was chosen for participation, a questionnaire on the nature and practice of the intensive care unit was completed by the unit's medical or nursing director. Questions were answered on staffing, organization, policies, procedures, educational affiliation, and extent of the critical care personnel's participation in patient care. Visits to each of the units confirmed the validity of the responses.

We then classified each hospital's intensive care unit by level of administration, as defined by the National Institutes of Health (NIH) Consensus Conference on Critical Care.[1] Assignment was made by two of the authors after visiting the units and reviewing the questionnaire. This classification was reviewed by a third observer after reading the questionnaires. In short, level I units had physician directors or qualified designees in the unit at all times, high nurse to patient ratios, and in-unit teaching and research commitments. Level II units had full- or part-time physician directors with qualified designees available in the hospital, and high to intermediate nurse to patient ratios. Level III units had designated part-time physician directors but relied on coverage by other in-house physicians and had lower but variable nurse to patient ratios. These assignments were based on administrative structure, not technical capability. All units had similar technologic abilities and could, when required, provide nurse to patient care on a one-to-one basis. Teaching hospitals were those with formal, close affiliations with medical schools; full-time residency training programs in internal medicine, surgery, and anesthesia; and regular patient care responsibilities for residents within the units.

Patient Data

Data were collected on either consecutive patients admitted to participating units or on a sample of every second or third patient until a specified number of patients was reached. These two sampling methods were used because the frequency of admissions of some of the hospitals was too high for one data collector to obtain accurate information on consecutive patients.

Excluded from the study were patients less than 16 years of age and patients with acute burns. Although information was collected on all patients who had coronary artery bypass grafts, these patients were also excluded from analysis because they represent a homogeneous group of patients whose outcome has been carefully scrutinized.

Information about each patient included age, sex, indication for admission to an intensive care unit, operative status (either postoperative for patients admitted directly to the unit from the operating or recovery room or nonoperative for all others), specific diagnosis, and daily therapeutic intervention (TISS) score. The treatment score gives a summary measurement of intensity and type of unit care.[13] To reflect the nature of treatment provided, we divided the 90 treatment courses used in this scoring system into categories of active treatment (for example, the use of ventilator and vasoactive drugs), unit monitoring (use of arterial or pulmonary artery catheters), and standard floor care (blood testing, intake and output).[14]

After patients had been in the unit for 24 hours, each clinical record was reviewed for physiologic data that would permit prognostic stratification using the APACHE II system.[11] The approach the APACHE system used to classify severity of disease was derived from general physiologic principles,[15-19] not from searching a data base, and its validity and reliability have been tested extensively.[4-9] The APACHE II system works as reliably as APACHE, but has the advantage of only requiring standard information on 12 routine physiologic measurements along with the patient's age and chronic health status.[11] This method eliminates the problem of missing values—a criticism of the original system.[20,21] Detailed definitions for the components of APACHE II are provided in Figure 13-1.

All data were recorded on standard forms and sent to a central location for editing, extensive error checking, and analysis. Strauss and colleagues[22] have reported a high degree of interobserver reliability for the APACHE system in prospective and retrospective data collection. Reported patient outcomes were also independently verified by cross-checking against hospital discharge summaries.

Analysis

In comparing the effectiveness of care in the intensive care unit, we used death in the hospital as a measurement of outcome. Although this determination excludes important considerations such as the quality and length of survival, we contend that differences in death rates can reflect specific and important differences in effectiveness of patient care.

For each patient, we estimated the probability of survival using a multiple logistic regression analysis[23] that included the patient's disease and first-day APACHE II score and information on whether the patient had come to the unit immediately after elective or emergency surgery. Diagnostic categories were specified by the most frequent appearance of 34 individual precipitating factors or causes prompting admission to a unit, combined

PHYSIOLOGIC VARIABLE	HIGH ABNORMAL RANGE				0	LOW ABNORMAL			
	+4	+3	+2	+1	0	+1	+2	+3	+4
TEMPERATURE - rectal (°C)	≥41°	39°-40.9°		38.5°-38.9°	36°-38.4°	34°-35.9°	32°-33.9°	30°-31.9°	≤29.9°
MEAN ARTERIAL PRESSURE - mm Hg	≥160	130-159	110-129		70-109		50-69		≤49
HEART RATE (ventricular response)	≥180	140-179	110-139		70-109		55-69	40-54	≤39
RESPIRATORY RATE - (non-ventilated or ventilated)		35-49		25-34	12-24	10-11	6-9		≤5
OXYGENATION: $A-aDO_2$ or PaO_2 - (mm Hg) a. FIO_2 >0.5 record $A-aDO_2$	≥500	350-499	200-349		<200				
b. $FIO2$ < 0.5 record only PaO_2					PO_2>70	PO_2 61-70		PO_2 55-60	PO_2<55
ARTERIAL pH	≥7.7	7.6-7.69		7.5-7.59	7.33-7.49		7.25-7.32	7.15-7.24	<7.15
SERUM SODIUM (mMol/L)	≥180	160-179	155-159	150-154	130-149		120-129	111-119	≤110
SERUM POTASSIUM (mMol/L)	≥7	6-6.9		5.5-5.9	3.5-5.4	3-3.4	2.5-2.9		<2.5
SERUM CREATININE (mg/100 ml) (Double point score for acute renal failure)	≥3.5	2-3.4	1.5-1.9		0.6-1.4		<0.6		
HEMATOCRIT (%)	≥60		50-59.9	46-49.9	30-45.9		20-29.9		<20

WHITE BLOOD COUNT (total/mm3) (in 1,000s)	○ ≥40		○ 20-39.9	○ 15-19.9	○ 3-14.9		○ 1-2.9		○ <1

GLASGOW COMA SCORE (GCS)
Score = 15 minus actual GCS

A Total ACUTE PHYSIOLOGY SCORE (APS):
Sum of the 12 individual variable points

Serum HCO_3 (venous-mMol /L) (Not preferred, use if no ABGs)	○ ≥52	○ 41-51.9		○ 32-40.9	○ 22-31.9		○ 18-21.9	○ 15-17.9	○ <15

B AGE POINTS:
Assign points to age as follows:

AGE(yrs)	Points
≤ 44	0
45-54	2
55-64	3
65-74	5
≥75	6

C CHRONIC HEALTH POINTS
If the patient has a history of severe organ system insufficiency or is immunocompromised, assign points as follows:
a. for nonoperative or emergency postoperative patients — 5 points
or
b. for elective postoperative patients — 2 points

DEFINITIONS
Organ insufficiency or immunocompromised state must have been evident prior to this hospital admission and conform to the following criteria:

LIVER: Biopsy proven cirrhosis and documented portal hypertension;episodes of past upper GI bleeding attributed to portal hypertension; or prior episodes of hepatic failure/encephalopathy/coma.

CARDIOVASCULAR: New York Heart Association Class IV.

RESPIRATORY: Chronic restrictive, obstructive, or vascular disease resulting in severe exercise restriction, i.e., unable to climb stairs or perform household duties; or documented chronic hypoxia, hypercapnia, secondary polycythemia, severe pulmonary hypertension (>40mmHg), or respirator dependency.

RENAL: Receiving chronic dialysis.

IMMUNOCOMPROMISED: The patient has received therapy that suppresses resistance to infection, e.g., immunosuppression, chemotherapy, radiation, long-term or recent high dose steroids, or has a disease that is sufficiently advanced to suppress resistance to infection, e.g., leukemia, lymphoma, AIDS.

APACHE II SCORE
Sum of **A** + **B** + **C** :

A APS points _____
B Age points _____
C Chronic Health points _____

Total APACHE II _____

Figure 13-1 Acute Physiology and Chronic Health Evaluation (APACHE) II System for Classifying Severity of Disease

with the major organ system (such as cardiovascular or respiratory) affected by the disease.[11]

Figure 13-2 illustrates the precision of this method of pretreatment risk stratification, which tabulates observed and predicted death rates for patients within three points of APACHE II scores. For patients with APACHE II scores of less than 3, observed and predicted death rates are 2 percent. For patients with scores greater than 40, the observed death rate was 93.9 percent compared with a predicted rate of 93.3 percent. Figure 13-2 also shows that, throughout the entire range of disease severity, rates derived from this method of individual risk stratification closely resemble actual death rates. To calculate a projected group death rate, we added individual patient estimates for each hospital using the APACHE II scoring system.[11] We then divided this sum by the total number of patients, compared the resulting ratios of projected and actual death rates,[24] and ranked each hospital correspondingly.

Using a multivariate logistic regression analysis, which had controls for the influence of APACHE II, emergency surgery status, and operative and nonoperative diagnoses, we tested for overall significance of differences in mortality rates across the 13 hospitals studied (chi square, 12 degrees of freedom). We tested differences in two ways. First, we used a t-test to determine the difference between the means of the observed and predicted death rates for each hospital. Second, the significance of the impact of

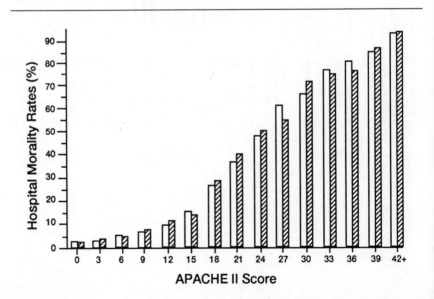

Figure 13-2 Acute Physiology and Chronic Health Evaluation (APACHE) II Scores and Mortality Rates in 5,030 Consecutive Patients Admitted to Intensive Care Units at 13 Hospitals. Actual (*shaded bars*) and predicted (*open bars*) mortality rates are indicated; $r = 0.995$.

individual hospitals was tested with partial chi-square tests (1 degree of freedom) after controlling for all the prognostic factors listed above. Hospitals selected as significantly different were compared with a reference group of all the hospitals that were not significantly different, with statistical significance defined as $p \leq 0.01$. After this comparison of outcomes, we examined how each hospital's structure and process of intensive care related to its overall performance, an analysis that follows closely the method suggested by Williamson.[25]

RESULTS

The age distribution and percentage of patients in severely failing health before hospitalization were similar at all 13 hospitals. For most units, cardiovascular-related diagnoses such as cardiac arrest, septic shock, or peripheral vascular disorders were the commonest reasons for nonoperative and postoperative admission.[11] With the exception of selected surgical procedures, differences in the frequency of individual diagnoses across the 13 hospitals were not substantial. The number of patients in the study ranged from 159 to 1,657 per hospital (Table 13-2), but only one hospital had more than 500 patients.

Outcome of Care: Predicted and Actual Mortality Rates

Table 13-2 contrasts projected and observed death rates for the 5,030 patients by ranking the 13 hospitals according to their ratio of actual to predicted deaths. This listing does not correspond to the alphabetic listing in Table 13-1 because each hospital's performance is confidential. A ratio of close to 1 implies the hospital's performance approximates the average for the sample, meaning that actual and estimated death rates are similar. A ratio of less than 1 implies an above average performance and a ratio of greater than 1, lower than average. The relative ability in two hospitals to treat acutely ill patients differed significantly. Hospital 1 did significantly better ($p < 0.001$) than all other hospitals, with a death rate 41 percent lower than predicted. Hospital 13 did significantly worse ($p < 0.01$), with 58 percent more deaths than predicted.

The overall influence of individual hospitals on outcome was highly significant (chi square = 62.9, with 12 degrees of freedom; $p < 0.0001$), when controlled for APACHE II scores, medical and postsurgical diagnoses, and emergency surgery status. Most important, outcomes in Hospitals 1 and 13 differed significantly ($p < 0.0001$) from those in a reference group of ten hospitals. Hospital 4 had a better outcome than the remaining

Table 13-2 Comparison of Actual and Predicted Hospital Deaths in 5,030 Patients in Intensive Care Units at 13 Hospitals

Hospital Performance Ranking	Total Patients	Hospital Mortality Rate	Nonoperative Patients			All Patients		
			Actual Deaths	Predicted Deaths*	Mortality Ratio	Actual Deaths	Predicted Deaths	Mortality Ratio
	n	%	n	n		n	n	
1	365	11.2	30	46	0.65†	41	69	0.59†
2‡	201	20.4	32	34	0.93	41	49	0.84
3‡	159	18.9	20	23	0.87	30	34	0.88
4	201	38.3	77	86	0.90	77	86	0.90§
5	500	9.8	20	17	1.18	49	53	0.92
6	426	8.9	21	21	1.00	38	41	0.93
7	412	17.2	54	58	0.93	71	74	0.96
8	198	19.7	33	37	0.94	39	39	1.00
9	1657	24.1	269	263	1.02	400	383	1.04
10	366	14.8	20	15	1.33	54	49	1.10
11	170	26.5	39	34	1.14	45	40	1.13
12	178	31.5	44	37	1.18	56	44	1.27
13‡	197	26.4	38	21	1.81†	52	33	1.58†

*Predicted deaths were computed as the sum of individual risks with a multiple logistic regression equation. Nonoperative predicted deaths were computed from a separate analysis of those patients.

†$p < 0.01$. Computed as a t-test of the difference between two means. An alternate analysis, including institutional effects in the estimated logistic regression equation, yielded similar differences and larger significance levels for each hospital (chi square = 24.6, $p < 0.0001$ for Hospital 1; chi square = 15.4, $p < 0.0001$ for Hospital 13).

‡Nonteaching hospitals.

§p = 0.03, chi square = 4.6 in the multivariate logistic regression equation.

ten hospitals but with a significance level ($p = 0.03$) greater than our statistical threshold.

We also evaluated the relative performance of the 13 hospitals for non-operative admissions alone. As shown in Table 13-3, the ratio of observed to predicted deaths for these 2,314 patients was consistent with that for all patients combined (correlation coefficient = 0.91). The only exceptions occurred in Hospitals 5 and 10 where the surgical units accepted and treated a small number of nonoperative patients. The resulting mortality ratios for these patients, 1.18 for Hospital 5 and 1.33 for Hospital 10, were greater than the total mortality ratios but were based on outcome in too few patients to represent valid exceptions.

Finally, we compared outcomes in all hospitals within six of the more frequently appearing diagnostic categories—four nonoperative and two postoperative (Table 13-3). Within each of these categories, the relative performance of the 13 hospitals is consistent with their overall ranking. Although the number of patients from a single hospital within a specific diagnostic group was too small for standard significance testing, hospitals with better overall performance rankings had fewer than predicted deaths

Table 13-3 Comparison of Actual and Predicted Hospital Deaths within Diagnostic Categories for 5,030 Patients in Intensive Care Units at 13 Hospitals

Hospital Performance Ranking	Patients with Diagnosis	Actual Deaths	Predicted Deaths
	←——————————— *n* ———————————→		
Postcardiopulmonary arrest			
1	21	4	11
4	40	28	27
7	19	8	10
8	16	8	8
9	65	46	44
13	9	4	3
Septic shock			
1	10	3	6
3	5	3	3
6	12	3	4
9	69	45	44
12	11	7	6
Gastrointestinal bleeding (nonoperative)			
2	11	1	3
4	11	4	4
5	10	4	3
11	14	7	5
13	15	6	3
Pneumonia respiratory failure			
4	18	7	7
9	66	24	27
11	11	4	3
12	11·	6	3
13	7	4	3
Peripheral vascular disorders (postoperative)			
1	61	2	4
3	34	1	2
5	176	5	9
9	71	9	7
10	40	3	3
13	21	3	2
Gastrointestinal perforation or obstruction (postoperative)			
1	8	2	3
2	7	1	3
6	23	1	4
9	32	17	15
13	10	5	4

in individual diagnostic categories, whereas hospitals with lower rankings generally had more than predicted.

Structure of Care

Use of Unit

We examined the relationship between the proportion of severely ill patients a hospital treated and that hospital's performance using an APACHE II score of greater than 15 as the threshold for defining a moderate degree of severity. For a nonoperative 60-year-old patient, an APACHE II score of 16 corresponds to a hospital death rate of 25 percent and usually indicates the need for active support of at least one major organ system. For a 60-year-old postoperative patient, an APACHE II score of 16 usually implies a mortality rate of 12 percent and a requirement for unique monitoring or treatment.

All 13 hospitals treated a substantial number of patients with a score of at least 15. Hospital 6 had the lowest proportion of patients with scores in this category, but 27 percent of its nonoperative patients still had scores in this range or higher. Hospital 4 had the greatest proportion, with 72 percent of its nonoperative patients scoring greater than 15. The proportion of patients at each hospital with scores greater than 15 did not correlate with its overall performance ranking.

At each hospital, however, the ratio of predicted to observed mortality for these severely ill patients matched its performance with the entire sample of patients. Similar to the results obtained with medical and surgical patients and within specific diagnostic categories (Tables 13-3 and 13-4), these findings suggest that the differences in outcome were not limited to one particular diagnostic or surgical group or to level of severity of illness, but involved several categories of patients.

Administration of Unit

Table 13-4 lists the self-reported organizational characteristics of individual units. Most units had designated full-time directors, but the amount of involvement and control these directors had with respect to admission, discharge, and treatment decisions differed, as did 24-hour, in-unit physician coverage. Only two level I units, Hospitals 1 and 4, gave complete control over admission, discharge, and most treatment decisions to full-time physician staff. In most hospitals, these responsibilities were shared with the attending physician on an individual patient basis. The two level III units, Hospitals 3 and 13, had no mechanisms for the unit director

Table 13-4 Structure and Process of Services Given in Intensive Care Units at 13 Hospitals

Hospital Performance	Full-time Unit Director	Controls Decision for Patient Therapy	Controls Decision for Admission/ Discharge	24-Hour In-Unit Physician Coverage	Consistent Senior Charge Nurse	Continuity of Care/ Primary Nursing	Problems with Adequate Nurse Staffing
Level I							
1*	Yes	Director/ staff	Director/ staff	Yes	Yes	Yes	None
4	Yes	Director/ staff	Director/ staff	Yes	Yes	Yes	None
5	Yes	Shared†	Director/ staff	Yes	Yes	No	None
6	Yes	Director/ staff	Shared	Yes	Yes	Yes	Minor‡
7	Yes	Shared	Shared	Yes	Yes	Yes	None
9	Yes	Shared	Director/ staff	Yes	Yes	Yes	Minor
10	Yes	Shared	Director/ staff	Yes	Yes	Yes	None
11	Yes	Shared	Director/ staff	Yes	Yes	Yes	Minor
12	Yes	Shared	Director/ staff	Yes	Yes	Yes	Minor
Level II							
2§	Yes	Shared	Attending physician only	Yes	Yes	Yes	Minor
8	No	Shared	Attending physician only	No	Yes	No	Minor
Level III							
3§	No	Attending physician only	Attending physician only	No	Yes	Yes	Minor
13*§	No	Attending physician only	Attending physician only	No	No	No	Major

*Indicates that standardized mortality rate significantly different ($p < 0.01$) from all others.
†Shared indicates that therapy or admission/discharge decisions are shared jointly by attending physician and director/staff.
‡All hospitals listed as having minor difficulties had organized contingency plans.
§Nonteaching hospitals.

to influence therapy, and all care was directed by primary attending physicians.

Most hospitals had experienced senior nurses who were consistently designated as charge nurses for each shift (Table 13-4). Most also had formal training programs for new nurses and continuing education for all nurses. All but one provided continuity of patient care through a system of primary nursing or its equivalent and had written provisions for dealing with nursing shortages.

The average mortality ratios of the nine level I units and the two level II or level III units were not statistically different. Also, we found no significant difference between the average mortality ratios of all teaching hospitals and nonteaching hospitals.

Process of Care

Amount and Type of Treatment

The total number of daily therapeutic intervention points given during the stay, when adjusted for the type and severity of illness of the patients treated, was similar at 12 of the 13 hospitals. Hospital 1, however, had an average of 40 percent more points per patient, even after controlling for diagnosis and severity of illness. This average differed significantly (t-ratio $= 4.74$, $p < 0.01$) from that in the other hospitals.

Examination of the type of treatment given showed that the proportion of points reflecting active treatment or invasive hemodynamic monitoring did not differ substantially for any of the units. Even when the hospitals were examined for individual variations in the use of pulmonary artery catheters and other invasive monitoring techniques, no substantial differences were found.

The major portion of increased therapy given at Hospital 1 came from frequent laboratory testing, dressing changes, and chest physiotherapy, which resulted from extensive reliance on clinical protocol and not from increased use of unique technologies such as ventilators or pulmonary artery catheters. In fact, controlling for categories of diagnosis and severity of illness of patients treated, Hospital 1 had one of the lowest utilization rates of pulmonary artery catheters in this sample.

Interaction and Coordination of Staff

Measuring and analyzing how treatment was provided is more difficult than evaluating the type of treatment. Nevertheless, we found substantial differences in the interaction and coordination of the intensive care teams among the 13 hospitals. These differences are shown best by contrasting individual hospitals, primarily Hospitals 1, 3, 4, and 13.

Hospital 1 relied on carefully designed clinical protocol implemented by senior level in-unit physicians. This hospital also had the most comprehensive nursing educational support system. Clinical specialists with Masters' degrees and extensive experience in intensive care units had as their primary responsibility the orientation and development of the nursing staff. Educational programs were targeted not only to the staff nurse as a care giver but also to the charge nurse as a manager. As a result of this educational program, the nursing staff at Hospital 1 had independent responsibilities within the clinical protocols. Excellent communication between physicians and nursing staff was ongoing to ensure that all patient care needs were met. For example, Hospital 1 was the only institution that had a routine policy to cancel major elective surgery if adequate unit nursing staff was not available—a decision that could be made by the unit nurse in charge. A similar degree of respect extended to other physician and nurse interactions.

Hospital 4 was the only other unit besides Hospital 1 that had all elements of structure and process graded positive (Table 13-4). This large teaching hospital also had a high degree of coordination of care among its intensive care staff, although it did not make use of clinical protocols. Hospital 4 was the hospital in which the mortality ratio (actual to predicted deaths) might have been significantly lower had we sampled a larger number of patients (Table 13-2).

Hospital 3, a nonteaching hospital without a full-time director, had no system for the part-time unit director to influence admission, discharge, or treatment decisions, and no clinical protocols were used. The nursing staff at this unit, however, did have an extensive educational program and cooperated closely with the private attending staff. On rounds each day, physicians at Hospital 3 met with their patients with both the patient's primary nurse and the charge nurse so that immediate and long-range goals could be established. The private attending staff was available to the nursing staff for consultations during the day, most had offices close to the hospital, and both admission and discharge decisions and treatment choices were discussed frequently.

Hospital 13, the other level III unit in our study, also had no dedicated unit physician staff to direct admission, discharge, or treatment policy. Unlike Hospital 3, however, Hospital 13 also lacked a comprehensive nursing organization and functioned without a consistent centralized nursing authority, formal educational program, or provision for continuity of patient care through primary nursing or other form of staff assignment. Also during this study, admitting physicians and unit nursing staff communicated poorly. No policy was established for routine discussion of patient treatment, and there was no direct coordination of staff capabilities with clinical demands. Frequent disagreements about the ability of the nursing staff to treat additional patients occurred, and there was an atmosphere of distrust. During the study, there were also staff shortages that necessitated care by nurses who were not trained in the intensive care unit.

Although the differences in interaction and coordination of intensive care in these four hospitals were the most dramatic found, contrasts in other hospitals also supported their relative rankings. Hospitals 2 and 12, for example, had very similar administrative characteristics in their units

(Table 13-4). At Hospital 2, however, information gathered from the questionnaire and the visit showed that the unit directors not only worked closely with the nursing staff but also had close, comfortable relationships with most of the admitting physicians. This hospital had a commitment to improving the quality of its tertiary care services. At Hospital 12, communication between physicians about patient care was frequently difficult and incomplete, apparently because of personality differences and the lack of an institutional structure in which to resolve them.

DISCUSSION

In comparing the outcomes in 5,030 patients from 13 hospitals, we found important differences between predicted and observed death rates for both nonoperative patients only and for all patients, as well as differences within specific diagnostic categories. These differences appeared to relate to the interaction and communication between physicians and nurses.

Our results support the belief that involvement and interaction of critical care personnel can directly influence outcome from intensive care.[26] In addition, a high level of intensive care can be provided by hospitals lacking a full-time, dedicated intensive care physician team if adequate attention is given to unit coordination, especially coordination between nursing and physician staffs. The highest quality of care, however, appears to require a high degree of involvement by both dedicated physicians and nurses in ongoing clinical care.

The findings also indicate that the use of invasive technologies for better patient care, although important, is not sufficient.[21] All hospitals in this study had similar technical capabilities and used invasive monitoring, ventilator therapy, and other specialized intensive care treatment with similar frequency.

Indications from visits to the hospitals and reviews of individual patient records supported our findings that differences in the process of care influenced outcome. Reviews of individual records at Hospital 13 showed a pattern of difficulty with the care of patients requiring long-term ventilation and frequent complications related to invasive procedures. Hospital 1 showed a consistent, coordinated response to patients' needs and a division of responsibility among physicians and nurses that precluded many problems. Results of these differences in process of care are reflected in Tables 13-2 and 13-3, which show consistent differences between predicted and actual outcome for various diagnostic categories as well as for total patients treated.

These results specifically suggest that the reduced mortality ratios in some units, as compared with others, are not limited to a single diagnostic category or level of severity of illness. Li and colleagues[21] previously reported that full-time physician staffing of an intensive care unit appeared to improve outcome only for patients in the mid-range level of severity of illness. This limitation implies that some patients are too ill to benefit, regardless of treatment, and others so stable that intensive treatment is not essential for survival. Although we do not disagree with this contention, our ability to rank a larger number of patients from many hospitals into more precise risk strata suggests that some patients at a very high risk of death as well as some at low risk may have different outcomes depending on where they are treated. These findings also are consistent with our hypothesis that outcomes differ due to the influence of unit staff interaction and coordination, and not to specific therapy used.

Possible Confounding Variables

The possibility that our findings could be attributed to other confounding variables that were not examined never can be excluded with certainty, but we think the probability is extremely small. The approach to stratification by risk used in this study is an improvement over previous attempts because it uses individually determined risks, incorporating information on both diagnosis and acute severity of disease. This approach has been shown to be more precise in estimating group death rates than using either diagnostic information alone or combining diagnostic information with mean physiologic values—one traditional way of contrasting patient groups.[8,12]

The severity of illness scoring system used, APACHE II, is objective and, when based on first-day data as was done in this study, independent of subsequent therapeutic decisions. It also was designed independent of this analysis. Identical results are obtained using the 33-physiologic-variable acute physiology score (APS) from the original APACHE system.[4] The logistic regression analysis used to compute estimated death rates works equally well in estimation and validation data using randomly split halves of the 5,030-patient data base.

We did not collect information describing severity of illness and therapy used either before or after treatment in the intensive care unit. Because the prognosis of many disorders in patients commonly admitted to these units depends on treatment before and after admission, this lack of data may be important. If treatment before admission varied among the 13 hospitals, however, the differences would have influenced the patient's severity of illness at admission. For example, if cardiopulmonary resuscitation had been poorly done or significantly delayed at 1 hospital, when compared with others, the patients would have been more hemodynamically unstable or have had a greater depression in the level of consciousness at admission. These differences would have been incorporated into the first-day APACHE II score, resulting in a higher estimated death rate.

To analyze the possible influence of differences in post-unit treatment, we compared each hospital's performance using unit rather than hospital death rates. Unit death rates are subject to the individual discharge and triage decisions of the units and are not as accurate as hospital rates. In this study, however, a separate analysis using unit death rates gave results similar to those in Table 13-2, with results from Hospitals 1 and 13 still significantly different from the norm.

Our reliance on hospital mortality rates, however, does ignore the possibility that one hospital might have been able to discharge patients with poor short-term prognoses sooner than other hospitals. A lower than predicted hospital mortality ratio would then have resulted, but little change would have occurred in overall quality of care. Only patient status after discharge from the hospital can adequately address this concern. Such information is not available for all hospitals, but a preliminary comparison of the status of patients 6 months after discharge from Hospitals 1 and 9 suggests no significant differences in long-term outcome.

Patient selection may also bias results. Although most differences in patient risk should have been found by diagnosis and APACHE II scoring, some units may have systematically excluded patients with especially poor prognoses or, conversely, admitted many patients to the unit for monitoring but not active treatment.[14] However, we reanalyzed the data after excluding from analysis all patients who had not received one or more unique active treatments in the unit and found results in Table 13-2 unchanged. The best way to examine selection by patient prognosis is to compare predicted and actual death rates for all patients eligible for intensive care, not just those ultimately selected. We lack such information, but none of the hospitals in this study had formal policies excluding patients with especially high severity of illness scores or poor prognoses.

Finally, to ensure that the hospital with the largest number of patients (Hospital 9) did not unduly influence results, we re-estimated results from a predictive equation excluding this hospital and recomputed predicted death rates. The results were identical to those reported in Table 13-2.

In summary, we could find no measurement biases that would have systematically favored one hospital over another. Therefore, we are confident that the results represent real differences in therapeutic efficacy that are related to differences in the process of care and, specifically, to the interaction and coordination of the unit staff.

Volume, Organization, Cost, and Teaching Status

Important institutional differences exist in the effectiveness of intensive care because its practice grew rapidly, with little scientific agreement about when and how to use its various techniques.[1] Many of these techniques, however, are complex, dangerous, and require skillful titration by knowledgeable nurses and physicians working closely together.

In a comparison of neonatal intensive care units, Paneth and colleagues[27] reported an association between treatment at highly organized neonatal care centers and decreased mortality rates for infants who had low birth weights. They suggested that coordination of care was also important in achieving good results. Baxt and Moody,[28] in comparing outcomes of trauma patients transported to hospitals by helicopter or land evacuation, concluded that the greater survival rates in the helicopter group were conceivably also due to "the continuity and standardization of care afforded by the highly trained physician/nurse teams"; in contrast, rotating physician/nurse teams were assigned to the land evacuation group.

In these studies, as in this survey, it was difficult to separate the relative contributions of volume of patients treated and staff interaction when comparing outcomes.[29] Realistically, the two are closely related, but a large volume of patients does not necessarily mean relatively fewer deaths. The results of this study emphasize the importance of the process of care— specifically, the interaction of physicians and nurses in achieving optimal results.

Although the number of teaching hospitals in this study is small, our findings also suggest that intensive care units do not have uniform results among large teaching hospitals. Large tertiary care teaching hospitals, although generally treating a greater number of severely ill patients and doing more complex operations, may not achieve optimal results based solely on teaching status. These hospitals must develop highly coordinated systems for management of their patients, similar to the one used in Hospital 1.

The incremental cost of implementing that quality of care is still uncertain and we would emphasize caution before any conclusions can be drawn. Hospital 1 clearly used the most resources of all hospitals studied. No statistically significant association was found, however, between the total amount of daily therapeutic intervention points provided, a reasonable estimate of unit cost,[30] and performance of the other 12 hospitals. Most important, no correlation existed between the total amount of invasive monitoring and patient outcome. Changes in national reimbursement policy, however, should be followed closely to see what impact they have on such high-cost, high-quality hospitals.[31] An important question is whether Hospital 1 could reduce its unit costs without changing its quality of care. Of equal importance for further investigation is our finding that busy nonteaching tertiary care hospitals, as exemplified by Hospitals 2 and 3, can provide a level of care equal to that of some teaching institutions.

Implications

These results should stimulate further investigation into how various elements of the process of modern hospital care may influence outcome from an acute illness. In the past, isolation of various aspects of care has been difficult because much of the difference in patient outcome could not be determined by traditional methods of prognostic stratification. Using methods described in this study, one can reduce variation in patient factors so that the influence of other variables becomes more apparent.

The first task is to validate prospectively the findings of this study—namely, that the interaction and communication within a hospital's intensive care unit staff directly influence patient outcome and that this impact can be measured. Measurement could be done by independently ranking a random sample of hospitals according to quality and extent of staff coordination and simultaneously monitoring mortality rates. Patients' conditions after discharge from the hospital should also be analyzed to ensure that improved in-hospital mortality corresponds with improved long-term outcome.

Such comparisons not only would help us determine the importance of differences in medical staff care, but could also lead to greater understanding of how patient and medical care factors influence outcome from a severe illness. In this sample, 2 of the 13 hospitals had statistically significant differences from the average. The use of a larger patient sample, such as the one at Hospital 4, might have resulted in other hospitals being identified as significantly different and strengthened our appreciation of the relationship between specific aspects of patient care, such as the use of clinical protocols and their performance. Attention to these aspects could improve the treatment of future patients.

NOTES

1. National Institute of Health Consensus Development Conference. Critical care medicine. *JAMA*. 1983;250:798–804.

2. Relman AS. Intensive-care units: who needs them [Editorial]? *N Engl J Med*. 1980;302:965–6.

3. Donabedian A. Evaluating the quality of medical care. *Milbank Mem Fund Q*. 1966;44:166–80.

4. Knaus WA, Zimmerman JE, Wagner DP, Draper EA, Lawrence DE. APACHE—acute physiology and chronic health evaluation: a physiologically based classification system. *Crit Care Med*. 1981;9:591–7.

5. Knaus WA, Draper EA, Wagner DP, et al. Evaluating outcome from intensive care: a preliminary multihospital comparison. *Crit Care Med*. 1982;10:491–6.

6. Knaus WA, LeGall JR, Wagner DP, et al. A comparison of intensive care in the U.S.A. and France. *Lancet*. 1982;2:642–6.

7. Wagner DP, Knaus WA, Draper EA. Statistical validation of a severity of illness measure. *Am J Public Health*. 1983;73:878–84.

8. Knaus WA, Wagner DP, Draper EA. The value of measuring severity of disease in clinical research on acutely ill patients. *J Chronic Dis*. 1984;37:455–63.

9. Wagner DP, Draper EA, Abizanda Campos R, et al. Initial international use of APACHE: an acute severity of disease measure. *Med Decis Making*. 1984;4:297–313.

10. Mosteller F. Improving the precision of clinical trials [Editorial]. *Am J Public Health.* 1982;72:430.

11. Knaus WA, Draper EA, Wagner DP, Zimmerman JE. APACHE II: a severity of disease classification system. *Crit Care Med.* 1985;13:818–29.

12. Horwitz RI, Feinstein AR. Improved observational method for studying therapeutic efficacy: suggestive evidence that lidocaine prophylaxis prevents death in acute myocardial infarction. *JAMA.* 1981;246:2455–9.

13. Cullen DJ, Civetta JM, Briggs BA, Ferrara LC. Therapeutic intervention scoring system: a method for quantitative comparison of patient care. *Crit Care Med.* 1974;2:57–60.

14. Knaus WA, Wagner DP, Draper EA, Lawrence DE, Zimmerman JE. The range of intensive care services today. *JAMA.* 1981;246:2711–6.

15. Cullen DJ, Ferrara LC, Gilbert J, Briggs BA, Walker PF. Indicators of intensive care in critically ill patients. *Crit Care Med.* 1977;5:173–7.

16. Pessi TT. Experiences gained in intensive care of surgical patients: a prospective clinical study of 1,001 consecutively treated patients in a surgical intensive care unit. *Ann Chir Gynaecol Fenn.* 1973;62 (suppl):3–72.

17. Shoemaker WC, Chang P, Czer L, Bland R, Shabot MM, State D. Cardiorespiratory monitoring in postoperative patients: I. Prediction of outcome and severity of illness. *Crit Care Med.* 1979;7:237–42.

18. Teres D, Brown RB, Lemeshow S. Predicting mortality of intensive care unit patients: the importance of coma. *Crit Care Med.* 1982;10:86–95.

19. Thibault GE, Mulley AG, Barnett GO, et al. Medical intensive care: indications, interventions, and outcomes. *N Engl J Med.* 1980;302:938–42.

20. Champion HR, Sacco WJ. Measurement of patient illness severity [Editorial]. *Crit Care Med.* 1982;10:552–3.

21. Li Tc, Phillips MC, Shaw L, Cook EF, Nathanson C, Goldman L. Staffing in a community hospital intensive care unit. *JAMA.* 1984;252:2023–7.

22. Strauss MJ, LoGerfo JP, Yeltatzie JA, Temkin N, Hudson LD. Rationing of intensive care unit services: an everyday occurrence. *JAMA.* 1986. (In press.)

23. Chambers EA, Cox DR. Discrimination between alternative binary response models. *Biometrika.* 1967;54:573–8.

24. Wolfe RA, Roi LD, Flora JD, Feller I, Cornell RG. Mortality differences and speed of wound closure among specialized burn care facilities. *JAMA.* 1983;250:763–6.

25. Williamson JW. Evaluating quality of patient care: a strategy relating outcome and process assessment. *JAMA.* 1971;218:564–9.

26. Safar P, Grenvik A. Organization and physician education in critical care medicine. *Anesthesiology.* 1977;47:82–95.

27. Paneth N, Kiely JL, Wallenstein S, Marcus M, Pakter J, Susser M. Newborn intensive care and neonatal mortality in low-birth-weight infants. *N Engl J Med.* 1982;307:149–55.

28. Baxt WG, Moody P. The impact of a rotorcraft aeromedical emergency care service on trauma mortality. *JAMA.* 1983;249:3047–51.

29. Luft HS, Banker JP, Enthoven AC. Should operations be regionalized?: the empirical relation between surgical volume and mortality. *N Engl J Med.* 1979;301:1364–9.

30. Wagner DP, Wineland TD, Knaus WA. The hidden costs of treating severely ill patients: a case study of charges and resource consumption in an intensive care unit. *Health Care Financ Rev.* 1983;5:81–6.

31. Relman AS. Are teaching hospitals worth the extra costs [Editorial]? *N Engl J Med.* 1984;310:1256–7.

ACKNOWLEDGMENTS: The authors thank the following people for providing essential data: Carolyn Bekes, M.D., George Kuhn, R.N., and W. Eric Scott, M.D., Cooper Medical Center, Camden, New Jersey; Peter E. Dans, M.D., Jeanne Keruly, R.N., and Warren R. Summer, M.D., Johns Hopkins Hospital, Baltimore, Maryland; Susan Brown, R.N., Paul Cox, M.D., and Phyllis Ogrodnik, R.N., Maine Medical Center, Portland, Maine; David J. Cullen, M.D., and Roberta Keene, R.N., Massachusetts General Hospital, Boston, Massachusetts; Robert Bevis, M.D., and David Mize, M.D., Medical College of Georgia, Augusta, Georgia; Robert C. Gilroy, M.D., and Carey Goodrich, R.R.T., Polyclinic Medical Center, Harrisburg, Pennsylvania; Helen Epstein, R.R.A., Gerald E. Gustafson, M.D., and Barbara Reynolds, R.N., St. Francis Hospital, Tulsa, Oklahoma; Jean Henderson, R.N., M.S., James M. Klick, M.D., and Kenneth W. Travis, M.D., South Shore Hospital, South Weymouth, Massachusetts; Judith Moran, R.N., Ph.D., Michael Rosenthal, M.D., and James F. Silverman, M.D., Standford University Hospital, Stanford, California; Mary McKinley, R.N., and Baekhyo Shin, M.D., University of Maryland Hospital, Baltimore, Maryland; Mike Flannagan and John W. Hoyt, M.D., University of Virginia Medical Center, Charlottesville, Virginia; and Jean Grube, R.N., Mary Kay Kohles, B.S.N., M.S.W., and Dennis G. Maki, M.D., University of Wisconsin Hospital and Clinics, Madison, Wisconsin.

The authors also thank David Abrams, Gladys Campbell, Agnes Courtney-Jenkins, Netta Fedor, Terry Kuznicki, Diane Lawrence Reba, Jerry Tietelbaum, Tom Wineland, Jean Wolff, Lauri Yablick, and Maxine Smith for research assistance and careful editing; Frank Harrell, Ph.D., Duke University, for assistance with statistical analysis; and Dr. David Rogers of The Robert Wood Johnson Foundation for his personal support and enthusiasm.

Grant support: in part by grants #HS 04857 from the National Center for Health Services Research, Office of the Assistant Secretary for Health, and #8498 from the Robert Wood Johnson Foundation, Princeton, New Jersey.

The opinions, conclusions, and proposals in the text are those of the authors and do not necessarily represent views of the sponsoring agencies.

Chapter 14

Variations in Medical Practice and Hospital Costs

John E. Wennberg

I am very pleased to be asked to testify on the topic of variations in medical practice. My research into geographic patterns of health care delivery reveals extensive variation in the use of hospital services from one community to another. The extent of variation in reimbursements to hospitals under the Medicare program is such that if the low cost patterns of care were the norm, we would not be faced with the pending bankruptcy of the Medicare Trust Fund nor would we be now concerned with the specter that medical care must be rationed. For many medical or surgical conditions, the variations suggest opportunities to reduce expenditures under the Medicare and Medicaid programs without reducing the benefits of medical care. For other conditions, the variations reveal a critical need to evaluate the outcomes of different approaches to treatment, so that patients and physicians may better understand the significance of their choices in using medical care. Before concluding my testimony, I will describe a plan to address the cost containment and outcome assessment imperatives revealed by the variations and make some specific suggestions as to how the Department of Health and Human Services can contribute.

THE PRACTICE VARIATION PHENOMENON

The practice variation phenomenon first came to my attention some 15 years ago, when my colleagues and I implemented a system for monitoring health care delivery among hospital markets in Vermont. A unique feature of our approach is that we can identify the amount of care consumed by individuals in a specific population and are thus able to calculate rates per capita. We noticed that the per capita expenditures for hospitalization in some areas were more than double those of others, even though studies

Note: Reprinted from *Connecticut Medicine*, Vol. 49, No. 7, pp. 444–453, with permission of Connecticut State Medical Society, © July 1985.

of the populations of Vermont communities showed that the patients were quite similar and differed little in terms of medical need. We repeated these studies throughout New England and found similar patterns of variation in each state. These variations are not explained by differences in population characteristics and there seems to be no clear association between the factors that one ordinarily thinks should contribute to high costs, such as a greater percentage of the elderly in the population or the presence of a teaching hospital. However, differences in hospital costs do closely follow the distribution of hospital beds and numbers of persons employed in the hospital industry. (See Table 14-1)

Let me give some examples. We found that hospital costs in Boston are about twice those of New Haven, even though most resident hospitalizations in each of these communities is to a teaching hospital and the percent

Table 14-1 The Quantity of Hospital Resources Expended on the Populations of New Haven, Connecticut, and Boston, Massachusetts, by Hospitals Providing Resources (1978)

Hospital	Percent of Admissions from the Local Pop.	Beds Allocated to Local Population	Market Share	Per Capita Rates†		
				Beds	Expend.*	Personnel
New Haven, Connecticut (pop. est. 372,900)						
Yale-New Haven Univ. Hosp.	68.3	541.6	54.8	1.5	124	5.5
St. Raphael	86.4	416.6	38.1	1.1	82	3.5
Out-of-area hospital	—	65.0	7.1	0.1	9	0.5
All hospitals	—	1023.2	100.0	2.7	215	9.5
Boston, Massachusetts (pop. est. 732,400)						
Boston teaching hospital (N = 7)	42.6	1828.0	59.0	2.5	322	13.1
Boston community hospital (N = 11)	50.6	843.0	23.3	1.2	84	3.3
Out-of-area hospital	—	524.4	16.7	.7	42	1.8
All hospitals	—	3195.4	100.0	4.4	448	18.2

Note: The estimates for the resources allocated to the New Haven and the Boston populations are made by multiplying the amount of resources provided by each hospital by the percent of admissions that are from the local population (column 2). For example, 542 of the Yale-New Haven University Hospital's total complement of 793 beds are used by the residents of New Haven. The estimate for the total numbers of beds is obtained by summing column 3 which, it will be noted, includes beds from out-of-area hospitals that provided services to the population of New Haven. For comparative purposes, we are particularly interested in per capita rates. The exhibit shows these for beds, numbers of personnel, and inpatient expenditures. All rates are corrected for boundary crossing.
*For inpatient services.
†Beds and personnel per 1,000 population, expenditures per person.

of the population over 65 is about equal. Boston had about 4.4 beds and, in 1978, about 18.2 employees per 1,000 residents, while New Haven had about 2.7 beds and 9.5 employees. For 1982, we found that reimbursements for hospitalization of the elderly were 74 percent higher in Boston than in New Haven. If hospital insurance reimbursements for 78,000 Medicare enrollees living in Boston were the same as in New Haven, the outlays from the trust fund would have been $85 million rather than the actual $148 million, a savings to the trust fund of $63 million.

Figure 14-1 summarizes the extent of variation in expenditures and hospital bed allocations we have observed in our New England studies.

These differences in the per capita rates of use of resources are not intuitively known by the doctors or the patients on the scene. They become apparent only when they are measured directly. For example, I have asked clinicians who practice in both Yale and Harvard teaching hospitals to estimate the per capita expenditures for hospitals in each market. Their answers indicate they have no awareness of the magnitude of the difference; what is more surprising, many do not accurately guess which of the two markets is more expensive.

In my research, I have been very interested in how hospital resources are used—the specific services the dollars, facilities, and manpower produce. Here the findings are clear and consistent. Some causes of hospitalization show very little variation in admission rates among hospital markets, no matter what the level of resource investment. Examples of low variation admissions include hospitalizations for fractures of the hip, acute myocardial infarction (heart attack), strokes, appendectomy, and inguinal hernia repair. But these are the exceptions. Most causes of admission are highly variable, including many common surgical procedures. For example, we have found that the rates for tonsillectomy have varied as much as eightfold: nearly 70 percent of children had their tonsils removed by age 15 in one area, while in the low rate community fewer than 8 percent experienced the operation. The probability of having a hysterectomy has varied from less than 15 percent to well over 60 percent of women by age 75, depending on place of residence. And the chances that a male will have a prostatectomy by age 75 have ranged from a low of about 15 percent to well over 50 percent in different hospital market areas.

Figure 14-2 shows the typical patterns of variation seen for common surgical procedures.

The variation phenomenon has been similarly documented in Europe and is not limited to health delivery systems based on fee-for-service financing. I have found the pattern of variation for common surgical procedures consistent among fee-for-service hospital markets in Iowa, Maine, Massachusetts, Rhode Island, and Vermont; among health maintenance organizations in the United States and among health care regions in Canada, England and Norway, even though obvious differences exist in the

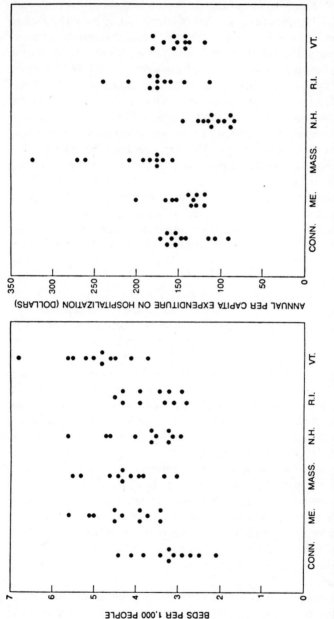

Figure 14-1 Number of hospital beds per capita and the annual amount spent per capita on hospital treatment also show the influence of geographic variations in medical care. The data are for the 11 most populous hospital areas in each of the six New England states. The number of hospital beds per 1,000 people (adjusted for the number of people who leave their hospital area for treatment) ranges from about two to more than six. The ratios thus range from well below to well above the four beds per 1,000 established by the Federal Health Planning Program as a standard. Furthermore, the variation in each state is so great that the number of beds per capita in the state or county as a whole (a measure often employed by health planning agencies) bears little relation to the conditions prevailing in each community. The average amount spent on treatment in hospitals in 1975 ranged from less than $100 per capita to more than $300 in the 66 areas.

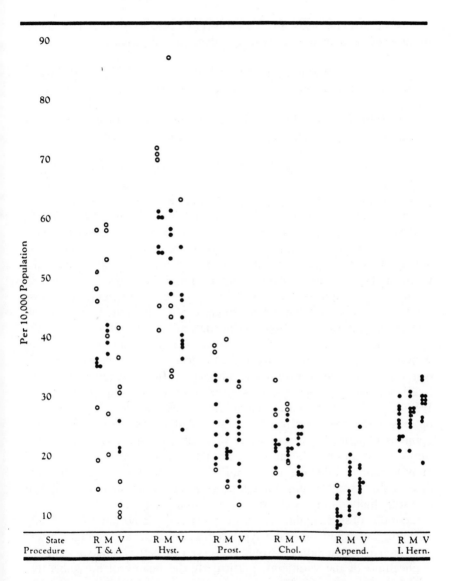

Figure 14-2 Age-Adjusted Rate of Procedure for Six Common Surgical Procedures in Rhode Island, Maine, and Vermont (1975). Note: Rates of surgical procedures vary greatly among hospital areas. The rates shown are for the six most common surgical procedures for the repair or removal of an organ in the 11 most populous hospital areas of Maine, Rhode Island, and Vermont (1975). The rate of tonsillectomy varies about sixfold among the 33 areas, the rates of hysterectomy and prostatectomy vary about fourfold. Moreover, many of the extreme rates for these procedures differ from the average rate for the state by an amount that is statistically significant (open circles). There is much disagreement among physicians on the value of the high-variation procedures. Similar patterns of variation for these procedures have been observed in Iowa, England, and Norway. R = Rhode Island, M = Maine, V = Vermont.

supply of hospital beds and surgeons, the organization and financing of services, and in the cultural and demographic characteristics of the residents.

Our more recent studies have been concerned with variations in hospitalization rates among medical as well as surgical admissions. We have found that *most* causes of admission as classified by Diagnosis Related Groups (DRGs) have highly variable admission rates. Indeed, nearly 90 percent of all nonobstetrical cases admitted to hospital have greater variation than hysterectomy.

The pattern of variation typical for medical DRGs is shown in Figure 14-3 and Table 14-2.

Why is it that such differences exist in the way medicine is practiced?

One reason is that for many common conditions, the necessary scientific studies that allow physicians to define the optimum treatment have not been done. Rather than consensus, there is controversy and disagreement among clinicians on what constitutes the best treatment for a particular problem. This is often the case when the clinical choice involves a medical versus a surgical approach to a given illness. The controversies arise because the natural history of the untreated or conservatively treated case is poorly understood and well designed clinical trials are notably absent.

Examples include surgical versus nonsurgical treatment for menopausal symptoms, for moderate urinary tract obstruction due to benign hyperplasia of the prostate, for recurrent sore throats related to hypertrophy of the tonsil, and for coronary by-pass surgery following myocardial infarction. Well-defined scientific norms simply do not exist to delimit the practice options physicians select to treat these maladies. As a consequence, the opinions of individual doctors can vary substantially, based upon their subjective experience. Because many of the conditions are extremely common, eventually affecting most if not all people to some degree, the candidates that could qualify for operative intervention sometimes appear upwardly limited only by the size of the population.

Examples of such conditions that are particularly important for the Medicare program include prostatic hypertrophy, cataracts, and coronary artery disease. The public interest would be served by better understanding the implications of the variations, particularly the quality of life gains that follow the use of surgical approaches as compared to more conservative treatments. This should be a compelling priority for operations that carry a high surgical mortality rate. One such operation is prostatectomy, where the postoperative mortality rate during hospitalization is about 1 percent or slightly higher. We calculated that if the conservative or low rate practice style seen in our New England studies were the national norm, one should expect about 1,900 deaths per annum in the United States following this operation. But if the national norm were the high rate, the number would be about 6,800. The responsibility for further research into the outcome

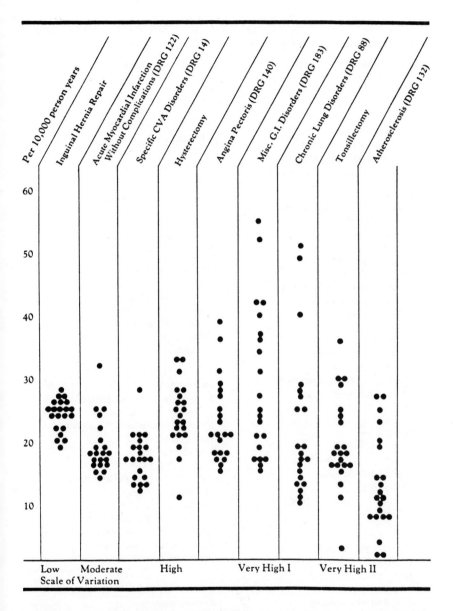

Figure 14-3 Age-Adjusted Incidence of Hospitalization (1980–82) for Selected Medical DRGs and Three Common Surgical Procedures for Maine Hospital Markets. Note: The DRGs with similar statewide rates were selected to demonstrate the spectrum of variation in the incidence of DRG-specific hospitalizations among Maine hospital markets. Each circle represents a hospital market area. The graph is limited to markets with 45,000 person years or greater. The incidence of hospitalization for most DRGs is more variable than for hysterectomy.

Table 14-2 Medical and Surgical Causes of Admissions Ranked in Ascending Order of Variation in Incidence of Hospitalization (1980–1982)

Medical Causes of Admission

Low Variation
None

Moderate Variation
Acute myocardial infarction
Gastro-intestinal hemorrhage
Specific cerebrovascular disorders

High Variation
Nutritional and metabolic diseases
Syncope and collapse
Respiratory neoplasms
Cellulitis
Urinary tract stones
Cardiac arrhythmias
Miscellaneous injuries to extremities
Angina pectoris
Toxic effects of drugs
Psychosis
Heart failure and shock
Seizures and headaches
Adult simple pneumonias
Respiratory signs and symptoms
Depressive neurosis
Medical back problems
Digestive malignancy
G.I. obstruction
Adult gastro-enteritis
Peripheral vascular disorders
Red blood cell disorders
Adult diabetes
Circulatory disorders etc., A.M.I. with
   card. cath.

Very High Variation
Deep vein thrombophlebitis
Adult bronchitis and asthma
Organic mental syndromes
Chest pain
Transient schemic attacks
Kidney and urinary tract infections
Acute adjustment reaction
Minor skin disorders
Trauma to skin, subcut, tiss. and breast
Chronic obstructive lung disease
Hypertension
Adult otitis media and URI
Peptic ulcer

Medical Causes of Admission (cont.)

Disorders of the biliary tract
Pediatric gastro-enteritis
Pediatric bronchitis and asthma
Atherosclerosis
Pediatric otitis media and URI
Pediatric pneumonia
Chemotherapy

Surgical Causes of Admission

Low Variation
Inguinal and femoral hernia repair
Hip repair except joint replacement

Moderate Variation
Appendicitis with appendectomy
Major small and large bowel surgery
Gall bladder disease with
   cholecystectomy
Adult hernia repairs except inguinal and
   femoral

High Variation
Hysterectomy
Major cardiovascular operations
Pediatric hernia operations
Hand operations except ganglion
Foot operations
Lens operations
Major joint operations
Stomach, esophageal and duodenal
   operations
Anal operations
Female reproductive system
   reconstructive operations
Back and neck operations
Soft tissue operations

Very High Variation
Knee operations
Transurethral operations
Uterus and andenexa operations
Extra-ocular operations
Misc. ear, nose, and throat operations
Breast biopsy and local excision for
   nonmalignancy
D & C, conization except for malignancy
T & A opertions except for tonsillectomy

Table 14-2 continued

Surgical Causes of Admission

Very High Variation	*Very High Variation*
Tonsillectomy	Dental extractions and restorations
Female laparoscopic operations except	Laparoscopic tubal interruptions
for sterilzation	Tubal interruption for nonmalignancy

[a]Causes of hospitalizations are taken from Diagnostic-Related Disease Classification system, but cases have been grouped without regard to presence or absence of significant complication. Obstetrical and neonatal causes of hospitalization are excluded. Ranking is according to the Systematic Component of Variation. Variations are measured across thirty hospital markets: The exhibit lists individually only those with more than 1,500 cases. More than 50 percent of hospitalizations are represented in the exhibit. Classes of variation are defined such that the variation associated with the first entry in a class is significantly more variable than the first entry in the previous class. For additional information see K. McPherson, J E Wennberg, O B Hovind, and P Clifford. *The New England Journal of Medicine* 307 (1982) 1310-4.

---

implications for this procedure seems to rest at least in part with the federal government since many of its activities promote the public's use of care and, for this procedure, most of the operations done in the United States are financed by the Medicare program.

There are other important reasons for variations that do not rest on scientific controversies and these provide the best opportunities for immediate savings on the cost of hospitalization. Physicians in some hospital markets practice medicine in ways that have extremely adverse implications for cost because they use the hospital for treating relatively minor illnesses or for performing minor surgery much more often than do most of their colleagues. The professional reasons that lead to a particular practice style are likely to be complex and idiosyncratic—involving matters of professional or patient convenience, inexperience or insecurity on the part of clinicians, individualistic interpretations of the requirement for "defensive medicine," and unexamined viewpoints about the relative risks associated with ambulatory versus inpatient treatment. To one degree or another, most of the medical causes of admission appear to fall into this class as do most minor surgical procedures. Common examples include admissions for virtually all pediatric medical diagnoses, and minor surgery such as a cystoscopy, teeth extractions, sterilization, or breast biopsy. These examples typically exhibit more than a tenfold variation in admission rates among hospital markets. Among the Medicare populations, the common examples include gastro-enteritis, chronic obstructive lung disease, atherosclerosis, bronchitis and asthma, and simple pneumonias.

The consequences for costs of practice styles that favor inpatient over ambulatory settings are large, indeed. Take as the first example the differences in pediatric medical hospitalization rates, which are reflective of the variations that may be expected under Medicaid's program for dependent children. In Maine, a state with about one million residents, the largest hospital market area had utilization rates only 55 percent of the state average over the 3-year period of our study. Based on an estimated cost per case of $1,300, we can project a net saving of about $2.5 million in this hospital market over average costs. If the practice styles seen in this area were emulated throughout the state, the costs of pediatric medical hospitalizations in Maine during the first 3 years of this decade would have been about $15.5 million, rather than the estimated $28.3 million—a saving of $12.8 million.

As a second example, consider medical admissions for the population over age 65, that is, those eligible for Medicare. One of the three most populous hospital markets in Iowa hospitalizes the elderly for medical admissions at a rate that is only 66 percent of the state average. Assuming an average cost per case of $2,000, we can estimate a net saving there of $2.2 million for Medicare medical admissions in 1980. If the hospitalization rate for this area were the norm for the state, the bill for medical admissions for the 190,000 persons over 65 years of age in our study would have been $72 million rather than the estimated $109 million—a saving of $36 million in one year alone.

Let me place these estimates of potential savings in a slightly different context. One hears a lot these days about how the cost crisis is leading to the need to ration medical services. This fear seems to me to be misplaced. The problem is that we are uninformed about the opportunities for real-locating existing resources. If the more conservative, ambulatory-oriented practice styles were to become the norm—and if hospital administrators and trustees translated the decrease in demand for specific services into a reduction in the capacity of the hospital system—then substantial cost savings would follow. Indeed, the resources that can be saved through the more judicious use of hospitals should more than meet the demands for investment in effective new technologies, such as liver transplants, for some time to come.

A PLAN FOR ACTION

What Needs to Be Done?

Let me state at the outset that the goal is emphatically *not* to obliterate all variations in the practice of medicine nor to reduce the practice of medicine to a cookbook. Obviously, physicians must have freedom to apply their skills as they and their patients see fit. Medicine is as much art as it is science and will always be so. An enterprise as large as medical care will always produce variations in approach. Rather, the goal should be to reduce variations that are highly aberrant, that reflect supply factors rather than scientific knowledge, or that reflect idiosyncrasies of physicians rather than the values, needs, or wants of their patients.

In the summer 1984 edition of *Health Affairs,* I suggested a three-part plan for dealing with the practice variation phenomenon in a way that improves health care outcomes and promotes cost-containment. I would like to review the outline of this plan and suggest steps the federal government could take to ameliorate the problems.

Monitoring Performances in Hospital Markets

The first part calls for a closer monitoring of medical practice in local markets, using epidemiologic techniques to create reports giving the numbers per capita of hospital beds, employees, and expenditures, as well as the rates of use of services and their outcomes. These reports provide an objective means for identifying variations, for assessing practice patterns, and for planning corrective actions. Without them, people are simply unaware of what is going on. The reports should be made available routinely to practicing physicians, to state and county medical associations, to Professional Review Organizations (PROs), to hospital administrators, and to others with interest in the measurement of hospital performance.

The data necessary to create the reports are, for the most part, generated already as part of the routine management of health insurance or regulatory programs and are contained in Medicare, Medicaid, and Blue Cross/Blue Shield claims systems and in hospital discharge abstracts similar to those used in the DRG program. Because of its national coverage and the richness of its data base, the Medicare program offers the best immediate opportunity to implement feedback in all parts of the country. The federal government now requires each hospital to record uniform information on the costs, reasons for hospitalization, and treatments for each hospitalization paid for under the Medicare program. When this information is linked to claims data under the Medicare part B program and to patient registration files, a registry is created of the medical care events and certain outcomes for virtually the entire population of the United States who are 65 years and older. The many problems for public policy concerning the equity and outcome of care that are illustrated by the variation phenomena, as well as the federal government's own need for effective cost containment, lead me to recommend that this very important national resource be used for this purpose.

Dealing with the Cost-Containment Problem

The second aspect of my plan calls for the use of the reports in a strategy to reduce the use of hospitals for highly variable medical admissions and minor surgery which can be treated effectively and safely in the ambulatory setting. The feedback reports give the information necessary for action:

they identify the hospital market areas with costly practice styles for specific discretionary admissions and costly administrative practices with regard to hospital expenditure, bed, and personnel rates. The shift of such patients to the ambulatory setting will neither disrupt the patient-physician relationship nor have a significant negative effect on professional income. If widely implemented, this shift will create the opportunity for an extensive reduction in the resources allocated to hospitals.

Given the current imperatives to contain the costs of medical care and to reallocate resources to more productive ends, it is in everybody's best interest to reduce the use of marginally effective or unnecessary hospitalizations. In some respects, this is already happening. Over the past 2 years, we have witnessed an important change in practice patterns in the United States as evidenced by a reduction in the long-term trend of increasing hospital utilization. This dimunition is the result of pressures from many sources, but the pivotal factor is that physicians are changing their attitudes about how medicine should be practiced. Our data suggest that the changes that have occurred to date should be viewed as just a beginning. We need to create and sustain an environment where cost-effective medical practice is the norm.

For this to happen, practicing physicians must take the lead by examining the pattern of utilization in their own communities and, when necessary, adapting their own practice styles and influencing their colleagues to adapt theirs to the more cost-effective practice patterns. A virtue of this approach is the recognition that decisions on cutbacks in service must be highly selective and specific, and that success depends on an informed and cooperative medical staff. It takes into account the nature of uncertainty concerning the value of most medical services and recognizes the need to make clinical choices that reduce demand for hospitalizations that are not worth the costs. It decentralizes the effort to the sites where clinical decisions are made and provides objective information on variations. Most important, the strategy offers a model for cost containment in which the profession can take a leading, not a defensive, role.

Will practicing physicians participate in such efforts? The evidence I have, based on my experiences in Iowa and New England, is that they will indeed respond. Given information on practice patterns in their local and regional markets, a consensus will emerge that it is safe and in the public interest to reduce hospitalization rates for many of the high variation cases I have listed in Table 14-2. Government officials, managers of benefit plans, and representatives of public or private interest groups have exercised important, sometimes decisive influences in persuading the medical profession of the need to respond to the challenge. But lacking as they must a detailed understanding of the nature of medical choices or the particular circumstances of a specific decision, they are in no position to deal with such issues as the necessity for hospitalization for a given patient.

The federal government can make two very specific contributions to promote market reforms based on feedback and review of high variation causes of admission. First, as indicated above, it can assure that the Medicare data base is available for the construction of market area-specific reports. Second, it can promote population-based utilization review in hospital markets as part of the strategy for implementing the PRO program.

There are important reasons why the federal government should act. With the adoption of the DRG system, new controls on unit costs are now in place. But the level of variation for utilization rates is generally much greater than for unit prices (Figure 14-4.) Since the DRG payments for services in any given hospital market depends upon diagnosis-specific admission rates, per capita reimbursements for most DRGs will typically show a three- and four- and often as much as a tenfold difference among neighboring areas. Many of these DRGs are highly variable because in some communities patients are cared for in the hospital while in others they are treated outside of the hospital.

Some of the variation in the medical DRGs may represent misclassification of patients, so I am reluctant to extrapolate from the variations seen for specific DRGs to predict the savings that might accrue to the Medicare Trust Fund if the PRO program were able to mobilize the physician community to adopt the more conservative practice styles. However, since hospital reimbursements for all causes vary by more than twofold, adoption of the conservative practice styles could easily result in savings that amount to more than 40 percent of the current outlay for hospitals.

Is there danger here of withholding necessary care or decreasing quality? Some expensive procedures are clearly necessary and costs for these will remain high. I am convinced, however, that it is both safe and in the public's best interest to reduce the use of hospitals for most high variation medical and surgical admissions. Many communities with first class medical care systems have low hospitalization rates. We find many examples of low cost markets where most hospitalizations occur within teaching hospitals. I mentioned already the case of the New Haven market area served by Yale teaching hospitals. Others include the local market area of the University of Wisconsin's teaching hospital in Madison where Medicare reimbursements for hospitalizations in 1982 were $876 per enrollee compared to $1,515 in Milwaukee and the University of Iowa's area where reimbursements were $734 compared to $1,320 in Des Moines.

Dealing with the Effectiveness Problem

The third part of my plan is to design and implement a program to deal with the unanswered questions concerning the outcomes of many common diagnostic and therapeutic interventions. The overriding question is whether a specific intervention undertaken to treat a condition with a known level

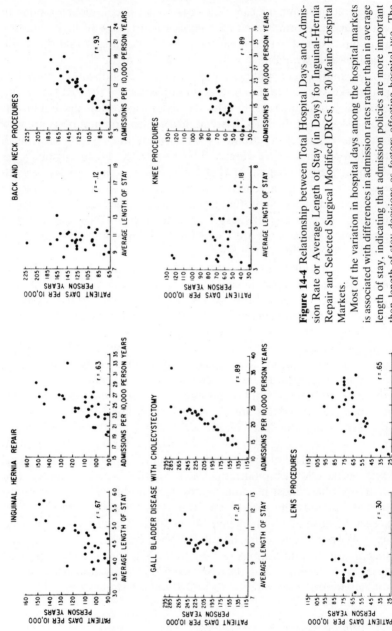

Figure 14-4 Relationship between Total Hospital Days and Admission Rate or Average Length of Stay (in Days) for Inguinal-Hernia Repair and Selected Surgical Modified DRGs, in 30 Maine Hospital Markets.

Most of the variation in hospital days among the hospital markets is associated with differences in admission rates rather than in average length of stay, indicating that admission policies are more important than length-of-stay decisions as factors affecting hospital use. The exception is inguinal-hernia repair, a low-variation procedure.

of morbidity gets a better result than an alternative treatment. High levels of uncertainty cost billions of dollars nationwide and involve potentially thousands of lives. Reducing the level of uncertainty demands a concerted effort on the part of the private sector as well as government, and we have the means to achieve that objective.

The extent of the variation in use of most medical and surgical treatments, as well as a critical review of the literature supporting the assertion for efficacy of specific treatments, indicates that the number of outcome studies to be done is very large. Priorities will need to be set, new cost-effective health services research methodologies for evaluating outcomes must be invented and adopted, resources to conduct the studies must be made available, and the interest of practicing physicians in carrying out the studies and responding to the results must be cultivated.

I think we can count on physician participation in the design and implementation of such studies. By virtue of their inclination as well as their training, physicians want to practice scientifically sound medicine. That is what is expected of physicians and what physicians expect of themselves. When resources are available to support their participation, they respond in a very positive way. I submit as evidence the program of the Maine Medical Association to evaluate practice variations and cite in particular their program to investigate the outcome implications of prostatectomies undertaken for benign prostatic hypertrophy. After becoming aware of the extensive variation in prostatectomy rates among Maine communities, the urologists in Maine, under the leadership of Dr. Robert Timothy, undertook an extensive examination of the indications for the operation. As is typical for many common treatments, they could find no studies that provided a longer term, systematic follow-up of unselected patients. Because of this defect in the literature, the probabilities for specific kinds of outcomes—both the good and bad ones—could not be estimated in a meaningful way. To correct the situation, the physicians have undertaken a prospective evaluation of the response of patients to this treatment in order to document the changes in morbidity and functional status that relate to the operation. The study, which will provide information on events for up to a year after surgery, is making an important contribution to reduce uncertainty and ignorance concerning the expected outcomes following this operation.

What Can We Do to Make Such Efforts Routine?

Let me deal first with the medical schools. While the country has made a massive investment in basic biomedical science, both the Congress and the nation's medical schools have largely ignored the disciplines that deal directly with the problems of improving clinical decision making and evaluating health care outcomes—clinical epidemiology, biostatistis, and clinical decision analysis. Research to improve medical decision making is an important part of the agenda of schools of Public Health and has received scattered interest from enlightened physicians in many parts of the country. Yet, career opportunities are extremely limited in these disciplines and funding for specific outcome studies seems to be the last on everyone's agenda, except perhaps for randomized trials in selected fields such as cancer chemotherapy. The underdevelopment of these quantitative disciplines in the faculties of the medical schools not only affects the quality and volume of research in this area; it also means that the medical students are receiving little training in the very subjects that promise to make them better evaluators of evidence concerning alternative choices of treatment and more sophisticated participants in studies designed to improve the knowledge base of clinical medicine. If we wish to deal systematically with the clinical dilemmas evidenced by the practice variation phenomenon, we must adjust this imbalance.

How could the federal government help? In addition to the mobilization of the Medicare claims data base I mentioned before, the Department of Health and Human Services could help in a very direct way. Let me close this testimony by suggesting some specific objectives.

Foremost, the topic must be given visibility and priority. I suggest that HHS should make the goal of reducing uncertainty about the outcome implications of commonly used medical and surgical interventions a high departmental priority.

Second, a lead agency should be designated with responsibility for organizing a national strategy for implementing a program of outcome evaluation. The recent expansion of its mandate to include technology assessment suggests the National Center for Health Services Research for the role of lead agency, but, at the same time, Congress appropriated funds at a level below that available last year. Further, I want to underscore that the evaluative effort I am calling for applies to existing and commonly used medical practices. While assessment of new technology is obviously important, the lack of understanding of the value of existing practices needs special and ongoing attention.

Third, the national strategy should include the development in the medical schools of the quantitative disciplines essential to this task, including epidemiology, biostatistics, decision analysis, and computer sciences. This will provide medical students the analytic tools they need to practice informed, cost-effective medical care. The government could promote this needed instruction by directly supporting educational programs in these areas and by linking government awards to medical schools to the establishment of training programs in these vital areas.

Fourth, as part of this strategy, HHS should design and implement an intra- and extra-mural research program that seeks specifically to improve the knowledge base for services purchased under the Medicare program. My suggestion is that a fixed percentage of the Medicare and Medicaid patient care dollars be earmarked for this purpose. In 1984, expenditure from the Medicare Trust Fund totaled about $33 billion, nearly all spent on hospital care. Industries commonly invest directly in development of better products. If one-half of one percent of this amount were invested to find out what portion of this $33 billion is well spent and what represents unnecessary and even harmful uses of public resources, the long-term cost containment strategies of the federal government would not only be more successful, they would truly promote better health.

Chapter 15

Quality Assurance in Ambulatory Care

Benjamin Chu

Providing health care in an ambulatory setting engenders greater uncertainty than does the care of patients in an inpatient setting. When patients are not "captive audiences" on a hospital ward, diagnostic assessments and therapeutic interventions cannot be monitored as closely for accuracy and effectiveness. In addition, when the patient is away from the watchful eye of the health care provider and nursing staff, uncontrollable factors such as compliance with care plans, abstinence from potentially harmful activities, habits, and other environmental influences make it difficult to predict favorable outcomes for the health care process. The reasons for ambulatory visits and the results of these encounters are often more ambiguous than those involving hospitalized patients. The nature of a patient's complaints frequently does not lend itself to definitive diagnosis. Good ambulatory care is often intimately related to the ability of the health provider to motivate a patient to comply with care plans, embark on important life style changes, and return for regular follow-up and preventive health visits.

Fortunately, most ambulatory patients are relatively healthy and resilient. The lack of proper health care will generally not impact on the health status of most outpatients, at least not in the short run. In contrast, hospitalized patients require more careful observation and greater adherence to prescribed therapies simply because the odds of an adverse outcome resulting from inattention or lack of proper intervention are much higher than in most ambulatory encounters. Similarly, favorable outcomes in the ambulatory care setting cannot always be ascribed to attributes of the health care process; good results may just as easily be due to certain characteristics

Benjamin Chu, MD, PhD, is an Assistant Professor of Clinical Medicine in the Department of Medicine at the State University of New York Health Science Center at Brooklyn and the Acting Director of the Adult Emergency Department of Kings County Hospital, Brooklyn, New York.

238

of the ambulatory population itself. However, this relative insensitivity of outcome to errors and to health care intervention should not be misconstrued to indicate that quality of care is less important in the ambulatory setting. Delays and errors of both omission and commission may substantially alter outcomes for some patients. The complexity and sheer volume of ambulatory care, much of which occurs in small private settings insulated from the scrutiny of quality assessment and assurance programs, present a huge challenge to quality assurance efforts in the ambulatory setting. Palmer aptly characterized this challenge when she wrote:

> The challenge to primary care practitioners is to distinguish in a timely manner those patients who are at risk but are concealed among the many not at risk. The task is made more difficult because patients are seen for brief visits spread over time, like picture frames moving in slow motion.[1]

QUALITY ASSURANCE IN THE AMBULATORY SETTING

The Joint Commission on Accreditation of Healthcare Organizations defines "quality" as "the degree of adherence to generally recognized contemporary standards of good practice and anticipated outcomes for a particular service, procedure, diagnosis, or clinical problem." "Appropriateness is the extent to which a particular procedure, treatment, test, or service is effective, is clearly indicated, is not excessive, is adequate in quantity, and is provided in the inpatient, outpatient, home, or other setting best suited to the patient's needs." A quality assurance program must "objectively and systematically monitor and evaluate the quality and appropriateness of patient care, pursue opportunities to improve patient care and clinical performance, and identify problems in care and in performance."[2]

Palmer and Nesson have suggested that quality assurance or medical care evaluation should proceed in a cyclical fashion, involving the following 11 steps:[3]

1. identify the problem to be evaluated
2. choose the problem for assessment
3. select the type of assessment (process or outcome)
4. choose the data source
5. define the topic and develop criteria
6. define the index for case identification
7. specify the unit of care for study
8. collect and analyze the data
9. intervene to correct deficiency

10. implement reassessment
11. repeat steps 8, 9, and 10 until deficiency is corrected

The Joint Commission on Accreditation of Healthcare Organizations also advocated such a cyclical quality assurance process, suggesting only minor modifications.[4] Quality assurance requires not only the systematic monitoring and assessment of quality but also active intervention to correct deficiencies and reassessment to ensure that the correction plan is successful.

Recognizing the complexity of health care in the ambulatory care environment, numerous authors have recommended health care parameters and indicators of quality that can be used in the ambulatory setting. Benson and associates stressed the "art of care" as the ability of practitioners to motivate patients to comply with health care plans, whose ultimate objective is to improve the health status of the patient. Quality assurance at the Methodist Hospital in Indianapolis centers on ten generic ambulatory care parameters that the staff believes have the capacity to affect patients' health. These parameters serve as the focus for monitoring and evaluation. The ten parameters described all impact upon some aspect of care and can be the objects of in-depth study and evaluation.

- "Practitioner performance" is a wide-ranging parameter that includes structural aspects such as credentialing, continuing medical education (CME), and clinical privileging, as well as performance aspects that encompass the practitioner's knowledge, skills, judgment, and interpersonal skills necessary to deliver good care.
- "Appropriateness of service" has implications both for quality and for cost of services.
- "Patient compliance" is a difficult parameter to control, but is nonetheless important to the overall success of care plans.
- "Support staff performance" underscores all those vital functions, such as laboratory and chart retrieval, whose absence may have deleterious effects on overall care.
- "Accessibility" defines the ease and timeliness with which health care services can be obtained.
- "Continuity of care" is a parameter that emphasizes the smooth and complete transfer of information between providers and consultants, as well as the condition upon which therapeutic and trusting relationships between providers and patients can be formed.
- "Patient health care minimization" encompasses those procedures and systems, such as infection control, drug profiling, and risk management activities, that are designed to minimize harm to patients.
- "Medical record system" includes the means to provide appropriate, accurate, and complete information about the patient.

- "Patient satisfaction" is an important barometer of the success of the provider-patient relationship. Because the diagnostic and therapeutic goals of ambulatory visits are often unclear or simply related to the value of reassurance, patient satisfaction may be an important measure of the success of the encounter.
- Finally, "cost of services" is suggested as a parameter that can reflect an important barrier to health care.

The use of these parameters is offered as a structured approach to quality assurance in the complex ambulatory care setting.[5]

Others have offered structured approaches to quality assurance that emphasize ambulatory care indicators broken down according to more traditional areas of care, such as laboratory utilization, radiology, drug prescription patterns, and specific clinical management areas.[6]

Armed with this clear definition of quality, a straightforward process to monitor for quality and correct deficiencies, and structured indicators of care, one might expect the path to implementing an effective program of quality assurance in the ambulatory setting to be relatively simple. However, the uncertainties and complexity of the ambulatory care encounter serve to obscure these clear conceptualizations of quality. In addition, the lack of uniform data on encounters, uniform definitions of units of service that would aid in indexing encounters, and uniform standards of record keeping make efforts to study quality of care difficult. Definitions of quality, sources of data for assessment, and the relationship of identified standards or indicators of good care to actual outcomes are problematic issues for any program of quality assurance in the ambulatory setting.

What Is Quality Care in the Ambulatory Setting?

Quality, according to the classic theoretical constructs offered by Avedis Donabedian and others, might be studied through examination of structure, process, and outcome measures of care. Structure refers to the nature of the providers and the resources of care. Types of providers, credentials of care givers, operating procedures, physical facilities, and so forth are the nuts and bolts of health care units. Process refers to the intermediate products of care. Patterns of diagnostic evaluations, medical therapies, rates of utilization, and algorithms for care all define how medical care is delivered. Outcome is the end product of care.

Improved health status, longer life, decreased morbidity, and greater patient satisfaction and comfort are the valued targets of health care. Structure, process, and outcome form a hierarchically related model from which to study quality of care. The complexity and difficulty of studying quality at each level presumably rise as one moves from structure to process to outcome measures of quality. Also underlying this theoretical model is the assumption that quality indicators at the structure and process levels imply quality at the outcome level. Similarly, favorable or unfavorable outcomes are often interpreted to implicate quality issues at the structure and process level rather than some other unknown aspect of the population studied.

Despite the implications that good structure and good process will result in good outcomes, significant questions have been raised about the validity of this relationship. Further, quality assurance using process assessments ensures a measure of standardization of the care given. One hopes that this standardization will ultimately lead to improved patient outcome. However, it is also possible that standardization may lead to a more uniform practice of useless or bad care. Berwick has warned that devising minimalist standards for quality without an overall commitment to a continued striving for excellence may produce unwanted consequences. Creating floors for quality of care rapidly invites their institution as ceilings. Since standards change and definitions of quality are often evolutionary, good quality control and assurance is less about the actual monitors of care and paper compliance with minimalist standards and more about the approach to the quest for excellence.[7]

In addition, if chart audits are used to evaluate process, the standardization of chart documentation may not, in fact, reflect measures that will ultimately lead to improved outcome. A number of authors have observed that despite general correlation of retrospective review using explicit and implicit criteria, the correlation between good process and good outcome is poor.[8] Others have noted that physicians judged to perform well in one diagnostic category do not always do well in other categories.[9] Romm and associates studied the correlation between compliance with peer-derived criteria for good care of diabetic and hypertensive patients in private practice and found no correlation between adherence with standards of care and level of control of the disease process.[10] In an emergency department setting, others have discovered little correlation between good charts in patients with asthma and good outcome.[11] Finally, Brook and Appel found that in evaluating emergency department visits for urinary tract infections and hypertension and for radiologically defined peptic ulcer disease, neither implicit nor explicit expert estimation of the adequacy of the process of care correlated with the implicit or explicit judgment of the adequacy of outcome.[12]

The implication of these studies, then, is that despite the relative advantages of process reviews, namely, the ease and unobtrusiveness of the audit process, there continue to be questions as to the relationship of the adequacy of the process of care with the outcome. On the other hand, outcome assessments may not reflect the adequacy of medical care but may instead reflect unrelated aspects of the patient's condition, such as general health or compliance with the care process. Process reviews should be combined with outcome reviews in order to assess the overall effect of the medical care encounter. Attempts should be made to relate process to outcome and to ferret out the factors that may contribute to unexpected findings. More complete quality assurance efforts that combine these aspects of the care process constitute de facto clinical research.

These studies have shown that there is only limited proof that good health care outcomes are tied to good structure and process. Berwick and Knapp have warned that making effectiveness a prerequisite for measuring quality is a sure formula for paralysis. Using health status outcome to define quality "burdens the exploration of quality with the agenda of virtually all clinical and health services research." The authors further maintain that the product of most health care is not tied to good outcome. The multidimensional aspects of quality care in ambulatory settings equally involves such intangible items as patient satisfaction, reassurance, and the human contact that results from caring interpersonal relationships. Tying quality to health status, to longer life for example, negates the value of this essential process of health care.[13]

Thus, the concept of quality in ambulatory care is not a notion that can be easily crystallized and quantified in, say, a level of blood pressure control or adherence to a diagnostic algorithm, although these measures may be one aspect. Quality in ambulatory care does not readily lend itself to analysis in the traditional structure, process, and outcome model of quality assessment. The complexity of care in the ambulatory environment is reflected in the complexity involved in defining ways to evaluate and assure the high quality of the care rendered.

How Is Quality Measured and How Can Measurement "Assure" That Quality Care Is Delivered?

If tying quality to definitive proof of improved outcomes is a formula for paralysis, then judging the methods of measuring quality against a similar standard will also lead to a paralyzing skepticism. Methods of measuring quality are reviewed in detail elsewhere in this book. They center on reviews of structure, process, and outcomes. Some rely on implicit criteria of quality as supplied by a panel of experts. Others rely on comparison with explicitly spelled-out criteria for care. Criteria maps are detailed and patterned forms of explicit criteria. Tracer studies of selected diagnoses are another form of review of care that uses explicit criteria. Other studies rely on the detailed analyses of adverse outcomes, the so-called sentinel events, to direct quality assurance efforts toward problem areas. Many studies use retrospective medical record reviews. These studies, however, are bound by the limitations of the records as an accurate reflection of the encounter. More recently, the use of direct observation, videotaping, exit interviews, questionnaires, patient surrogates, and other methods to judge the quality of encounters has been described in the literature. Studies can be performed by trained personnel, peers, programmed analysis of computer records, and a variety of other means.

Feedback, staff involvement, and staff investment in the provision of quality care are the ingredients necessary to translate accurate assessment of quality into assurance that health care will be provided on the highest possible plane.

IMPLEMENTING QUALITY ASSURANCE PROGRAMS IN THE AMBULATORY CARE SETTING

Understanding the multidimensional aspects of quality assessment and assurance in the complex ambulatory setting and the limits of the methodology for measuring quality, various authors have approached the challenge of implementing programs for quality assurance in different ways.

Whitcomb et al. have suggested that successful quality assurance programs require multiple methodologies, including review of complaints, generic screening, and process audits. They further suggest that an effective system is one that is educational and constructive, *not* punitive and judgmental. "Success will depend on the respect with which the QA process treats physicians who find themselves criticized. Anonymity allows changes in behavior without loss of face." Therefore, once these approaches have been instituted in the emergency department, the results of daily generic screening, investigation of patient complaints, results of telephone follow-ups, lobby questionnaires, paramedic feedback forms, focus groups, and problem-oriented review can be returned to providers for comments and input. The authors offered the postulate that awareness of these extensive reviews of physician behavior created by a nonthreatening system of peer-reviewed feedback will ultimately lead to improved care. To make the system work, however, the authors noted that a substantial institutional commitment of time and personnel is required.[14]

In support of this thesis, Harchelroad et al. reported on a 3-year daily review of over 108,000 emergency department records that provided immediate corrective feedback to all ER physicians. Two certified nurse practitioners performed these audits. The study found that the yearly percentage of errors recorded on a standard problem checklist declined from 5.47 to 3.57 percent. The authors conceded that the major problem with this process audit methodology was the possibility that the medical records may inadequately reflect the care given and that the methodology was unable to assess the final outcome. Only those patients who were identified as mismanaged were evaluated for outcome.[15]

Overton offered a microcomputer-based method for simplifying peer review data, using a popular spreadsheet. Physicians working in an emergency department reviewed representative samples of the 65,000 visits to that facility per year. Each physician reviewed two charts per shift, utilizing a standard process-oriented checklist. Every physician was given a code to ensure anonymity. The resulting information was entered onto the spread-sheet, which recorded performance records for each physician. Graphic feedback on performance compared to group norms and to other physicians was provided on a timely basis. To date, no data have been collected on improvement in performance.[16]

Flint et al. suggested that successful quality assurance programs in the emergency department require the active participation of all staff members, clinical and nonclinical. Describing the program in operation at the Michael Reese Hospital in Chicago, the authors noted that measures moni-toring structure (inventory, staff qualifications, etc.), process (workups, waiting times, therapies, etc.), and outcome (morbidity and mortality, complications, patient satisfaction and understanding, etc.) were divided among the entire staff. Flint and colleagues further emphasized the utility of criteria lists and audit results in improving care.[17] Maxwell et al., also writing about the Michael Reese program, demonstrated that those ER staff who participated in criteria and audit committees as part of the QA program gained increased knowledge, as assessed by objective test scores. A range of medical innovations relevant to peer participation followed these activities.[18]

The literature on the beneficial effects on behavior of peer review and feedback programs in the ambulatory care setting provides some basis, though not entirely conclusive support, for these assertions. As part of the Ambulatory Care Medical Audit Demonstration Project conducted from 1978 to 1982, Palmer and associates measured compliance to certain task performance (process) in 16 primary care group practice settings in a ran-domized controlled crossover trial of cycles of quality assurance. Their methods included meetings and mailings of the tasks to be reviewed, circulation of criteria lists, journal discussions, and active feedback of per-formance. The authors found task performance improved in two of the tasks (6.7 percent and 9.8 percent) over controls during intensive QA cycle intervention. There was marginal improvement in a third task and no improvement in three other tasks. The authors concluded that the quality assurance effort resulted only in limited improvement, even in highly mo-tivated practices where there was general agreement with criteria.[19]

Payne et al. postulated that simple feedback on performance does not change behavior. Noncoercive methods that involve health care providers in problem identification, problem solving, and solution implementation were felt to be more effective in changing behavior. The QA cycle of problem identification, consensus-building regarding significance and cor-rectability, action planning for correction, and remeasurement of deficiency was used to test this thesis. Physician panels developed optimal explicit criteria for specific diseases, and a physician performance index was devised using weighted scores for audited items. University and solo practice set-tings served as control and experimental groups for various levels of interventions. Control groups received feedback only. Experimental groups received either feedback and seminars (conducted in a retreat-like atmosphere) or feedback and seminars with postseminar consultations on implementing changes for improved performance. In this quasi-experimental study, physician performance indexes improved in both the intensive intervention and the control groups, but the increases were greater in the intensive intervention groups.[20]

Winickoff and associates reported the results of a study of compliance with colorectal screening criteria, using the computerized records in the Harvard Community Health Plan. Three different intervention strategies were employed in a randomized clinical trial utilizing a crossover design. Educational meetings, retrospective feedback of group compliance rates, and retrospective feedback of individual compliance rates compared with peers were used in the experimental group. Compliance rates improved from a baseline of 66 to 79.9 percent in the experimental group, as well as 67.7 to 76.6 percent in the control group. These results might reflect the spillover effect from the experimental group to the control group, since physicians in the two groups practiced in the same setting. In the second phase of the study, the experimental and control groups were reversed. The new control group (the first experimental group) stabilized its compliance rate at 80 percent, while the new experimental group improved from 76.6 to 84 percent. The authors offered this study as an example of the effectiveness of peer comparison feedback in improving quality of care. The costs of the study were considerable, however.[21]

Using a tracer methodology, HIP of Greater New York developed explicit process criteria for hypertension, otitis media, and breast lesions. An extensive and expensive 3-year audit of over 6,800 records at multiple sites and reaudits of over 700 records demonstrated that the quality of records had improved. Initial audits were followed by meetings with physician groups, open discussions of the findings and the criteria, and a letter of response for corrective action from medical directors for the sites. Outcome assessment was not performed in the HIP study. The process audits used were performed by trained abstractors. The cost of the project was estimated at 35.7 cents per enrollee.[22-23]

Hastings et al. compared the use of a simple peer review checklist for quality assessment to assessments using explicitly defined disease-specific protocols devised by expert reviewers who used re-examination of the patient by an expert physician as a gold standard. The authors found that peer review checklists performed as well as or better than the disease-specific protocols. Further, they found that even the physicians who actively engaged in developing the criteria failed to apply them uniformly to their practices.[24]

Kemeny and associates used a criteria map for chronic obstructive pulmonary disease and compared videotaped observation, chart audit, exit interviews with physicians, and exit interviews with patients to determine which method provided the best gauge of the adequacy of care as defined by the criteria map. The authors concluded that no method was perfect. The interviews were found to cover more aspects of the map than either the video or the chart audit.[25]

Finally, recognizing the complexity of the ambulatory care setting and the need for a simple, easily applied instrument for quality assessment and assurance, Oswald and Winer developed a uniform quality assessment form that has been applied to all 60 clinics at the University of Chicago on-site ambulatory care system. The data collected provide a blend of standard administrative indicators of performance, such as waiting times, missed appointments, patient satisfaction, clinic-specific procedures, complications, and clinic-specific criteria for quality. This uniform, centralized system allows for a streamlined methodology that can be applied to a large number of clinics. Data can be more easily collected, standardized, and analyzed. The emphasis on clinic-specific information encourages greater staff participation in a relatively centralized process.[26]

CONCLUSIONS AND DIRECTIONS

Striving for quality assurance in ambulatory care is not an easy task. Notions of quality and standards of care are often nebulous at best. The multiplicity of objectives for ambulatory visits renders it difficult to define successful outcome in a systematic fashion. Dependence on medical records of variable quality, the lack of a uniform data base for recording encounters, and the huge variability in patient characteristics make careful assessments of quality difficult. Finally, the uncertainty of the relationship between traditional notions of structure, process, and outcome of care challenges the researcher in quality assurance to accomplish the difficult task of developing valid methods for measuring quality.

These seemingly insurmountable barriers need not lead the health care worker concerned with providing quality care into deep despair. Instead, recognition of the multidimensional aspects of care in the ambulatory setting allows us to strive for improvement at multiple levels. Gains at each level should significantly contribute to the improvement of the overall "product." Cast in this light, quality assurance becomes an integral part of the culture of health care. Drawing from the literature of industrial quality control, Berwick has characterized this philosophical orientation with the Japanese word "kaizen," which can be translated to mean "the continuous search for opportunities for all processes to get better." An approach to quality assurance based on what he terms the "Theory of Continuous Improvement" holds every defect to be a treasure that allows for insight into the ways to improve the production process. Carefully implemented, "kaizen" shifts the entire curve over to a higher standard. In contrast, quality assurance efforts based on a regulatory model, what Berwick terms the "Theory of Bad Apples," search only for the outlier. The curve becomes more compressed, but the mean remains the same. This search for the bad apples encourages a wholly defensive posture rather than a communal striving to do better.[27] Knowledge and understanding of truly high quality ambulatory care are simply not sophisticated enough to support a stubborn defense of the status quo.

What requirements support these broad efforts to improve overall quality of care in the ambulatory setting? Quality must be a top priority of health care leaders. There must be substantial investment of resources, technical expertise, managerial time, and research. Valid instruments for data collection and objective assessments must be developed. All individuals involved in the health care process must receive feedback on all quality assurance efforts. Without staff training, education, and active participation in a partnership to improve care, quality assurance in ambulatory care can be of only limited benefit to the population at large.

NOTES

1. R.H. Palmer, "The Challenges and Prospects for Quality Assessment and Assurance in Ambulatory Care," *Inquiry* 25 (1988):119–131. (Quote p. 120.)

2. Joint Commission Forum. "Monitoring and Evaluation of the Quality and Appropriateness of Care: An Ambulatory Health Care Example," *Quality Review Bulletin* (January 1987):26–30.

3. R.H. Palmer and H.R. Nesson, "A Review of Methods for Ambulatory Medical Care Evaluations," *Medical Care* 20 (1982):758–781.

4. Joint Commission Forum, "Monitoring and Evaluation of the Quality and Appropriateness of Care."

5. D.S Benson, C. Gartner, J. Anderson, H. Schweer and R. Kirchgessner, "The Ambulatory Care Parameter: A Structured Approach to QA in the Ambulatory Care Setting," *Quality Review Bulletin* (February 1987):51–55.

6. E. Flanagan, "Indicators of Quality in Ambulatory Care," *Quality Review Bulletin* (April 1985):136–137.

7. D.M. Berwick, "Continuous Improvement As an Ideal in Health Care," *New England Journal of Medicine* 320 (1989):53–56.

8. B.S. Hulka, F.J. Romm, R.T. Parkerson, N.G. Clapp, and F.S. Johnson, "Peer Review in Ambulatory Care: Explicit Criteria and Implicit Judgement. Summary and Recommendations," *Medical Care* 17 (March 1979 Supplement):66–73.

9. P.J. Sanazaro and R.M. Worth, "Measuring Clinical Performance of Individual Internists in Office and Hospital Practice," *Medical Care* 23 (1985):1097–1114.

10. F.J. Romm and B.S. Hulka, "Peer Review in Diabetes and Hypertension: The Relationship between Care Process and Patient Outcome," *Southern Medical Journal* 73 (May 1980):564–568.

11. T.O. Stair, "Quality Assurance," *Emergency Medicine Clinics of North America* 5, no. 1 (February 1987):41–50.

12. R. Brook and F. Appel, "Quality of Care Assessment: Choosing a Method for Peer Review," *New England Journal of Medicine* 288 (1973):1323–1329.

13. D.M. Berwick and M.G. Knapp, "Theory and Practice for Measuring Health Care Quality," *Health Care Financing Review* (Annual Supplement 1987):49–55. (Quote p. 51.)

14. J.E. Whitcomb, H. Stuevenen, D. Tonsfeldt, and G. Kastenson, "Quality Assurance in the Emergency Department," *Annals of Emergency Medicine* 14, no. 12 (December 1985):1199–1204.

15. F.P. Harchelroad, M.L. Martin, R.M. Kremen, and K.W. Murray, "Emergency Department Daily Record Review: A Quality Assurance System in a Teaching Hospital," *Quarterly Review Bulletin* (February 1988):45–49.

16. D.T. Overton, "A Computer-Assisted Emergency Department Chart Audit," *Annals of Emergency Medicine* 16, no. 1 (January 1987):68–72.

17. L.S. Flint, W.H. Hammett, and K. Martens, "Quality Assurance in the Emergency Department," *Annals of Emergency Medicine* 14, no. 2 (February 1985):134–138.

18. J.A. Maxwell, L.J. Sandlow, and P.G. Bashook, "Effect of Medical Care Evaluation Program on Physician Knowledge and Performance," *Journal of Medical Education* 59 (January 1984):33–38.

19. R.H. Palmer, T.A. Louis, L.N. Hsu, H.F. Peterson, J.K. Rothrock, R. Strain, M.S. Thompson, and E.A. Wright, "A Randomized Controlled Trial of Quality Assurance in Sixteen Ambulatory Care Practices," *Medical Care* 23 (June 1985):751–769.

20. B.C. Payne, T.F. Lyons, E. Neuhaus, M. Kolton, and L. Dwarshius, "Method of Evaluating and Improving Ambulatory Medical Care," *Health Services Research* 19 (June 1984): 2219–2245.

21. R.N. Winickoff, K.L. Coltin, M.M. Morgan, R.C. Buxbaum, and G.O. Barnett, "Improving Physician Performance through Peer Comparison Feedback," *Medical Care* 22 (June 1984):527–534.

22. J.M. Deuschle, B. Alvarez, D.N. Logsdon, W.M. Stahl, and H. Smith, "Physician Performance in Prepaid Health Plan: Results of the Peer Review Program of the Health Insurance Plan of Greater New York," *Medical Care* 20 (1982):127–142.

23. "Implementation of a Peer Review System for Ambulatory Care. Experience of the Health Insurance Plan of Greater New York," *Public Health Reports* 93 (1978):258–267.

24. G.E. Hastings, R. Sonneborn, G.H. Lee, L. Vick, and L. Sasmor, "Peer Review Checklist: Reproducibility and Validity of a Method for Evaluating the Quality of Ambulatory Care," *American Journal of Public Health* 70 (March 1980):222–228.

25. M.E. Kemeny, W.A. Hargreaves, B. Gerbert, G.C. Stone, and D.S. Gullion, "Measuring Adequacy of Physician Performance: A Preliminary Comparison of Four Methods of Ambulatory Care of Chronic Obstructive Pulmonary Disease," *Medical Care* 22 (July 1984):620–631.

26. E.M. Oswald and I.K. Winer, "A Simple Approach to Quality Assurance in a Complex Ambulatory Care Setting," *Quality Review Bulletin* (February 1987):56–60.

27. D.M. Berwick, "Continuous Improvement As an Ideal in Health Care."

SUGGESTED READING

Berman, S. "Quality Assurance in Ambulatory Health Care." *Quality Review Bulletin* 18–21, January 1988.

Morehead, M.A., and Donaldson, R. "Quality of Clinical Management of Disease in Comprehensive Neighborhood Health Centers." *Medical Care* 12:301–315, April 1974.

Palmer, R.H., Strain, R., Mauer, J., Rothrock, J.K., and Thompson, M.S. "Quality Assurance in Eight Adult Medicine Group Practices." *Medical Care* 22:632–643, 1984.

Strain, R., Palmer, R.H. et al. "Implementing Quality Assurance Studies in Ambulatory Care." *Quarterly Review Bulletin* 168–173, June 1984.

Part V

Organizational Issues

Nancy O. Graham

In Chapter 16, Lois Bittle stresses that health care institutions are being held accountable to demonstrate their ability to provide high quality health care. Management's role is to create an environment that is conducive to planning, controlling, and improving service. The importance of leadership, attitude, accountability, role clarification, standards, and systems is also discussed. The chapter emphasizes that attention to quality begins with people, not things.

Integrated Quality Assurance (IQA) is a model for concurrent review that seeks to integrate the medical staff review component of quality assurance and data collection with risk management, utilization review, and infection control. IQA is an approach for streamlining procedures for systematically reviewing quality. In Chapter 17, Dr. Longo describes this quality management system and how it integrates the full spectrum of quality-related review activities.

In Chapter 18, Dr. Fifer states that quality assurance is evolving from an age of criterion-based peer review to the computer age—an era of norms, data bases, and statistical analysis. The analytic power of computers has helped shed light on Wennberg's small area variation. HCFA's mortality data and the volume/quality of surgical death rates point to the fact that the challenges for the future will be to maintain data quality and to adjust form–case mix, while giving special emphasis to severity of illness. Computers may provide what Dr. Codman advocated in 1914, that is, a means to assure quality by analyzing the results of the care that is provided.

In Chapter 19, Lois Bittle and Mitchell Curtis discuss the concept of information management. With the growing need to demonstrate the quality and efficiency of services provided and with the increasing cost of obtaining information, the health care industry is looking at what data exist and what data can be reused to support the organization in its quality management quests. Technology, personnel, and organizational issues are discussed.

Chapter 16

Quality Management: The Infrastructure for Quality Assurance

Lois J. Bittle

MANAGING QUALITY THROUGH CONFORMANCE TO ESTABLISHED STANDARDS AND PRINCIPLES

Organizations at the federal, state, and private levels are joining forces to collect data on the quality of health care to determine whether the services provided are clinically effective, afford patient satisfaction, and are clinically efficient. More specifically, the American Hospital Association, American Medical Association, Joint Commission on Accreditation of Healthcare Organizations, government agencies, and business coalitions are defining quality from several perspectives. This redefinition of quality has led to the beginning of quality measurement through the use of hard data such as mortality, surgical complication rates, infection rates, inappropriate admissions, and readmissions.

This environment further suggests that business and industry will impact the health care delivery process dramatically. According to the Health Care Financing Administration, expenditures for health care services in the United States topped $500 billion in 1988. The move toward giving employees the power to ask questions based on the use of computerized data categorized by practitioner, by procedure, and by health care institution will support decisions and essentially control the flow of health care dollars into the system.

Today, in response to this environment and public demand, health care institutions are being held more accountable to demonstrate their ability to carry out their role as providers of quality health care. Measuring quality will remain the job of the organization and the provider. Purchasers, on the other hand, will continue to set their own expectations and reward providers by using their services.

Lois J. Bittle, RN, MPA, is President of Bittle & Associates, Inc., Baltimore, Maryland.

Setting the Stage for Performance

Quality management is conformance to requirements that are defined in specific terms, measurable, and cost-effective. An accountability system, which is well-defined in corporate documents and introduced throughout the organization by an extensive educational effort, provides the basis for problem resolution at the lowest level and holds all individuals accountable for their own performance and those they supervise. Management's role is to create the expectations and the environment for planning, controlling, and improving services through appropriate leadership, training, and application.

The delivery of health care is guided by a number of standards, regulations, and legal requirements. For example, the Joint Commission identifies standards and required characteristics applicable to the health care environment. These selective standards provide established guidelines to assist health care organizations to achieve their basic mission. Such guidelines and other licensing and regulatory requirements aid in setting the stage for performance.

Within the health care organization, additional guidelines are defined based on corporate law and internal policy. Organization bylaws are critical to the process of defining the purpose of the organization and determining what services will be provided or exist, who will be providing the services, how the efficiency and effectiveness of those services will be measured, and what recourse is available when the standards set forth by the institution are breached.

In order to effectively set the stage for performance, those at the executive level must have a clear understanding of quality. Quality for the institution is defined at the board level in the mission statement. For example, *the provision of services will be appropriate to the needs of the community, provided by competent, well-trained staff, and provided efficiently within the parameters of the available resources of the institution. The care provided will be in a safe environment, utilizing current technology and affording access to all.*

Policies and procedures at the administrative level and within each department provide parameters for performance. This establishment of parameters is followed by a selective hiring process to ensure that competent individuals are providing the service. Focused orientation of each employee establishes corporate philosophy, the mission and goals of the organization, and individual accountability for maintaining these goals. To ensure conformance, objective performance appraisals at all levels, first on a provisional basis and then annually, will ensure the organization's commitment to quality.

Emphasis on "Zero Defect" Prevention

As previously stated, the Joint Commission, professional societies, state and federal agencies, and the courts have defined minimal standards for hospital performance. More specifically, the Joint Commission's standards outline the roles of the governing body, administration, medical staff, nursing, and support services. These guidelines are designed to provide parameters for health care organizations to support appropriate performance, to measure performance (against the prescribed standards), and to define areas in need of improvement.

According to the literature, 85 percent of poor quality results from the "system" and 15 percent can be clearly attributed to individuals. From a management perspective, it becomes apparent that monitoring conformance to established guidelines can preclude the occurrence of an unanticipated event.

Multiple approaches have been used to identify those areas in the health care delivery process that need improvement. Audits, incident reporting, and "mass inspection" have proven to be ineffective and, in some cases, cost-prohibitive. Further, the process of "finding and fixing," in many instances, may only restore the problem to its original state. Preventing the problem, however, *is* cost-effective and efficient. It precludes the unanticipated outcome, which creates a perception of poor quality and the potential for litigation in a health care setting. Prevention also precludes the unnecessary use of scarce resources to repeat a process of care caused by nonconformance to procedure.

According to Deming's philosophy, the process of inspecting every part of the health care delivery process is inefficient. Deming argues that if the "production system" is good, quality is built into the process, not inspected in. The "zero defect" concept, then, relies on a well-established infrastructure created through well-conceived bylaws, rules, regulations, policies, procedures, and job descriptions, followed by conformance in order to prevent events from happening in the first place. This "zero defect" concept focuses on those problems or errors that are preventable, establishes a sense of common purpose, and provides for quality service within the parameters of the individual's control.

ORGANIZATIONAL ENVIRONMENT

Commitment to Quality Performance

Nothing short of top level commitment and leadership will make quality a reality. Institutional elements, such as quality of the work and work environment and proper attitudes, support the policy of doing the job right the first time. This sense of pride and corporate caring filters down through the organization—attention to quality begins with people, not things. Therefore, education of all members of the organization, demonstrated commitment, the development of plans to assure that quality service is provided, and the maintenance of quality performance as an organizational culture all serve to create an environment for total quality management.

Quality management in health care is, above all, a systems approach to ensuring that patient care delivery proceeds according to policy, procedure, and protocol; it is a management discipline that creates the climate for preventing the unanticipated outcome.

Historically, however, while there may be precise administrative direction for establishing budgets, services, and the like, management's role in the assessment of quality of care may be poorly defined. The administrative functions that support quality service may be defined in broad terms, e.g., "oversee the budget, staffing and services provided within the ancillary department," and no guidance is given on defining the specific role of management in organizing this functional discipline. Traditional established social communication depersonalizes and/or blurs accountability, and without adequate direction or definition, each individual makes up his/her own rules.

In addition, quality management is not outcome-oriented; rather, it is one aspect of planning, is interactive, and is process-oriented. The end result of quality management, therefore, is a critical review of the structure, process, and outcome of service delivered.

According to Juran, quality management encompasses a three-part process: quality planning, quality control, and quality improvement. *Quality assurance* only becomes tangible as the fourth element or when it incorporates itself into the planning, control, and improvement processes.

To establish an effective quality management program, inaccurate assumptions regarding quality must be altered (e.g., quality is good or bad, not measurable, hard to define; health care delivery is different; quality is the QA department's job). Changing attitudes begins by defining the perception of quality within the organization and focusing facility-wide education on the accepted internal definition.

Management As Role Models

Successful management recognizes that the worker provides the impetus for quality improvement. Second level administrative personnel (e.g., vice presidents, assistant administrators, etc.) should begin to view quality as a continuum, not a destination, and should understand that, as leaders, they are ultimately accountable for what happens within their span of control. It becomes critical, then, to view a move toward quality improvement as a continuous educational process, with management aware that listening to reports from workers is mandatory. Further, management must realize that these discussions of quality are not merely words, but are demonstrations that by doing it right the first time the cost of rework is eliminated, which translates into bottom line dollars.

Management as role models serves as the infrastructure for providing cost-effective, efficient quality services. Quality planning, quality control, and quality improvement fall within the confines of each managerial level and each individual's defined job description, albeit in different degrees.

This attitude at the leadership level sets the stage for organizational performance. If an employee thinks management is uncaring, inconsistent in its requirements for conformance, or uncertain of its own role, that employee will respond accordingly. Management's demonstrated commitment, support, and intervention, however, can move the patient care delivery process toward a cost-effective, prevention-oriented environment conducive to improving outcomes.

True quality management places less emphasis on data collected through traditional quality assessment, utilization review, and risk management activities. It has become clear that these functions, when performed based on compliance with external agency requirements, merely create a stockpile of unrelated data, which accomplishes little in terms of quality improvement. Quality management places more emphasis on the role of individuals to perform in the manner prescribed.

Managers visibly striving for quality will foster the appropriate behaviors within their personal span of control. Ultimately, quality will be measured and reported by conformance, and quality improvement will be noted in outcomes, both bottom line and patient care.

INFRASTRUCTURE AS THE DETERMINANT OF QUALITY

Building Quality into the Product

A successful organization requires leadership, quality-directed dimensions, a culture within the organization to support and encourage response from other participants, the ability to communicate, and the talent to orchestrate activities. Additionally, a successful organization needs middle managers with both knowledge and value systems to make the organization work. An effective way to begin building quality into the product, not unlike the credentials process, is to selectively hire the individuals who are the infrastructure for quality assurance. These individuals must be able to "think systems" and must be committed to focusing on performance as an acceptable framework within which all elements of service are provided.

To achieve this end, expectations must be clarified at the outset. Leadership in organizations seeking excellence create a favorable attitude toward and impart the philosophy and value system of the organization, thereby creating expectations on the part of both administration and middle management. In doing so and where members of management provide the behavior role models, an unconditional commitment to quality is created, with more emphasis on doing it right the first time and less emphasis on "finding and fixing."

Organizational Behavioral Performance

The management philosophy used in Japanese business after World War II was rejected by the American business community. However, industry experts such as Deming, Juran, and Feigenbaum saw the potential of the Japanese approach and developed a new philosophy that worked from the premise that each department and each individual contributes to the overall quality of the product and everyone is accountable for the outcome. In industry, these techniques have proven their merit and have demonstrated that the most important determinant of quality is the degree of interaction among the individuals involved.

Hospitals must move toward developing an interpersonal support system that will view employees as clients as well as physicians and patients. Where there is evidence that management is personally committed to participating in quality management, the quality level is raised and the likelihood of everyone's participation is enhanced.

Quality assurance programs may be ineffective if too much effort is expended in settling real or imagined problems on a day-to-day basis, and not enough time is spent in planning positive actions and/or approaches that would preclude such problems from developing in the first place.

Orchestrators and Providers of Care

Human interface is a predictor of performance. Quality is an institutional culture dominated by individual response. Performance is based on knowledge, experience, competence, supervision, *and attitude*. Management's role, then, is to create expectations, establish requirements for each job/position, orient employees on how to meet these requirements, and demonstrate management's commitment to accomplishing these goals by assisting and encouraging employees to meet these requirements. This interface continually educates the employees as to their individual roles and promotes the recognition that inappropriate interventions create untoward outcomes.

In the health care setting, physicians are the orchestrators of care. Both orchestrators *and providers* of care determine the level of quality. It is commonly perceived that poor quality, high costs, and medical malpractice stem largely from the performance of the medical staff. However, statistics show that only a small percentage of physicians are involved in actual malpractice. Industry has found that the high cost and poor quality of service often partially result from inefficiencies within the organization. Moreover, in the well-published *Darling* and *Misericordia* cases, the courts clearly identified the hospital as a major contributor to the adverse outcomes. This exemplifies the importance of the infrastructure and the "system" of patient care delivery.

Employees are "customers for the organization's services." Well-trained, satisfied employees can be expected to comply with performance guidelines established by the organization. Each individual, each department, and each manager is accountable for both the quality of the service performed and the resulting "product." In the health care industry, this "product" is the treated and discharged patient.

Accountability for quality care in nursing practice begins with management and rests ultimately with the hands-on provider of care. The process of quality management is most obvious in this setting since nursing activities are *planned,* i.e., defining the ends to be achieved and the means to achieve them; *organized,* i.e., defining the nature and content of each job, grouping jobs, and delegating authority; and *controlled,* i.e., ensuring that planned outcomes and actual outcomes are consistent.

Each of the components of quality management mentioned has broader applications, but for the purpose of this chapter, they demonstrate the vital role nurses play in determining the quality of patient care. Thus, commitment from nursing administration is critical. Nurses provide round-the-clock services and therefore create a substantive infrastructure for providing safe, efficient, cost-effective care.

This group, more than any other in the hospital setting, has the greatest potential to set the stage for performance and accountability by defining parameters for its own performance and also by upholding the parameters set forth in comprehensive hospital policy related to the nursing profession *and* the organization as a whole.

Relationship between Structure, Process, and Outcome

Donabedian emphasizes the importance of structure, process, and outcome in the evaluation of health care delivery. He argues that outcomes reflect the result of the total intervention, i.e., the effectiveness of the intervention. Structure is more a predictor of outcome than an indicator of quality. Thus, elements of the organizational environment and qualifications of the providers, those human and technological elements that support or propel behavior, must be considered powerful influences that govern patient outcome.

In regard to nursing's role in quality assurance, it is generally perceived that nursing measures nursing performance and that the results of these evaluations remain within the confines of the nursing organization. Little has been done to effectively eradicate the lines of division between the orchestrators and the providers of care. In summary, the fundamental responsibility of nursing is the administration of hospital policy as it pertains to patient care.

Nursing is the infrastructure for comprehensive, effective quality assurance, risk management, and utilization management. In nursing, as with the facility-wide QA program, commitment from both the administration and nursing leadership is essential. Evidence of this commitment is demonstrated by:

- documented ongoing, systematic monitoring and evaluation processes that encompass major clinical functions
- education of the nursing leadership and staff on their legal and ethical responsibilities for problem-oriented patient care assessment
- support by nursing leadership in effective implementation of and adherence to policies and procedures
- periodic privilege and skills inventory
- established, documented communication processes
- effective procedures for taking action

It is well-known that multiple factors often contribute to an undesired "bad" outcome. There are, in fact, systems problems that, if "managed," would/could support the development of a quality product. The concept of "managing" quality has been evident in the business and industry sectors largely since the inception of manufacturing. This concept resulted in the development of quality control mechanisms to ensure product reliability.

In the health care industry, these mechanisms translate into bylaws, rules and regulations, policies, procedures, protocols, and job descriptions. These well-defined mechanisms set the parameters for performance. Using these parameters at every level in the health care delivery process creates an environment in which quality can be built into the "product" (the treated and discharged patient).

Each individual is held accountable for producing a quality service and adhering to established parameters for performance. This application produces a continuum of *assess, apply, stop,* or *proceed* for each aspect of service provided to the patient.

One example of how this quality management activity supports "building quality into the product" is provided below.

Case scenario: A patient expired during an elective cataract removal procedure.

Quality management:

1. Prior to surgery, the patient had laboratory studies, an EKG, and a chest X-ray performed.
2. These laboratory values were not available in the patient's medical record:
   (a) when the history and physical were performed
   (b) at the time of preoperative medication administration
   (c) upon entering the operating suite
   (d) at the time of anesthesia induction
   (e) at the time surgery began

The missing laboratory values and EKG demonstrated major cardiac changes that, if reviewed, would have canceled surgery. An effective quality management program (i.e., building quality into the product) would have assessed the situation and stopped the process at any juncture noted in step 2.

FRAGMENTED QUALITY ASSESSMENT

For most hospitals, the process of "*quality assurance*" follows prescribed accrediting body or other external agency guidelines. In many cases, *risk management* is perceived as insurance or administratively related; *utilization management* is viewed as a federal mandate. Thus, less attention is focused on responding to the internal needs of the organization. Moreover, within the organization, direction for each of these activities comes from separate and distinct areas of administration, further adding to the confusion.

Defining Quality Assurance, Risk Management, and Utilization Management (QA, RM, and UM)

Quality assurance, simply defined, is a program designed to evaluate and improve patient care through identification, evaluation, and correction of problems in the patient care delivery process.

Risk management is a comprehensive program for the identification, evaluation, and control of risks that affect patient, staff, and visitor safety, as well as the hospital's assets.

Utilization management is a program that plans, organizes, directs, and controls the delivery of the health care product in a cost-effective manner.

The entire integrated program is usually referred to as "QA programs"; this term and the letters QA, RM, and UM are used interchangeably in this text. "QA programs" should be designed to enhance patient care through the ongoing objective assessment of important aspects of care and the correction of identified problems. Such programs, if well organized, will emphasize integration and coordination (to the degree possible) of quality assurance and related activities, such as utilization management, risk management, infection control, nursing QA, and required medical staff peer review functions.

As management tools, these interventions control not only the quality of the "product," but also the use of unplanned resources. Envision this case scenario: if the patient survived the surgery in the previous "case scenario" and was unexpectedly transferred to ICU.

Further, these interventions reduce the potential for unanticipated events that lead to malpractice claims. Envision this same "case scenario" where, with appropriate quality management, the surgery would have been postponed until the patient was stabilized.

In summary, QA can serve as an effective tool to help hospital management assure cost-effective, good quality patient care. As a management tool, a QA program offers the following significant benefits:

- QA improves production processes. QA evaluates prospective or intermediate outcomes and thus identifies the individual risk factors and their influence on outcomes.
- QA influences the organization's decision-making processes to improve performance. Objective QA, RM, and UM financial data can improve strategic planning, resource consumption, and physician behavior.
- QA review of the process of patient care lowers risk. QA helps reduce the hospital's financial risk through problem identification and resolution.
- QA utilizes senior medical staff time more efficiently. An effective QA structure, using criteria-based review, saves time by using physicians to review the results of the patient care review process.
- QA utilizes support staff more productively. Current UR, QA staff, and others who review charts for select purposes are trained to review records for multiple purposes and to collect data for multiple issues.

Structure and Perceptions That Support Fragmentation

Fragmented quality assessment programs stem from structure as well as perception. Some major factors that contribute to this fragmentation are as follows:

- Confusion over the roles of the professional and clinical staffs. These two principal groups function in different organizational structures. The medical staff, through its own committee structure, reports directly to the board, while the nursing and support staffs report to the hospital administration. The medical staff is "self governing," but hospital staff personnel are controlled by the administration. This blurred relationship occurs primarily in voluntary hospitals where physicians are self-employed practitioners or members of group practices and maintain no employee relationship with the hospital.

- The perception within the medical staff that the Medical Executive Committee, as the action body of the medical staff, is accountable solely to the medical staff, not the governing body.

- The perception that administratively motivated quality monitoring requirements interfere with efforts to support or implement a sound quality management program.

Regarding structure, the Medical Executive Committee is responsible for overseeing that the medical staff carry out their responsibilities for the "functions" designed to monitor clinical performance. These functions include surgical case review, blood utilization, medical records assessment, and review of the credentials of applicants for staff appointment and reappointment.

Typically, the supervisory structure of the medical staff is based on the *appointment of department chairmen and chiefs of staff. Appointed committees* oversee these "functions." These committees review the assigned topic to determine appropriateness; the information generated usually remains within the confines of the committee and/or is reported directly to the Medical Executive Committee. In such a structure, the derived data rarely interface with and/or are communicated directly to the clinical departments where the services are actually rendered. The extent to which professional performance is reviewed through this structure is minimal, and, historically, these activities have not modified behavior. Medical staff bylaws continue to reflect an outdated perspective. In the past, the need for complete medical records was not as great as in today's environment in which complete documents are required for third party payments. Sanctions designed to curb these inappropriate behaviors are not suited to an environment in which financial viability is a necessity, not an option, and in which it is less of an ethical or clinical performance issue.

Credentials and Privileges

The process of credentialing and privileging on the basis of training and competence is the cornerstone of a successful quality management program. Despite the case law that has evolved supporting inappropriate credentials procedures in hospitals, little change has occurred in the actual activities. While this function has the potential to support appropriate quality, not only case law but statistics from the Joint Commission demonstrate that this process is not meeting its potential.

More recently, however, the initial credentials process is moving toward its potential, with new applicants being critiqued in a more systematic, thorough way. Barriers that continue to exist, however, include:

- willingness of physicians to be candid about the applicant's shortcomings
- lack of data to demonstrate appropriate or inappropriate performance
- lack of clear understanding of "qualified privilege" and immunity statutes to protect the individuals providing the information
- conspiracy of silence

Generally, credentials review is performed by the hospital administrator, the medical staff coordinator, and the credentials committee. These individuals act on behalf of the medical staff to fulfill the responsibility for evaluating candidates' credentials for suitability of appointment or reappointment to the medical staff and to submit their findings to department chairmen and the governing body. This process is the fundamental step in quality management. It is the entry point not only to membership to the medical staff but also to defining the scope of practice through delineation of privileges.

Despite the changing environment little attention is focused on the applicant's awareness of quality management during the credentials process. When this process ignores the business of managing quality, we lose a significant opportunity to elicit a commitment that the applicant will pursue staff functions in line with the organization's established objectives. We also lose an opportunity to foster a positive attitude toward quality management, thereby preventing future problems.

Roles and Responsibilities

The argument that good quality management programs do not exist because physicians are reluctant to participate is no longer valid. The role of the medical staff in quality management activities is critical. However, the true role of the medical staff should be considered advisory; the staff should support these programs with both clinical guidance and assistance in formulating the standards and/or criteria used for evaluation.

The role of the administrator in traditional quality assurance, risk management, and utilization management programs is generally poorly defined.

The president of the medical staff and the hospital administrator appear to have equal status. Moreover, the administrator's direct accountability to the board is clearly mandated. The accountability of the medical staff to the administrator, however, is generally less clear. Consequently, the medical staff feels no obligation to keep the administration informed of its quality assessment findings. (Exceptions occur where assessment identifies problems of a critical nature.) This lack of communication is further reinforced by the administrator's lack of willingness to confront the medical staff on quality issues. The administrative staff, on the other hand, is required to report directly to the administrator, and the decision-making authority is clear.

Another factor that diminishes the administrative role in quality management is the fact that quality assessment activities are often not considered to be a budgetary item. Professional staffs are asked to collect, analyze, report, and/or otherwise participate in extraneous quality assessment activities *as part of their work process.* (In true QM, IT IS THE WORK PROCESS!) In business and industry, quality assessment activities represent 5 to 15 percent of the annual budget. Specific responsibilities are assigned to a high administrative level within the organization and there are specific requirements for program implementation, monitoring, and effectiveness. In the health care industry, on the other hand, this function is delegated to managerial or below managerial levels. In some instances, only one individual is accountable at the administrative level (often representing 10 to 20 percent of the job function); in most instances, responsibilities are spread over a number of administrative personnel, e.g., Director of Finance/medical records, Vice President, patient care services/QA, and President/risk management.

Responsibilities for coordination of facility-wide activities are usually delegated to one individual; however, the role in general has been poorly defined. In many cases, these responsibilities have been assigned without providing appropriate training; individuals are hired and/or assume the position with minimal knowledge, and the program design is often not compatible with the philosophy, personality, or structure of the organization.

This exemplifies management's understanding of and attitude toward quality management. In this scenario, there is no comprehension of quality assessment as a management tool, problems will be addressed as they occur, and quality management is not viewed as an essential part of the organization. Such an approach also indicates that quality improvement activities are crisis-oriented, rather than part of the normal work process.

THE MEDICAL-LEGAL CLIMATE

Rise of Claims

Attempts at monitoring the quality of care through peer review have often failed. Perhaps out of fear, concern, or reluctance to "point the finger," hospitals have been unwilling to address the real issues of quality.

In any given circumstance, mistakes may be made, care delivery systems may break down, and a few incompetent doctors may still manage to move from hospital to hospital and state to state because of poor credentialing processes. It is then the goal of clinical RM to objectively identify systems, areas, and personnel that impede either the delivery of quality care or the effective response to patient needs.

While hospital risk management programs are only beginning to evolve, the severity and frequency of claims against hospitals continue to rise. For example, in its 1986 report, the American Hospital Association Task Force on Professional Liability cited the following increases for claims filed per 100 occupied beds between 1976 and 1985:

- average number of claims against physicians: from 7.9 to 17.8
- average paid award or settlement from physician claim: from $17,600 to $70,200
- average number of claims against hospitals: from 1.5 to 3.4
- average paid award or settlement from hospital claim: from $7,500 to $40,300.

Other major changes occurring in the health care environment include:

- *Institution of tort reform bills.* Many state legislatures have examined professional medical liability tort reform bills and, in some instances, have then passed comprehensive legislation or liability-related bills.

- *Mandatory QA and RM programs.* In 1986, the state of New York ordered that a QA and RM program be in place in every hospital and that "adverse" events be defined and reported to the New York Department of Health.

- *New required conditions for hospital malpractice insurance.* Many major malpractice insurance companies are considering no longer insuring hospitals for medical liability if the hospitals do not, in turn, require their physicians individually to have a specified amount of malpractice insurance.

- *Subsidized physicians' insurance premiums.* Possibly as a result of the above, some hospitals have begun to subsidize their staff physicians' insurance premiums.

- *Federal intervention.* The Health Care Quality Improvement Act of 1986, legislation designed to provide immunity from damages arising under state or federal law to persons or entities participating in or providing information for peer review, includes the creation of a National Data Bank. The proposed rules require that hospitals and all other health care entities must report to the appropriate state medical board and to the "Bank" all settlements and adverse peer review determinations. Additionally, the rules call for hospitals to request such information routinely as part of physician credentials review.

The Courts' View

After years of excluding hospitals from actions, the courts have increasingly taken a hard line on a hospital's responsibility to protect its patients and staff. This new stance can be shown dramatically by considering the well-known *Nork* and *Darling* cases. In *Darling,* the highest court of the state of Illinois considered a case in which a young man was treated in a hospital emergency room for a leg fracture. Complications that were felt to reflect improper care ultimately led to the amputation of the leg. In the *Nork* case, Dr. Nork was found to have improperly performed spinal fusions on a number of patients for several years, with no evidence of any hospital intervention. In 1972, the California court found that the hospital was liable because it had failed to meet its duty to protect its patients from malpractice by a member of its medical staff, when it knew or should have known that malpractice was likely to be committed.

The legal impact of these and other court decisions has placed increased emphasis on accountability and the need to look more critically at the organizational culture as a whole. It is no longer sufficient for a hospital merely to state what is expected as an outcome of appropriate medical care. The hospital must now take a direct role to assure that outcome, including ongoing review of those responsible. Although the responsibility for quality of care is delegated, the hospital board remains ultimately accountable, and will need to focus on both the clinical and administrative roles and responsibilities of managing the quality of care provided.

Hospitals portray themselves to the community as providers of health care services and, as such, have the duty to "first do no harm." Therefore, the same public pressure that increased the number of lawsuits filed against medical institutions has led to an even greater demand for effective quality assessment. In upholding the public trust, hospitals must be prepared to demonstrate a commitment to Quality Management.

SUGGESTED READING

Bittle, Lois J. *The Manual for Quality Assurance: Integrating Quality, Risk and Utilization Management Programs and Criteria Based Review.* Baltimore, Md.: Bittle & Assoc. Inc., 1989.

Burda, David. "Providers Look to Industry for Quality Models." *Modern Healthcare* 18(29) (July 1988): 24–26.

Carroll, Jean Gayton. *Restructuring Hospital QA, The New Guide for Health Care Providers.* Homewood, Ill.: Dow Jones-Irwin, 1984.

Case, John. "Zero-Defect Management." *INC* Magazine (February 1987): 17–18.

Crosby, Philip B. *Quality Is Free.* New York: McGraw-Hill Book Co., 1979.

Darling v. Charleston Memorial Hospital 33 Ill. 2d 326,211 N.E. 2d 253 (1965) cert. denied 383.U.S.946 (1966).

Donabedian A. "Evaluating the Quality of Medical Care." *Milbank Mem. Fund Q,* 44(3) Part 2 (1966): 166–203.

Greyic MD, S.D., O'Sullivan MD, JD, D.D., and Whermacher MD, W.H. "Organizational Control of Hospital Infrastructure Determines the Quality of Care." *Quality Assurance and Utilization Review* 4(1) (February 1989).

Johnson v. Misericordia Community Hospital, 294 N.W. 2d501 (Wis. Ct. of App., May 12, 1980).

Joint Commission on Accreditation of Healthcare Organizations. *Accreditation Manual for Hospitals.* Chicago, Ill., 1988.

Kirk, Roey. *Healthcare Quality & Productivity: Practical Management Tools,* Rockville, Md.: Aspen Publishers, Inc., 1988.

Peters, Thomas J., and Waterman, Jr., Robert H. *In Search of Excellence.* New York: Warner Books, 1982.

Shroeder, Partricia S., and Maibusch, Regina M. *Nursing Quality Assurance—A Unit-Based Approach.* Rockville, Md.: Aspen Publishers, Inc., 1984.

Walton, Mary. *The Deming Management Method.* New York: Putnam, 1986.

Chapter 17

Integrating Quality Assurance into a Quality Management Program

Daniel R. Longo

INTRODUCTION

The origin of the Integrated Quality Assessment (IQA) model lies in the need of the three Chicago-affiliated hospitals of the Ancilla System (a multihospital system headquartered in Elk Grove Village, Illinois) to develop an effective and efficient Quality Management System. Later, the pressing need of hospitals in New York State to implement a concurrent review system caused the initial developer to work closely with New York hospitals to blend the stringent regulatory requirements of the New York State Public Health Law as it applies to hospital quality assurance into the IQA approach. Finally, the developer collaborated with the Director of Quality Assurance, U.S. Navy and Joint Commission Consultant, Dr. Jonathan Lord, to develop the IQA model more fully. The IQA Workbook was initially produced by the Hospital Association of New York State and subsequently was published nationally by American Hospital Publishing. This chapter summarizes the major components of the model, which is more fully described in *Integrated Quality Assessment: A Model for Concurrent Review.*

Accordingly, the purpose of this chapter is to provide a comprehensive summary of the IQA model as it relates to hospitals' medical staffs and

Note: Based on *Integrated Quality Assessment: A Model for Concurrent Review* by D.R. Longo, K.R. Ciccone, and J.T. Lord, published by American Hospital Publishing, Inc., © 1989.

Daniel R. Longo, Sc.D., is President of The Corporation of the Hospital Research and Educational Trust, American Hospital Association, Chicago, Illinois.

their quality management review functions. Basically, this guide will address two questions:

- What is IQA?
- What is the medical staff's role in the IQA model?

WHAT IS IQA?

Integrated Quality Assessment (IQA) is a suggested model for concurrent review that integrates into one system four basic components: Quality Assurance (QA), Risk Management (RM), Utilization Management (UM), and Infection Control (IC). In Figure 17-1, IQA is represented by the shaded area where the four different functions overlap.

Because these functions developed independently to meet different operational needs, they are usually treated as distinct and separate functions in many of today's hospitals. Historically, the fundamental objective of Quality Assurance has been to identify and take advantage of opportunities for improvement in care. Risk Management's primary purpose has been to protect the financial assets of an organization and to prevent untoward events. Utilization Management has been concerned traditionally with appropriate utilization of resources and length of stay issues. Finally, Infection Control focuses on the prevention, identification, and resolution of all types of problems associated with infections. In most hospitals, these programs have settled either into one-person departments or narrowly defined functions (such as departmental review).

The IQA model seeks to integrate the medical staff case review component of quality assurance and the data collection and review components of risk management, infection control, and utilization review. The advantages of this system are that it

- reduces redundancy of chart review by allowing one reviewer to identify issues pertinent to four functions at the same time
- identifies relevant issues while the patient is still in the hospital or at least under treatment
- coordinates the concurrent review process with retrospective review
- assists the hospital in the reappraisal and reassessment of physicians in the credentials process

To meet the practical demands of such a review system, it is necessary to have coordinated collection and reporting of data. In the IQA model, this is accomplished by centralizing authority in a Quality Management Department and delegating basic data collection responsibility to a number of Quality Management (QM) Coordinators.

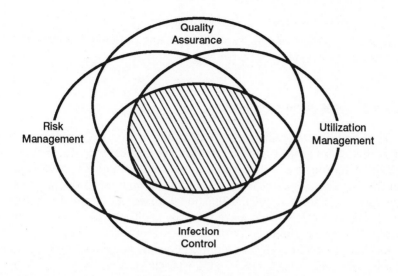

Figure 17-1 Basic Components of the Integrated Quality Assessment Model

The Quality Management Department

The IQA function is best organized in an operating unit or department that can effectively and efficiently cut across traditional "territorial" boundaries within the hospital. For purposes of this guide, we will refer to this unit as a "Quality Management Department." This department would be responsible for:

- collecting data
- providing administrative/clerical support for department chairpersons before, during, and after monthly meetings
- assisting in developing agendas for monthly meetings
- ensuring that the QA, RM, UM, and IC* functions are performed and reported to department chairpersons
- acting as a clearinghouse for hospital and departmental QA committees for monthly minutes and ensuring that appropriate information is provided
- tracking problems and coordinating follow-up action on recommendations

---

*Depending on organizational needs, it is also possible to fold medical record review and discharge screening into the IQA model.

- consulting with hospital and medical staff
- ensuring timely and appropriate reporting to the QM committee and Board of Trustees.

Quality Management Coordinators

The Quality Management (QM) Coordinators are key personnel in the IQA model. The QM Coordinators conduct medical record reviews using specific indicators and criteria; collect data and document this information on the appropriate worksheets; convey these findings to the appropriate QM Specialist for each of the functional areas (the hospital experts for QA, UM, IC, or RM); and make referrals to physician advisors and managers of other departments. Under a concurrent review schedule, the QM Coordinators review each case within 24 hours of admission, every 72 hours during the stay, and within 24 hours of discharge.

The Coordinators may also be involved in other activities such as communicating with patients and families, analyzing data, preparing reports, and participating in committee work. Since concurrent review of the medical record alone cannot convey a complete picture of care, QM Coordinators are encouraged to incorporate observations and discussion with the patient, family, and other staff members into the concurrent review process. These types of "rounds" not only enable the Coordinator to note potential problems but also to evaluate the progress of preventive measures or policies already introduced.

Overview of Information Flow

Basic data on patient care are collected by the QM Coordinators using IQA Worksheets (Exhibit 17-1). The top part of the worksheet contains patient demographic and billing information; the lower portion gathers coded data for specific functional areas. Several of these areas (e.g., infection control) may require the use of additional worksheets, but only when specific problems (e.g., a postsurgical wound infection) are identified. The IQA worksheet also allows for concurrent collection of utilization information generally in the form of severity of illness (SI) and intensity of service (IS) data, e.g., Interqual or whatever Utilization Management screens (such as Health Care Financing Administration (HCFA) screens) a hospital may use. This coded information is compiled by the QM Department for use in subsequent summary reports to the appropriate reviewing departments. Space is provided for comments by the physician, or the QM Coordinator may enter the appropriate data. Physician advisor review should occur when a QM Coordinator identifies a problem that

Exhibit 17-1 IQA Review Worksheet

Room and bed	Patient name			Sex	Age	Medical record no.		Financial class	
Adm. date	Adm. time	Service	Attending physician			Discharge date	Status	Total LOS	
Admitting diagnosis					Last admit				
Occurrence screens	Medical staff monitors	Specialty screens		Utilization mgmt		Infection control		Focused review	

ADMISSION REVIEW   Date: QMC code:

Preadmission screening?   Y   N   Date: By: PAS w/s attached?   Y   N

BODY SYSTEM	SI	IS	PHYSICIAN'S ADVISORY REVIEW		
Generic			Discharge prior to review		Y N
Other			Attending physician contacted	Date	Y N
Discharge screen			Additional physician(s) consulted Date		Y N
Vital signs			M.D. code _____		

COMMENTS

Case approved   Y N

Date _____ M.D. code _____

DISCHARGE REFERRAL

Discharge barriers _____

Social services needed?   Y N

Date contacted _____

Next review date   Date seen _____

CONTINUED STAY REVIEW   Date: QMC code:

Occurrence screens	Medical staff monitors	Specialty screens		Utilization mgmt		Infection control		Focused review	

BODY SYSTEM	SI	IS	PHYSICIAN'S ADVISORY REVIEW		
Generic			Discharge prior to review		Y N
Other			Attending physician contacted	Date	Y N
Discharge screen			Additional physician(s) consulted Date		Y N
Vital signs			M.D. code _____		

COMMENTS

Case approved   Y N

Date _____ M.D. code _____

DISCHARGE REFERRAL

Discharge barriers _____

Social services needed?   Y N

Date contacted _____

Next review date   Date seen _____

continues

Exhibit 17-1 continued

Patient name	Hospital number	Financial class	Room number

CONTINUED STAY REVIEW   Date: QMC code:

Occurrence screens	Medical staff monitors	Specialty screens	Utilization mgmt	Infection control	Focused review

BODY SYSTEM	SI	IS	PHYSICIAN'S ADVISORY REVIEW

Generic			Discharge prior to review		Y N
Other			Attending physician contacted	Date	Y N
Discharge screen			Additional physician(s) consulted	Date	Y N
			M.D. code _____		
Vital signs					

COMMENTS

Case approved   Y N

Date _____ M.D. code _____

DISCHARGE REFERRAL

Discharge barriers _____

Social services needed?   Y N

Date contacted _____

Next review date   Date seen _____

CONTINUED STAY REVIEW   Date: QMC code:

Occurrence screens	Medical staff monitors	Specialty screens	Utilization mgmt	Infection control	Focused review

BODY SYSTEM	SI	IS	PHYSICIAN'S ADVISORY REVIEW

Generic			Discharge prior to review		Y N
Other			Attending physician contacted	Date	Y N
Discharge screen			Additional physician(s) consulted	Date	Y N
			M.D. code _____		
Vital signs					

COMMENTS

Case approved   Y N

Date _____ M.D. code _____

DISCHARGE REFERRAL

Discharge barriers _____

Social services needed?   Y N

Date contacted _____

Next review date   Date seen _____

From *Integrated Quality Assessment: A Model for Concurrent Review*, published by American Hospital Publishing, Inc., copyright 1989.

requires prompt intervention at any point in the review process. Sections are set aside for physicians' review during the admission review and each subsequent continued stay review. The discharge review should be the last review completed on the sheet. This final review should be documented not only as to discharge screens but also noted in the "Comments" box.

The hospital's Quality Assurance Plan should outline the referral process for acting on and resolving identified problems, as well as specifying the particular committees that review different types of occurrences. Under IQA, specialists from the specific functional area involved usually report to the department-level committees, and the Administrator of the QM Department reports to the hospital-wide QA Committee, to Administration, and ultimately to the Governing Board.

WHAT IS THE MEDICAL STAFF'S ROLE IN THE IQA MODEL?

Before discussing the specific responsibilities of the medical staff under IQA, it is important to understand the multifaceted objectives of an integrated quality assurance system. Building on a foundation of methodically accumulated and coordinated data, the IQA Model is designed to meet five basic goals:

1. the systematic review of the quality and appropriateness of care
2. improved patient care through enhanced practitioner effectiveness and efficiency
3. the assembling of useful and timely management information
4. the aggregation of objective data that can be used in credentialing and the granting of privileges
5. compliance with the standards and requirements of external review groups such as the Joint Commission on Accreditation of Healthcare Organizations

Each of these five aspects is discussed in turn in the following sections, which outline physicians' roles in relation to Clinical Case Review, Medical Staff Monitors, Peer Review, Reporting Lines and Credentials Review, and Delineation of Privileges.

Clinical Case Review

The first step in any review process is to identify the untoward events or conditions that warrant additional scrutiny. These occurrences are termed "indicators" or "screens" and are used in this process to identify cases for review. Indicators should be accompanied by "criteria." Whereas indicators are often called "flags," suggesting further review, criteria may be thought of as "yardsticks" or measures against which the quality and appropriateness of care can be measured.

For a given indicator, criteria define what a department or service considers to be (based on professionally recognized standards) "acceptable" quality or "appropriateness." Both criteria and indicators should be objective and measurable and for that reason should be carefully developed as a cooperative effort between administration and the clinical and medical staffs. It is equally important that they be clearly defined and factual in nature because QM Coordinators must have a firm basis for screening the medical record and flagging appropriate cases for review and follow-up.

The following sections describe different types of indicators and their review functions in more detail.

Volume Indicators

Ongoing monitors of the frequency and scope of services (e.g., number of cardiac catheterizations performed each month) are often referred to as volume indicators. The volume indicators selected by a clinical department or service should encompass all significant clinical activities and should include data specific to all individuals with defined clinical privileges. These data help the department delineate the scope of care or services and focus on the high volume, high risk, or problem-prone areas that are most important to review. Volume indicators provide valuable denominator data that are used in calculating rates of incidence.

Occurrence Screens

Currently, there is no firm national consensus on precise distinctions among clinical indicators, generic screens, and occurrence screens. For purposes of the IQA Model, indicators are defined as "professionally developed, clinically valid and reliable, measurable dimensions of the quality and appropriateness of care." (The term "indicator" is also considered to be interchangeable with the word "screen.") An indicator may describe measurable care process, clinical events, complications, or outcomes for which data can be collected. Examples include unexpected death, return to the operating room, or adverse drug reaction.

Clinical Indicators

In contrast to occurrences that may cross specialty lines (also known as hospital-wide or "generic" screens), clinical indicators are developed and collected for individual specialties represented on the medical staff. These indicators should target key aspects of care provided by each clinical specialty in the hospital. Because they may vary from hospital to hospital, indicators should be developed after a review of the hospital's scope of service and each clinical department's high volume, high risk, known, or suspected problems. An example of a clinical indicator for obstetrics might be an Apgar rating of less than 7 five minutes postdelivery.

Focused Review

Another aspect of clinical case review is the focused review. This process is designed so that departments or services can examine key areas of care identified by one or more of the first three review indicators (volume indicators, occurrence screens, or clinical indicators) as warranting further evaluation and review. It may, for example, evaluate in depth a single occurrence that exceeded its threshold for evaluation. A focused review may concentrate on a representative sample of high volume diagnoses or procedures, target a finite period of time or case series, or span the entire year for low volume but high risk care.

Development of indicators and criteria for a particular type of focused review should be a consensus-building exercise involving all department staff members. It must be stressed that the focused review is NOT a medical audit; rather, it is a comprehensive process that remains in place until actual performance attains the level of "expected." Data collection for a focused review is concurrent and follows the same procedure for data evaluation. When properly employed, focused reviews gently contribute to improvement in care—first, through the educational value of the consensus-building exercise in review development and, second, by comparing "ideal" and actual care.

Medical Staff Review Monitors

Since the late 1970s, the Joint Commission's Accreditation Manual for Hospitals has required medical staff monitors that are review functions over and above the monitoring and evaluation functions of clinical departments. These functions have undergone some revision and refinement since originally introduced into the Standards and currently consist of five basic reviews:

1. surgical case review
2. blood usage review
3. drug usage review
4. pharmacy and therapeutics (p&t) review
5. medical records review

Surgical Case Review

The surgical case review function addresses the indications/justifications for all invasive surgical procedures and tissue, nontissue, and invasive diagnostic procedures performed in both inpatient and ambulatory care settings. This type of review is the responsibility of the medical staff and should be performed monthly. As noted above, the surgical case functions can be performed by department, committee, or both. Surgical cases in which potentially diagnostic or diagnostic tissue is removed can easily be reviewed by the pathologist at the time of tissue examination by comparing the surgeon's preoperative diagnosis. Cases demonstrating an inconsistency between preoperative and pathologic findings would require further review at either the committee or departmental level.

Blood Usage Review

The blood sugar review function consists of five major tasks:

1. justification/indication for transfusion episodes for all blood products
2. review of all confirmed transfusion reactions
3. approval of transfusion policies and procedures
4. monitoring of adequacy of transfusion services
5. review of blood product ordering practices

The blood usage review function should be conducted by the medical staff and reported at least quarterly. As noted previously, each hospital has great flexibility in organizing this activity. For hospitals choosing to have a committee perform this function, suggested membership would include at a minimum a pathologist, blood bank/transfusion service chief technologist, surgeon, hematologist, and members of appropriate clinical services. The review group's primary function is the review of transfusions for justification/indication and identification of suspected transfusion reactions.

Drug Usage Review

The drug usage review (formerly termed "antibiotic review" by the Joint Commission) involves the review of all major classes of drugs used in the hospital. Results of this review function should be reported at least quarterly. For most hospitals, the selection of drugs for review and the adoption of review criteria are best done at the department level, with oversight by a medical staff committee. Drugs should be reviewed for all uses (empirical, therapeutic, and prophylactic) and for the following parameters:

- appropriateness—indications/justifications for use

- safety—reflecting appropriate evaluation and/or monitoring of the physiologic state of the patient and monitoring of drug levels where indicated
- effectiveness—defined here as the correct dosage in the indicated form (e.g., IV or p.o.) at appropriate intervals

It is important to note that this function does not require review of all drugs. Drugs selected for review should be considered "important" by the medical staff, i.e., they represent either high volume or high risk drugs or drugs that have been identified as presenting problems in the past.

Once the medical staff has selected the drugs for review, clinical indicators/criteria should be developed that address the appropriateness, safety, effectiveness, and outcome of use. Criteria for these reviews are available from a variety of sources, one example being a handbook of the American Society for Hospital Pharmacists, entitled *Drug Audit Criteria for Drug Usage Evaluation*. Drug reviews should encompass all areas of the hospital (inpatient, ambulatory, and emergency room) and all persons authorized to write doctors' orders/prescriptions in the hospital. Review can be spread throughout the year.

Data collection can be accomplished through the IQA model, in much the same way as focused reviews are conducted. Reports of drug usage that fails to meet established criteria are submitted to the responsible clinical department for review. Results are reported to the medical staff oversight committee, and practitioner-specific data are entered into the practitioner activity profile.

Pharmacy and Therapeutics Review

Although the pharmacy and therapeutics function is viewed as a medical staff function, participation by pharmacy, nursing, and hospital administration is required. Reports of the activities of this function should be made quarterly. In many respects, the scope of the pharmacy and therapeutics function is analogous to blood usage review. Required activities include the following:

- approval of pharmacy policies and procedures
- development, maintenance, and modification of the hospital formulary
- evaluation/approval of experimental or investigational drugs (Note: This function may be performed by a hospital's Investigational Review Board.)
- review of serious, untoward drug reactions

In the case of the last element, the medical staff is charged with the responsibility of defining both possible untoward drug reactions and serious untoward drug reactions.

Medical Record Review

Of the five monitoring functions, medical record review is probably the most misunderstood and least liked by the medical staff. This function should focus on two major elements: (1) timeliness of record completion and (2) clinical performance. In this instance, review of the record should not be for the quality of the care but rather the quality of the record. Again, while medical records review is classified as a medical staff function, these reviews should be performed in conjunction with the nursing service, hospital administration, other clinical service, and staff from the Medical Record Department. Results of this activity should be reported at least quarterly. For larger hospitals, this function is often best performed at the departmental level, with results forwarded to a medical staff committee charged with oversight responsibilities.

The medical staff has the primary responsibility for determining the clinical pertinence of the record, i.e., deciding whether the record is adequate. In adopting criteria, the medical staff may choose to consider such factors as the adequacy of the documentation of the history and physical, substantiation for admission diagnosis and therapy, description of the response to treatment, delineation of risk factors, documentation of continuity of care, and the caliber of the final summary. Often, hospitals require physicians to review records randomly in order to comply with these requirements.

Ideally, physician review of records for clinical pertinence should occur and be documented any time a physician reviews a record for any purpose (e.g., surgical case review, generic screen, blood review) in order to optimize the time physicians spend performing peer review activities. This approach also has the advantage of providing the hospital and medical staff with a "double-check" on those records identified because of an untoward event or unexpected outcome.

Peer Review

In light of recent court challenges, it is essential that the peer review process be carefully structured, impartial, and open to participation by all departmental staff. All criteria must be applied uniformly so as to avoid any suggestion of personal bias that might have antitrust implications. The IQA model is useful in this case because it provides a structured process for data collection; the department, under the guidance of the department chairperson, serves as the mechanism for data evaluation.

Concurrent data collection occurs in parallel with the same review schedule established for the IQA reviews by QM Coordinators: within 24 hours of admission, every 72 hours during the stay, and within 24 hours of discharge. (Records of patients admitted to special care units are reviewed by QM Coordinators every 24 hours.) The cases identified during medical records review should be noted by the QM Coordinator in the appropriate box of the IQA worksheet.

Referral Process

If, when reviewing a case, the QMC identifies an occurrence that requires immediate notification, the case should be referred at once to the QM physician advisor for review. If, upon the physician advisor's review, the case is not "approved," it should be referred to the attending physician. The physician advisor and attending physician should then discuss this case and reach a conclusion. If these two physicians cannot come to an agreement, the case should be referred to a designated physician peer or departmental chairperson for review. Data on both types of cases, those resulting in agreement and disagreement, should be maintained for trending purposes.

Once an event is referred to a department for review, a physician is assigned to review the record and document findings, conclusion, recommendations, and actions. Exhibit 17-2 represents the clinical care review worksheet. Each clinical department designates one member of its medical staff to serve as a reviewer for the department; this assignment may be time-limited (daily, weekly, or monthly) or the responsibility for initial review may be retained by the department chairperson. If corrective action is required, the reviewer should contact the attending physician to discuss the case. In extremely unusual cases, immediate intervention by the department head, medical director, or other medical staff leader, may be necessary to ensure that the patient receives appropriate care.

Categorizing Cases

The reviewer should next identify the responsible practitioner (attending staff and fellow, resident, or intern) and attempt to place the case into one of the following categories:

- *Not Practitioner-Related*: These are events that are causally related to factors intrinsic to the patient (e.g., underlying disease, biologic/anatomic variation, hypersensitivity reaction in the absence of allergic history); to institutional support (e.g., delay in turnaround time for lab/X-ray studies, unavailability of CT/MR scans); or to care provided outside the hospital.

- *Practitioner-Related*: The four subcategories listed below should include events that either individually, or in aggregate, are related to specific health care practitioners. Data derived from these categories

Exhibit 17-2 Case Review Worksheet

☐ Generic   ☐ Specialty   ☐ Drug   ☐ Surgical   ☐ Blood   ☐ Pharmacy   ☐ Medical
  screen   specific   usage   case   review   and   records
                                  review   review   therapeutics   review
                                                                           review

Patient name _____ Dept. _____ Meeting date _____

QMC No. _____ Chart No. _____ M.D. No. _____ Reason for review _____

Admission date _____ Discharge date _____ Financial class _____

R.N. Review

☐ Routine review

Findings _____ male/female admitted to _____ direct/from ED/from OPD with admitting diagnosis of _____

_____

_____

_____

Date _____ Signature _____R.N.

M.D. referral for _____ :

Findings _____

_____

_____

_____

_____

Determination: ☐ Approved ☐ Refer to _____ ☐ Departmental review

Date _____ Signature _____M.D.

Departmental referral for _____

Findings _____

_____

_____

_____

_____

Determination: ☐ Approved ☐ Not approved ☐ Undetermined

Action recommended/taken: _____

_____

_____

Date _____ Signature _____

From *Integrated Quality Assessment: A Model for Concurrent Review,* published by American Hospital Publishing, Inc., copyright 1989.

will allow department chairpersons and practitioners to identify opportunities to enhance their practice in terms of quality, effectiveness, or efficiency.

Category I—Predictable Event within the Standard of Care
"PREDICTABLE" refers to events that are anticipated, well-known, widely reported in the literature, and relatively frequent.
"WITHIN THE STANDARD OF CARE" means that care was provided in accordance with contemporary standards of the specialty and departmental staff.

Category II—Unpredictable Event within the Standard of Care
"UNPREDICTABLE" means that events in this category are infrequent and unanticipated, but have been described in the literature or are known by departmental medical staff to occur in cases where the standards of care are met.

Note: *Category II* does not represent an escalation in seriousness over *Category I*; they are both within accepted standards of care.

Category III—Marginal Deviation from the Standard of Care
"MARGINAL" events reflect care that is minimally outside of the contemporary standards of the specialty or the expected standards of the department staff.

Category IV—Significant Deviation from the Standard of Care
Events in this category usually speak for themselves. These events represent gross departures from expected standards.

Departmental Meetings

One of the benefits of instituting the IQA model is that cases have already been reduced to their objective essentials. Because reviews are conducted concurrently, many events have been identified and resolved while the patient is still in the hospital. Only cases that demonstrate opportunities for improvement in care (either because of the problems identified or because of their educational value) or cases that are particularly complex need to be discussed at the monthly departmental meetings.

At the time of the departmental meeting, the staff member who initially reviewed the case or the departmental chairperson should present a synopsis. Depending on the nature of the case, the practitioner(s) responsible for the patient's case, if present, may wish to provide additional relevant information. These comments should be followed by a general discussion of "lessons learned," after which summaries of the presentation are documented in the departmental minutes. Initial presentation by a single reviewer is recommended in order to keep the review as impartial as possible. In addition to discussing specific review cases, monthly meetings should discuss pertinent results of peer review from either medical staff monitors or hospital-wide functions.

The peer review process is only as sound as the actions taken to improve patient care. In the vast majority of cases, the responsible practitioner recognizes both the issues and the measures required for correction; in other instances, additional support or counseling may be required. In either case, adequate documentation of the measures taken should be included in the practitioner's activity profile.

Reporting Lines

Hospitals are expected to have in place adequate systems and processes for monitoring quality of care and correcting problems identified during the monitoring process. Effective quality management requires that relevant information be communicated in a timely manner to the appropriate individuals, departments, and committees. The IQA model meets these requirements by integrating the reporting functions of all the affected departments (Quality Assurance, Utilization Management, Infection Control, and Risk Management) into a coordinated system. This consolidation streamlines the reporting process and thus facilitates evaluation of the data.

Reporting to Committees and Departments

Information gathered through the IQA process has to be reported to the appropriate committees and departments. In the IQA model, it is the responsibility of the Quality Management Department to "manage" the data and guide these data through the process from the point of initial documentation (on IQA worksheets), through committee and department review, and, ultimately, to the governing body.

The QM Department may serve as staff to a number of committees or departments that should receive QA information. Generally, specialists for each function will report to their respective committee/department. Thus, the Utilization Management specialist will report to the Utilization Management Committee, the Infection Control specialist to the Infection Control Committee, and so forth.

Each hospital will need to develop its own guidelines specifying the format and types of data required for different committee reports. It is recommended, however, that a status report be attached to the numerical data summary to provide an additional description of variances or adverse trends and the actions taken to resolve them. Only important information should be documented on this form, and all documentation should be as succinct as possible. The appropriate monitoring committee (e.g., Utilization Management) reviews and acts on the report. A copy of the report should be attached to the committee minutes and forwarded to other hospital committees as outlined in the hospital's QA Plan. At times, formal written communications are necessary to alert individuals, departments, or committees about a specific problem. Once completed, a copy of the form should be retained as part of the committee minutes and department review.

Role of the QA Committee and the ECMS

Depending on hospital complexity and organizational structure, many different hospital-wide QA Committee models have been developed. In some hospitals, each clinical and ancillary department or service has established its own oversight committee to carry out the QA functions as defined by the hospital-wide QA plan. Each of these committees, in turn, reports to the hospital-wide QA Committee. Sometimes, medical staff committees report to the Executive Committee of the Medical Staff (ECMS), with the ECMS referring concerns to the hospital-wide QA Committee. At other times, the opposite occurs, with medical staff QA committees reporting to the hospital-wide QA Committee, which then refers problems to the ECMS. Also, some hospitals have established a separate QA Board Committee to which the hospital-wide QA Committee and ECMS report their QA activities. This QA Committee of the Board then reports to the full Board on a quarterly basis.

Whatever organizational structure is adopted, it is usually the QM Department Administrator who assists with the overall coordination, tracking, scheduling, and integration of these reports. The QM Administrator serves as staff to the QA Committee and may also assist with preparation of reports to the ECMS and governing body.

Integration of Reports

Since the QA Committee is responsible for the hospital-wide QA programs, it must receive summary reports regarding each of the QA committees and their review functions. (The QA Committee does not need to review the details of every case that failed to meet screening criteria.) It is suggested that the QM Administrator coordinate and present these reports, although it is the responsibility of each department/committee to prepare the individual report.

Reporting to the Governing Body

The governing body or Board of Trustees has the ultimate legal responsibility for the operations of a hospital. Various external groups emphasize the governing body's ultimate responsibility and accountability for the performance of the hospital, as well as the leadership and management of their institutions. The Board relies upon reports generated by the various departments and committees to provide meaningful information that will guide them in their decision making and development of hospital policies. Just as it is not necessary for the QA Committee to review the specifics of every case, it is also not necessary for the Board to review every case detail. Few Board members are clinicians, and such data would not be meaningful to them. Rather, the Board must have information verifying that the quality management process is in place and working. Board members should receive reports describing the following:

- overall patterns, trends, or significant events (e.g., confirmed PRO quality citations)
- results of the peer or department evaluation
- corrective actions taken
- any recommendations for further action

It may be helpful for the QM Administrator to prepare a summary highlighting the major issues/activities of each of the peer review/monitoring committees and attach this report as a cover to the committee minutes that are routinely forwarded to the Board. Any outstanding items should be identified so the Board is alerted to the need for continued follow-up.

When properly prepared and presented, quality management reports are invaluable tools for helping the hospital, medical staff, and governing body to fulfill their individual responsibilities for quality of care. These reports should address important aspects of patient care, summarize important actions taken and patterns identified, and generally be presented to the governing body only after hospital and medical staff department members have had the opportunity to address any concerns. It is important that the reports be viewed as a vehicle of communication in the quality management process—a byproduct rather than the end product of the process.

CONCLUSION

Quality assessment and assurance begins by focusing on the quality of the provision of health care. Starting with a review of individual cases, through hospital-wide monitors of broader functions, and finally to individual credentials review and privilege delineation, the IQA model comes full circle to ensure accountability and quality of patient care.

The methodology outlined in the preceding pages is designed as a clinically relevant and systematic approach to the evaluation of the quality of care. To be successful, it relies on the ongoing commitment and personal involvement of all members of the hospital team—the governing body, administration, medical staff, nursing staff, and other professionals. Ultimately, however, the provision of care and assessment of its quality remain the responsibility of each hospital and every provider.

SUGGESTED READINGS

Donabedian, Avedis. *Exploration in Quality Assessment and Monitoring.* Vol. I, *The Definition of Quality and Approaches to Its Assessment.* Ann Arbor, Mich.: Health Administration Press, 1980.

Joint Commission on Accreditation of Healthcare Organizations. *Accreditation Manual for Hospitals.* Chicago: JCAHO, 1988.

Longo, Daniel R., Ciccone, Kathleen R., and Lord, Jonathan. *Integrated Quality Assessment: A Model for Concurrent Review.* Chicago: American Hospital Publishing, Inc., 1989.

Chapter 18

Quality Assurance in the Computer Era

William R. Fifer

The story of how thalidomide was discovered to be the cause of pho-comelia—a condition causing infants to be born with rudimentary arms and legs—dramatically illustrates the usefulness of computers. Epide-miologists suspected that some agent encountered by the mother during pregnancy caused the birth defect, but they were dismayed by the almost limitless number of variables that might be the cause of the tragedy. The urgency of discovering a cause was frustrated by the painstaking work of classical epidemiology, but a computer solved the dilemma quickly: When all the variables were fed into the computer, only one—the ingestion of thalidomide during pregnancy—was common to all the mothers and, there-fore, was the cause of the infants' deformities. The power of the computer had provided an insight not otherwise possible.

Just as our society has progressed from the age of agriculture, via the industrial age, to the information age, so quality assurance (QA) is evolving from an age of peer review, via the criterion age, to the computer age. The purpose of this article is to trace this evolution briefly, review signif-icant developments and publications that explain the concept, and indicate why the current revolution in methodology is timely.

WHERE WE HAVE BEEN

The first era of QA was the era of "peer review," which can be traced from the beginnings of medical care. The word *peer* (from the Latin mean-ing "an equal") implied that appropriate review of a piece of work, be it a ballet or a cholecystectomy, could only be done by someone with training

---

Note: Reprinted from *Quality Review Bulletin*, August 1987. Copyright 1987 by the Joint Commission on Accreditation of Healthcare Organizations, Chicago. Reprinted with per-mission.

in that field. While this may be true, the method was found to have flaws. First, it was extremely time-consuming; second, it was inherently subjective, with considerable variation in the judgments rendered between judges or peers. Also, because the evaluation was carried out one case at a time, no patterns or statistical associations could be discovered.

The era of subjective peer review gave way to the era of criteria, which held the promise of eliminating interobserver variation by creating objective measures for judging quality. These measures or standards could be prescriptive (those things considered necessary or useful) or proscriptive (things to be avoided). Donabedian divided them into three categories: structures, processes, and outcomes[1]; and a lively debate ensued as to which category was most appropriate for a given evaluation and whether there was reasonable correlation among the categories. McAuliffe,[2] Brook,[3] and others demonstrated quite clearly that the correlation was poor to nonexistent and that the judgment reached about the quality of the care provided depended heavily on the category of criteria used. For example, examining the processes used in a particular situation (e.g., what tests the physician ordered) might result in an entirely different evaluation of the quality of care than would examining the outcome (e.g., whether the patient got better).

Regardless of category, criteria presented other problems, such as weighting (all criteria are not equally important), relevance (criteria are not relevant to all situations), and sensitivity (criteria cannot always discriminate between good and bad care). All of these problems limit the usefulness of criteria or require extensive methodologic treatment.

Now, thanks to the analytic power of computers, QA is entering the era of norms—a time to dust off statistical concepts, such as measures of central tendency, standard deviations, and levels of significance. QA is entering the age of the "bell-shaped curve" so familiar to statisticians.

SIGNIFICANT EVENTS AND DEVELOPMENTS

Two recent occurrences have cast long future shadows. One occurrence was the realization that Wennberg's "small area variations"[4] in the rates of surgical procedures were at once a unique insight of the information age and a profound dilemma crying out for clinical analysis. Wennberg found that the rates at which surgical procedures were performed varied within small geographic areas (e.g., between counties in a state) more than could be explained by population characteristics. If low rates indicate that communities are getting shortchanged on medical care and high rates represent waste, such data bases are useful to buyers and third parties. Currently, the Codman Research Group (Philip Caper, MD, president) is using small area analysis to help Aetna Life and Casualty Company and Blue

Cross/Blue Shield find hospitals that provide the best mix of quality and efficiency.

The other occurrence that has had a far-reaching effect was the release in March 1986 by the Health Care Financing Administration (HCFA) of lists of hospitals with mortality rates for Medicare patients significantly higher or lower than the national average. The list was intended to help the professional review organizations (PROs) identify hospitals with problems; but, to the consternation of the hospital industry, it was released to the press. In addition to the principal list released, which showed 269 hospitals with abnormal overall mortality rates, HCFA released mortality data for nine common medical problems, from pneumonia to coronary artery bypass procedures. The lists were derived using case records from 10.7 million Medicare patients treated in 1984. The comparative national statistic was adjusted for 89 possible variables; but the statistic could not be adjusted to fully account for the severity of the patient's illness and, thus, was viewed by hospitals that treat more severely ill patients as an unfair analysis.

HCFA also released data on surgery death rates by procedure, which indicated that at 33 hospitals in which fewer than 100 coronary bypass operations were performed in 1984, 14 percent of patients who underwent the procedure died, while at hospitals in which more than 350 procedures were performed, the death rate was seven times lower. To say that the data were controversial is an understatement, but to say that the release of the data was the "handwriting on the wall" is apparent. HCFA plans to release data from 1985 shortly, and the information is eagerly awaited by consumer groups, buyers of health care, and an increasingly well-informed public.

The volume/quality relationships mentioned previously have been the subject of several important publications. Luft, Bunker, and Enthoven examined the mortality rates for 12 surgical procedures in 1,498 hospitals using Professional Activity Study (PAS) data on almost 850,000 surgical patients during 1974 and 1975.[5] The authors found that mortality from open-heart surgery, transurethral resection of the prostate, and coronary bypass decreased as the number of operations, adjusted for case mix and severity of illness, increased. Their finding—that hospitals in which 200 or more of these operations were performed annually had death rates (adjusted for case mix) 25 percent to 41 percent lower than hospitals in which lower volumes of these operations were performed—led them to recommend that certain operations be performed in regional centers.

Farber, Kaiser, and Wenzel used a statewide program for the surveillance and reporting of nosocomial infections to examine the relationship between surgical volume and the incidence of postoperative wound infection.[6] Analyzing more than 25,000 surgical procedures, the authors found a highly significant inverse relationship between the logarithm of the frequency with which a surgical procedure was performed and the wound infection rate for appendectomy, herniorrhaphy, cholecystectomy, colon resection, and abdominal hysterectomy. They concluded that hospitals in which surgery is performed relatively infrequently have higher morbidity rates, as judged by the incidence of wound infection.

Flood, Scott, and Ewy found strong and consistent evidence that high surgical volume is associated with better outcomes for surgical patients.[7] They examined 500,000 patient records from more than 1,200 hospitals to search for other explanatory variables, such as hospital size, teaching status, and hospital expenditures. After adjustment for such variables, the outcome/volume relationship remained strong; significant for both medical and surgical patients; and true for low-risk, medium-risk, and high-risk patients.

Several authors have used data base analyses to determine the relationships among a variety of independent variables and case outcomes. This method was used by Garber, Fuchs, and Silverman, who found that the in-hospital mortality rate was significantly lower on the faculty service than on the community service at Stanford University Hospital, after adjustment for case mix and patient characteristics.[8] Shortell and Logerfo studied 50,000 acute myocardial infarction patients and more than 8,000 appendectomy cases using Commission on Professional and Hospital Activities data collected from 96 hospitals.[9] The authors then merged these data with those collected by the American Hospital Association concerning medical staff organization and found that medical staff organization factors (such as physician participation in hospital decision making) were more highly correlated with clinical outcomes than such characteristics as hospital size or academic activities or physicians' specialty board certification.

Flood and others studied 8,000 surgical patients of 500 surgeons in 15 hospitals and concluded that hospital features had more impact on surgical outcomes than did surgeon characteristics (such as board certification).[10] An interesting finding was that the "measure of commitment" (the percentage of each surgeon's practice at a given hospital) was significantly associated ($p < .05$) with quality of care.

Finally, a recent, elegant study of Manitoba data by Roos and others analyzed patient, surgeon, and hospital characteristics associated with serious postdischarge complications of hysterectomy, cholecystectomy, and prostatectomy.[11] Manitoba is an example of an excellent data substrate because, owing to the person-specific system in effect in Canada, patients can be traced as individuals through a series of encounters with different hospitals and physicians. Such elegant epidemiology is not often possible in the United States where payer-specific or physician-specific systems are used. For example, in the United States it would be difficult to track a patient who was hospitalized first through a health maintenance organization (HMO) and later under Blue Cross coverage, perhaps at a different hospital, under the care of a different set of physicians.

These authors, using multiple logistic regressions, found that hospital variables were not important predictors of complications, but that physician surgical experience accounted for relatively large differences in the probability of patient complications following cholecystectomy.

Roos and others also commented on the importance of the reliability and validity of claims data, which deserves elaboration. There is a substantial set of hospital utilization data bases maintained by about one-third of the states in the United States. In 1979, agreement was reached on a national level about those elements that constituted a minimal hospital utilization data set which would be useful for health policy and planning. This agreement resulted in the Uniform Hospital Discharge Data Set (UHDDS), which consists of diagnosis, procedure, and certain demographic data. In 1985, the Washington Business Group on Health recommended that UB-82, the uniform billing form currently required by Medicare and Medicaid, be used by major insurers and hospitals as well. According to a survey conducted at the National Center for Health Services Research and Health Care Technology, 24 states now collect patient utilization data (12 use UB-82, 7 use UHDDS, 3 have unique systems, and 2 are undecided). Should five states that have introduced legislation mandating collection of patient-specific utilization data join those already collecting such data, 70 percent of all hospitals, 79 percent of all admissions, and 80 percent of the population would be under data surveillance.[12]

THE IMPORTANCE OF CASE-MIX VARIABLES

All of the data bases previously mentioned, and especially the data used for the HCFA Medicare Mortality Report, may be subject to misinterpretation unless they are adjusted for severity of illness.

Medicare has attempted to adjust for severity by assigning diagnosis-related groups (DRGs) on the basis of surgical procedures, comorbidities, complications, and, in some cases, age and sex. But, as pointed out by Horn and others, patient classification by means of unadjusted DRGs does not adequately reflect severity of illness, and prospective payment based on DRGs alone may be unfair to certain hospitals.[13]

Horn's interest in case-mix measures was demonstrated by her consultation with Roveti and Kreitzer, who developed a severity-of-illness index called AS-SCORE, which divided five attributes of the index (age, systems involved, stage of disease, complications, and response to therapy) into one of four classes to produce a cumulative severity score.[14] Horn later developed a new Severity of Illness (SOI) Index, which uses four levels determined from the values of seven variables related to the patient's burden of illness.[15] She has most recently combined her work with that of Richard Averill to produce the Computerized Severity Index (CSI), which adds a sixth digit to the ICD-9-CM codes to reflect severity.[16]

Space does not permit a full discussion of the lively topic of severity measures, but several systems are most prominent. MedisGroups™ (Medical Illness Severity Grouping System) gives a severity score to patients on admission based on a set of physiologic variables and key clinical and X-ray findings and divides patients into five severity groups. Medis-Groups™ was developed by Brewster et al.[17] as a QA method; a second set of measurements, taken after the patient has been in the hospital for several days, could distinguish patients showing clinical improvement from those whose conditions were worsening. Like Horn's SOI Index, MedisGroups™ can demonstrate the relationship between severity of illness and resource use.

Gonnella developed a severity classification system called Disease Staging,[18] which, like the systems described above, has been computerized. Like the DRG system and the SOI Index (but unlike MedisGroups™), Disease Staging classification is based on the UHDDS. In Gonnella's system, each diagnosis is assigned to one of 400 conditions and to one of four stages of severity. Like the SOI Index, Disease Staging groups exhibit greater homogeneity in resource consumption than do DRGs and exceed the variance explained by DRGs by large margins in all cases.[19]

Wanda Young at Blue Cross of Western Pennsylvania developed patient-management categories (PMCs), which group patients into disease classifications based on the key admitting diagnosis and then into a specific PMC based on comorbidities and multiple diagnoses. PMCs also run on computers using UHDDS data.[20]

Knaus and others have used an intensive care unit-specific severity classification called APACHE II, which uses admission values on 12 physiologic variables to rank severity of illness.[21] This system also is independent of diagnosis and does not use UHDDS data. In a recent publication,[22] these authors illustrated the application of case-mix adjustment to quality-of-care evaluation. They compared the outcome of intensive care, as measured by the mortality rate, in 13 tertiary care hospitals and found significant differences that they related to organizational variables. What was important about their conclusions was that—unlike HCFA's Medicare Mortality Report, which failed to adjust for case mix and thus was assailed as comparing "apples to oranges"—Knaus et al. found significant differences in outcomes after adjustment for case mix by APACHE II stratification.

The other side of the coin is illustrated by a study of comparative mortality rates in pediatric intensive care units by Pollack et al. who found that after adjustments were made for severity of illness the differences in mortality rates noted in the raw data from nine hospitals disappeared.[23]

The importance of case-mix variables in the analysis of health care data bases for quality is clear. After differences in outcomes are determined by analysis of unadjusted, raw data (from claims or utilization files), the differences must be subjected to case-mix analysis to disclose "net" variations. Whatever difference remains after the application of explanatory variables is likely to be a true difference in quality of care.

WHO CARES AND WHY?

It is clear that QA is entering a major new era, but is the new era important and, if so, why? Certainly, the new agenda at the Joint Commission on Accreditation of Healthcare Organizations will be of signal importance to the hospital industry. The Joint Commission plans to require hospitals to report clinical outcomes; those reports can then be used to assemble a national data base of performance norms. In switching from an evaluation of the capability of a hospital to provide good care to the actual measurement of the clinical outcomes, the Joint Commission is recreating the dream of E. A. Codman at the beginning of this century— that is, that "hospitals, if they wish to be sure of improvement, must find out what their results are, must analyze their results, must compare their results with those of other hospitals."[24]

In addition to the renewed emphasis placed by health care professionals on the quality of care, greater concern about quality is being shown by consumers and buyers.[25] Thus, the U.S. Congress created the PRO program to monitor the care provided to Medicare beneficiaries and, in the second round of contract negotiations, considerably strengthened the emphasis on quality.[26] Consumer groups, such as the Public Citizen Health Research Group, have called for public disclosure of hospital mortality figures.[27]

Private buyers, such as General Motors (GM), in conjunction with the United Auto Workers, are developing QA monitoring systems for the HMOs used by GM employees.[28] Honeywell recently contracted for benefits for its 12,500 employees by publishing a request for proposal (RFP) to which potential contract providers were required to respond. Of interest in the RFP were reporting requirements relative to quality of care, which, among other things, mandated the periodic reporting of outcomes, such as infection rates, mortality rates, and readmission rates by DRG, institution, and profession.[29]

State hospital associations, such as that in Maryland, have embarked on projects to monitor quality measures across a spectrum of hospitals, using such indicators as rates of hospital-acquired infections, newborn mortality, and perioperative mortality.[30]

Why all the concern? Because medical care has become a more complex enterprise administered more quickly on sicker patients than in the past.

Because there is concern that "payment reform" (i.e., HMO capitations and hospital reimbursement based on prospective payment rates) may have altered the incentives for providing care in a direction that would compromise quality. Because data confirming widespread "small area variation" in the use of medical care raise serious questions about quality. Because the "dumping" of indigent patients with unstable clinical situations has been documented.[31]

Friedman commented recently that "quantitative information will prove invaluable to providers in the debate over the quality of health care—perhaps medicine's hottest topic these days."[32]

CONCLUSION

QA is entering the computer era—an era of norms and data bases and statistical analyses. Large claims and resource utilization data bases are available and can be analyzed in nanoseconds by powerful computers to provide insights not possible in times past. The challenges for the future will be to maintain data quality and to adjust data for case mix with special emphasis on severity of illness. In the midst of a flurry of concern for quality born of cost-containment measures, computers may provide the means for accomplishing what Codman advocated in 1914—that is, assuring quality by analyzing the results of the care that is provided.

NOTES

1. Donabedian A: *The Definition of Quality and Approaches to Its Assessment,* vol. 1 of *Explorations in Quality Assessment and Monitoring.* Ann Arbor, Mich.: Health Administration Press, 1980.

2. McAuliffe WE: Studies on process-outcome correlations in medical care evaluation: A critique. *Med Care* 16:907–930, Nov. 1978.

3. Brook RH: *Quality of Care Assessment: A Comparison of Five Methods of Peer Review.* Washington, DC: Department of Health, Education and Welfare, Publication no. HRA-74-3100, 1974.

4. Wennberg JE, Gittlesohn A: Variations in medical care among small areas. *Sci Am* 246:120–134, Apr. 1982.

5. Luft HS, Bunker JP, Enthoven AC: Should operations be regionalized? The empirical relation between surgical volume and mortality. *N Engl J Med* 301:1364–1369, Dec 20, 1979.

6. Farber BF, Kaiser DL, Wenzel RP: Relation between surgical volume and incidence of postoperative wound infection. *N Engl J Med* 305:200–204, Jul. 23, 1981.

7. Flood AB, Scott WR, Ewy W: Does practice make perfect? Part 1: The relation between hospital volume and outcomes for selected diagnostic categories. *Med Care* 22:98–114, Feb. 1984.

8. Garber AM, Fuchs VR, Silverman JF: Case mix, costs and outcomes—Differences between faculty and community services in a university hospital. *N Engl J Med* 310:1231–1237, May 10, 1984.

9. Shortell SM, Logerfo JP: Hospital medical staff organization and quality of care: Results for myocardial infarction and appendectomy. *Med Care* 19:1041–1055, Oct. 1981.

10. Flood AB, et al.: Effectiveness in professional organizations: The impact of surgeons and surgical staff organizations on the quality of care in hospitals. *Health Serv Res* 17:341–366, Winter 1982.

11. Roos LL, et al.: Centralization, certification, and monitoring: Readmission and complications after surgery. *Med Care* 24:1044–1066, Nov. 1986.

12. Larks M: State systems gather more health care data but lack uniformity. *Business and Health* 3:49–50, Apr. 1986.

13. Horn SD, et al: Interhospital differences in severity of illness. *N Engl J Med* 313:20–24, Jul. 4, 1985.

14. Roveti GC, Horn SD, Kreitzer SL: AS-SCORE: A multi-attribute clinical index of illness severity. *QRB* 6:25–31, Jul. 1980.

15. Horn SD, Sharkey PD, Bertram DA: Measuring severity of illness: Homogeneous case-mix groups. *Med Care* 21:14–30, Jan. 1983.

16. Commercial severity scaling puts pressure on DRG system. *Prospective Payment Guide* 4:3, Jul. 1986.

17. Brewster AC, Jacobs CM, Bradbury RC: Classifying severity of illness by using clinical findings. *Health Care Financing Review,* Annual Suppl, pp. 107–108, 1984.

18. Gonnella JS, Louis DZ, McCord JJ: The staging concept—An approach to the assessment of outcome of ambulatory care. *Med Care* 14:13–21, Jan. 1976.

19. Severity of illness and hospital payment. *Washington Report on Medicine and Health,* 39(*Perspectives* suppl):1–4, Mar. 11, 1985.

20. Young WW: Incorporating severity of illness and comorbidity in case-mix measurement. *Health Care Financing Review,* Annual Suppl, pp. 23–31, 1984.

21. Knaus WA, Draper EA, Wagner DP: Toward quality review in intensive care: The APACHE system. *QRB* 9:196–204, Jul. 1983.

22. Knaus WA, et al.: An evaluation of outcome from intensive care in major medical centers. *Ann Int Med* 104:410–418, Mar. 1986.

23. Pollack MM, et al.: Accurate prediction of the outcome of pediatric intensive care: A new quantitative method. *N Engl J Med* 316:134–139, Jan. 15, 1987.

24. Codman EA: The product of a hospital. *Surg Gynecol Obstet* 18:491–496, Apr. 1914.

25. Fifer WR: They're talking about quality again! *Penn Med* 90:24–35, Mar. 1987.

26. National Council of Community Hospitals (NCCH): *Scope of Work for PRO Contracts: Final Regulation.* Washington, DC: NCCH, Feb. 25, 1986.

27. Employers push for higher quality measures. *Medicine and Health,* 40(*Perspectives* suppl):3, Sep. 8, 1986.

28. HMOs' quality comes under GM's watchful eye. *Hospitals* 60:40, Jul. 20, 1986.

29. Honeywell tries a new contracting approach. *Business and Health* 4:2, Dec. 1986.

30. Personal communication between the author and Steven J. Summer, Vice-President, Professional Activities, Maryland Hospital Association, Baltimore, Maryland, Apr. 1, 1987.

31. Schiff RL, et al.: Transfers to a public hospital: A prospective study of 467 patients. *N Engl J Med* 314:552–557, Feb. 27, 1986.

32. Friedman E: Will the art of medicine survive the numbers? *Medical World News* 28:38–51, Mar. 9, 1987.

Chapter 19

Information Management: Reusing Existing Data for Quality Assessment

Lois J. Bittle and Mitchell S. Curtis

THE CONCEPT OF INFORMATION MANAGEMENT

Recognizing the need for data and the value of computerization brings about new challenges in the health care industry. While systems for collecting data in health care have evolved over the years, most were designed for single specific reasons. Therefore, the resulting information is not easily accessed and/or shared. To be effective and critical in today's environment, these data must be translated into usable profiles of performance through an effective mechanism of combining the knowledge of individuals with the capabilities of computers. The ability to corral the proliferating data through technology and reduce them to more common usable information forms the concept of information management.

As the health care industry begins to look at various types of data and to consider their utility to this particular environment, so must the information manager look at various ways to respond to this new demand. The ever-growing recognition that usage patterns have changed, different users need different kinds of information, and new technology exists causes some data processing departments to rethink their traditional roles on managing information.

With the growing need to demonstrate the quality and efficiency of services provided and with the cost of obtaining information continually on the rise, the health care industry is critically examining what data exist, what data can be reused, and how management of multiple sources of data can be translated into useful information to effectively support the organization in its quality management quests.

Lois J. Bittle is President of Bittle & Associates, Inc., Baltimore, Maryland.

Mitchell S. Curtis is associated with Presbyterian University Hospital of Pittsburgh, Pittsburgh, Pennsylvania.

TECHNOLOGY AND PERSONNEL

Product Evolution and Enhancement

Over the years numerous computerized systems have been created to collect data for various reasons. These systems evolved for specific purposes and, in many cases, rendered the data collected incomplete and/or incompatible for use beyond their original specific design.

Revolutionary changes in technology have provided the health care industry with greater access to existing data. By virtue of increased capabilities and lower cost, users in the industry have the ability to become more independent, with more flexibility to collect and analyze data and expand their applications into areas such as enhanced data base management.

Technologies once relegated to finance departments have now been extended to almost every area in the health care arena. This growth in product evolution and enhancement, however, has created a new fragmentation of data. Computerization, without information management, could very well be the Achilles heel of facility-wide information systems. The creation of isolated computerized data bases undermines the effort to create an integrated, coordinated data base to demonstrate performance. With this growth comes a challenge to coordinate and manage information in a productive, cost-effective way.

The Role of Clinical Information Managers

Because of the influx of technology and data from various sources, hospitals are defining the need for individuals with computer savvy, information management skills, and health care knowledge to enable the organization to efficiently assemble, coordinate, integrate, and utilize the various pieces of data and information in the organization. The role of the clinical information manager has been defined and includes:

- identifying and affecting the information needs of the organization
- identifying and evaluating the information resources that exist both internally and externally, as well as those that are currently evolving
- developing practical recommendations for appropriate information products and services suited to the needs of the organization
- managing the access to the organization's information
- developing detailed plans covering cost, staffing, training, technology required, and implementation to support improved information management

• assisting in the implementation of these plans and/or information systems

INSTITUTIONAL RESPONSE TO DEMANDS FOR DATA FOR QA, RM, UR, AND RELATED PEER REVIEW ACTIVITIES

System Fragmentation

The health care industry is reacting to the cry for more data/information to be supplied to more users for more reasons. As an example, the Joint Commission on Accreditation of Healthcare Organizations, in its Agenda for Change, will require specific data elements to be reported at a national level; state data commissions are calling for a move toward severity assessment and state mandates for quality and risk management programs and are pushing for more aggressive internal programs that tend to produce volumes of paper to display the state of the art of their respective programs.

Coupled with the growth of data systems is the ever-changing needs of the user. For example, clinical departments may need department-specific information requiring repeated access to similar kinds of information. Administration may require targeted, specific, and/or comprehensive consolidated information. Multilevel requirements may call for specific linkages in order to tailor the information pertinent to their needs. Trustees need information to support decisions in this competitive, litigious environment that reflect, e.g., cost, quality, and strategic planning information.

Just as the advent of Diagnostic-Related Groups (DRGs) and the prospective pricing system (PPS) proliferated DRG coordinators, the need for information management/computerization is spawning the growth of data analysts/managers in the health care industry. In many instances, however, these individuals are not responsible for assisting in generating a comprehensive data base on clinical performance. Hence, the QA, RM, UR, and medical staff credentials and peer review programs are left to expand on their own. This fragmented decision making propagates the growth of separate, individual pockets of computerized data in direct contradiction to attempts to centralize, coordinate, and organize data reflecting both clinical and organizational performance.

Decentralizing the Decision-Making Process

From the hospital's perspective, the responsibility for establishing computerized systems for QA, RM, UR, and medical staff credentials is generally decentralized. This leaves the ultimate pursuit of software programs to individual users whose focus is generally centered on their own priorities. The outcome is the sale and/or purchase of a system incompatible with other resources and, from a strategic perspective, potentially incomplete.

From an external perspective, individuals involved in developing computerized systems for QA, RM, and UR for health care and/or vendors may or may not have in-depth knowledge of the internal workings of these programs in health care settings. The backgrounds of these individuals vary, and most "clinical" expertise is gained through the use of isolated groups of individuals working in hospital-based QA, RM, and/or UR programs. The result is a system based on the designer's area of expertise or focus (e.g., insurance, claims, or incident-oriented programs) or based on isolated input from users that is either incomplete or lacking in a comprehensive application.

Currently, most hospitals have various and sundry data bases, each with its own focus, e.g., admission, discharge, and transfer systems (ADT), finance, medical record abstracting, pharmacy profiles, laboratory data, etc. These systems evolved over the years and frequently resulted in the creation of information responsive to individual users rather than to the organization as a whole; thus, it is incompatible with other systems and, again, incomplete.

The health care industry is rapidly moving into the arena of more complete information systems. In doing so, it becomes vital for health care organizations to know what information is important to efficiently and effectively support their current needs, what information is presently available, how the information is to be used and communicated, and what is necessary to respond to tomorrow's needs.

Identifying Existing Data Bases: Reusing Data

As previously stated, in many cases the evolution of health care information systems was unplanned and uncoordinated. These systems evolved for specific purposes, e.g., to support patient billing or to abstract data from medical records.

Because of more recent emphasis on data and hospital information systems, however, these existing isolated pockets of data warrant review to determine whether the data elements can be extracted or managed to support QA, RM, and UM activities. What is needed is a comprehensive assessment of what exists and what can be efficiently extracted or "reused" from these sources.

In general, three major sources of health care information exist in most health care institutions:

1. data from the organization's own financial, clinical (medical records abstracting, laboratory, etc.), and administrative systems (Exhibit 19-1)

Exhibit 19-1 Existing Data Bases

Existing computerized internal data bases generally include:

In General:
Demographic (ADT)
Clinical
Financial

More Specifically:
Billing data
Case mix
Medical record abstract service
DRG grouper/assignment
Laboratory systems
Scheduling systems
Infection control
Employee health/accident
Pharmacy

Data bases prepared manually might include:

Results of concurrent criteria-based review
Medical staff required functions, e.g.,
   Surgical case review
   Blood and blood product usage
   Mortality review
   Pharmacy/drug usage review
   Medical record pertinency review
   Utilization review data
   Risk and claims management
   Incident reports
   Patient complaints/satisfaction surveys
   Nursing quality review
   Support service quality review
   Results of focused studies

---

2. purchased proprietary data (Exhibit 19-2)
3. other externally generated information purchased from a variety of government or private sources (Exhibit 19-2)

Organizations wanting to enhance internal health care information should perform a self-assessment. In order to determine the existing situation, the following actions should be taken:

- consider where current computerized data operations and data-gathering strategies are in progress or in the planning stage
- determine users of data and who is charged with information management responsibilities
- define manual data bases that exist relative to QA and related activities

Exhibit 19-2 Existing Information from External Sources

Existing information from external sources generally includes reports by:

Third-party payer(s)
Professional Review Organizations (PRO)
Abstract service
Data commission
Claims data/insurer
Centers for Disease Control (CDC)
National or state safety agencies
Insurance inspections
State licensing agencies
Contract services
HCFA (mortality)
Etc.

- determine the need for certain information used in addition to existing data (automated or manual)

Next, a matrix should be prepared that includes:

- existing source
- producer
- internal or external
- type of data
- user
- consistency/quality of information (levels 1–5, with 5 equaling always accurate and correct)
- confidentiality level (levels 1–5, with 5 equaling strict confidentiality)
- other, e.g., centralization of data with QA office

Once the data sources are defined, it is necessary to ascertain what data can be "reused" to support a comprehensive QA, RM, and UM program and reflect both practitioner and organizational performance. The intent is to reduce duplication of data collection and focus on gaps in the data base; for example:

- Is the pharmacy profile used to provide data on drug utilization by practitioner, which would serve to "flag" the high volume, high cost user?
- Does the infection control profile provide data by practitioner or hospital department as well as by organism?

- Do existing data bases define areas of overlap and/or major gaps in the data/information system?

If these data bases exist, consideration should be given to whether any QA, RM, or UM software under review has the capability to interface with each system to demonstrate more comprehensive practitioner performance and to eliminate duplication of effort. Additional consideration should be given to modifying existing systems as necessary to support the creation of an integrated, coordinated, usable information system.

DEFINING DATA REQUIRED TO DEMONSTRATE COMPREHENSIVE INSTITUTIONAL AND PROFESSIONAL PERFORMANCE

The information that supports both individual and organizational performance exists in remote data bases. Additionally, hospitals tend to re-isolate these data by implementing additional manual systems to collect data to profile physician behavior or to be used along with computerized programs.

After determining what exists, it is possible to proceed toward a more definitive approach in developing a comprehensive information management system—one that is flexible in meeting the needs of the organization and compatible to external requirements.

The data required (Exhibit 19-3) to demonstrate comprehensive interrelated QA, RM, and UM performance assessment by physician, department, and the institution, as well as to establish clinical experience, education, and competence, now must be assembled into a framework of reports that is used to process the clinical information to the appropriate user.

FRAMEWORK FOR MOVING TOWARD INFORMATION MANAGEMENT

Recognize the Institution's Final Needs

In determining an institution's final needs, it is first necessary to recognize that two generic categories of information are needed to demonstrate quality. One set of information deals with the quality control elements and includes:

- bylaws, rules, and regulations
- QA, RM, and UM plans and program organization

Exhibit 19-3 Data Needed To Support Comprehensive Performance Assessment

Physician
Demographics
Training/education
Licensure/certification
Verification
  Inquiry
  Letters of recommendation
Staff status
Privilege delineation
  Privileges defined
Professional liability/insurance
  Limits
  Expiration data
  Claims
  Suits/Settlements
Health status
Results of peer review

Clinical departments
Number of physicians by:
  Staff status
  Types
  Board certification
Results of peer review
Use of resources
Results of internal and external assessment

Institution
ADT
Census
Categories of patients
Case mix
DRG profiles
UR data
Financial
  Accounts payable
  Patient accounts
  Cost accounting
  Budgeting
  Etc.
Complication rate(s)
Infection rate
Mortality rate
C-section rate
Pharmacy profiles
Laboratory profiles

- the organization's policies, procedures, and job descriptions
- the credentials process

The other set of information demonstrates performance:

- volumes, utilization of resources
- processes of care, e.g., protocols
- outcomes including complications, mortality, and infections
- external agency findings
- results of QA, risk management, and claims management review

As data are generated and compiled, the results raise key questions regarding objectivity, comprehensiveness, and whether the findings demonstrate significant patterns/events. Further, it is important to know how the information is used, by whom, and whether the available information contributes to changes in practice and behavior.

The institution next must centralize the responsibility for determining the needs of the QA and related activities, e.g., RM, UM, infection control, credentials, etc. A task force can be used to determine:

- What functions need to be supported?
- What data are currently collected?
- What information is most essential?
- Who will use the data?
- What kinds of reports will have to be generated?
- Will the system grow with the needs of the organization?

Assemble the Information To Demonstrate Performance Precisely and Concisely

One of the weakest areas in health care organizations having substantive QA, RM, UM, and medical credential programs is the ability to display data. Formats vary from month to month, committee to committee, report to report. It is difficult if not impossible to track issues to conclusion. In many cases, existing data are unattainable because of lack of retrievability and/or the fact that each area collects and prepares data for its own purposes.

The reports and formats must be designed to accommodate the respective users. For example, a composite summary for credentials review at the clinical department level might include all physician codes, with numbers representing the results of peer review; at the board level, a brief summary by practitioner with recommendations by the department chairman, credentials, and medical executive committee may be in order; and a graph or pie chart may be the best tool to present the current QA, RM, and UM picture.

The following guidelines should be considered in report design:

- determine the needs (not the whims) of the user
- display data in a meaningful way:

  1. standardize report formats to ensure consistency and objectivity and to support "tracking" of problems to conclusion
  2. include all necessary, relevant items, e.g., dates, times, name of person report sent to . . . , prepared for, signatures, etc.
  3. enhance relevance by including scope of activity, denominators, e.g., 2 of 20 is more relevant than 2 of 200
  4. use charts to condense/replace pages of narrative
  5. be able to identify the report "at a distance"
  6. maintain flexibility/capability in the system to generate subreports
  7. delete pages of "zeros"

Define Guidelines and Prepare for More Inquiries into Quality Data Reflecting Quality of Care

We are in a dynamic information era. The external environment surrounding the need (demand) for information is in flux. As mentioned previously, major organizations, in addition to purchasers and providers, "have a need to know" and will attempt to satisfy this need in ways that may not be in the best interests of the health care industry. Hospitals, in particular, can be better prepared to share data by:

- designating an individual or task force to keep track of how the hospital manages information about quality
- having a written policy that defines how data will be shared
- designating a spokesperson to respond to questions about quality
- knowing how the hospital collects, analyzes, and uses QA and related data
- being prepared to cooperate with other hospitals in gathering and analyzing information
- organizing regular sessions with local reporters and editors
- responding promptly and accurately to requests for information

SUGGESTED READING

Bittle, L.J., and Bloomrosen, M. *Quality Assurance, Risk Management and Utilization Management Functions Require Coordinated Information Management,* 1989 (unpublished).

Carroll, J.G. *Restructuring Quality Assurance—The New Guide for Health Care Providers.* Homewood, Ill.: Dow Jones-Irwin, 1984.

Eisele, C.W., Fifer, W.R., and Wilson, T.C. *The Medical Staff and the Modern Hospital.* Englewood, Colo.: Estes Park Institute, 1985.

Hewson, T.S. "Managing the Growth of Microcomputers in Health Care." *Health Care Financial Management* 41(6) (June 1987):68–73.

Hospital Trustee Association of Pennsylvania. *Keys to Better Hospital Governance through Better Information,* 1983:48–71.

Joint Commission on Accreditation of Healthcare Organizations. *Agenda for Change Update,* Vol. 3, No. 1. Chicago, Ill., February 1989.

Krantz, G.M., Doyle, J.J., and Stone, S.G. "Costs, Needs Must Be Balanced When Buying Computer Systems." *Health Care Financial Management* 43(6) (June 1989):50–54.

Lemon, R. and Crudele, J. "Systems Integration: Tying It All Together." *Health Care Financial Management* 41(6) (June 1987):46–54.

Mohlanbrock, W.L. "Quality and Cost Efficiency Data to Support Physicians' Clinical Decisions." *QRC Advisor* 5(5) (March 1989).

Pivnicny, V.C. and Carmody, J.G. "Criteria Help Hospitals Evaluate Vendor Proposals." *Health Care Financial Management* 43(6) (June 1989):38–48.

Part VI

Cost / Quality Issues

Nancy O. Graham

With the implementation of the prospective payment system (PPS) in 1983, concerns have been raised in both the public and private sectors about the potential for compromised quality of care resulting from the financial incentives inherent in the system. Chapters 20 and 21 address some of these issues.

In Chapter 20, Russell states that the dominant question for health care providers is—How can we get the most health from the resources available? This question must be broken down into three parts: (1) Is the medical intervention effective? (2) If effective, how much does it cost? and (3) What is the balance of costs and effects or does the measure bring a reasonable return in health for the expenditure?

Methods available to help answer these questions have advanced considerably in the past 2 decades. Progress has been made in synthesizing information, measuring health outcome, and evaluating the balance between costs and effects. These advances in cost-effective analysis will help us make better decisions in balancing both the cost and quality of medical care. The final decision, however, about which investment to make depends on how we as individuals and society *value* the effort.

Concerned with learning whether cost containment and quality can coexist, the Health Care Financing Administration has initiated several studies related to quality of care issues. Currently, there are a variety of efforts dealing with issues of access to inpatient care, the quality of inpatient care, and access to posthospital care. In Chapter 21, Eggers discusses some of these results. Early results do not suggest that implementation of PPS is associated with problems of access to inpatient care or with increases in mortality. Future research will refine the analysis, as well as provide data on access to posthospital care services, severity of illness levels, and analysis of the process of care in the inpatient setting.

SUGGESTED READING

Clifford, L.A. and Plomann, R.N. "Cost and Quality: Two Sides of the Coin in Cost Containment." *Healthcare Financial Management* (September 1985): 30–32.

Donabedian, A. "Quality, Cost and Cost Containment." *Nursing Outlook* 32 (1984): 142–145.

Enthoven, A. and Kronick, R. "A Consumer-Choice Health Plan for the 1990s." *New England Journal of Medicine* 320 (1989): 94–107.

Guterman, S. and Dobson, A. "Impact of the Medicare Prospective Payment System for Hospitals." *Health Care Financing Review* 7 (1986): 97–114.

Horn, S.D.; Buckley, G.; Sharkey, P.; Chambers, A.F.; Horn, R.; and Schramm, C.J. "Interhospital Difference in Severity of Illness." *New England Journal of Medicine* 313 (1985): 20–24.

Roper, W. "Perspectives on Physician Payment Reform." *New England Journal of Medicine* 319 (1988): 865–867.

Shortell, S. and Hughes, E. "The Effects of Regulation, Competition, and Ownership on Mortality Rates among Hospital Inpatients." *New England Journal of Medicine* 318 (1988): 1100–1107.

Stern, R.S. and Epstein, A.M. "Institutional Responses to Prospective Payment Based on Diagnosis-Related Groups." *New England Journal of Medicine* 312 (1985): 621–627.

Vladeck, B.C. "PPS and Quality Care: Can They Coexist?" *Health Span* 3(1986): 15–18.

Chapter 20

Balancing Cost and Quality: Methods of Evaluation

Louise B. Russell

The title of this panel, Balancing Cost and Quality, succinctly describes the fundamental dilemma of cost containment. The dilemma is that doing all, or even most, of the good things possible in medical care entails the kind of growth in expenditures experienced during the last 20 years, but slowing the growth of expenditures means going without some of those good things. Containing costs means giving up at least a little quality. It is an unpleasant but unavoidable dilemma. And as medical expenditures have pressed harder on personal, corporate, and government budgets, the nation has reluctantly moved to slow their growth.

The dominant question for health care providers and consumers is thus shifting from "How can we get more resources?" to "How can we get the most health for the resources available?" The goal is, as it always has been, to provide as many people as possible good health for as long as possible. But what is possible is clearly constrained by the nation's growing reluctance to continue diverting resources from other uses.

The change is having a profound effect on investments in health. The major effect comes from the slowdown in the growth of resources available to medical care. The details of how that slowdown is brought about, whether through DRGs, HMOs, PPOs, or other mechanisms, are less important. The fundamental change is that resources now lag noticeably behind opportunities to use them. Each new opportunity must be judged more care-

*Presented in a panel, The Continuing Government Task: Balancing Cost, Quality and Innovation, as part of the 1985 Annual Health Conference, *The Role of Government in Health Care: A Time for Reappraisal,* held by the Committee on Medicine in Society of the New York Academy of Medicine, May 2 and 3, 1985.

This paper was based on research that was funded in part by the National Center for Health Services Research under Grant HS04392.

Note: Reprinted with permission from *Bulletin of the New York Academy of Medicine,* Vol. 62, No. 1, pp. 55–60, © January-February 1986.

fully. It is not enough to show that a service or procedure is effective, that is, that it works and improves health. Instead, each service or procedure must bring a reasonably good return in health for the required expenditure.

The standard is comparative, not absolute. The better investments will be kept; those that are less good will be used more selectively or not at all. Cost-saving innovations will spread faster than before since they free up resources for other uses. But most innovations are not cost-saving, or are cost-saving in only a few applications. These cost-adding innovations will be slowed in their diffusion to some degree, less if they produce a lot of health for the expenditure, more if they produce relatively little.

An increasing number of articles in the medical literature spell out some of the choices. They have yielded illuminating results. Equally promising, they reflect the enormous development in evaluation methods over the last 2 decades. The decisions ahead are difficult, but the techniques have been developed that will make the process of sorting through them easier and more accurate. I shall review just a few studies and then sketch the techniques that are available.

SOME STUDIES

The examples extend across the entire spectrum of medical care. Fineberg and his colleagues[1] showed that, for patients with a low probability of myocardial infarction, admission to a coronary care unit offered only small advantages over an intermediate care unit and at high cost: $139,000 per year of life saved. With less formal analysis, but a keen sense for the same dilemma, Turnbull and his colleagues[2] reported on the introduction of a tighter admissions policy at the critical care facility of the Memorial Sloan-Kettering Cancer Center. The change, which required consultation between the patient's physician and the attending staff of the unit before a patient could be admitted, was intended to focus resources more precisely on those for whom real improvement was possible.

Bunker and his colleagues[3] published a volume of papers appraising surgical procedures, primarily those for which the indications are imprecise and a matter of some controversy. Many of the procedures considered are quite common and affect hundreds of thousands of people. The editors of the volume note the wide variations across geographic areas in the rate at which a procedure is done. Others observed (and reported) the variations. These authors noted the fact of variation and discussed its implications. These variations carry substantial differences in cost, but it is less clear that higher costs bring substantially better health. To quote the authors: "Thus, nationwide policies of appendectomy for narrow indications or for broad indications differ only slightly in the number of expected lives saved or lost, but the substantial difference in morbidity and hospitalization costs is estimated to amount to several million days of patient hospitalization per year. Similar arguments can be made about other operations where the indications are marginal." Similar arguments can be made as well about other kinds of medical intervention and recently were, for example, in a paper showing that routine chest roentgenograms rarely had any effect on the treatment given patients in a VA hospital.[4]

In preventive medical care, choices can be equally difficult. In spite of hopes to the contrary, prevention rarely reduces medical expenditures.[5] It almost always involves the same weighing of additional costs against improvements in health as most other choices in medical care. In some cases, such as childhood immunizations, evaluation shows that the investment is an excellent one. In others, such as many screening procedures, the cost per year of healthy life gained is high. Calculations such as these persuaded the American Cancer Society a few years ago to alter its recommendations about the appropriate frequency for some cancer screening tests.[6]

METHODS OF EVALUATION

The balancing of cost and quality is the balancing of cost against health outcomes. Whether the evaluation is formal or informal, this requires some sort of assessment of costs and effects. Methods available to help with these calculations have advanced considerably in the last 2 decades. It is exciting to realize how great the advances have been. Cost containment means that cost-effectiveness evaluations have become truly valuable for the first time—until cost is accepted as important, cost-effectiveness is irrelevant—and the methods are ready, with some exceptions, to support the kind of work that needs to be done.

One major step in the evolution of cost-effectiveness analysis in health has been its expansion beyond the original and rather narrow use of the term. Originally (and often still) cost-effectiveness was applied in a situation where a specific decision to spend had already been made—to put in a new telephone system or start an intensive care unit, for example. Then the analysis is directed toward finding the least expensive way to make the investment. Hence cost-effectiveness has become equated with cost-saving, with finding the cheapest way to make the investment. But note that the decision itself is not necessarily cost-saving; it would usually be cheaper not to make the investment at all, but the effects have been judged worth the expense at the outset. Further, the decision has been set up so that the effect is much the same—a telephone system or an intensive care unit—and only the costs of achieving it differ. Actually, this statement oversimplifies. The alternatives rarely produce exactly the same result, but the results are close enough that differences can be handled intuitively or ignored.

Most investments in health (or anything else) differ in effects as well as costs. Evaluation methods must be tailored to fit this more common situation. And it is useful, and intuitively more comfortable and understandable, to represent effects by some measure of health rather than to try to translate them into dollars. Over the last 2 decades cost-effectiveness analysis has developed to permit the comparison of investments with different effects as well as costs.

Cost-effectiveness must proceed by answering three questions: First, is the medical intervention effective? If not, the analysis need proceed no further. If the measure is effective, the second question is, How much does it cost? Measures that add nothing to costs or that save more than they cost can be accepted without going further; they not only improve health, but free resources for other uses. But most measures add to costs at the same time that they improve health. For these a third question must also be answered: What is the balance of costs and effects? Put another way, does the measure bring a reasonable return in health for the expenditure? In this broader use of the term, to say that a measure is cost-effective means that it is a good investment in health.

Most of the development of cost-effectiveness for health has focused on measuring effectiveness, that is, on health outcomes. This is understandable since effectiveness is extremely important, particularly difficult to measure, and was, until cost containment became a reality, almost the only concern. An important series of methods have been developed for combining information from different sources to arrive at an overall conclusion about the effectiveness of an intervention. It is not possible, and would not make economic sense if it were possible, to mount large, randomized, controlled trials to provide a definitive test of every issue in medical care. At the same time, large amounts of highly imperfect and incomplete information are available about many of these issues. The problem is what sense to make of it all. Methods to synthesize information, especially the methods grouped under the heading meta-analysis, have been developed which give guidelines for reviewing the literature and statistical techniques for calculating the size and significance of average effects.[7] A more recent methodology, developed at Duke University, employs Bayesian techniques and emphasizes the importance of synthesizing information about each link in the causal chain between disease and treatment outcome.[8]

A second series of developments, equally important, have explored how to measure health outcomes in ways that both capture the effects of very different interventions and allow them to be compared. These methods try to represent health outcomes in terms of a common, objective set of descriptors having to do with ability to function. The Sickness Impact Profile, for example, is based on questions about physical and psychosocial functioning derived from people's descriptions of the effects illness had on them.[9] The quality-adjusted life-year describes levels of physical function and symptom/problem complexes (e.g., a persistent cough).[10] The analysts who developed these approaches have used surveys to develop weights for each descriptor. Thus, health effects can be described in terms both important and readily understandable and that allow improvements in health to be included as well as changes in life expectancy. Further, the results can be aggregated into an equivalent number of healthy years to facilitate comparisons of different interventions.

Costs and their measurement have been taken for granted, in part because economics already provides some guidance as to how to handle them. The economic concept of opportunity cost—the payment necessary to induce the owner of the resource to make it available—is central although not always easy to put into practice in an area such as health where market prices are suspect. There has been progress toward agreeing on the specific costs that should and should not be included.[11] But I think that this part of the methodology needs further attention to bring it up to the standards reached in measuring health outcomes. Costs need to be measured more carefully and completely if cost-effectiveness evaluations are to be reliable guides for decision making.

The third step is to evaluate the balance between costs and effects. To help with this final step the analyst usually calculates a cost-effectiveness ratio in addition to presenting the estimates of costs and effects in detail. The need here is to continue to standardize the approaches and, where possible, the assumptions made in different studies so that their results can be compared.[12] Comparison is the essence of cost-effectiveness evaluation and, as the method becomes more widely used, it should also become more standardized so that comparisons are easier. Comparing the results for different interventions shows which are more or less cost-effective, that is, which produce additional health at lowest cost.

The final decisions about which investments to make depend, however, on values. The information about costs and effects is essential to good decisions, but the decisions depend on how we as individuals and as a society value the effects, which represent what we get, as against the costs, which represent what we must give up elsewhere to get those effects. The new methods help to make those values explicit and ensure that they are consistent with our other values, but the decisions must be made by real human beings, by us, not by technical methods.

Nonetheless, the advances that have been made in methods are exciting and impressive. They can be of enormous help in making the decisions that lie ahead. With their help we shall do a better job of balancing cost and quality in medical care.

NOTES

1. Fineberg, H.V., Scadden, D. and Goldman, L.: Care of patients with a low probability of acute myocardial infarction: Cost effectiveness of alternatives to coronary-care unit admission. *N. Engl. J. Med.* 310: 1301–07, 1984.

2. Turnbull, A.D., Carlon, G., Baron, R. et al.: The inverse relationship between cost and survival in the critically ill cancer patient. *Crit. Care Med.* 7: 20–23, 1979.

3. Bunker, J.P., Barnes, B.A. and Mosteller, F., editors: *Costs, Risks, and Benefits of Surgery.* New York, Oxford University Press, 1977.

4. Hubbell, F.A., Greenfield, S., Tyler, J.L. et al.: The impact of routine admission chest x-ray films on patient care. *N. Engl. J. Med.* 312: 209–13, 1985.

5. Russell, L.B.: The economics of prevention. *Health Pol.* 4: 85–100, 1984.

6. American Cancer Society: *ACS Report on the Cancer-Related Health Checkup.* July 1980.

7. Light, R.J. and Pillemer, D.B.: *Summing Up: The Science of Reviewing Research.* Cambridge, MA, Harvard University Press, 1984.

8. Eddy, D.M.: The Evaluation of Medical Practice: A Language for Combining Medical Evidence. Presentation before the U.S. Preventive Services Task Force, Denver, Colorado, April 18, 1985.

9. Bergner, M., Bobbitt, R.A., Carter, W.B., and Gilson, B.S.: The sickness impact profile: Development and final revision of a health status measure. *Med Care* 19: 787–805, 1981.

10. Kaplan, R.J. and Bush, J.W.: Health-related quality of life measurement for evaluation research and policy analysis. *Health Psych.* 1: 61–80, 1982.

11. Weinstein, M.C. and Stason, W.B.: Foundations of cost-effectiveness analysis for health and medical practices. *N. Engl. J. Med.* 296: 716–21, 1977; Warner, K.C. and Luce, B.R.: *Cost-Benefit and Cost-Effectiveness Analysis in Health Care: Principles, Practice, and Potential.* Ann Arbor, Mich., Health Administration Press, 1982; Russell, L.B.: Issues in the Design of Future Preventive Medicine Studies. In: *The Value of Preventive Medicine.* Ciba Foundation Symposium 110. London, Pitman, 1985.

12. Russell, idem.

Chapter 21

Prospective Payment System and Quality: Early Results and Research Strategy

Paul W. Eggers

INTRODUCTION

With the passage of Public Law 98-21 in 1983, Congress initiated the most sweeping change in payment for hospital services in the history of the Medicare program. The major rationale for this system is to reverse the financial incentives inherent in the original cost reimbursement system. Under cost reimbursement there is little, if any, incentive to control costs. Under a system of prospectively set rates, there is every incentive to economize and institute efficiencies.

At the time of the passage of this act, Congress was aware of the potential for economizing at the expense of the patient. Consequently, section 603(a)(2)(A) of that legislation requires the Secretary of the U.S. Department of Health and Human Services to:

> ". . . study and report annually to the Congress at the end of each year (beginning with 1984 and ending with 1987) on the impact of the payment methodology under Section 1886(d) of the Social Security Act during the previous year, on classes of hospitals, beneficiaries, and other payers for inpatient hospital services, and other providers . . . ." *

The impact of the prospective payment system (PPS) has, subsequently, been interpreted to encompass the issue of quality of care. Various organizations such as the Office of Technology Assessment (OTA);[1] the Pro-

---

*More recently the Omnibus Reconciliation Act of 1986, Public Law 99-509, has extended the annual reports through 1989.

Note: Reprinted from *Health Care Financing Review*, 1987 Annual Supplement, HCFA Pub. No. 03258, Office of Research and Demonstrations, Health Care Financing Administration, U.S. Government Printing Office, Washington, D.C., December 1987.

spective Payment Assessment Commission;[2] the General Accounting Office;[3] the Assistant Secretary for Planning and Evaluation, U.S. Department of Health and Human Services;[4] and Lohr[5] have pointed out the need for in-depth evaluations of the impact of PPS on the quality of health care.

Despite a near unanimous opinion that there is a need for research on the quality of care under PPS, there is little guidance on how to measure PPS impacts or what specific problems to look for. OTA states, "How hospitals and other providers actually will respond to the financial incentives inherent in PPS is by no means well understood . . . . Thus, the magnitude and direction of PPS effects on health care costs and benefits cannot be predicted with confidence . . . ."[1] For instance, it is entirely possible that a single response could have both negative and positive effects on Medicare beneficiaries. Specialization of services is an example. Should hospitals respond to PPS by increased specialization, it is generally believed that quality of care would improve as the volume of services increases in fewer hospitals. However, this specialization could also result in a centralization of needed services in hospitals farther removed from many beneficiaries, in which case, access to care could be compromised.

The Office of Research and Demonstrations (ORD), Health Care Financing Administration (HCFA), has adopted an evolving approach to assessing PPS impacts. Initially, the plan centered on issues of access to hospital care and quality of care within the hospital setting. However, more recent events have led to the addition of other areas of interest. In particular, the large reductions in length of stay occurring with the introduction of PPS have raised the "sicker and quicker" issue. That is, concerns have been raised that shorter lengths of stay (quicker) will lead to patients being discharged in a less stable medical condition (sicker). Thus, efforts have been included to assess access to post-hospital subacute health care services. Additionally, the unanticipated drop in admission rates has raised the possibility of changes in case severity that could impact on outcome measures such as mortality and rehospitalization rates. Thus, there is a need for work in the area of severity adjustment research, as it relates to quality of care issues.

Finally, the Omnibus Reconciliation Act of 1986 (section 9313(d)) has mandated that the Secretary of the U.S. Department of Health and Human Services, ". . . shall arrange for a study to design a strategy for reviewing and assuring the quality of care for which payment may be made under title XVIII of the Social Security Act." ORD's response to this mandate is currently in the development phase.

CURRENT WORK IN PROGRESS

The Office of Research and Demonstrations (ORD) has 13 extramural efforts in the area of PPS quality impact and a significant intramural effort as well. Essentially these efforts are directed at three major issue areas within the quality of care domain: access to inpatient care, the quality of inpatient care, and access to post-discharge services, that is, the "aftercare" issue.

Access to Inpatient Care

The concern in this area is that one of the incentives of PPS is to encourage providers to selectively market to patients who are relatively easy and inexpensive to treat and avoid those patients who are difficult and more expensive to treat. That is, hospitals could avoid some of the high costs of expensive patients either by not admitting them in the first place or by discharging them earlier than other patients. This could show up either in admission rates or average lengths of stay.

ORD is approaching this problem through an intramural analysis of utilization rates such as discharges per 1,000 Medicare beneficiaries and average lengths of stay. Because there are no acceptable standards of what constitutes appropriate use rates, the analysis is directed toward changes in utilization rates that are disproportionately large. For instance, there have been large decreases in average length of stay. To the extent that these decreases are consistent across types of patients—aged, disabled, and those with end stage renal disease (ESRD), and demographic breakdowns of age, sex, and race—there is no evidence that specific groups have been denied access to inpatient care. In other words, the impact of PPS on access to care—whether good, bad, or indifferent—would be at least consistent across beneficiary groups. Early results from this analysis are presented later in this article.

There is one extramural effort in this area that is being conducted by the Urban Institute, Learning from and Improving DRG's for End Stage Renal Disease (ESRD) Patients. In that study, the utilization patterns for ESRD patients prior to and after the implementation of PPS to determine the potential adverse consequences of PPS are examined. Because ESRD patients are a potentially high-risk and high-cost group, it was felt to be important to examine them in some detail.

Quality of Inpatient Care

Originally, this was the area in which it was thought that quality of care problems might occur. That is, with the fixed PPS payment, the concern is that hospitals might cut back on needed services as well as unnecessary care, to the detriment of the patient. This could occur as reductions in ancillary services, reductions in staff levels, or as premature discharges.

There are a number of studies in this area to determine if such changes have taken place. First, there are intramural studies in which hospital-related mortality, overall population mortality, and rehospitalization rates are examined. The mortality analyses use both Medicare and National Center for Health Statistics time trend data to determine if death rates are changing for the Medicare population. Rates of rehospitalization (usually within 30 days) are being examined to determine whether there has been an increase since PPS went into effect. Such an increase could indicate that patients are being discharged too early and require additional hospital care as a result.

There are limitations to using the Medicare data bases for these kinds of analyses. First, the amount of clinical detail available from the administrative claims data is somewhat limited. Each inpatient stay can have up to five diagnoses and up to three procedures. Additional clinical data that could indicate important risk factors (such as blood pressure, serum creatinine levels, and hematocrit) are not available from the billing system. Second, the change in coding and data collection that occurred with the advent of PPS makes it difficult to do time trend analyses. Therefore, the intramural analyses have been supplemented with a number of extramural efforts.

ORD has cooperative agreements with the Commission on Professional and Hospital Activities (CPHA) to do two studies on quality of care. In the first study, Impact of the Prospective Payment System on the Quality of Inpatient Care, CPHA uses their Professional Activities Study (PAS) data set to examine trends in inpatient care prior to and after PPS implementation. It has two major advantages over what ORD can do intramurally. First, the PAS data system is considered to be more consistent over time. The data elements collected did not change at the time PPS was implemented. Of course, the more general problem of diagnosis-related group (DRG) creep could affect this study as well as studies based on Medicare data.[6] (DRG creep is a term used to describe changes in the distribution of DRGs that are a result of changes in coding practices.) Second, CPHA data include information on the non-Medicare patient population. Thus, this study will compare Medicare trends with trends for persons not directly affected by changes in reimbursements because of PPS. In the second study, Develop Indexes of Hospital Efficiency and Quality, CPHA is using a multivariate classification approach (data envelopment analysis) to assess the changes that have occurred in the process of care (to measure efficiency) and to relate these to changes that have occurred in patient outcomes (to measure quality). Data envelopment analysis is a mathematical procedure for making comparisons between units (in this case, hospitals) delivering similar services with similar resources. It constructs a set of weighted values for inputs (staff, capital, etc.) and outputs (days of care, procedures, etc.) that maximize differences among hospitals. Efficiency, as measured by a ratio of outputs to inputs, is then compared with patient quality (measured as inpatient mortality). This procedure has been used in the health care field by Sherman and Nunamaker.[7-8] This study also uses the PAS data set.

ORD also has cooperative agreements with the Rand Corporation to do two studies related to quality of care assessment. The first, Impact of the DRG-Based Prospective Payment System on Quality of Care for Hospitalized Medicare Patients, is a large-scale effort to examine changes that have occurred in the process of care provided to patients in the inpatient setting that might be attributable to PPS. Rand has selected conditions for which the acceptable standards of care are well-known and have remained more or less constant in the past few years. These include myocardial infarction, congestive heart failure, hip fracture, depression, pneumonia, and cerebrovascular accident. Criteria sets of appropriate care have been developed for these six conditions through consensus panels of physicians. A total of 17,000 inpatient medical records in these six categories are being sampled for data abstraction and analysis, one-half in the pre-PPS period (1981–1982) and one-half in the post-PPS period (1985–1986). The study is being carried out in five states: California, Florida, Indiana, Pennsylvania, and Texas. The results of this study, although not strictly generalizable to hospital care nationwide, will be a major in-depth assessment of how the care provided to patients may have changed since PPS was introduced.

The second Rand study is the Non-Intrusive Outcome Measures: Identification and Validation. The intent of this study is to determine the extent to which the administrative data base maintained by HCFA can be used as a monitoring tool for quality of care. Both ORD and the Health Standards and Quality Bureau already use the administrative system for this purpose. However, this study will relate outcomes as measured by administrative data with more clinically oriented data from discharge record abstractions. Rand is using myocardial infarction and congestive heart failure as tracer conditions, and the study is being carried out in the states of California, Illinois, Minnesota, and New York.

One issue that has recently become more evident is the extent to which changes in admission rates may indicate changes in patient mix. In 1984, there was a reduction in Medicare admissions for the first time since the Medicare program began. In 1985, there was an even larger reduction. It is likely that these reductions came at the expense of the easier, less problematic cases. For example, it is well-known that certain surgical procedures, such as lens extractions, are being shifted to outpatient settings. Because these procedures have very low mortality rates, this shift will tend to increase the overall mortality rate. This increase may have nothing to do with quality changes but may merely be the result of a more severe case mix. It is unlikely that DRG mix changes will be adequate to measure the more subtle indicators of case mix. Therefore, ORD has contracted with SysteMetrics, Inc., to assess case-mix changes in a study entitled A Mortality Based Case-Mix Severity Index. The purpose of this study is to determine any shifts in case mix that have occurred within diagnostic categories that would affect mortality rates. SysteMetrics is using their staging methodology to conduct this analysis.

In Summer 1987, ORD awarded two additional studies directed toward refining the analysis of case-mix effects on quality of care evaluation. The first is Patient Classification Systems: An Evaluation of the State of the Art being conducted at Queens University. This study will compare 15 patient classification systems in terms of their usefulness both for refining the DRG payment system and for the monitoring of and research on the quality of care. These systems will be compared in terms of reliability, predictive validity, and cost, using a data base constructed from 30,000 abstracted medical charts. The second study is An Automated, Data-Driven, Case-Mix Adjustment System for Studies of Quality of Care being conducted at the University of California at San Francisco. The main objectives of this project are to develop and validate predictors of medical outcomes based on patient status at admission. Patient status will be assessed based on early lab tests, diagnostic codes, and demographic data.

Access to Post-Discharge Services

This is the area in which many of the more recent efforts have been channeled. The concern in this area is that because patients are being discharged earlier than before, they still have rehabilitative and subacute care medical needs for which services may not be available. A number of extramural efforts have been initiated to examine this issue.

Among these is the health status at discharge research project being conducted by the Northwest Oregon Health Systems Agency. The purpose of this study is to develop an instrument for measuring dependency at discharge and then to determine the extent to which dependency has changed since PPS was introduced. The results so far indicate that there has been an increase in discharge dependency since PPS was begun. It does not indicate, however, whether this increased dependency indicates an increased need for subacute care or the extent to which subacute care needs are being met. To address these concerns the Office of Research and Demonstrations has three other extramural efforts.

The first is the study, Changes in Post-Hospital Service Use by Medicare Beneficiaries, being conducted under contract by Abt Associates. The purpose of this study is to examine Medicare post-hospital use patterns pre- and post-PPS implementation to determine whether any changes have occurred. The analysis will examine skilled nursing facility (SNF), home health agency (HHA), and physician use patterns. This analysis will be a longitudinal assessment of these patterns from 1981 through 1986. It is, however, confined only to Medicare covered services. An inherent shortcoming is that much of aftercare needs are long-term care needs that Medicare does not cover. Most long-term services are paid for out of pocket or by Medicaid.

The second study, the Impact of Medicare Prospective Payment on Post Hospital Care among Medicaid Recipients, conducted by SysteMetrics, Inc., is an attempt to fill in this gap. Using state Medicaid data, the intent of this study is to determine the extent to which use of Medicaid covered services (post discharge) have changed as a result of PPS. The analysis will be limited to persons with entitlement to both Medicare and Medicaid in Michigan and California. Although not strictly generalizable to the nation as a whole, it will provide some important information on the impact of PPS on Medicaid covered services.

These two studies have several major limitations. First, neither study will have measures of the need for aftercare services. That is, even if the rates of aftercare use remain constant over time, there could be a problem if the need has increased (as suggested by the health status at discharge research project). Second, neither study will provide any information on the provision of informal care services. That is, to what extent are informal caregivers (wives, husbands, children, and neighbors) providing care to patients after discharge from the hospital? Nor will either study be able to identify the types of patients who encounter aftercare problems or the causes of these problems (e.g., financial, travel, access).

These issues are being addressed in the pilot study Development of a Study Plan for the Appropriateness of Post-Hospital Care Received by Medicare Beneficiaries under the Prospective Payment System. This study, being conducted by System Sciences, Inc., and Mathematica Policy Research, Inc. (and jointly sponsored by the Assistant Secretary for Planning and Evaluation and HCFA), is an attempt to design a study to address patient aftercare needs at discharge and the subsequent use of services, including Medicare, Medicaid, and informally provided care. This pilot project is intended to develop the methods necessary to conduct a national study of these issues. Key tasks under this project include the following:

- developing a classification scheme of patients based on the need for skilled and unskilled aftercare services
- constructing professionally developed guidelines of minimally acceptable aftercare service needs
- developing a plan to sample patients at varying risks of receiving inadequate aftercare
- developing an overall study plan that uses the above methodologies in a national study of aftercare use

This study relies heavily on primary data collection including telephone interviews and patient health assessments. Because it requires primary data collection, a pre- and post-PPS study is not feasible. That is, it is not possible to interview patients and determine their aftercare needs and use patterns for a hospital stay that occurred 4 years ago. Consequently, the goal of this study is to determine current aftercare needs and access to needed services, not whether these needs and access have changed over time with respect to PPS.

In Summer 1987, ORD awarded a cooperative agreement to Duke University to do a study of the use of post-hospital subacute care services; the study is entitled Trends in Patterns of Post-Hospital Service Use and Their Impacts on Outcomes. Grade of membership analysis will be used to categorize patients according to mortality risk levels and need for skilled nursing and home health care. This analysis will then be integrated into basic life table analyses to determine the changes that have occurred over time (pre- and post-PPS implementation) in mortality, in site of death, and in the use of post-hospital services.

FINDINGS

Findings on utilization of inpatient services and mortality analyses from the Impact of the Medicare Hospital Prospective Payment System 1985, Report to Congress are presented in this section.[9]

Utilization of Inpatient Services

Medicare discharge rates and average length of stay for the years 1980 through 1984 are shown in Table 21-1. From 1980 through 1983, the discharge rate in the United States increased from 371 per 1,000 beneficiaries to 394 per 1,000, an average annual rate of increase of 2.1 percent. This was a continuation of the trend since 1968. The rate of increase was somewhat lower in PPS states (2.0 percent) than in the four waiver states (2.5 percent).* In 1984, the discharge rate declined for the first time since the beginning of Medicare. The decline was 2.9 percent. However, the change was markedly different between PPS and waiver states. The discharge rate declined by 3.5 percent in PPS states and increased in waiver states. The increase in the waiver states was, however, much less than the pre-PPS

---

*Hospitals in Maryland, Massachusetts, New Jersey, and New York were waived from inclusion at the inception of the PPS, because they were participating in demonstrations of other payment systems. Currently, Maryland and New Jersey retain waiver status, and New York and Massachusetts have been incorporated into the PPS.

Table 21-1 Discharge Rates per 1,000 Aged Medicare Beneficiaries, Average Length of Stay, and Annual Percent Change by Area: 1980–84

						Annual Percent Change	
Area	CY 1980	CY 1981	CY 1982	CY 1983	FY 1984	1980–83	1983–84
			Discharge rate per 1,000				
United States	371	371	388	394	386	2.1	−2.9
PPS States	380	382	398	403	393	2.0	−3.5
Waiver States	322	316	338	346	349	2.5	1.0
			Average length of stay				
United States	10.3	10.1	9.9	9.6	8.7	−2.3	−11.5
PPS States	9.9	9.7	9.5	9.2	8.3	−2.3	−13.2
Waiver States	12.9	12.5	12.3	12.1	11.5	−2.1	−5.7

Notes: PPS is prospective payment system; CY is calendar year; FY is fiscal year.
Source: Health Care Financing Administration, Bureau of Data Management and Strategy. Data from the Office of Statistics and Data Management.

---

trend had been. It would appear that the slower rate of growth in the discharge rate in waiver states represents a spillover effect of PPS and that providers in these states were reacting to the PPS changes in ways similar to providers in PPS states.

This decline in the PPS states was contrary to expectations, and it has raised considerable speculation as to the causes. Some analysts have suggested that it is a temporary phenomenon and that, once hospitals and physicians adjust to the PPS system, there will be a return to increasing rates. Others have argued that the decreased hospitalizations represent a change in the basic practice of medicine (in part a result of the PPS). Primarily, this line of reasoning contends that closer attention is now being paid to possible alternatives to inpatient care and that there will be a continuing trend toward less costly alternatives such as ambulatory surgery. A related explanation is that the peer review organizations are taking a more effective role in admission review and that hospitals and physicians are adopting more stringent criteria for admission.

It was in the area of length of stay that PPS had its greatest apparent effect. Unlike discharge rates, average length of stay had been declining every year prior to the start of PPS. From 1980 through 1983, it declined from 10.3 days per stay to 9.6 days per stay, an average annual decline of 2.3 percent. In 1984, the decline was 0.9 days, or 11.5 percent. Waiver states (actually, the entire northeast section of the country) have historically had longer lengths of stay than the rest of the country. In 1980, there was a 3.0-day differential (9.9 days in PPS states and 12.9 days in the waiver states). During the 1980 to 1983 time span, lengths of stay declined somewhat more rapidly in the PPS states (2.3 percent) than in the waiver states (2.1 percent). However, in 1984, there was a 13.2 percent decline in the PPS states, and a 5.7 percent decline in the waiver states. Although not as large as the PPS state decline, the 5.7 percent decline in the waiver states is still almost three times as great as the historical trend, suggesting that there was again some spillover effect from PPS. As a result, the mean length-of-stay difference (3.2 days) between waiver states and the rest of the country was greater in 1984 than it had been in 1980.

A major concern is whether or not any changes in utilization rates fell disproportionately on high-risk groups or on groups with potential access problems. Discharge rates and average lengths of stay by age, sex, and race in PPS states are shown in Tables 21-2 and 21-3. The data in Table 21-2 indicate that changes in discharge rates were not borne disproportionately by the highest risk groups. To the contrary, in 1984, persons in the oldest age group (85 years of age or over) had a lower rate of decline (1.2 percent) than those in the younger age groups (5.7 percent for persons aged 65–69). Further, the declines were greater for males (3.9 percent) than for females (3.2 percent) and for white persons (3.6 percent) than for persons who are not white (2.3 percent).

Table 21-2 Discharge Rates per 1,000 Aged Medicare Beneficiaries in PPS States, and Annual Percent Change, by Sex, Race, and Age: 1980–84

| | | | | | | Annual Percent Change | |
Sex, Race, and Age	CY 1980	CY 1981	CY 1982	CY 1983	FY 1984	1980–83	1983–84
	Discharge rate per 1,000						
All persons	380	382	398	403	393	2.0	−3.5
Sex							
Male	409	409	421	428	415	1.5	−3.9
Female	361	363	382	387	377	2.4	−3.2
Race							
White	387	388	403	409	398	1.9	−3.6
Other	437	440	471	483	475	3.4	−2.3
Age							
65–69 years	294	295	300	302	289	0.8	−5.7
70–74 years	353	354	368	374	362	1.9	−4.0
75–79 years	424	426	445	453	442	2.2	−3.2
80–84 years	487	493	518	526	514	2.6	−2.9
85 years or over	532	531	561	569	564	2.3	−1.2

Notes: PPS is prospective payment system; CY is calendar year; FY is fiscal year.

Source: Health Care Financing Administration, Bureau of Data Management and Strategy. Data from the Office of Statistics and Data Management.

Table 21-3 Average Length of Stay for Aged Medicare Beneficiaries, in PPS States, and Annual Percent Change, by Sex, Race, and Age: 1980–84

Sex, Race, and Age	CY 1980	CY 1981	CY 1982	CY 1983	FY 1984	Annual Percent Change	
						1980–83	1983–84
	Average length of stay						
All persons	9.9	9.7	9.5	9.2	8.3	−2.3	−13.2
Sex							
Male	9.5	9.4	9.3	9.0	8.1	−2.0	−12.6
Female	10.1	9.9	9.7	9.3	8.4	−2.6	−13.7
Race							
White	9.7	9.6	9.4	9.1	8.2	−2.4	−13.1
Other	10.9	10.8	10.6	10.2	9.1	−2.2	−14.2
Age							
65–69 years	9.1	8.9	8.8	8.5	7.7	−2.2	−12.4
70–74 years	9.5	9.4	9.2	8.9	8.0	−2.3	−12.8
75–79 years	10.0	9.9	9.7	9.3	8.4	−2.4	−13.4
80–84 years	10.5	10.3	10.1	9.7	8.6	−2.6	−14.3
85 years or over	10.9	10.7	10.5	10.0	8.9	−2.7	−14.3

Notes: PPS is prospective payment system; CY is calendar year; FY is fiscal year.
Source: Health Care Financing Administration, Bureau of Data Management and Strategy. Data from the Office of Statistics and Data Management.

The trend in average length of stay for Medicare beneficiaries for the years 1980 through 1984 by age, sex, and race is shown in Table 21-3. Lengths of stay are directly related to the age of the patient. However, the trend has been to narrow the age difference. In 1980, persons 85 years of age or over had a length of stay 1.8 days longer than persons 65–69 years of age (10.9 days and 9.1 days, respectively). By 1983, this difference had decreased to 1.5 days (10.0 days and 8.5 days, respectively). All age groups experienced large declines in average length of stay in 1984, with the largest decline experienced by persons 80 years of age or over (14.3 percent). By 1984, there was only a 1.2-day differential in length of stay between the oldest and the youngest aged Medicare beneficiaries.

The changes in discharge rate and average length of stay by age, sex, and race largely offset each other in terms of total days of care.* That is, males had a larger decline in the discharge rate, but females had a larger decline in length of stay. The result is that there is virtually no difference between males and females in the decline in the days of care rate. The

---

*Total days of care is the product of the discharge rate and the average length of stay. As such, it is an indicator of total hospital use.

same is true for race. Minority persons had a slightly smaller decrease in discharge rates, but white persons had a smaller decline in average length of stay. By age group, persons 65–69 years of age had a slightly greater decline in days of care than persons 85 years of age or over did.

In summary, the trends in use of inpatient services indicate that there has been little change in the relative utilization levels (or access) across age, sex, or race categories. To the extent that the reductions in discharges and length of stay represent decreased access, the decreases have been relatively evenly distributed across demographic categories. Similarly, to the extent that these reductions represent decreases in overuse, the decreases have been equitable (in a purely statistical sense).

MORTALITY

Interpreting death rates is not the straightforward task it might appear to be. First of all, death is the most extreme outcome that one can relate to the provision of health care. To the extent that changes in mortality rates can be attributed to changes in the practice of medicine, then, indeed, there are quality of care problems. However, poor quality of care could result in increased disability, discomfort, or hardship without having a measurable effect on mortality. Thus, the absence of a measurable change in mortality does not necessarily mean that there has been no change in the quality of care. In a sense, testing for changes in mortality represents a worst-case scenario. If one finds increases in mortality that appear to be related to the introduction of PPS, then there is likely to be a severe quality of care problem. No change in mortality does not necessarily mean that quality has not changed, however.

A second problem with using mortality rates to test for changes in the quality of care because of PPS is the issue of attribution. There are many other factors that will have an impact on mortality independent of the effectiveness of medical care. These include changes in general standards of living, personal health practices, as well as periodic events such as influenza epidemics. During the 20th century, mortality rates have generally declined. This has been not only because of improvements in health care but because of improvements in standards of living and advances in public health measures (water purification, better sanitation, vaccines, etc.). Currently, PPS seems to be the major payment reform occurring in the U.S. health care system. However, there are other societal changes over which the health care system has little or no control. One example is the acquired immune deficiency syndrome (AIDS) epidemic. New cases of AIDS have doubled each of the last few years. Given this rate of increase and the fact that AIDS is considered fatal, it will not be many years before overall mortality rates will be affected by AIDS deaths (although probably not for the aged). A second example is lung cancer among women. The first year in which deaths resulting from lung cancer exceeded deaths resulting from breast cancer among women was 1985. This was in large part because of the increase in smoking among women that began back in the 1950s. Even if the rate of smoking among women were to decrease immediately, the lagged effects of a 30-year increase in smoking will push up lung cancer deaths among women for the next few decades. The health care system (including the payment methods) will have little effect on this type of mortality.

Three measures of mortality follow. The first is population mortality. This is usually expressed as deaths per 100,000 population. It is a measure of total deaths, irrespective of place of death or hospitalization experience. An advantage of this measure is that it is based on the total population at risk and is not directly affected by variations in utilization rates or practice patterns, both of which can affect hospital mortality, irrespective of levels of quality. It also has the advantage of picking up any effect PPS might have on mortality for those persons not admitted to hospitals. On the other hand, it has the disadvantage of including mortality unrelated to the provision of health care.

The second measure is post-admission mortality. This is usually expressed as post-admission deaths per 1,000 hospitalizations. For the purposes of this analysis, a 6-week post-admission period was used to capture mortality rates. This measure is used in preference to the more commonly used discharge mortality rate because of a bias in discharge mortality rate caused by variations in lengths of stay. To some extent, differences in discharge mortality rates are caused by practice patterns that result in patients dying in hospitals in some areas and patients dying in long-term care institutions or at home in other areas. Thus, variations in discharge mortality are in part the result of where people die as well as the fact of death itself. Mortality at a fixed interval from date of admission avoids biases caused by regional patterns of length of stay and possible constraints on the placement of patients to alternative settings because of variations in the supply of skilled nursing facilities, intermediate care facilities, or home health care.*

Post-admission mortality, nonetheless, is not a measure that can be interpreted in a fully straightforward manner. It can be influenced by the volume of services. As shown in Tables 21-1 and 21-2, the number of admissions per 1,000 population declined with the advent of PPS. If the reductions come at the expense of relatively nonsevere cases (e.g., the

---

*Using a fixed interval from admission is a special case of the more general actuarial life table methodology. Picking a fixed point to measure mortality is a somewhat arbitrary decision. Life table analyses are preferable in that they enable one to examine the entire distribution of time until death.

shift of lens extractions and other procedures to the outpatient setting), then the overall case severity of the remaining hospitalizations will increase and with it, mortality. To counteract this potential bias of post-admission mortality, another measure of mortality is used that is a hybrid of the population base and the post-admission death rates. It is the number of post-admission deaths per 1,000 population. The numerator is the same as in the post-admission mortality measure (that is, the number of deaths occurring within a fixed length of time from admission), but the denominator is the total population, not just the hospitalized population. The advantage of this measure is that it helps control for changes in case mix. As will be shown, this measure shows a different pattern than does the post-admission rate based on hospitalized patients only.

Data from the National Center for Health Statistics were used to track population mortality among the aged for the years 1968 through 1983. The yearly rates were age adjusted to the age distribution of Medicare beneficiaries in 1980. The expected 1984 mortality rate for the U.S. aged population was calculated using a linear time trend model. The dependent variable (the year-by-year mortality) was expressed as a log function, so that the trend would appear as a rate of change. The independent variable, time, was divided into two separate time trends.[10] The two trends intersect in 1976. Essentially this model allows one to use all 15 years of mortality data and at the same time provide estimates of two rates of change, one prior to 1976 and one since 1976. This allows full use of the data and allows for an apparent leveling of the downward trend in mortality.

The results of this analysis are shown in Table 21-4. The regression model fits the data very well, with an R-squared value of .96. The estimated rate of change coefficient for the 1968-to-1976 time period was -2.3 percent; and for the 1976-to-1983 time period, the coefficient was -1.2 percent. Thus, it is estimated that since 1976 mortality rates have been improving less rapidly than previously. Also shown in Table 21-4 are the actual mortality rates for each of the years 1968 through 1984, as well as the predicted rates from the model and an estimated confidence interval of plus and minus two standard deviations from the predicted rate. If an actual value lies outside the confidence intervals, then one would be 95 percent certain that that value was off the trend line.

In 1984, the predicted mortality rate for aged persons was 5,017 deaths per 100,000. The actual rate was 5,100, or 1.7 percent higher than predicted by the model. However, as shown by the confidence intervals, the 5,100 was clearly within the bounds of year-to-year variations experienced in previous years. The upper end of the 95 percent confidence interval in 1984 was 5,206. Thus, the actual mortality rate was not statistically different from the previous trend of declining mortality.

The difficulty in projecting expected mortality rates can be further illustrated by a closer examination of the trends in Table 21-4. Looking over

Table 21-4 Estimated and Actual Mortality Rates per 100,000 Aged Population: United States, 1968–84

Year	Actual Mortality Rate per 100,000	Low Estimate (−2 Standard Deviations)	Predicted Mortality Rate per 100,000	High Estimate (+2 Standard Deviations)
1968	6,637	6,385	6,625	6,873
1969	6,449	6,239	6,473	6,715
1970	6,152	6,095	6,324	6,561
1971	6,141	5,955	6,179	6,411
1972	6,171	5,819	6,037	6,263
1973	6,101	5,685	5,898	6,120
1974	5,857	5,555	5,763	5,979
1975	5,550	5,427	5,631	5,842
1976	5,527	5,303	5,502	5,708
1977	5,357	5,242	5,439	5,643
1978	5,336	5,182	5,376	5,578
1979	5,170	5,123	5,315	5,514
1980	5,367	5,064	5,254	5,451
1981	5,186	5,006	5,194	5,389
1982	5,101	4,949	5,134	5,327
1983	5,130	4,892	5,076	5,266
1984	5,100	4,836	5,017	5,206

Note: Data are age adjusted to the 1980 age distribution of aged Medicare beneficiaries.

Source: National Center for Health Statistics: Annual Summary of Births, Marriages, Divorces, and Deaths: United States, 1984. *Monthly Vital Statistics Report.* Vol. 33, No. 13. DHHS Pub. No. (PHS) 85-1120. Public Health Service, Hyattsville, Md., Sept. 26, 1985.

an even shorter time frame (1979 through 1983), it appears that mortality rates may have almost stopped declining. From 1979 through 1983, there was only a .2 percent average decline in mortality. The model was rerun using 1979 as the year in which a change took place in the long-term trend in mortality (not shown). The model fit very well (R^2 was .96), and the predicted mortality in 1984 was 5,114, somewhat higher than what actually occurred.

The major point to be made from these various examinations of the data is that the mortality rate in 1984 was well within historical trends for mortality among the aged. Tracking mortality in future years against a projected rate will become more and more suspect, however. As the projected figures get farther and farther away from 1983, the validity of the projection declines. For instance, how would one interpret the mortality rates if they continue to exhibit the rate of change shown between 1979 and 1983? Was the 1979-to-1983 trend a real leveling off of the historical trend, or was it a short-term aberration in the longer trend that goes back at least to 1968? There is no simple answer to this question. In essence, the assessment of the PPS impact on population mortality rates will have

Table 21-5 Number of Deaths per 1,000 Hospitalizations (First Admissions Only) Occurring within 6 Weeks of an Admission, and Annual Percent Change by Area: 1980–84

Area	CY 1980	CY 1981	CY 1982	CY 1983	FY 1984	Annual Percent Change 1980–83	Annual Percent Change 1983–84
	Deaths per 1,000 hospitalizations						
PPS States	80.0	74.9	72.4	74.0	76.1	−2.5	3.7
Waiver States	89.3	85.1	82.3	81.9	81.7	−2.8	−0.3
	Deaths per 1,000 beneficiaries						
PPS States	29.2	28.5	29.7	30.3	29.3	1.2	−4.1
Waiver States	27.5	27.0	29.1	29.2	29.1	2.1	−0.7

Notes: CY is calendar year; FY is fiscal year; PPS is prospective payment system.
Source: Health Care Financing Administration, Bureau of Data Management and Strategy. Data from the Office of Statistics and Data Management.

to be taken within the context of other measures of quality such as post-admission mortality and rehospitalization rates.

Post-admission mortality rates for aged Medicare beneficiaries are shown in Table 21-5. In PPS states, a decline in post-admission deaths per 1,000 hospitalizations in 1981 and 1982 was followed by increases in 1983 and 1984. Overall, there was an average annual decrease in this measure between 1980 and 1983 of 2.5 percent. The increase in 1984 was 3.7 percent. In waiver states the pre-PPS decline was 2.8 percent per year, with a very small decrease of .03 percent in 1984. The second part of Table 21-5 (post-admission deaths per 1,000 beneficiaries) shows the impact of the decline in admission rates in 1984. In 1984, mortality declined by 4.1 percent in the PPS states to 29.3 per 1,000 beneficiaries and declined by 0.7 percent in the waiver states to 29.1 per 1,000. The banks of data in Table 21-5, taken together, support the hypothesis that declining admission rates are associated with increasing case severity. Although the mortality rate increased in 1984 (per 1,000 hospitalizations), the number of deaths within 6 weeks of a hospitalization actually decreased.

SUMMARY

The assessment of quality of health care in the United States has received increased attention in recent years, primarily because of the implementation of PPS. The research agenda on quality of care, developed within ORD, has evolved since the implementation of PPS to deal with additional quality issues as they have arisen. Currently, there are a variety of intramural and extramural efforts dealing with issues of access to inpatient care, the quality of inpatient care, and access to post-hospital care.

Early results from utilization and mortality statistics do not suggest that the implementation of PPS is associated with problems of access to inpatient care or with increases in mortality. Future research will refine these initial analyses, as well as provide information on the trends in access to post-hospital care services, further refinements on changes in inpatient severity levels, and more detailed analyses of any changes in the actual processes of care in the inpatient setting.

NOTES

1. Office of Technology Assessment, U.S. Congress: *Medicare's Prospective Payment System: Strategies for Evaluating Cost, Quality, and Medical Technology*. Pub. No. OTA-H-263. Washington. U.S. Government Printing Office, Oct. 1985.

2. Prospective Payment Assessment Commission: Report and Recommendations to the Secretary, U.S. Department of Health and Human Services, Apr. 1, 1986.

3. General Accounting Office: Efforts to Evaluate Medicare Prospective Payment Effects Are Insufficient. Pub. No. GAO/PEMD-86-10. Washington. U.S. Government Printing Office, June 1986.

4. Assistant Secretary for Planning and Evaluation: *Research Agenda: The Impact of PPS and Capitation on Quality and Access to Care*. Prepared for the Office of Health Planning and Evaluation by Lewin and Associates, Inc., Sept. 1986.

5. Lohr, K. N., Brook, R. H., Goldberg, G. A., et al.: Impact of Medicare Prospective Payment on the Quality of Medical Care: A Research Agenda. The Rand Corporation. Pub. No. R-3242-HCFA, Mar. 1985.

6. Carter, G. M., and Ginsburg, P. B.: The Medicare Case Mix Index Increase: Medical Practice Changes, Aging and DRG Creep. The Rand Corporation, 1985.

7. Sherman, H. D.: "Hospital efficiency measurement and evaluation: An empirical test of a new technique," *Medical Care* 22(10):922–938, 1984.

8. Nunamaker, T. R.: "Measuring routine nursing services efficiency: A comparison of cost per patient day and data envelopment analysis," *Health Services Research* 18(2):183–205, 1983.

9. Health Care Financing Administration: Impact of the Medicare Hospital Prospective Payment System, 1985 Annual Report. *Report to Congress*. HCFA Pub. No. 03251. Office of Research and Demonstrations. Washington. U.S. Government Printing Office, Aug. 1987.

10. Draper and Smith: *Applied Regression Analysis*. New York. John Wiley and Sons, 1966, p. 139.

Part VII

Research

Nancy O. Graham

With the rising costs of medical care and the increasing concerns about the effects of cost containment, we can no longer provide health care without knowing more about its successes and failures.[1] Research is needed to produce the information required to make medical care decisions that are both efficacious and effective.

Dr. Brook and Dr. Lohr discuss the future directions for quality assessment research. In the past 20 years health services research has grown and matured. It is their hope that future quality assessment research will play a larger role in the areas of public policy, planning, and evaluation. To do this, Brook and Lohr state that there must be a commitment to integrate efficacy studies with measures of effectiveness; with measures of structure, process, and outcome of care; and with epidemiologic studies of variation in the use of services. Advances in computers and information handling in the next 2 decades should greatly enhance the quality assessment research tools available.

The remaining challenge is to expand our knowledge about the costs and benefits of different options, to design standards, and to monitor against these standards. Accomplishing these objectives will require not only specific actions but also strong leadership and the development of a common vision.[2]

With constant questioning, heightened awareness, and continuing research, there is an unique opportunity to make major advances in improving the quality of health care.

NOTES

1. A.S. Relman, "Assessment and Accountability—The Third Revolution in Medical Care," *New England Journal of Medicine* 319 (1988): 1220–1222.

2. D.M. Eddy, and J. Billecy, "The Quality of Medical Evidence: Implication for Quality of Care," *Health Affairs* (1988): 19–32.

SUGGESTED READING

Caper, P. "Defining Quality in Medical Care." *Health Affairs* (1988): 49–61.

Donabedian, A. "The Epidemiology of Quality." *Inquiry* 22 (1985): 282–292.

Eddy, D.M. and Billings, J. "The Quality of Medical Evidence." *Health Affairs* 7 (1988): 19–32.

Ellwood, P.M. "Shattuck Lecture Outcomes Management." *New England Journal of Medicine* 318 (1988): 1549–1556.

Greenfield, S. "The State of Outcome Research: Are We on Target?" *New England Journal of Medicine* 320 (1989): 1142–1143.

Lohr, K.N. "Outcome Measurement: Concepts and Questions." *Inquiry* (1988): 37–50.

Lohr, K.N.; Yordy, K.D.; and Their, S.O. "Current Issues in Quality of Care." *Health Affairs* (1988): 49–61.

Roper, W.L. and Hackbarth, G.M. "HCFA's Agenda for Promoting High-Quality Care." *Health Affairs* 7 (1988): 19–32.

Roper, W.L.; Winkenwerder, W.; Hackbarth, G.M.; and Krakauer, H. "Effectiveness in Health Care: An Initiative to Evaluate and Improve Medical Care." *New England Journal of Medicine* 319 (1988): 1197–1202.

Winslow, C.M.; Solomon, D.H.; Chassin, M.R.; Kosecoff, J.; Merrick, N.J.; and Brook, R.H. "The Appropriateness of Carotid Endoarterectomy." *New England Journal of Medicine* 318 (1988): 721–727.

Chapter 22

Efficacy, Effectiveness, Variations, and Quality: Boundary-Crossing Research

Robert H. Brook and Kathleen N. Lohr

The title of this article telegraphs our judgment about the future of health services research as it relates to quality-of-care assessment: Returns from research will come more from integrating efficacy, effectiveness, variations in population-based rate of use, and quality of care into an operational model for policy, planning, and evaluation needs than from continuing to treat them as isolated subjects. We have been asked, however, specifically to consider future directions for *quality assessment* research and the uses to which its products should be put, and that is the main focus of this article. Nonetheless, our views of the directions research in this area should take are shaped by the hope that it will serve a larger policy purpose and reach beyond the health services research audience.

Ten years ago, and certainly 20, conceptual and practical questions pertaining to these topics as individual subjects were important health services research concerns. Not all of them are so central today. Health services research has grown and matured; with it, these fields have ripened as well.

We can, *if we want,* accurately measure the efficacy of procedures or drugs, assay their effectiveness in the everyday world, examine per capita variations in their use, and even evaluate the quality of the care process

Supported in part by the Health Insurance Study grant 016B80 from the U.S. Department of Health and Human Services, Washington, D.C. Other support was provided by the Commonwealth Foundation, the Robert Wood Johnson Foundation, and the Hartford Foundation through their funding of the Health Services Utilization Study.

The opinions and conclusions expressed are solely those of the authors and should not be construed as representing the opinions or policy of The Rand Corporation, of sponsors of its research, or of any agency of the United States Government.

Note: Reprinted from *Medical Care,* Vol. 23, No. 5, pp. 710–722, with permission of J.B. Lippincott Company, © May 1985.

337

in which use of these services is embedded. Indeed, in some cases we may know more about the appropriate way to treat or measure the impact of an illness than we do about its pathophysiologic causes: the correct "steps" of detecting and treating high blood pressure, for instance, are better understood than are the consequences of essential hypertension.

Health services research can profitably be focused on issues of efficacy, effectiveness, variations in use, or quality of care. Our argument, however, is that tomorrow's important issues require that information from all these areas be integrated into a "macro" model that will address continuing problems in the medical system. Changes in health systems may come through a regulatory model or a procompetitive model, but without an integrated flow of information about all four areas, evaluating or recommending alternative strategies of medical delivery will be difficult.

A BRIEF DEFINITION OF TERMS

Efficacy, effectiveness, variations in use, and quality of care are familiar ideas, so familiar, perhaps, that imprecision as to their meaning in this context impedes thinking about them "in the whole." In this article, we mean the following:

"Efficacy" refers to "the probability of benefit to individuals in a defined population from a medical technology applied for a given medical problem under ideal conditions of use."[1] This benefit (i.e., what a technology *could* do, not what it does) should be judged as comprehensively as possible, reflecting positive and negative aspects of physical and mental health. We can currently weight these outcomes and account for patient preferences for various states of ill (or good) health; a decade or more of significant research into health status measurement has given us many such tools.

"Effectiveness" has all the attributes of efficacy except one: It reflects performance under ordinary conditions by the average practitioner for the typical patient. In quality-of-care terms, what your doctor or mine does for you or me in the daily course of events is measured in terms of effectiveness.

"Variations in use" most commonly refers to different observed levels of per capita consumption of a service, especially hospital care, office visits, drugs, and specific procedures. Generally, these variations are seen as especially significant when all the usual explanations for use, such as demographic, social, economic, and health status factors, have been controlled, leaving no obvious explanation for differences except those related to practice style of the individual provider. Typically, variation studies do not concern themselves with the outcomes of care (i.e., variations in effectiveness).

Avedis Donabedian, dean of the "quality-of-care" field, defined quality of care as ". . . that kind of care which is expected to maximize an inclusive measure of patient welfare, after one has taken account of the balance of expected gains and losses that attend the process of care in all its parts."[2] Within a research framework, the quality of medical care is that component of the difference between efficacy and effectiveness that can be attributed to care providers, taking account of the environment in which they work. "Quality assessment" is the act of detecting and measuring that difference, including variations across regions and peoples. In practical terms, it is the measurement of the technical and interpersonal aspects of medical care.*

THE PAST AS PROLOGUE

The Efficacy of Medical Practice

We do know something about the efficacy of medical practice, but not as much as we would like.† For regulatory needs (e.g., establishing efficacy and safety of a new drug) and research reasons (e.g., testing a chemotherapy protocol in a cancer patient) the efficacy of many drugs and drug combinations has been tested. In other therapeutic realms, we tend to know more about the efficacy of costly or innovative surgical procedures or other technologic breakthroughs than about traditional or ordinary practices, simply because the latter became widely accepted well before concerns with efficacy entered the policy or research domain and before appropriate research methods were available to investigate them. We know less about the efficacy of many diagnostic tests and procedures, and certainly less about tests and procedures used in combination or about using a given test or combination of tests more than once in a defined time

---

* Lohr and Brook distinguish between quality assessment and quality assurance and define the latter as ". . . the formal and systematic exercise of identifying problems in medical care delivery, designing activities to overcome the problems, and carrying out follow-up steps to ensure that no new problems have been introduced and that corrective actions have been effective."[3] See Komaroff for a more complete discussion of quality assurance.[4]

† In 1978, the Office of Technology Assessment (OTA) reviewed the efficacy of 17 different services, ranging from a variety of preventive services (e.g., Pap smears for cervical cancer, chicken pox vaccine) to diagnostic procedures (e.g., mammography, electronic fetal monitoring) and therapeutic interventions (antibiotics in otitis media, cast application in forearm fractures) and surgical procedures (e.g., hysterectomy, tonsillectomy).[1] Among other things, OTA concluded that many technologies are not adequately assessed for efficacy (or safety) before they come into widespread use. Even among practices that are deliberately studied, findings may be equivocal. The situation has not changed appreciably in the intervening years.

period. Finally, we know next to nothing about the efficacy of "cognitive" practices, such as listening to, counseling, or reassuring patients.

Efficacy is often established with regard to patients who are not representative of those for whom the service is ultimately intended. To illustrate the point, consider the literature on two diagnostic procedures: colonoscopy of the lower gastrointestinal track and endoscopy of the upper gastrointestinal tract.‡

In terms of physician charges, colonoscopy ranks among the 50 procedures done most frequently for the Medicare population, yet no randomized controlled trial has tested the efficacy of this procedure in general, for a specific diagnostic purpose, or in the elderly. A few prospective studies have followed patients who have undergone this procedure. Almost all information on colonoscopy comes from retrospective studies carried out mainly by physicians who do the procedure.

Endoscopy is another popular procedure for which our knowledge of efficacy is meager. A few randomized controlled trials have tried to establish its efficacy for patients with bleeding from the upper gastrointestinal tract. However, for the majority of patients who receive this procedure (i.e., patients with dyspepsia or nonbleeders), data about efficacy in terms of information gained or in relation to an upper gastrointestinal X-ray series or a trial of medication to relieve symptoms are nonexistent.

The lack of information on efficacy is so obvious that more and better clinical trials and other efforts to establish efficacy will be needed. Research will also be needed for developing (a) better methods for conducting randomized clinical trials (e.g., experimental design, ways to measure and assign values to patient outcomes, disease severity, and comorbidity) and (b) better quasi-experimental designs, when using randomized trials is not feasible. With regard to the latter, improved ways to exploit secondary data bases or insurance claims files and to follow patients who are potential candidates for a procedure will be needed.

The Effectiveness of Medical Practice

If we accept for the moment the supposition that the medical profession knows less about the efficacy of what it does than it would like to know, then that problem is compounded as regards the ordinary course of patient care because even less is known about effectiveness than about efficacy.

---

‡ As part of a current study on variations in use of services, extensive literature reviews have been prepared for six major procedures: coronary artery bypass surgery, cholecystectomy, gastrointestinal endoscopy, fiberoptic colonoscopy, carotid endarterectomy, and coronary angiography. Comments here and elsewhere on these services are taken from those publications.[5,6]

Granted, we know a good deal about the effectiveness of many preventive practices such as immunizations provided in a community setting; similarly, we know which antibiotics are efficacious against which organisms, so by implication we should know for which patients they are likely to be effective. We know the efficacy of setting broken legs, replacing hips, or carrying out intraocular lens procedures *when judged against the outcomes expected if one does nothing.* We might even be comfortable with saying that the efficacy of surgical procedures such as hernia repair, cholecystectomy, and appendectomy are established for patients with a classical clinical presentation, as are modes of care for patients with angina, hypertension, or diabetes.

Having evidence about the efficacy of a given intervention does not mean we can translate that knowledge appropriately into guidance about the daily practice of medicine. Take, for instance, treatment of Stage 1 cancer of the cervix. Studies of the efficacy of radiotherapy for cervical carcinoma show that it provides the same cure rate as surgery but with lower complication rates,[7] suggesting it should be the recommended therapy. What is not known is whether the same holds true in the community, because differing skills of the average surgeon or the typical radiotherapist or varying attributes of the hospital may attenuate or magnify the outcomes expected on the basis of efficacy studies. In other words, we cannot be sure that what is learned in the best possible circumstances provides a reliable guide in ordinary circumstances. Just as we may be uncertain about the efficacy of much medical practice today, we may be equally uncertain as to effectiveness *even when* we know something about efficacy.

What is needed might be characterized as an epidemiology of effectiveness: some way of routinely collecting information that describes the outcomes of tests, procedures, drugs, and other services as they are customarily used in everyday practice. Current health services research resources would never permit the study of both efficacy and effectiveness of the wide array of services about which our knowledge is sparse, let alone investigation of why gaps between the two appear. Our view is that better returns from health services research dollars would come from examining the effectiveness of medical care and describing the magnitude of the difference between efficacy and effectiveness when efficacy is known.

The goals would be to reduce the range of uncertainty facing physicians in their day-to-day practice of medicine and to illustrate the limited utility of efficacy studies in the absence of effectiveness studies. If these goals were accomplished, perhaps a longer-range outcome would be more research funding to study both efficacy and effectiveness.

Finally, concerns with effectiveness should shift away from services per se to *patients* and their problems, to *combinations* of services that may produce the best outcomes, or to *interactions* of variables (region of the country, type of hospital market area, type of patients, class of hospital, skills of physicians, attributes of other care providers, and so forth) that may modify or moderate the "average" effectiveness of the service under investigation.

Variations in Use of Services

Variations in use and outcomes of medical services are large and ubiquitous, as empirical evidence amply shows.§ Throughout the developed world, the per capita use of procedures varies by two- to 12-fold in ways that are not satisfactorily explained by population characteristics or differences in available resources. Rates of hospital admissions for medical reasons may also vary by eight-, ten-, or even 12-fold across hospital market areas.

Such large variations are seen irrespective of the mechanisms used to pay providers and of differences in national health care delivery systems. Moreover, some evidence from the United States, Canada, and other developed countries suggests that variations within geographic areas in per-person use or medical expenditures is as great as those across areas, reinforcing the notion that differences in practice style and organization at the level of individual practitioners may lie at the heart of variations in use of services.

Uncertainty about the appropriateness or effectiveness of a given service provided to a given patient for a specific condition or complaint allows for differences of opinion and thus may account for much of the high rates of variation in use. Hence low variation rates may reflect a fairly high degree of consensus about effectiveness of a given procedure or service (although this conjecture remains to be proven). The very lowest rates, however, could represent underuse and failure to provide needed services. The highest rates, by contrast, may often represent overuse of services, the effectiveness of which is at best incompletely demonstrated or at worst very questionable.

These phenomena imply, virtually by definition, that the quality of medical care may vary markedly across population groups. What we do not know, at this juncture, is the range of variation in quality of care (let alone the explanations for it).

Let us be clear about the problem: We know little about the effectiveness of many aspects of medical practice, so we have little to go on in establishing quality-of-care standards. That is, we cannot easily judge the degree to which patient outcomes are optimized. We know that use of many services

---

§ For an up-to-date compendium of articles on this topic, see the summer issue of *Health Affairs*[8-14]; data on medical admissions were reported by Wennberg.[15,16] Articles included in the section on practice patterns provide more information on this topic.[17]

varies tremendously throughout the nation, often for no obvious reasons; amorphous notions about practice style, group consensus, and tradition are thus offered as possible explanations. Without good measures of quality (i.e., expected levels of effectiveness), we cannot readily evaluate what low or, especially, high rates of variation mean in quality-of-care terms. Hence we cannot sensibly decide where medical care consumption can or cannot justifiably be constrained.

We emphasize that investigating the *clinical* appropriateness of such variation is crucial on two scores. First, documenting wide ranges of "unexplained" per-person use of specific services essentially tells us where to concentrate resources for research into the effectiveness and quality areas, on the reasoning that reducing physician uncertainty about expected benefits could lead to better decisions about optimal therapeutic choices. Second, decisions about health care financing still must be made. In the absence of good clinical data that would justify use of specific services, cuts may be made arbitrarily in high-use and/or high-cost services. Good quality-of-care research will help guard against ill-advised reductions in the use of those services that are more effective (i.e., bring about demonstrably better patient outcomes) than their alternatives.

Assessing the Quality of Medical Care

Two decades of research support for quality assessment, much of it by NCHSR, have vastly improved the tools of our trade.¶ What has not yet happened is the application of those tools beyond rather narrow confines of assessing quality of care for specific diagnoses, particular groups of patients, or types of institutions. That is, quality assessment has not been integrated into larger models of health care delivery that would allow us to understand the meaning or ramifications of variations in the use of services or to specify the permissible ranges of effectiveness.

Conceptualization of Quality of Care

Much progress has come just in the definition and refinement of the concepts of quality of care. In this regard, the classic work by Donabedian

---

¶ We could not possibly review here the vast literature in quality of care measurement that accrued during the 1960s and 1970s. Seminal work has been done by Brook, Donabedian, Egdahl, Greenfield, Kane, Kessner, Palmer, Payne, Rutstein, Sanazaro, Starfield, Ware, Williamson, and their several associates; selected citations appear in the notes.[18-44] For related work, see the article by Bergner on health status measurement.[45] We thank Jim McAllister of NCHSR for providing some information about work the Center has supported in the past. We have restricted ourselves to discussing the quality of *medical* care in this article, but it should be clear that many of the same points might be pertinent for dental, mental health, and other forms of care.

was especially important. The constructs of structure/process/outcome are well established, as is the notion that the science and the art of care are interrelated but distinguishable.

Evaluating the Medical Process

Probably the greatest advances have come in ways to evaluate the process of medical care (i.e., what is done to or for a patient with respect to his or her particular disease or complaint). The concept of diagnosis- or problem-specific "tracers" has won wide acceptance; an alternative approach that might be characterized as applying "comprehensive criteria sets" to randomly selected patient records is also gaining prominence.

Twenty years ago few, if any, diagnosis- or symptom-specific criteria sets could be "pulled off the shelf." Today, one would not have to search far to find at least a few criteria sets for a variety of common conditions that afflict adults, children, or both. Work by Heather Palmer and her colleagues at Harvard on the Ambulatory Care Medical Audit Demonstration is a case in point. Unfortunately, as of this writing, no system is in place to generate such criteria on a continuing basis, to update them, or to validate them against proximate or ultimate outcomes.

"Criteria maps," which were developed through the UCLA EMCRO,** incorporate decision logic (i.e., contingent or branching criteria).[25,26] They provide a powerful tool for quality assessment and quality assurance programs, and they may also lend themselves to development of protocols for use by both physicians and nonphysicians. This promising technique has thus far been applied only to a few conditions; hence criteria maps (validated or not) are not widely available.

Computer-Based Information

Our ability to carry out secondary analyses on large data bases, such as insurance claims files, for quality assessment purposes has improved drastically over the years. We can, for instance, apply fairly detailed criteria to episodes of care for acute conditions, as shown in work based on data from the New Mexico EMCRO. As another example, we can evaluate whether hospital admissions following surgery have been caused by a previous operative complication. Furthermore, various computerized information systems such as Computer-stored Ambulatory Record (COSTAR) permit information on patient/provider ambulatory encounters to be entered directly in a computer file.

** EMCROs, or Experimental Medical Care Review Organizations, were established as part of an NCHSR-initiated program to foster local peer review in the early 1970s.[31-33]

Methods Effects

Different quality assessment methods will produce different conclusions regarding the level of quality. Because we now know something about the effects of "methods" on results, however, sources of potential bias and error can be postulated and tested. Moreover, specific clinical models that relate process to outcome can be built, along the lines of ones developed for measuring the quality of care given to children with iron-deficiency anemia.[41]

Outcomes of Care

Our fundamental concern in quality assessment is the end result of care (i.e., the patient's eventual outcome or health status). Much progress has been made in measuring health status, and we note here only the broad areas of development.

First, we think about patient outcomes differently than we used to: Over the years, our understanding of what health means to people and of the factors that might interact (i.e., need to be controlled for in a research sense) to produce a good or poor outcome has improved tremendously. Insights into the multifaceted nature of health status prompted much methodologic work that produced reliable and valid outcome measures. These include functional status and physical capacity measures, mental health inventories, the Sickness Impact Profile, and measures of a person's perceptions and ratings of his or her general health.[45–48] Unfortunately, progress in measuring disease-specific outcomes, especially for people with a chronic disease, has not kept pace with measurement of overall health status.

Second, we know a good deal more about measuring a patient's satisfaction with care.[49–51] Some aspects of patient satisfaction relate directly to quality of care, although this construct is neither a necessary or sufficient measure of the outcomes of care. As in the field of health status measurement, much of this developmental work was supported by NCHSR.

Third, a great deal of progress has been made in developing measures of hospital case mix and severity of illness.[52–59] Although these measures may be relatively specific (e.g., those developed for assessing the seriousness of condition of patients admitted into intensive care units), others attempt to deal with the full range of problems causing a hospital admission. In all these cases, incorporating such indexes into research will permit better understanding of the links between processes and outcomes and better comparisons of outcomes across providers.

Deficiencies in the Quality of Care

Quality assessment research has identified major deficiencies in medical care; many persist to this day. Poor care is seen in ambulatory and hospital settings alike. It is just a matter of time before deficiencies in newer settings such as surgi-centers or freestanding emergency centers begin to be documented.

Some deficiencies are well-known and of long standing; inappropriate use of antibiotics is a good example. Other suspected problems that are not well documented involve the applications and uses of psychotherapy, the high rate of nosocomial infections in hospitals, and inappropriate use of "intensive" technology such as intensive care units. The quality of nursing home care, roundly and deservedly criticized in the past, will continue to be a salient problem as the population ages.

WHERE DO WE GO FROM HERE?

Research Needs in the Quality Assessment Field

Process and Outcome

Quality assessment ultimately should serve to improve the level of health in this country. No government agency, hospital system, or medical practice can afford to judge quality of care solely on the basis of outcomes. To discover some adverse outcomes produced by poor quality of care, for instance, might require collecting data from hundreds of patients. Moreover, assessing patient outcomes alone provides little opportunity to influence medical practice patterns; conversely, modifying medical practice on the basis of normative process criteria has not always yielded demonstrable improvements in patient health status.

Thus one critical gap in the quality assessment field is our inability to establish the linkages between the process and outcomes of care. We often are unable to say with confidence that the services rendered to the patient bear some medically plausible relationship to the patient's subsequent health status.

Establishing the *clinical* validity of process measures (i.e., the degree to which process predicts outcome) is a significant area of future research. Disease models that include comorbidity, stage, process, and outcome measures need to be built, tested, and validated so that they (or their components) can be used to evaluate quality of care. This area will need continuing attention.

Nonintrusive Outcome Measures

There remains a need for outcome measures that do not rely on obtaining information directly from patients or physicians and that do not require medical record data. Research into so-called "nonintrusive outcome measures" may be aimed primarily at large secondary data bases, often insurance claims files such as those included in the Medicare Statistical System, those maintained by Blue Cross/Blue Shield, or state Medicaid systems. Computer-based ambulatory or hospital medical records offer another potentially important source of data.

Developing nonintrusive outcome measures requires linking such files with other, population-specific statistical files (such as eligibility files or death certificates); it also requires testing simple and complex measures (e.g., death, complications of surgery, or recurrent signs and symptoms following hospitalization). Validating "candidate" measures calls for use of expert review, process-of-care data, and directly measured outcome variables.

Such work may show, of course, that outcomes really need to be measured directly, that is, nonintrusive measures as presently conceived are too nonspecific, insensitive, unreliable, or invalid for quality assessment or program monitoring. If that is so, the point needs to be made explicitly, so that further research can be directed toward improving how nonintrusive measures can best be used and so that major policy decisions about health care financing and delivery will not be made on indefensible quality-of-care grounds.

The Evolution of Disease and Patient Outcomes

The need continually to refine our definitions of patient outcomes is prompted by the evolution of our understanding of disease in clinical terms. For example, conditions once thought incurable are now curable; or, at a minimum, we can say that for some illnesses, death is no longer an acceptable outcome (e.g., cervical cancer, bleeding ulcer, malignant hypertension). The population is aging, and the elderly population is itself aging. With more attention being turned toward this population, diagnoses (e.g., senility, Alzheimer's disease, and depression) that could not be made reliably 5–10 years ago are now being made. These necessitate wholly new ideas about appropriate patient outcomes. The advent of new technologies forces us down a similar path: as "experimental" procedures such as liver transplants or artificial organs become more fully accepted or disseminated into medical practice, we are forced to redefine the outcomes of care that the nation should legitimately be able to expect.

In some cases, this may essentially be an issue of efficacy, when such procedures or services are regionalized to only a few "best" centers. We should be alert, however, to the degree and speed with which medical practices tend to diffuse into the community, because then the question becomes one of effectiveness. In this regard, the need for good process and outcome measures to use in larger "technology assessment" efforts, especially those that are disease- or problem-specific, should be clear.

The Art of Care

Implicitly, much of what has just been discussed concerns the technical (i.e., technologic or mechanical) aspects of care. Perhaps as important are issues relating to the art of care and to the "cognitive" services that physicians and other care-givers provide. We need to know more about physician-patient communication and interaction and how, for instance, physicians can best communicate reassurance and hope about their patient's prognosis. The strong push for recognition of and appropriate compensation for cognitive (as opposed to procedure-oriented) care by some physician specialty groups argues for early research in this area. Finally, how the art of care or physician style affects patient outcomes deserves much more critical attention.

An Epidemiology of Quality of Care

One important area of research may be simply to develop an "epidemiology of the quality of medical care." Just as we will continue to explore and document variations in per capita use of services across the nation, we will need to know how quality is distributed in the population. Describing the distribution of quality of care in epidemiologic terms means, first, knowing how to measure quality and, second, knowing something about the relationship of physician characteristics to the process of care and, eventually, to the outcomes of that care.

For example, certain types of health financing mechanisms (e.g., prospective payment in Medicare) may foster "regionalization" of complex or costly procedures into high-volume institutions. Restricting some services to high-volume facilities has been shown to be positively associated with better outcomes (e.g., lower death rates), but high-volume centers could also achieve that volume by performing such services inappropriately often.

Research should be aimed at improving our understanding of the epidemiology of quality and at answering a number of important policy questions. For example, would regionalization of common surgical procedures, or of invasive diagnostic tests, or of *noninvasive* diagnostic services result in better patient outcomes? What physician characteristics or institutional arrangements are directly associated with these better outcomes? Finally, are there interactions between patient characteristics or disease variables and provider variables that augment or detract from the effect of regionalization?

Furthermore, addressing questions of both equity and efficiency requires knowledge of the levels of quality of care (a) among patients who use medical care and (b) among all individuals in the population. In research or program evaluation terms, we should know how good the care is for "recipients" and for "eligibles," if we are to make reasoned choices about ways to finance and deliver medical care.

We make the point about studying both users and eligibles here because nonuse of medical care can itself be a quality-of-care issue. Nonuse is not by definition poor quality of care: avoiding unnecessary hospitalizations, invasive diagnostic procedures, excessive use of drugs, and so forth may be positive aspects to lower use of medical care. For some population groups, however, nonuse of care may be an important problem, leading to poorer health status generally and poorer outcomes once care is sought.

We need more work on population-based models of quality assessment, such as that used by Nutting in the Indian Health Service.[60] These models will help us pay greater attention to the quality of care for many groups: populations enrolled in Medicare and Medicaid; persons in alternative health plans (especially those established to control the costs of publicly funded medical care); and individuals choosing preferred provider organizations. In general, the quality of care received through *any* innovative financing scheme that is based on economic incentives to curb the use of services merits attention.

Costs and Quality of Care

It is trite to say that the overriding problem of the day concerns the nation's health care expenditures, not the quality of the services received. We know a great deal about costs of and expenditures on medical care; we know a fair amount about what individual services may "cost" or at least what price they command in the market. We recognize there is a direct relationship between the price of medical care faced by the patient and the level of use of services. Finally, we know that the major public debates in the health field for the rest of the century will focus on medical care financing issues.

What we still do not know much about is the relationship, indeed the tension, between costs and quality—the so-called cost-quality trade-off. Further conceptual and empirical research will be needed on how to measure the direct and indirect costs and benefits of medical care, where benefits in this context refer to expected patient outcomes. Added to this is the need to be able to take into account patient "utilities" or preferences for alternative states of health and alternative levels of financial burden. Derived from this is the need to look at how to weight the preferences of different factors (i.e., the utilities of patient versus family versus provider versus community versus society as a whole).

Choosing among alternative forms of care, when they differ in costs, requires knowledge about the expected benefits of those forms of care. Further, knowing when to provide more care and when to stop requires knowing something about the *marginal* costs and returns to care. In short, the domain of quality assessment research of the future must be defined to include these cost–quality relationships, focusing on the question of what dimensions of health and patient outcomes to put on the benefits side of the balance scale.

AN INTEGRATED MODEL

A Simple View of the Policy Context

We have briefly outlined important quality assessment issues that in our view should form the heart of the third decade of health services research. Reasonable people may differ with our selection and recommendations, believing, for instance, that more (or less) resources should go to policy-oriented work or to refining methods and measures. Those debates we leave for another forum.

We would like here to return to the theme introduced at the outset of the article: research into quality of care (or any other topic, for that matter) can no longer be carried out in splendid isolation from other issues. We have suggested that a large research effort (perhaps the most important one) should attempt to integrate (a) the efficacy of care where circumstances are most favorably disposed to produce good outcomes, (b) the effectiveness of care in the daily course of events, (c) population-based variations in the use of services and the intimately related variations in quality of care (measured in terms of patient outcomes), and finally (d) levels of quality of care in the broadest possible terms. Proposing, testing, and investigating a model of this sort implies attention to the current and future policy context of health care delivery and financing.

For purposes of this discussion, we would argue that the policy context involves continuing alarm about medical expenditures and a myriad of public and private sector efforts to control costs, increasing reliance on an as-yet unproven "competitive" approach to cost containment, a growing acceptance of the notion that medical care will be rationed (whether or not the care is needed), and a perception (strong in some quarters, dim in others) that members of society at greatest risk of harm from rationing (the elderly, perhaps the very young, the poor) need special protection as the financing issues work themselves out. Within this policy context, obviously, the interesting research questions are legion.

Planning a Research Agenda

Developing an explicit "hierarchy" of research needs will itself be an important step as the health services research community sets its agenda for the rest of the century. In the quality assessment area, criteria for making those choices should reflect the following points: (a) the population groups most affected by actions elsewhere in the policy arena; (b) the most common medical problems; (c) the problems we think research could do the most to solve; (d) the topics we know the least about; and (e) the external factors we think will provoke the most serious future problems in the delivery of care (such as growth of transplant and artificial organ technologies or marked aging of the population).

Clinical Trials

One special arena of research calling for careful preparation concerns efficacy—more precisely, the planning and conduct of clinical trials. Better research tools and measurement techniques, including more reliable and valid measures of patient outcomes, are needed. Work in these areas can contribute to stronger bridges to the biomedical community over which existing and new knowledge can be more effectively passed. Research on how best to disseminate the products of such trials to the medical community and the policymaking branches of government should also be done.

The "Macro" Model

A second point is that the planning process for clinical trials must itself be integrated with an "operational" system that will track the use of services under investigation in the country as a whole. That is, clinical trials of the *efficacy* of a service should not be performed without prior attention to how *effectiveness* will be monitored, should the trial show positive results.

From the beginning attention should be given to whether outcome measures will be suitable for long-term monitoring. For instance, detailed physiologic variables that require direct patient contact and perhaps even invasive testing, although probably considered by clinicians to be the best efficacy measure, are likely to be unsuitable for measuring effectiveness and for long-term monitoring of the use of that service. Other less intrusive outcome measures should be sought from the beginning and validated against the physiologic variables tracked during the clinical trial. Perhaps the integration of clinical trials with evaluation of effectiveness and quality, coupled with greater attention to variations in population-based rates of use, will be the hallmark of the next level of activity in health services research.

SUMMARY

Ideally, we need a fully integrated system of data collection and information dissemination. We need to be able to discard those medical procedures or services that are not efficacious and to quantify and understand the effectiveness of efficacious services. When efficacy and effectiveness diverge dramatically, then we need to understand issues relating to the quality of care rendered by the average physician.

Differences in efficacy and effectiveness are measured in terms of patient outcomes, but explanations of *why* patient outcomes differ partly reside in measures of the technical and interpersonal aspects of the care process (other things such as patient compliance more or less equal). When differences in the process of care do not explain differences in outcomes, we may look to structural characteristics of the medical delivery system as a whole for clues. Finally, we need to ensure that effective services are being provided to the appropriate groups of patients in ways that minimize inequitable variation in per person use of those services across geographic regions and population groups.

One crucial requirement for such a system is that research be designed to be internally valid, generalizable to the outside world, and important in a policy sense. To do this presupposes a commitment to integrate efficacy studies with measures of effectiveness, with measures of the structure, process, and outcomes of care, and with epidemiologic studies of variations in the use of services. In the long run, this research might serve to unite the epidemiologic and clinical approaches into one—a clinicoepidemiologic model of health—and produce the information and insights needed to help prevent the rationing of effective medical care.

NOTES

1. Office of Technology Assessment. *Assessing the efficacy and safety of medical technologies.* Washington, DC: Congress of the United States, Office of Technology Assessment, OTA-H-75, 1978, p. 16.

2. Donabedian A. *Explorations in quality assessment and monitoring. Vol. 1. The definition of quality and approaches to its assessment.* Ann Arbor, MI: Health Administration Press, 1980.

3. Lohr KN, Brook RH. *Quality assurance in medicine: experience in the public sector.* Santa Monica, CA: The Rand Corporation, R-3193-HHS, 1984.

4. Komaroff A. Quality assurance. *Med Care* 1985;23:723.

5. Kahn KL, Fink A, Roth CP, et al. *A review of the literature on fiberoptic colonoscopy: findings, complications, utilization rates, costs, efficacy, and indications.* Santa Monica, CA: The Rand Corporation, R-3204/4-CWF/PMT/HF (In press).

6. Kahn KL, Roth CP, Fink A, et al. *A review of the literature on gastrointestinal endoscopy for diagnosis: findings, complications, utilization rates, costs, efficacy, and indications.* Santa Monica, CA: The Rand Corporation, R-2304/3-CWF/PMT/HF (In press).

7. Casciato DA, Lowitz BB. *Manual of bedside oncology.* Boston, MA: Little, Brown & Co., 1983.

8. Wennberg JE. Dealing with medical practice variations: a proposal for action. *Health Affairs* 1984;3:6.

9. Sammons JH, Rubin R, Hackbarth G, et al. ReViews *Health Affairs* 1984;3:33.

10. Brook RH, Lohr KN, Chassin M, et al. Geographic variations in the use of services: do they have any clinical significance? *Health Affairs* 1984;3:63.

11. Eddy DM. Variations in physician practice: the role of uncertainty. *Health Affairs* 1984;3:74.

12. Schwartz JS. The role of professional medical societies in reducing variations. *Health Affairs* 1984;3:90.

13. Vladeck BC. Variations data and regulatory rationale. *Health Affairs* 1984;3:102.

14. Caper P. Variations in medical practice: implications for health policy. *Health Affairs* 1984;3:110.

15. Lohr KN, Lohr WR, Brook RH. Update. A London conference. *Health Affairs* 1984;3:139.

16. Wennberg J, McPherson K, Caper P. Will payment based on diagnosis-related groups control hospital costs? *N Engl J Med* 1984;311:295.

17. Hulka B, Wheat J. Patterns of utilization. *Med Care* 1985;23:438.

18. Brook RH, Davies-Avery A, Greenfield S, et al. Assessing the quality of medical care using outcome methods: an overview of the method. *Med Care* 1977;15(Suppl):1.

19. Brook RH. *Quality of care assessment: a comparison of five methods of peer review.* Rockville, MD: National Center for Health Services Research and Development, (HRA) 74-2100, 1973.

20. Brook RH, Davies-Avery A. *Mechanisms for assuring quality of U.S. medical care services: past, present, and future.* Santa Monica, CA: The Rand Corporation, R-1939-HEW, 1977.

21. Brook RH, Williams KN, Avery AD. Quality assurance today and tomorrow: forecast for the future. *Ann Int Med* 1976;85:809.

22. Donabedian A. *Explorations in quality assessment and monitoring. Vol. 2. The criteria and standards of quality.* Ann Arbor, MI: Health Administration Press, 1982.

23. Egdahl RH, Gertman PM. Technology and the quality of health care. Rockville, MD: Aspen Publishers, 1975.

24. Egdahl RH, Gertman PM, eds. Quality assurance in health care. Rockville, MD: Aspen Publishers, 1976.

25. Greenfield S, Nadler MA, Morgan MT, et al. The clinical investigation and management of chest pain in an emergency department: quality assessment by criteria mapping. *Med Care* 1977;15:898.

26. Greenfield S, Cretin S, Worthman LG, et al. Comparison of a criteria map to a criteria list in quality-of-care assessment for patients with chest pain: the relation of each to outcome. *Med Care* 1981;19:255.

27. Kane RL, Gardner G, Wright DD, et al. A method for assessing the outcome of acute primary care. *J Fam Pract* 1977;4:1119.

28. Kane RL, Bell RM, Hosek SD, et al. *Outcome-based reimbursement for nursing home care.* Santa Monica, CA: The Rand Corporation, R-3092-NCHSR, 1983.

29. Kessner DM, Kalk CE. A strategy for evaluating health services. In: *Contrasts in health status.* Vol 2. Washington, DC: National Academy of Sciences, Institute of Medicine, 1973.

30. Kessner DM, Snow CK, Singer J. Assessment of medical care in children. In: *Contrasts in health status.* Vol. 3. Washington, DC: National Academy of Sciences, Institute of Medicine, 1974.

31. Brook RH, Williams KN. Evaluation of the New Mexico peer review system. *Med Care* 1976;14(Suppl 12):1.

32. Lohr KN, Brook RH, Kaufman MA. Quality of care in the New Mexico Medicaid program (1971–1975). *Med Care* 1980;18(Suppl 1):1.

33. Lohr KN. *Quality of care in episodes of common respiratory infections in a disadvantaged population.* Santa Monica, CA: The Rand Corporation, R-6570, 1980.

34. Lohr KN, Winkler JD, Brook RH. *Professional standards review organizations and technology assessment in medicine.* Santa Monica, CA: The Rand Corporation, R-2820-OTA, 1981.

35. Palmer RH, Strain R, Maurer JVW, et al. Quality assurance in eight adult medicine group practices. *Med Care* 1984;22:632.

36. Palmer RH, Strain R, Maurer JVW, et al. A method for evaluating performance of ambulatory pediatric tasks. *Pediatrics* 1984;73:269.

37. Payne BC. *The quality of medical care: evaluation and development.* Chicago: Hospital Research and Edcuational Trust, 1976.

38. Payne BC, Lyons TF, Neuhaus E. Relationships of physician characteristics to performance quality and improvement. *Health Serv Res* 1984;19:307.

39. Rutstein DD, Berenberg W, Chalmers TC, et al. Measuring the quality of medical care. A clinical method. *N Engl J Med* 1976;294:582.

40. Sanazaro PJ. Quality assessment and quality assurance in medical care. *Annual Review of Public Health* 1980;1:37.

41. Starfield B, Scheff D. Effectiveness of pediatric care. *Pediatrics* 1972;49:547.

42. Williams KN, Brook RH. Quality measurement and assurance. *Health and Medical Care Services Review* 1978;1:1.

43. Williamson JW. *Assessing and improving outcomes in health care: the theory and practice of health accounting.* Cambridge, MA: Ballinger Publishing Company, 1978.

44. Williamson JW. *Improving medical practice and health care. A bibliographic guide to information management in quality assurance and continuing education.* Cambridge, MA: Ballinger Publishing Company, 1977.

45. Bergner M. Measurement of health status. *Med Care* 1985;23.

46. Bergner M, Bobbitt RA, Carter WB, et al. The sickness impact profile: development and final revision of a health status measure. *Med Care* 1981;19:787.

47. Ware JE, Jr., Brook RH, Davies AR, et al. Choosing measures of health status for individuals in general populations. *Am J Public Health* 1981;71:620.

48. Brook RH, Ware JE, Jr., Rogers WH, et al. Does free care improve adults' health? Results from a randomized controlled trial. *N Engl J Med* 1983;309:1426.

49. Ware JE, Jr., Davies-Avery A, Stewart AL. The measurement and meaning of patient satisfaction: a review of the literature. *Health and Medical Care Services Review* 1978;1:1.

50. Ware JE, Jr., Synder MC, Wright WR, et al. Defining and measuring patient satisfaction with medical care. *Evaluation and Program Planning* 1983;6:247.

51. Ware JE, Jr., Davies AR. Behavioral consequences of consumer dissatisfaction with medical care. *Evaluation and Program Planning* 1984;6:291.

52. Horn S, Horn R, Sharkey P. The severity of illness index as a severity adjustment to DRGs. *The Health Care Financing Review.* 1984 annual supplement. HCFA Publ. No. 03194, 1984.

53. Young W. Incorporating severity of illness and comorbidity in case mix measurement. *The Health Care Financing Review.* 1984 annual supplement. HCFA Publ. No. 03194, 1984.

54. Kominski G, Williams S, Mays R, et al. Unrecognized redistributions of revenue in diagnosis-related group-based prospective payment systems. *The Health Care Financing Review.* 1984 annual supplement. HCFA Publ. No. 03194, 1984.

55. Gertman P, Lowenstein S. A research paradigm for severity of illness: issues for the DRG system. *The Health Care Financing Review.* 1984 annual supplement. HCFA Publ. No. 03194, 1984.

56. Wagner D, Knaus W, Draper E. Acute physiology and chronic health evaluation (APACHE-

II) and Medicare reimbursement. *The Health Care Financing Review.* 1984 annual supplement. HCFA Publ. No. 03194, 1984.

57. Smits H, Fetter R, McMahon I. Variation in resource use within DRGs. The severity issue. *The Health Care Financing Review.* 1984 annual supplement. HCFA Publ. No. 03194, 1984.

58. Conklin J, Lieberman J, Barnes C, et al. Disease staging: implications for hospital reimbursement and management. *The Health Care Financing Review.* 1984 annual supplement. HCFA Publ. No. 03194, 1984.

59. Thompson J. The measurement of nursing intensity. *The Health Care Financing Review.* 1984 annual supplement. HCFA Publ. No. 03194, 1984.

60. Nutting P, Shorr GI, Burkhalter BR. Assessing the performance of medical care systems: a method and its application. *Med Care* 1981;19:281.

Appendix A

Glossary of Terms

Concurrent Review: a method of reviewing both the process and outcome of patient care during the course of the patient's hospital stay.

Criteria: predetermined elements of health care against which the quality and appropriateness of an aspect of care can be measured.

Effectiveness: concerns the level of benefit when services are rendered under ordinary circumstances by average practitioners for typical patients.

Efficacy: reflects the level of benefit expected when health care services are applied under ideal circumstance.

Focused Review: concentrated review of key areas in a department or service based on high volume, high risk, or a history of an identified problem.

Generic Screen: review of display of medical records that utilizes criteria that apply to all patients, regardless of source or persons responsible for care ordered or given.

Indicators: professionally developed, clinically valid, and reliable dimensions of the quality and appropriateness of care. The distinction between "indicators" and "screens" has become blurred and these terms are often used interchangeably.[1]

Monitoring: the planned, systematic, and ongoing collection, compilation, and organization of data about an indicator of the quality and/or appropriateness of an important aspect of care, and the comparison of those data to a pre-established level of performance (threshold for evaluation) to determine the need for evaluation (Joint Commission definition).

Occurrence Screen: used for concurrent identification of signal events that warrant review—either as individual events or in the aggregate.

Quality Assessment: the measurement of the level of quality at some point in time with no effort to change or improve the level of care.

Quality Assurance: the measurement of the level of care provided (assessment) and, when necessary, mechanisms to improve it.

Reliability: reproducibility of the findings.

Retrospective Review: review that focuses on the collection and analysis of data typically gathered from a review of the medical record. Unlike concurrent review, retrospective review relies on data collected after the patient has been discharged.

Severity of Illness: a term used to describe the acuity of a patient's condition from clinical evaluation and evidence.

Trending: the evaluation of data collected over a period of time for the purpose of identifying patterns or changes.

Threshold: a pre-established level, attainment of which triggers an intensified review of a specific component of care.

Utilization Review: formal, prospective, concurrent, or retrospective critical examination of appropriate parts of the health care system such as hospitals, nursing homes, etc.

Validity: ability of a test to measure what it purports to measure.

NOTE

1. D. Longo, K. Cicione, and F. Lord, *Integrated Quality Assessment—A Model for Concurrent Review* (Chicago: American Hospital Publishing, Inc. 1989).

Appendix B

Sampling Design and Selection

An important part of a research design is the selection of probability samples that will represent the groups to be studied. A *probability sample* is a randomly selected sample of a sampling frame where the probability of the selection of each element is *known*. A *sampling frame* is an available list of sampling units that represent the population to be studied. Examples of sampling frames for quality assessment studies are (1) all patients with a specific diagnosis who were hospitalized in a specific facility during an indicated time period; (2) all patients who received care in a specific facility during an indicated time period; (3) all inpatients discharged with a specific primary diagnosis from designated hospital(s) during an indicated time period; or (4) all members of a health maintenance organization on a particular date.

The methods of obtaining the desired sampling frames from computer or written records should be determined. A sampling statistician should be consulted to (1) estimate the minimum sample size needed from each sampling frame, (2) develop the sampling design, and (3) write detailed procedures for sample selection.

There are four types of probability samples:

1. A *simple random sample* is a sample selected from a sampling frame in which each element has an *equal* probability of being selected. Tables of random numbers by computer or hand procedures are usually used to select simple random samples, but other methods may be used.
2. A *systematic sample* is a sample of an array of names on cards, lists, folders of cases, or computer records. The number of units in the sampling frame divided by the sample size equals the sampling ratio, called k. A random start of a number less than or equal to k (called m) is selected from a table of random numbers, and the sample is

the *m, m + k, m + 2k, m + 3k,* etc. elements from the list. For example, if *k* equals 10 and the random start is 6, the sample will be the 6th, 16th, 26th, 36th, etc. cases from the list. The systematic sample is easy to select and is usually similar to a simple random sample of the same list. The main consideration in using systematic sampling is to be sure that there are no periodic characteristics of every *k*(th) case on the specific list that is being used.

3. A *stratified sample* is selected from a sampling frame allocated to different strata, either for convenience or for assurance of allocation among important characteristics. Strata may be defined by facilities, time periods, or conditions. Two major types of allocation among strata are proportional allocation and equal allocation. *Proportional allocation* among strata should be used whenever possible so that the statistical measures based on the sum of the strata equal the statistical measures of the group sampled. *Equal allocation* among strata is used when strata are to be compared and it is necessary to have sufficient cases from each stratum. Proportional allocation yields self-weighting samples; the data obtained by equal allocation must be weighted to make estimates of each sampling frame.

4. A *cluster sample* is needed for convenience as one step in a sample design when it is not convenient to use a sample from the entire sampling frame. For example, a cluster sample for quality assessment may be obtained by random selection of days of the week that a clinic is open or random selection of wards. When cluster sampling is used, one or more of the other types of sampling is used for random selection of the elements for study.

Multistage probability sample designs are frequently used to combine the advantages of each type of sample. An example of a multistage sample of patients of one clinic for quality assessment would be clusters of days and systematic sampling of patients in the order of arrival at a specific desk on the sample days.

The formulas for sample size required are based on the results of previous studies or estimated results, desired level of accuracy, and available funds. Formulas for Optimum Allocation that will estimate sample size for the best possible accuracy or for the lowest possible costs are available.

Index

Note: Page numbers in *italics* indicate material in figures or tables.

361